So You Think You're A Good Person

By Cal Seban

Unless designated otherwise, all Scripture taken from the HOLY BIBLE, NEW INTERNATIONAL VERSION, Copyright © 1973, 1978, 1984, 2011 by International Bible Society. Used by permission of Zondervan. All rights reserved worldwide. www.zondervan.com The "NIV" and "New International Version" are trademarks registered in the United States Patent and Trademark Office by International Bible Society. Use of either trademark requires the permission of International Bible Society.

All rights reserved. No part of this publication may be reproduced in any form, except for brief quotations in reviews, without the written permission of the publisher.

Cover Design by Aaron Muther and Mike Swenson

Copyright © 2013 Cal Seban
All rights reserved.
ISBN: 1490925058
ISBN 13: 9781490925059

Acknowledgements

There is a very special group of people who have been instrumental in helping this passion to become a reality, and without whom this work would not be what it is, if it would have ever been finished at all. My brother Rich and dear friend Mike Swenson provided invaluable feedback and input that, while being supportive, was honest, candid, pointed and so very necessary. Oh that we all would be blessed with those in our lives who we can count on to be honest with us when we ask them, and who call it as they see it—because they care.

At just the right time along came Sharon Granke to help with the proofreading. It is amazing to have the gift of finding the grammar and spelling mistakes after four others have already read a document. The clincher was Nate Cox, a friend of our son Tim, whom we have known since his days in college. It turns out is he an experienced pro when it comes to Microsoft Word. He compensated for my limited ability in ways that I could not have begun to imagine. Finding Nate and Sharon during the process were two unexpected and delightful surprises.

The best gift of all is the one who has been the best thing to happen to me for the past 48 years—my wife, Karen. She has been my friend, confidant, reader and proofreader, supportive and generous in giving me the time needed to make this project a reality and walking with me each and every step of the way. As we are about to celebrate our 48th wedding anniversary, I so much look forward to spending the years ahead with my girl, who throughout this process was able to be objective and constructively critical in her unique way that combines candor and sensitivity. She still thinks Chapter 4 is too long and involved, like most of my sermons.

All of these folks have been very special blessings, and I will remain forever grateful. It would never have come together without them.

Most of all I can not begin to put in words what it means to have a God who knows me as an indifferent, greedy and unfaithful follower, and yet continues to love me, graciously forgives me and empowers me through his Spirit to be his loving presence in the lives of others.

This book is dedicated to

those whose compassion and selflessness have helped to relieve the misery and suffering of the poor, needy, broken, abandoned, vulnerable, sick and starving, and in so doing have given them some small measure of comfort, hope and peace.

So You Think You're A Good Person

Preface

Chapter 1 – "My Bad—Totally!".....1

Chapter 2 – Humanity's Capacity for Unthinkable Darkness and Evil.....27

Chapter 3 – The History of American Greed: from the "Robber Barons" thru 2007.....51

Chapter 4 – Close Call: The Near Economic Meltdown of 2008.....69

Chapter 5 – "They" is "We".....95

Chapter 6 – Christians and the Calculus of Indifference.....121

Chapter 7 – With Basin and Towel.....137

Chapter 8 – The Sermons Nobody Wants to Hear.....159

Chapter 9 – The Sermons Nobody Wants to Preach.....183

Chapter 10 – The Morality of Capitalism: There's Good News and There's Bad News.....209

Chapter 11 – The Morality of Government.....245

Chapter 12 – What in the World Do You Do with Mother Teresa?.....281

Chapter 13 – Power, Leverage and Advantage.....307

Chapter 14 – Is There a Message for Me in All This?.....327

Endnotes.....349

Preface

This book is about us—our humanity and our inhumanity, our selflessness and our self-centeredness, our compassion and our indifference. It is about the age old question of what we're really like in the depths of our being. Most assume that, "basically, we're good people." Isn't that just the way it is? Isn't that what everybody thinks? If someone feels like their self-image, integrity or reputation is being threatened, we often hear them say, "I'm a good person!" It would be pretty hard to live with yourself if you weren't able to maintain some semblance of self-worth. My intent is to call into question the validity of a belief about human nature that enjoys almost universal acceptance.

We've taken it for granted that, "basically, we're good people." Something we've just assumed to be a given has been elevated to status of truth. The reader will be asked to do some soul searching as to the validity of that widely held belief. While being overwhelmingly accepted as conventional wisdom, I would maintain it is not an assumption we can take for granted. I will suggest that perhaps we are delusional in our perception of the truth, and that quite possibly the opposite is true.

Without wanting or intending to be judgmental, critical or blaming, I will ask some tough, penetrating questions about what we're really like. Discount what I have to say and you may continue to live in a world of delusion. The tragedy would be that you have missed out on a chance to live in a real world where caring, compassion and sacrifice lead to more peace and contentment than you ever imagined. On the other hand, you may believe I find comfort in my own delusion. If so, then we have something to talk about.

This is in essence the story of my own personal spiritual journey, one that I have found to be profoundly meaningful and satisfying beyond measure. I thought that it might be helpful to share it with others. It was my hope to share the experience of writing with the person who was most excited about my undertaking the venture, our oldest son, Scott. He died on August 30, 2008 at the age of 38, the result of a tragic accident while tubing on a north Wisconsin lake.

After my retirement as pastor at St. John's Lutheran Church, West Bend, Wisconsin on January 1, 2006, Scott was the one who kept encouraging me to put my mind to it and start writing. But first I wanted to take some time for my wife, our boys and their families, visit Karen's mom in Wausau regularly and spend time with relatives and friends. For me the one downside of ministry was having responsibilities almost every weekend and missing out on being able to spend time with so many of the people who over the years have been wonderful blessings in our lives. But while trying to make up for some lost time in these relationships, I kept reading, reflecting and jotting down drafts of key concepts. I was just starting to get into high gear when Scott died very suddenly. Now the person who was most excited about it would not be able to continue on the journey with me. He and I did not agree on every issue, but we could always talk about them. He forced me to ask questions and examine my views and opinions, which was especially helpful in thinking through the tough, provocative issues that challenge conventional wisdom. We did agree on the core thesis of this book. He is the one who was most familiar with what I was about to write.

Not only did he understand, he was trying to live it. While he was in some ways still trying to get his life together, he was a very caring person. His tragedy was that he allowed too many people to use him. Yet, through it all his warm and kind heart never changed. For most of the last 10 years of his life, he lived in an upstairs apartment, while the owner, Ann, lived downstairs. A part of their arrangement was that he would help Ann. At first it included running errands, driving her around and taking care of the outside chores. As she grew older, weaker and had her physical issues, he began to help more and more. She had no toilet on the first floor, and used the basement toilet as long as she could get up and down the stairs. When that was no longer possible, he emptied her portable toilet and kept it clean. He was the one who seized the initiative, made the arrangements and took her for her weekly shower at the nearby Lutheran Home for the Aging. He could have bailed, but he didn't.

When she died, he had more time and said he wanted to join my wife and me on the Stephen Ministry Team in our congregation. While Stephen Ministers are not counselors, they are given extensive training as listeners and taught to resist the inclination that most of us have to want to jump in and fix "it," rather than come alongside as the care receiver works through their issues for themselves. As my wife Karen said, "We were so blessed to have him in our lives as a gift for as long we did." He has left our presence and is now in the eternal presence of our loving Lord.

Preface

The day they returned to St. Louis after Scott's funeral, our middle son Tim's wife, Wendy, was hospitalized with complications relating to her pregnancy. When Wendy became pregnant, she and Tim had been married 12 years and weren't sure they would ever have a child. So the 45 days she was in the hospital on almost complete bed-rest were a time of prayer and concern before she gave birth to a healthy 3 pound, 14 ounce baby boy. After Scott's funeral, we traveled to St. Louis almost weekly to help and support, both before and after the baby was born. Twenty-three days after Scott died and while Wendy was still in the hospital, we also lost Mom Otto in Wausau. Karen and I were overwhelmed with emotion, especially Karen who had lost her oldest son and her mom. We were unable to deal with so much of the grief and loss and sadness we were feeling. Tim and Wendy named the little guy Samuel Joseph Scott Seban.

It was about a year after we lost Scott that I was able to return to writing. When I would get bogged down and discouraged, it was often Scott's memory that helped to lift me up and keep me going. He knew my heart. He knew what I wanted to write about. Tim and Matt, our youngest son, and their wives had a good sense of it too; but I wanted to clearly spell it out for our grandchildren and future generations.

It would have been easy to just forget about writing by getting involved in a life full of activity, helping out at our church and others in the area (pastors and congregations currently without a pastor are always looking for retired guys who can help out), playing golf, biking, traveling and spending time with family, friends, relatives and our faith family at St. John's. While there will always be that empty place in our lives that can never be filled, our God is a loving God who blesses us with a little more healing each day. We had so much of life to live. There were still so many people to serve and help and so much to be written about. Only now there was more meaning than ever attached to my writing and our living of each day, serving our Lord together and being with those who are closest to us.

Listening to my parents and grandma tell stories about what it was like as they grew up was so helpful in understanding their past and in seeing how that past shaped their lives. In our family, we kids called them the "poor" stories. I want to do the same for our grandchildren. Were I to pass it on in the form of oral tradition, much of what will be told in these pages would be lost. Writing down what is on my heart will make it more likely that our grandchildren will know who I was, what made me tick and what I was about. It is my prayer that many others might also find it to be helpful in doing some soul searching of their own about the meaning of life. Hopefully it can serve as a path of discovery that will lead to finding new meaning and purpose.

Now back to the task at hand. Suggesting there is a huge gulf between the good people we think we are and what we're really like is painful for the reader and risky for the writer. Defenses are triggered. Just who do you think you are? Do you think you're better than we are? Those who are already sensitive about their self-image—and that includes most of us—just plain don't want to take the risk of opening up enough to really find out if this is true of them and possibly get hurt again. Try as you will to speak difficult truth in a manner that is non-blaming, non-judgmental and non-critical, many will still take offense. While this has been by far the biggest challenge in trying to write about this sensitive issue, it was clear to me that I had to take the risk.

So I tried as hard as I could to write in a way that conveys understanding, kindness, caring and sensitivity, hoping that you too will risk opening the door to your heart just a little, leave the chain fastened and find that nobody wants to get on your case. My sincere intent is to speak the truth as gently as possible so that at some point you feel safe enough to take off the chain and open the door to have a conversation with those you trust. After having a number of conversations over a period of weeks, you may find that one day you can let them into your living space, and when you do find that it is safe, that you will be treated with respect and that nobody is going to overturn the furniture and tear up the place.

Trying to address this issue is also risky for me in another way. Opening yourself up makes you vulnerable to others who now know your weaknesses, shortcomings and vulnerabilities, and can detect self-righteousness in a heartbeat. They know just where and how they can hurt you. I do not look forward to that any more than you would. Who knows where the journey will take us? Nevertheless, I'm going to take the chain off the door, open it, let you stick your foot in the door, let you look around and then let you come in and visit, trusting that my place won't get trashed.

Nevertheless, I'm inviting the reader to also hold me accountable. It is tough enough to have one or two people holding you accountable. But throwing the door wide open is flat-out scary. Yet, it was either be true to self or put the mask back on and chain on the door once again. This is the risk I had to be willing to take before beginning this project and starting to walk farther on down the path to finding out who I really am and what I'm really like. Does this guy really practice what he preaches? So, you're invited to come in. I hope you will consider the possibility of joining me on the journey. While neither of us knows where it will end, my hope is that it will open us up to where everyday will be a joyful celebration of life.

Several observations are in order before we begin. First of all, since I'm a preacher, my primary mode of communication is the sermon. It is just who I am. It is how I have been trained. It is just how I think. It would be tough to avoid using some semblance of that model. Since preaching conjures up all sorts of images and reactions, using that model as the construct for this message could be a turn-off for many. It may reinforce what you already think about sermons, or, it may give you a new and perhaps helpful perspective. However, this may be more than a bit presumptuous, since even though I prayed a lot while preparing my sermons, was conscientious and worked very hard on them, I was not a very good preacher. On top of that my wife has been telling me for years that my sermons are way too long. Knowing they were mediocre and that I would continue to preach too long must have been punishing for those who came to services. I am so thankful for patient, accepting, forgiving parishioners. My sense, however, is that they are far more tolerant of a sermon that is too long, than one that steps on their toes— one that addresses the issue of what we're really like.

Secondly, as a student of theology and pastor I can't help but use some of the models and concepts with which I'm familiar. However, I am aware that the use of some of the constructs of Christianity could be a turn-off for those affiliated with another religion, those who aren't sure there is a God or those who believe there is no God. One of the most painful parts—if not the most troubling part of this journey—has been the growing intensity of the painful awareness and conviction about why others are not drawn to Christianity. Observing us from the outside, there are many reasons why others would not have a favorable impression of us and would not want to be a part of our fellowship. If you do come along on the journey and that is your experience, than I have done a terrible disservice to you and to my church. But I do hope you will come along, that it will be a meaningful passage in your personal journey and that you will have found that it was well worth your time.

Finally, while this book is written for a broad mainstream audience, it is my hope that many of my brothers and sisters in the faith will listen in and participate in the conversation. I pray that you too will grow and be blessed.

Chapter 1
"My Bad—Totally!"

"Are people born Wicked? Or do they have Wickedness thrust upon them?"
— *"Wicked"*

"I know that nothing good lives in me, that is, in my sinful nature. For I have the desire to do what is good, but I cannot carry it out. For what I do is not the good I want to do; no, the evil I do not want to do—this I keep on doing" (Romans 7:18-19).

You Can't Restore What Was Never There

The title caught my eye: *Glenn Beck: Restoring Love.* Tuning in the program in progress I heard a message based on a worldview and belief system very different from my own.

> When someone is hungry, we will give them food. When someone is hurt we will heal them, help them. We are Americans. . . . We are helpers. And if there is one thing our government should never do, it is this: don't even try to stop us from helping and feeding and healing. We will serve. . . . We are not selfish people. We are selfless. And you are living proof of this. You are living proof that Americans are good.
>
> We want love and we want it for all mankind. And here's the thing, there are millions of people just like you—millions ready to act, ready to stand, ready to take up a struggle, to commit, to activate, to live it, to create, to restore love in our hearts and in America. . . . We will not give up the right to feed the hungry, to care for the sick. . . . With malice toward none and charity

toward all, let us tonight restore love. For love will hold us together. Love will make us a shelter from the storm. I will be my brother's keeper, and the world will once again know that they are not alone. Because . . . Americans have stood up and arrived again, with honor, and courage, and love.[1]

I wanted so very much to be able to shout, "Amen, brother." I wanted the words to be true. I desperately wanted to be able to agree with what he was saying. I wanted to be wrong and for Beck to be right. I want to see Americans as he sees them. It would be unbelievably satisfying to live in the America he envisions, and to share his view of human nature.

My belief about what people are like is fundamentally different. My perception is that we are not selfless and not very good at being our brother's keeper. We don't come anywhere near realizing our potential to feed the hungry, care for the sick, help, serve and love. Beck's presentation is representative of the belief system that is almost universally accepted. It reflects a view of human nature that says that "basically, we're good people." My thesis expresses a point of view that is different from the one that is taken as a given in our culture and is one of the fundamental tenets of popular religion. I see the world so differently. I would like to be able to see people the way Beck and almost everybody else does. Yet for me it just doesn't compute. I think I'm right, but I don't want to be.

So what are my beliefs about human nature and how do they shape my worldview? Trying to separate out the blending of the political and religious implications of Beck's message and focusing only on his presuppositions and beliefs about human nature, I'll note the fundamental differences we have and how those differences influence my beliefs and worldview. "My bad" is a phrase that recently has been used as a way of acknowledging that something is your fault. You are owning responsibility for a mistake. It conveys a nuanced version of "I'm sorry." Yet, it lacks a deep sense of seriousness or gravity as a description of human nature. In the bigger picture of life and love and family, it is not intended to convey any sense of an earth shattering flaw or mistake.

Another of today's colloquial expressions is "Totally!" My view of human nature might well be expressed by combining the two in a manner that conveyed both emphasis and passion: "My bad, totally!" Rather, most see themselves as basically, good people, who excuse our mistakes. In one way that is a good thing. We do need to be able to come to terms with our mistakes, learn from them and move on. We aren't perfect and we don't want to get dragged down and depressed just because we mess up.

There are some critical issues, however, where moving on without pause for serious reflection results in our being much less caring and compassionate than we would ever want to admit. A phrase like, "My bad, totally!" amplified to express serious concern about how good, or nice or loving I really am gives a hint about my beliefs and convictions about human nature. The reality that I will share and discuss is that basically, we are not good people. We are not selfless, loving helpers and servants who do a commendable or even acceptable job of being our brother's keeper. We live under the illusion that, "basically, we're good people," and I would like so very much to believe it is true. I just can't. My heart aches too much for all of the pain and suffering that has resulted from the way we treat each other in the human family.

Does this mean that my personal outlook on life is negative, pessimistic, depressing and that the future looks grim? Does this mean that I am not positive, optimistic and hopeful about my personal future? Not at all! I am, however, not encouraged when considering the vast majority of my brothers and sisters in the human family. Garrison Keillor appeared at the Milwaukee Arena several years ago. The show began when a spotlight focused on Keillor about a third of the way back on the main floor, just a few rows in front of us. He makes a distinction between sad Lutherans and happy Lutherans based on his experience living in Minnesota. When He appeared just a few feet away I was hoping for some audience participation and the opportunity to say that there are indeed many joyful, happy Lutherans who celebrate a life filled with hope and promise.

Asking people to consider the validity and truth of a belief system that includes an unfavorable opinion of human nature and the perception that all in the human family, Americans included, are for the most part indifferent to the plight of others, is going to encounter strong objection and stiff resistance. It goes against the culture and the basic tenets of popular religion. You're quite sure it will not be well received. It is a tough sell. If in the process you question the validity of the widely held notion that, "basically, we're good people," it gets even tougher. A whole lot of folks are going to get perturbed. How can anyone possibly make that claim? How can anyone suggest something so outrageous?

In what sense is it true that, "basically, we're good people"? In what sense is that perception fatally flawed? Clearly, working through the issue depends on how one defines the word "good." So right from the beginning it is important to start thinking about how we're going to define the word "good." How much meaning do we pack into it? The meaning of the term starts to get fuzzy when caring, kindness and compassion are added to the mix. Where there is the assumed inclusion of concepts like self-sacrifice and selflessness, the discussion really gets mucked up. So there is much to consider when attempting to carefully evaluate the validity of the statement, "basically, we're good people."

You often hear people say, "He was a good person," or "He was always ready to help," or "He would do anything to help anyone," or "He would give you the shirt off his back." In a sense it may be true—in the sense that *culture* defines goodness. The confusion I see in the use of the term is the result of watering down its meaning so much that it now conveys only a minimal standard of goodness. Those who make statements like these are simply not aware of the culture's influence in emptying the term of most of its meaning. There is no reason to expect folks to think any differently, or feel the need to carefully consider the precise meaning of what they are saying. Why would they even question something everyone knows to be true? It's a non-issue for almost everybody, an issue I'm admittedly introducing into the conversation. This is just how it is understood in our culture. Everybody knows that.

Then why even raise the issue at all? What is it going to accomplish? What possible rhyme or reason could there be in doing so? Bingo! The reason is to initiate a conversation about how we in the human family treat each other, and to bring into our awareness the phenomenal amount of untapped potential to do so much more to help and care for each other. If we really don't care all that much about the well-being of others, that's one thing. If we are not caring and not helping simply because of the cultural blinders we are wearing, that is quite another. If we have honestly never stopped to think about it, that's one thing. If the issue has been surfaced and brought into our awareness, and then we don't do anything different, and don't make any changes, that is another matter completely.

My intent is to initiate a discussion about an issue that nobody really gives much thought to, and yet is so absolutely essential in making an accurate assessment of human nature. Are we, basically, good people, or not? Are we just the human race? Or, are we family? My sense is that agreeing with the grand delusion, that, "basically, we're good people," has a pervasive influence on how we live. For the most part we are able to block out the pain, misery and suffering that are all around us, and consequently do not touch nearly as many people as we could in ways that could lighten their burdens. By not doing so, we tragically miss out on so much of the joy, fulfillment, contentment and peace that is out there for all of us.

Core Issues and Core Values

When you are concerned enough about someone that you feel you have to share your heart with them, it helps if you can do so gently. Try as you may to be humble and to come across as caring, sensitive and kind, it doesn't always help. When you start to get close to what might be perceived as a threat to a person's self-image, alarm-bells go off. The closer you get to core values, the more intense the reaction. Get too close and they will defend with the intensity of a mother-bear protecting her cubs. When chop after chop chips away piece after piece of our self-image and self-respect, and the structural integrity of the trunk is in danger of being compromised, we fight ferociously to defend whatever sense of self-worth we have left. Questioning the belief that, "basically, we're good people," gets right to the core.

However, when you have a genuine and heart-felt concern for the well-being of others, there is no choice but to speak. It would be unloving and uncaring to remain silent. While it goes without saying that we certainly do not want to knowingly say anything that will hurt someone's feelings, then as long as it is intended for good, the truth as you perceive it must be shared. You also know upfront that when you step out and speak the truth in love, you are going to step on somebody's toes. You know upfront that there will be negative, defensive responses. You just hope that what is shared will be received as an invitation to conversation and study, not the last word from a self-righteous, pompous, arrogant fool who thinks he has all the answers.

A part of my intent in what follows is to initiate a give-and-take that may be enlightening to readers, while also being helpful to me as I am blessed by the wisdom of others in revealing my blind spots. If you never say it out loud, you'll never know for sure whether you're way off the wall or not. I do hope that when speaking the truth in love to me that you will try to be as gentle with me as I will try to be with you.

We Live in Our Own "Reality"

Describing ourselves as, "basically, good people," no longer seems to me to be an accurate description of who we are and what we are about. It just doesn't feel right. It doesn't check out with my experience. It just doesn't compute for me. My sense is that the commonly held perception of the phrase is both dishonest and misleading. On the inside our hearts do not burn with care and compassion. Our external appearance conceals a "survival of the fittest," "every man for himself" mentality.

These assertions are a threat to the commonly held notion of what we are really like. Core beliefs are being called into question. We are being asked to reconsider our understanding of *self*, of *life* and of *meaning*. It is understandably difficult to step back and respond in a calm, collected, detached, rational way, when the very foundation of everything we have come to believe is being questioned. Will the integrity of our belief system be compromised as it is shaken to its very foundation, or will the structure remain intact and stable?

My contention is that we are delusional in the sense that we see ourselves as being kinder and gentler than is reflected in our behavior. As we gain more of an awareness of who we are and what we are really like, we have to be able to live with ourselves just as we are. Living with yourself once you sense that on some level you are much more cold-hearted and uncaring than you used to think, isn't easy. How difficult is a function of your self-image and the one being offered as an alternative.

Sometimes the gap between the two is big enough to be very painful. In some cases the pain is so intense that we are not able to tolerate it, at which point we have to create our own reality in order to survive. You have to find a way to insulate yourself from the truth. Sometimes the pain of the suggested reality is so great that you have to find a way to escape. The defensive strategy that seems to best describe this process is delusional thinking. Delusion is a means whereby one can evade the truth by misleading the mind into believing something that is not true. In the process of creating a new reality what gets lost is an accurate and realistic perception of who we are. Not having been made aware of what we're really like is one issue. Becoming aware of and then repressing, denying and distorting reality is quite another. I am suggesting that our perception of our ethics, morals and values does not come close to approaching reality.

The process of how we have been misled so much that we are able to evade the truth about ourselves—the delusion that, "basically, we're good people"—is not difficult to understand. We all have our views about what life is all about. Who are we? How did we get here? Why are we here? What is our purpose in life? What we believe about the meaning of life reflects the philosophies, beliefs, convictions and perspectives of the people who have taught us and shaped our lives, as well as the ideas and belief systems to which we have been exposed.

All of us have integrated the various elements of life that we have been taught and experienced into our very own world view, belief system, philosophy of life, or organizing principle. Each of us has a framework for what we perceive as reality. We become accustomed to that reality, accommodate ourselves to it and get very comfortable living in it. These are the principles and convictions that become the anchors in our life, and that give our life purpose and direction.

We all have our own goals, hopes and dreams, and we live life in pursuit of them. As we go about our daily life in pursuit of our dreams, we seek to maintain an outward presence of being kind, caring, charitable, decent and respectable. Yet, all of these characteristics are relative terms that we have to define both for ourselves and as a community; there is a whole continuum of meaning for each.

We are caught up in a delusion that is so widespread and pervasive that it permeates the culture in which we have been nurtured. We naturally accommodate ourselves to the conceptual framework and belief system of our culture. This helps explain why we adopt the cultural description of us as "basically, good people." We have no reason to question the culturally accepted view that we are kind, caring, charitable people. Cultural assumptions about what we're like make it easy to avoid even thinking about what I am suggesting is the truth about how kind, caring and compassionate we are, on the one hand, and how evil we really are, on the other.

A continuum with numeric values attached to ethics, morals and values will provide clarification. Both the descriptive terms chosen to categorize human nature and the ranges attached to them are admittedly arbitrary and subjective.

1-8	primative
9-15	barbaric
16-30	civilized
31-40	decent
41-50	good
51-60	kind, caring, considerate and charitable
61-73	compassionate and generous
74-95	selfless
96-99	saints

For purposes of discussion, my sense is that the perception of those who believe that, "basically, we're good people," would correspond to something in the 35-77 range. The reality I'm suggesting would correspond to the 19-44 range. This gives you a pretty good (no pun intended) sense of where I'm coming from and how I see people.

My intent is to challenge a common thread that runs through the American psyche: the part of our reality that incorporates the culturally validated delusion that, "basically, we're good people." Within the framework of our own set of organizing principles or worldview we have all come to share the bottom line conviction that we are kind, caring, charitable people. In order to get to that place we have to distort, repress and deny so much about ourselves. We simply are not being honest. We have done a fantastic job of creating a philosophy of life or belief system that includes a foundational conviction that, while not perfect, we're not all that bad either.

For example, let's examine the word "kind." Some of the nuances noted in Webster are benevolent, tender, gracious, loving, gentle and humane. There is a whole continuum of meaning for the word "kind" and for all the terms that help define it more specifically. Where you fall on the continuum—how kind is kind—is something we decide for ourselves. Bottom line, we define what "kind" means for us. We can choose a narrow definition of kindness in the purest sense, in which case it is more difficult to include the assumption that we are kind in our belief system or world view.

Or we can choose a more inclusive definition, one that doesn't hold us to as high a standard and allows for our inclusion in the category. In order to come to terms with ourselves and be at peace, we need to have a definition of kindness that allows us to be able to incorporate kindness into our self-image. Will we choose a narrow definition, or one we dumb down, dilute and spin in ways that show us in a more favorable light?

The process works the same way for Christians. While Christians have God's standard, which clearly defines kind, caring and charitable, the Biblical meaning of these concepts has been compromised significantly. My sense is that these terms have lost so much of their intended meaning and have been so watered down in our preaching and teaching that they have become bland and innocuous. Much of Christian teaching uses mental gymnastics to do a flip-flop that allows us to see ourselves as kind and retain our self-esteem. Rather than clinging to Christ, asking for forgiveness and celebrating his grace (the undeserved gift of love and forgiveness rooted in Jesus life, death and resurrection), we see ourselves as, "basically, good people," who do not have all that much of a need for forgiveness.

We are kind to one another when it is doesn't inconvenience us too much, when it fits our agenda or when it goes along with our program. We are caring when it doesn't involve too much sacrifice, or compromise our vision of the American Dream. We put our own spin on God's Word—we call it interpretation. We redefine the words. We're kind in the way we want to be kind. We put limitations on God's definitions of love and compassion.

Are we kind when our kids and grandkids have so much more than they need, and we repress and block out the anguish of parents whose hearts are breaking because they can't provide food, clean water or basic health care for their children? Are we kind when we consider our spending in the context of looking on as anguished parents hold their kids while they starve to death? Are we kind when our kids have all kinds of advanced electronics and opportunities to go to athletic camps or participate in club sports, while other parents are struggling with disease and can't even begin to imagine their children getting an education? Can such behavior really be described as caring and kind, loving and compassionate—the literal meaning of which is spilling out our guts in order to help others?

What does our Christian God think about all this? How does He feel about it? He is shocked, devastated and heart broken. He weeps and sobs in sadness and disbelief, overcome with heartache and disappointment. I can imagine these being his thoughts.

> After all I have done for my people I was hoping their response would be so different from what it is. Yes, I know. I loved them, forgave them, cared for them, and then set them free. It had to be that way. Unless you let them go, they can never bring you the joy and celebration that comes when, moved by your love for them, they respond by showing their love to me by being kind and caring in their relationships with others. So I hurt.

I'm vulnerable to the anguish felt when the children you love grow up and hardly ever come to visit. This just isn't how I wanted it to be. I hoped they would have responded differently to my self-sacrificing love on the cross. I thought they would understand why they were here. It is devastating when you know you raised them the best you could, and then the way they are living does not reflect the way they were raised.

There is such a huge disconnect between the way we see ourselves and the way God sees us.

"Fess Up! This Is a Sermon, Isn't It?"

As a pastor, the model of communication that I am accustomed to and comfortable with is the sermon. No, what follows is not going to be a sermon. Rather, my intent is to adapt the process of sermon preparation that I use as the vehicle for communicating, rather than making it a sermon. What is it that happens during the process of prayer, study and reflection that in the end emerges as the "message"? Wait a minute! Now I'm the one who is delusional! Certainly it is a sermon. How could it not be?

That being said, what kind of a sermon will it be? It will be one of those sermons that nobody likes, one of those sermons that nobody wants to hear. It will be a sermon that calls a spade a spade and tells it like it is. It will be one of those sermons where you get very uncomfortable and start to squirm. It will speak to our conviction that, "basically, we're good people."

It is always my prayer to preach in a way that lifts up, supports and encourages. In the end I believe it does. However, you have to deal with some disturbing and unsettling issues before you can get to a place of healing and peace. The dishonesty involved in sugar-coating the truth results in a short term high. Whitewashing the reality of what we're really like does not bring lasting joy and celebration. Facing the truth, as painful as that may be, is the only way to find lasting peace and contentment. The more intensely you resist, the more you dig in your feet, the more you repress, deny and distort truth and reality, the more you become insulated from the vitality and fullness of all that life was meant to be.

These are reflections about life written from a winter window that looks out on a landscape of a freshly fallen snow. It looks cold, but when you go outside, it feels warm in the sun. It is treacherous under foot, yet what a beautiful blanket of white. It is exhilarating when you are young and adventurous, but invites caution for seniors who don't want to slip and fall. The metaphor of competing emotions in a chilly landscape is descriptive of what I am currently experiencing as the fabric of a fantastic life. This is who I am. This is what I am about. This is me. This is where I am right now, feeling so very much alive, excited and full of anticipation just to be able to try to share with you what all this is about, to share what all of this means to me. At the same time I feel uneasiness and ambivalence knowing that my perceived reality is different from the perceived reality of most.

Being called out of the seminary to a small congregation afforded the blessing and opportunity for this young pastor to take time to pray, study and reflect while sitting with his wife on a porch swing in the sweltering heat of a central Illinois summer. What a great place to ponder how to preach and teach what it means to be a kind, caring, compassionate follower of Christ. It was during those early years in ministry that a number of related issues kept surfacing again and again. Over time it became clear that we Christians had strayed farther from the path of being faithful followers of Christ than I ever imagined. We as pastors and people needed to have a conversation that would describe with much greater specificity what it would look like if we were transformed into passionate, dedicated committed servants of Christ, willing to sacrifice and do whatever necessary to follow in his steps and do his will. It was during that process that I began to question the validity of the assumption that, "basically, we're good people."

Fortunately, I had the sense to realize that if you didn't slow down and tone down the message to soften the impact, a young, whippersnapper of a preacher could be tarred and feathered and run out of town on a rail for "preaching" about what it means to sell out for Christ. Consequently, my attempts to do so from the pulpit were feeble and weak, lacking the specificity and clarity needed to make it difficult for my parishioners to discount and dismiss the message. To put it bluntly, I bailed.

To be sure, at that time in my life my thoughts were in their early formative stages, lacking in clarity and focus. I did not have an understanding of the gravity of the issue or the conceptual framework needed to address the issue effectively. Perhaps that's an excuse. It would also be easy to hide behind the fact that except for my first congregation, I served as associate pastor and therefore it wasn't appropriate for me to set the vision for the congregation, or to pursue my agenda and upset the applecart by causing an uproar that would derail the vision of the senior pastor.

Truth is it took years for all of this to become clear to me. And there is still time to share the whole package. I couldn't live with myself if I bailed again. It was a choice between being authentic, or retreating into delusion. This is the first comprehensive attempt to share my perceptions about what I had at first assumed was the basic goodness of the people in our country and in the congregations I served. And, in the process, Christians certainly will not be given a pass.

While on the journey I have also come to understand the need to share with any Christians who may be interested a message rooted in the part of the pastoral role that includes prophetic proclamation of what it means to be and to live as a faithful follower of Christ. Early encouragement came from three notes written upon leaving my first congregation, St. Paul, Shobonier, Illinois. All three said in effect that as a result of my faithfulness in preaching and teaching, their lives as Christians would never be the same. Wow! They heard the Word. They understood. They got it. The notes were heaven sent and helped to relieve a growing sense of frustration and discouragement.

I thought that I had only marginally challenged a long term practice in the congregation, encouraged only minimal movement in what it meant to be transformed, and did so gently and patiently—taking two years to lay the groundwork for the proposed change. It didn't matter. I had made erroneous assumptions, and misread both the importance of the issue to them as well as how to go about the process needed to foster Christian maturity. Since I didn't feel as if my preaching and teaching were all that effective, it seemed best to leave and serve another congregation. Maybe someone else could be used by God to get through to the faithful at St. Paul. But what reason did I have for thinking it would be different anywhere else? Through the notes, God provided the blessing of encouragement I so very much needed at that time. Today the affirmation isn't needed and the desire to share my heart is stronger than ever.

Attitude Adjustment Hour

In church circles "attitude adjustment hour" is shorthand for going to church, with emphasis on the sermon." The opinions, feelings and attitudes worshippers have about sermons are all over the board. "Here we go again." "I hope that just once it will be less than 25 minutes." "It will probably be just as boring this week as it is every week." All the while, those who are broken and discouraged are desperately waiting for a word that will help bring healing and wholeness, strength and support.

There are all kinds of reasons folks don't like sermons. What I heard repeatedly from my wife was, "It was too long. You just have to shorten it up." She was right. Yet, you would expect a preacher would try to have the last word and defend the length. In defense of some of us, it needs to be said that long sermons aren't always a bad thing. All of us can remember long sermons where the time just flew by. You didn't even notice. It was a great message. You were fully engaged and hung on every word. You didn't mind the length a bit, unless it was the late service and kickoff for your favorite NFL team was at noon.

When you're not rushed and the sermon has a "spot on" message that is well prepared and well delivered, most of us don't mind if it is 20-25 minutes long. However, most preachers will admit that sermons fitting into this category are the exception rather than the rule. When the preacher is not prepared or starts rambling, the sermon seems like it is going to go on forever. It is easy to tune out and turn off. One of the professors who taught preaching at our seminary emphasized that we only have the whole congregation together once a week for twenty minutes, and we better make the most of every minute. We needed to be thoroughly prepared and know exactly what we want to say. He added, "And don't gas off."

Another thing parishioners don't like is when the pastor reads most of the sermon. While that is prevailing wisdom, my favorite preacher read large portions of his sermons. The reason was that you knew when he entered the pulpit, he was thoroughly prepared. The structure, outline and progression were easy to follow as he carefully developed the central thought.

It was always my intent to have a well prepared sermon with a clear outline and logical progression of thought that could be functionally memorized paragraph by paragraph. How well I succeeded is a whole different question. While you couldn't say that I wasn't prepared, my sermons were tightly written and I read too much of them. A good friend recently told me that my sermons and voice would be great on the radio, but lost something when delivered in front of a congregation. And, please, don't ask my wife.

Many believers really don't like it when the pastor preaches about stewardship. It is at or near the top of the list of excuses why people don't belong to a church or don't attend church regularly. "All they talk about in church is money: money, money, money." Most members don't like stewardship sermons either. If you want a whole bunch of your members to get their dander up, preach a stewardship sermon. It really gets their goat. If you're passive-aggressive and want to have a little fun by tweaking the parishioners, just preach a hum-dinger of a stewardship sermon. Oops, the punishing part of my wickedness has just surfaced again.

It is a preacher's calling to help the congregation grow in spiritual maturity to the point where all clearly understand what the Bible teaches. It is the preacher's hope and prayer that all members will come to a place in their relationship with God where they are not offended or upset by sermons about giving. A preacher hopes they will welcome the reminders of those ways in which they have strayed in their walk with the Lord, and that they will be led by the Holy Spirit to become cheerful and generous givers.

It may come as a surprise to many that those hell, fire and brimstone sermons are not at the top of the list of sermons people don't like. Actually, they like to hear a good one every once in a while. Members know they are guilty of some sins and deserve to be chastised—at least a little. But they don't want us to get carried away. Having to sit through a hell, fire and brimstone sermon is like getting disciplined by a parent for something you know you had coming. And it's a relief when it's over. You got what you deserved. Your slate is clean. You don't have to feel guilty any more, if you ever really did in the first place. So you look forward to a hell, fire and brimstone sermon every once in a while. I'll take my punishment. It isn't all that bad. Then I can get on with living my life just as before.

So if the hell, fire and brimstone sermons are not the ones that hurt the most when the preacher is carrying out his prophetic role in leading people to see themselves as they really are, then what—besides the ones about stewardship—are the ones we really don't like to hear? Actually, congregations are very patient and accepting—and so forgiving of the pastor's shortcomings as a preacher; believe me, I would know. However, what they do not appreciate at all and what they will not tolerate is when the preacher gets too close to the truth, steps on their toes too hard and it starts to hurt real bad. When the sermon makes them really uncomfortable, when it makes them squirm and sweat because their sin, when evil and wickedness are exposed in such a clear and compelling manner that they can't avoid taking responsibility, they really get mad.

When the hearer's wickedness is exposed, when they get undressed and stand naked before God, they get out the fig leaves and look for someplace to hide. About that time the preacher also better try to find a place to hide and seek refuge from irate parishioners. This holds true for gifted, charismatic, exceptional preachers, as well as for those of us who simply tried our best to faithfully proclaim the saving truth of God's Word and then relied on the Holy Spirit to work through our mediocre efforts. When we wear the mantle of the prophet, we better be ready to head for the hills, or if we keep it up, to another congregation.

So what are the kinds of sermons that really get good church folk upset—the biggies, the ones that send them right through the roof? They are the ones where the preacher directs a message about sinfulness at the very folks present in worship, those who consider themselves to be good Christians and good people. What many of our members want is for us to preach about "them there sinners out there," and about all of the moral decay that is ruining our country. Instead the preacher includes those present in the same category as "them there sinners out there," and when he does, they become irate and indignant. They freak out! "How dare he question our Christianity? Who does he think he is? We know him long enough to know that he's no saint either." They continue to complain on out into the parking lot. The pastor has crossed the line into territory where their spiritual self-image is threatened. These are the sermons the faithful don't like one bit. They don't think that they're all that bad. Actually, they think that, "basically, we're good people."

On a summer afternoon several years ago we were doing some planting and trimming out in the yard. Our neighbor two doors away was also out in his yard. They had this gigantic Great Dane named Excalibur. You hardly ever knew he was around. He didn't bark. When unleashed, he didn't roam. For some reason that day he grazed over toward our yard. I didn't know he was there. Then Larry saw him and yelled, "Cal, get over here!" I'm not sure who jumped more, "Cal" or me. I hadn't heard those words in years.

What was it that I reacted to? Clearly it triggered memories of similar messages heard as I was growing up, feelings deeply imbedded in my psyche—formative components of my personality and self-esteem. Clearly, my self-image was fragile. Larry's shout triggered a reaction to internal tapes recorded years before. If the relatively low intensity experience with Excalibur hooked me enough emotionally to make me jump and yelp, how much more strongly would I react when presented with a serious threat to my spiritual self-image? When the preacher makes it perfectly clear that he is addressing the sinfulness of those who are present in worship, it triggers a response far more intense than my "Excalibur experience". The hearer gets hot under the collar. The part of the sermon that convicts us is like a heat seeking missile that threatens the very core of our spiritual being. These are the kinds of sermons members don't like.

When our beliefs about life and reality are challenged, it is unnerving. When someone rocks the boat and the equilibrium surrounding foundational beliefs is threatened, we become very anxious. When our reality is threatened, we get defensive. My intent in this book is to stir the pot and rock the boat as hard as I can. Where it appears to me that there is a false and artificial sense of peace and tranquility resulting from delusional thinking, I will try to create chaos and uncertainty. It is my hope to motivate you to question beliefs based on conventional wisdom and a "reality" in which we have all become quite comfortable.

Atheists and agnostics will point out that religious beliefs about the afterlife and the supernatural origins of our doctrines are also evidence of delusional thinking. While it may not be possible to separate issues as clearly as I am suggesting, my attempt is to address that part of our being that is a common denominator for all, religious and non-religious. When it comes to the part of each of us that holds "I'm a good person," all of us classify ourselves within the range of what is acceptable. This is the perception that I intend to challenge.

Bursting My "Truth and Reality" Bubble

A recent Office Max commercial highlights what it calls "heart wrenching moments of truth, like when you see your dad shooting a basketball, when you see your DJ in person for the first time or when your printer runs out of ink." A moment of truth occurs whenever the integrity of our self-created belief system is challenged.

Indeed, my sense is that we live in a world that we have created for ourselves, that we live in a reality that is formed over time through a process that includes repression, distortion and denial in a magnitude of the first order. We live in a reality based on a reframing and spinning of the truth that fits with our preconceived ideas about what people are like and what life is all about. Our reality has its own belief system, conceptual framework or organizing principle. Within that belief system we acquire a self-image that makes it possible to maintain our integrity and self-respect, a self-image that is sacred and becomes holy ground. We accommodate ourselves to this new reality, live in it and become very comfortable, feeling safe and secure. The task is complete. We have reframed reality to fit with our perception of truth and reality.

Then along comes someone like me who suggests that the truth is that we are not anywhere near the kind, caring, compassionate folk we have convinced ourselves that we are. When someone takes a pin and becomes a threat to the bubble that is our reality, we react intensely, because facing the truth can be quite painful—at times almost too painful to bear. This book is a long, sharp pin that seeks to burst the bubble of distortion and illusion that define our culture and the reality we have created for ourselves—including our self-image.

Many among us don't feel all that good about ourselves. From early on most of us have internalized negative messages. "Why can't you be like your sister?" "How many times have I told you?" "If I've told you once, I've told you a thousand times!" "When will you ever learn?" "You'll never amount to anything!" "You are so stupid!" "You are pathetic!" "You're no damned good!" When we hear messages like these, we defend ourselves in order to preserve whatever sense of worth and value we have left. It is like taking an ax to the trunk of a tree and chopping out one chunk of self-esteem after another. After repeated blows the tree is in danger of falling. We move into crisis mode in order to protect the integrity and strength of whatever is left of our self-image.

Then along comes one more voice in the chorus suggesting that, basically, we're not the good, kind, caring people we think we are. We feel it in our gut, in the very core of our being. Someone has tread on our personal holy ground. You can mess with a lot of things, but don't mess with this acceptable picture of self that I have carefully nurtured and staunchly defend. We have repressed and distorted and denied reality in order to maintain an image of self that was developed to protect and insulate us from any more damage and pain to our perception of who we are in the very core of our being. When backed into a corner and our integrity and self-image are challenged, we come out fighting to retain whatever semblance of dignity, integrity and self-respect we have left.

We intensely resist those who would seek to expose our self-deception, quickly responding with arguments that defend the reality we have created and embraced in order to survive. The task of bursting the bubble of self-created truth and reality is the preacher's responsibility. It is part of the essence of what we are called to do. Upsetting the applecart, disturbing the equilibrium, and exposing the fallacies in the thinking, reasoning and arguments upon which we have built our belief system is the first of two primary objectives for a sermon.

In my head I know what I'm called to do. Saying that doing so is no fun is an understatement. You know you are going to meet with intense resistance. Yet, that part of the office when you wear the prophet's mantle calls you to attempt to smash into smithereens the belief systems and reality of those who think that, basically, they're good people. While I have this punishing part of my personality that surfaces far too often, initiating this conversation in the sermon is not a process in which I find any sadistic pleasure. I will try as hard as I can not to be judgmental, critical or blaming. The Lord knows I have enough issues of my own to confess and deal with. If I come up short in my desire to be non-blaming, non-judgmental or non-critical, having it in writing will make it easy for others to bring it to my attention.

So in effect I'm going to attempt to prepare a sermon designed to expose us for who and what we are, to expose the delusion that we are not the kind, loving, caring souls we think we are and to facilitate soul-searching and conversation about this issue. My hope is for us to honestly face the truth about ourselves, and consider beginning a process of self-examination and introspection that can lead us to a much better place than where we started—a place of joy, contentment, peace, fulfillment, meaning and purpose.

The Sermon as Conversation

As just noted, my views are not presented as the last word. They are intended to be the start of a conversation. I welcome the input of those who will help me carefully examine my beliefs, convictions and perceptions. The conversation includes the age old questions about the meaning of life. Who am I? Where did I come from? Why am I here? What is the meaning of my existence and all of life? What is my purpose in life? I too still "see in a glass darkly" (1 Cor. 13:12; King James Version)" and appreciate feedback and assistance in sorting it all out. I would like to suggest the same would be true for all of us. I would like to think that we all want to do some soul-searching and examine the presuppositions of the worldviews we have blended into the personal worldview we have adopted as our own. But I can't. The truth is that we are not all looking for feedback and assistance in sorting it out, and don't want to do any soul-searching. "We're just fine the way we are. So why don't you just leave well-enough alone."

The bottom line for Christians is that when the preacher is wearing the mantle of a prophet and teaches that God's call to be a disciple, a faithful follower of Christ, is a call to a life of complete surrender to the will of God, many still don't get it. And if they do, they don't like it. Living a life of sacrifice, commitment and dedication to Christ means living to honor and serve Him with all that you have and are. It means that you live to serve and praise Him from the time you arise in the morning until you close your eyes in peaceful sleep in the evening. It includes your personal devotional life, weekly worship with a congregation and service to the Lord in your vocation in the community, as a plumber or truck driver, dental hygienist, nurse, supervisor or executive. It includes using your time, your gifts and abilities in service to the Lord through the mission of the church. It includes the financial support of your congregation's ministry plan and the church's mission of healing and service throughout the world. In broad strokes this is what it means to be a disciple. This is what it is that those who consider themselves good Christians often don't like to hear. The understanding of what it means to be a disciple will be spelled out with detailed specificity and become crystal clear in Chapter 7.

Prophetic teaching and sermons that call people to be followers of Christ are met with deafening silence, convenient denial, angry resistance and parking lot insurrection. This is not what most folks are looking for in a church, and if that is the pastor's vision for the congregation, he should probably be looking for another place to serve. One could put the best possible interpretation on it and say that these folks are still spiritually immature. Sermons that teach and preach the fullness of these Biblical truths are the ones that people really don't like and don't want to hear. This is the biggie, the elephant in the room. As members are encouraged to own those parts of themselves they don't want to acknowledge, let alone confess, they begin to repress, deny and tune out. These are the sermons nobody likes.

It was always a source of great consolation to me when I would catch one of the parishioners nodding their head and snoozing before the sermon even began. Then it was easy to rationalize that it wasn't my sermon that put them to sleep. Actually, I didn't mind. If in the midst of the trouble and turmoil in their lives they were able to find in worship a place of quiet and a peace, a refuge from everything else that was swirling around them, God bless them. I always appreciated the early snoozers. I looked for them. In retirement it is so tempting to want to join their fellowship. Since we remained in the congregation and the other worshippers know who I am, I'm very grateful for the coffee served during the fellowship that precedes worship. With a cup or two—it depends on the sermon—I can usually stay awake. My wife is "Plan B." Our pastors should be grateful for the coffee. Yet, how easy it is to give in to temptation, find a place of calm and peace in worship and join the "fellowship of the snoozers." Perhaps our pastors are also happy that I too can find in worship a place of peace.

You don't go church because of the preacher. You don't stay away because of the preacher. To put it in the kindest possible way, not all pastors are gifted preachers. However, God has blessed us all with gifts. Each pastor is gifted in at least one aspect of ministry, and usually several. But there isn't one of us who is gifted for all of the ministry tasks for which we are responsible: preaching, teaching, outreach, administration, youth ministry, family ministry, counseling and pastoral care. But we are gifted in one or two and it is a part of God's plan that the current pastor has just the right gifts to meet the congregation's needs at that time. He is just the right one to be there with God's comfort, reassurance, encouragement and strength, and in just the way they need it. Your current pastor might be the right person to be with you if you are grieving the loss of a loved one, have just found out you have cancer or that your husband is leaving you or when you've been arrested, need bail and haven't told your wife yet.

While on vacation out east, we left Gettysburg early one Sunday morning and stopped to worship at a congregation on the outskirts of Pittsburgh—not an easy thing to do for citizens of the Raider nation who simply cannot erase the memory of Franco Harris and the "Immaculate Reception." The congregation was vibrant and alive. You could see it. You could feel it. They radiated the joy and love that we Christians have as we come to know and develop a close, personal relationship with Jesus Christ. They were very welcoming to us as visitors. The liturgy and music were uplifting, the pastor's sermon delivery was easy and relaxed and the message was both spiritually moving and profound. We were truly blessed to have been there. After sharing a few words of affirmation and encouragement with the pastor, we headed on our way. The Lord had blessed us richly by being in his service, as he always does.

We chatted about the service as we headed on down the road. My wife said, "That was one of our kind of sermons." I knew exactly what she meant. The sermon was both prophetic and challenging. All of us were called to a life of surrender and sacrifice. It was a call to discipleship. It was a call to be more faithful followers of Jesus Christ. The pastor didn't mince words. He laid it out there gently and tactfully, yet at in a manner that was compelling and unapologetic. The level of commitment and dedication that he was describing was way beyond that with which most Christians bargain for when they are looking to join a church. It was the kind of sermon most people don't like, not because it was too long, not because it wasn't well prepared, not because he stayed too close to his manuscript, not because he wasn't dynamic or charismatic, but because it agitated and irritated and made us all feel extremely uncomfortable.

It was a prophetic call to a life of sacrifice, self-denial and service, in response to all that Christ has done for us.

The Christian life he described probably didn't fit with the kind of relationship with God most people have in mind. It is really tough to accommodate the comfortable lifestyle of most Christians into the lifestyle he was describing. It was too intrusive, too inconvenient. But without a doubt he was proclaiming Biblical truth. My hunch is that his people were somewhat farther along the journey to spiritual maturity than most. Later I'll explain my sense that most preachers are very hesitant when it comes to preaching sermons like his, even though they are an essential part of the process of spiritual nurture which seeks a more radical expression of the Christian faith—one that begins to approach the Biblical model of discipleship. It is a moment of truth. As the preacher gets closer and closer to the truth, exposing us for who and what we really are, he crosses the threshold that triggers a "DEFCON 1" response. He hit the nail on the head as he proclaimed the truth of God's Word and exposed us for who we are. He crossed the line that separates the spiritual comfort zone from a life of discipleship.

"Wicked"

It was a cold and blustery December day as we boarded the bus to Chicago with a tour group from Concordia University, Wisconsin. The roads were clear, but snow was expected later in the day. Everyone was looking forward to a performance of "Wicked" at the Oriental Theatre. I was looking forward to the day, mostly because I knew how much my wife wanted to go, and how much she would enjoy it.

On our way in we were given a brief a tour of the north Loop area, including the "Magnificent Mile." I was born and raised in the city, and always enjoyed going downtown. We were dropped of at the Renaissance hotel, where they had an excellent lunch buffet in a room overlooking Wacker Drive, the Chicago River, the Marina City towers, the Trump Tower, the Tribune Tower, the Wrigley Building and what was the old Pure Oil Building. As part of a high school writing project they allowed me to go to the very top of the Pure Oil Building— to the outdoor porch under the dome. It is now dwarfed by the skyscrapers that surround it. There are many spectacular views in downtown Chicago; the one from the restaurant at the Renaissance was a first for me, and an unexpected treat. After lunch we were taken on a tour of the south Loop area: Millennium Park, the remodeled Soldier's Field, Lakeshore drive and the

Kodak moment view of the downtown skyline from Planetarium Drive. Then we turned west on Randolph Street toward the Oriental.

When in high school, we sometimes went downtown for a late movie at the State and Lake, the Chicago, the Woods or the Oriental. Afterwards we'd stop at one of the restaurants where you could get a steak dinner for $1.98. We usually managed to go in shortly before closing time, and were often given extra baked potatoes and garlic bread.

The Oriental didn't seem as elegant back then. Maybe it was because the frescoed ceiling and walls were already getting dingy. It has since been refurbished and was magnificent. From my perspective it was already a great day, and the performance had yet to begin. Looking forward to an enjoyable and relaxing afternoon had an appeal all of its own. There would be time to just sit back and take it all in. Being there was like going back to the way it used to be for me, to another time and another place that was less turbulent and less complicated, before many of the experiences and awareness's that had shattered my relatively safe little world and opened my eyes to so much that I didn't want to see and wished that I knew nothing about.

I hadn't paid much attention to what "Wicked" was about, and just thought it was a take-off on the wicked witch in the Wizard of Oz. This story about the Witches of Oz was a pleasant surprise. Maybe pleasant isn't the best word. It was delightful and painful, funny and sad, and wonderful and tragic. Early on the lyrics and dialogue caught my attention. "Are people born Wicked? Or do they have Wickedness thrust upon them?" It was going to be about the question, where does "wicked" come from? A rush of adrenalin kicked in. The body and mind which were just starting to relax shifted into my active, cognitive mode, reflecting and ruminating about what it all meant. I hurt most about the transformation of crippled Nessarose into physical wholeness and spiritual wickedness.

I was now fully engaged in anticipation of what "Wicked" had to say that would help inform my interest in human nature, and what being "wicked" really means. After years of study, reflection and prayer it was just recently that I had come to new levels of awareness in my understanding of human nature and its implications for life and relationships, including a much better grasp of what being "wicked" is all about. As with the word "good" there is a whole range of meaning when defining "wicked". Since the manifestation of wickedness in our lives is what this book is about, it is imperative that I share my understanding of "wicked" as the baseline from which the conversation can begin. **"Wicked" is our tendency to look out not just for the needs of ourselves and our own,**

but also for our wants, at the expense of the unmet needs of others, many of whom are living in misery and despair.

For some time I have been pondering my perception of human nature as it relates to the needs of others. I see it as the core issue that has to inform our study of all the other disciplines: anthropology, history, theology, philosophy, sociology, psychology, government, politics and international relations. In any study of the theories of personality, a key component is one's understanding of human nature. Being clear about my understanding of human nature is foundational to all that follows.

Most of us believe that, basically, we're good people. My hope is to bring out into the open the rationalizations and justifications that make it possible for us to maintain that delusion, while repressing and denying what we're really like. What happens once the fig leaves are dropped and we again stand naked and exposed for who and what we are? Are we going to continue on down the river of cultural tradition in which we have been carried along, going with the flow of the ethics, morals and values in which we have been living? Or, do we start fighting the strong currents that seek to pull us along with the vast majority. My hope is to make it more difficult to repress and deny, distort and reframe, rationalize and justify, as we are looking out not just for the needs, but also for the wants of ourselves and our own at the expense of the unmet needs of others.

There is a saying well known to preachers: *The task of the preacher is to comfort the afflicted and afflict the comfortable.* It is my intent to try to do just that, to "preach the sermons" nobody likes and nobody wants to hear. We have this image of ourselves as basically good people. My sense is that we are just kidding ourselves. Our self-concept is so favorable as to be totally out of touch with reality. It may be fairly accurate when measured by widely accepted standards of decency in our culture, but so inaccurate as to be almost totally unrecognizable when evaluated by anything resembling a higher standard.

Providing for the needs of those for whom we are responsible is absolutely essential, commendable and the right thing to do. But there is that oh, so, important distinction between needs and wants. We seek to satisfy the wants of our own, often in abundance, while so many in our world are struggling and finding it unimaginably difficult to meet even their most basic needs and maintain any sense of dignity. They courageously try to keep themselves and their children alive, and often just can't. This is so tragic! Again, looking out for not just for the needs of ourselves and our own, but also for our wants at the expense of the unmet needs of others is the essence of wickedness. And, as I see it, wickedness is the essence of who we are. These are issues and choices that each of us have to deal with in our hearts. These are the sermons nobody likes.

An Invitation to Come to Services

What I'm asking you to do is to come to services where the sermons are too long, the preacher reads too much of the message, and he is right in middle of a sermon series dealing with stuff you really don't want to hear. The preacher is going to try very hard not to be judgmental or critical in a punishing way, but he will speak the truth. You may not like what you see in yourself. But skipping church will most likely mean that you will continue to live in the delusion of a never-never land, out of touch with reality. You will miss out on an opportunity to be more fully alive in the real world, rather than continuing to live in the make believe world that exists only in your mind.

Human nature expresses itself in the real world. Based on our observations, what are we like in our essence? What makes us tick? Some would say that, "basically we're good people." Others would say we are rotten to the core. Bottom line, this conversation is what this book is all about. It is a way of providing those who mean the most to me a window into my soul, together with an invitation to explore the very depths of my being, to discover the essence of who I am and what I am about, to have a sense of my passion and to feel the fire in my belly as they come to understand my perception of what people are really like.

The reader is invited to come to services and listen to the rest of the sermons in this series over the coming weeks. They will include themes that address our understanding of the nature of man and how that understanding becomes an essential structural component of the foundation upon which we build our belief system.

Tragically, most of us seem to be able to live life without being aware of the core philosophical and religious issues that determine our worldview. Life gets a whole lot more complicated for those of us who do. Sadly, my sense is that even those who do understand end up distorting, repressing and denying the truth about what we are really like. On some level not only are we unconcerned about the unmet needs of others, but we are able to justify our attempts to manipulate, control and use others to further our own agenda.

My belief and thesis is that how I have just described human nature fits all of us, and to a degree that is far greater than we are aware of or want to admit. This is the sermon nobody likes. This is the homily nobody wants to hear. We resent the insinuation. We want to hear about the good in us. We want to hear about the potential and possibilities for our lives. Truth be known — we care about "the least of these" only when it doesn't inconvenience us too much or require much sacrifice. When we do help them, it is often out of a sense of duty, obligation or guilt. But we sure don't want anyone suggesting that we're not the good people we think we are.

My purpose is to surface and expose the rationalizations and justifications that make it possible for us to repress and deny what we're really like in the hope of making it more difficult to maintain a favorable impression of ourselves. Most of us think, "I'm a good person." Clearly, I see us so very differently. For me the bottom line is that we are greedy, self-serving people who look out not just for the needs of ourselves and our own, but also for our wants at the expense of the unmet needs of others, many of whom are destitute and living in misery and despair.

Addressing this issue is so necessary and important. If one of our foundational beliefs about self and about life turns out not to be true, then all of the structure built on that foundation is unstable and could collapse. Our worldview and the principles that define our reality are called into question, and maintaining our belief system intact requires that we become delusional. The perceptions, beliefs and convictions we have constructed for ourselves make it difficult to see things the way they really are. What it all adds up to is that in essence we are living in a reality that we have created for ourselves- a world that exists only in our mind, a world that has no basis in reality. We want so much to be able to see the world a certain way. Doing so, however, necessitates that we live in some sort of delusional state that bears little resemblance to the reality that is out there.

I am very much aware that my views are the ones that do not represent conventional wisdom, and most would say that I am the one who is delusional. So what if I'm the one who's wrong? What if the delusions about life and reality are of my own making? How do I find out? It seems to me that I have to share my beliefs, ask the questions and start the conversation. So that's just what I'm going to do. I am going to open up and share my beliefs and perceptions, asking the reader to be a sounding-board, offering input and feedback, and letting me know where you think that I need to re-examine my beliefs and perceptions.

Within the context of my worldview and beliefs the painful truth that has to be surfaced is that for most of us, our lives are being lived in a way that borders on the wilderness of meaninglessness and futility. The truth about commonly accepted notions of reality carries along with it the deeply disturbing and troubling corollary that the meaning and impact of much of the love that is shared is so shallow as to be at best marginal, and at worst meaningless and irrelevant. If everything happens in an environment or culture that is imagined rather than real, then ultimately relationships are doomed to superficiality.

No matter how it turns out, this is a conversation that we have to have. What is at stake is an authentic experience of life. There have been times when my personal journey has been almost unbearably painful. As the beliefs and perceptions about life and love and reality began to wash over me in waves, I was at times overwhelmed by the magnitude of the challenge to my beliefs, especially the deep-down perceptions about what kind of a person I am. At times the anxiety generated by addressing these issues was almost debilitating. Gradually, over time, my experience was transformed into hopefulness and celebration. I am more fully alive than ever. So please, don't burst my bubble! Obviously I don't mean that. What I'm hoping for is quite the opposite. I'm looking forward to a spirited conversation, as only then can fuller, richer more meaningful lives be the outcome.

It is only when we find and face the truth about our own human nature that we can truly experience joy and celebration, and live lives of meaning and purpose, as we use our time, ability and abundance to help those in need. We are making a journey to find and face the truth. We begin by remembering mankind's capacity for unthinkable evil and how that evil envelops us in darkness. The journey will hopefully shine some light on truth that has been hidden in that darkness, the truth that we are not the kind, caring, compassionate people we think we are. We can't see very well in the darkness. Hopefully, this narrative will shine some light into the depths of the darkness in our souls. Maybe we don't want to see it. Not seeing it serves to insulate us from the pain, suffering and misery of others, and allows the wiggle-room needed to be able to pursue our own goals, hopes and dreams without having pangs of conscience strong enough to make us feel guilty.

We will begin the journey by reminding ourselves of the darkness and evil in the history of the human race. In the 40's and 50's there was an early evening radio broadcast on Sundays called "The Shadow." It had a memorable introductory tag line: "Who knows what evil lurks in the hearts of men! The Shadow knows," followed by this haunting laugh. We need to know too—we just have to!

Chapter 2
Humanity's Capacity for Unthinkable Darkness and Evil

"You ask, what is our policy? I say it is to wage war by land, sea and air. War with all our might and with all the strength God has given us, and to wage war against a monstrous tyranny never surpassed in the dark and lamentable catalogue of human crime." Winston Churchill

"At this (being called out for their sin—big time) they covered their ears and, . . . they all rushed at him, dragged him out of the city and began to stone him. . . . While they were stoning him, Stephen prayed, "Lord Jesus, receive my spirit." Then he fell on his knees and cried out, "Lord, do not hold this sin against them." When he had said this, he fell asleep. . . . And Saul was there giving approval to his death. On that day a great persecution broke out against the church at Jerusalem, and all except the apostles were scattered. . . . Saul began to destroy the church. Going from house to house, he dragged off men and women and put them in prison" (Acts 7:57-8:3).

Throughout history man has been asking questions about his origin and nature, and about the meaning and purpose of life itself. This chapter will surface fundamental issues and questions about the nature of man, and how the drama of life plays out in terms of meaning and purpose in our relationships with others. Religious leaders, philosophers, theologians and scientists hold to a variety of belief systems. Some would say that we are basically good: kind, caring and altruistic. Others would say that we are evil. Then there is Skinner who says we are born neutral, with a *tabula rosa*, a blank slate shaped by our environment and experience. Are we born with tendencies toward discord, cruelty and barbarism, or tendencies toward fairness, kindness and gentleness? This chapter sets the table for all that follows. It offers the presuppositions and conceptual framework for a discussion that seeks to ask, deep down, what are we are really like?

Little Monsters

Mention the "Terrible Twos" and all kinds of thoughts and images come to mind. Conventional wisdom is that kids that age are little terrors: contentious, mischievous and strong-willed. Those who hold to this behavioral model for two-year olds wince when they hear about a very different model, wondering whether its proponents have lost their minds.

Some experts in parenting and some parents view the two year old as demonstrating the very qualities we value in adults: energy, curiosity, inquisitiveness and assertiveness. Getting into everything because you are in discovery mode and want to know how it works are traits that we value in grown ups. Once their child is finally asleep these parents run to the middle of the family room, jump up and give each other high-fives. They have this kid who is so very much alive and wants to learn about everything in his environment, and they are ecstatic. These kids watch when you're using your computers, cell phones, iPads and remotes, making mental notes so they can see if they can make them do the same thing. The computer in their little noodle has an extraordinary capacity for memory and operates at lightening speed. Some parents are excited and totally delighted as they watch their children grow and learn. Others see them as little monsters who get into everything.

Parents who see the fantastic potential in a two-year-old's behavior are ecstatic to know their child is off to a great start along the road to becoming a happy, fun-loving, well balanced, interesting, stable adult who will probably live a joyful and exciting life filled with meaning and purpose, comfortable with themselves and secure in themselves. This doesn't at all mean that children should be left to their own devices and allowed to become little demons. Having limits and boundaries and not allowing them to be out of control helps make them feel safe and secure. Indeed, parents of these children are always guiding, leading, shepherding and teaching. Exhausted at the end of the day, they hardly have the energy to finish with the celebratory high-five.

Shadows of Light and Darkness

Just as there are at least two different perceptions about the behavior of two-year olds, there are number of perceptions of the nature of man and explanations for his behavior. Throughout history consideration of the nature of man has been the subject of so much of what has been expressed in philosophy, theology, literature and the arts. Historically human nature has been viewed as fundamentally evil and selfish; I share this view, which shapes my worldview and belief system. Others have a more positive opinion of man's nature. Recently, social neuroscience researchers have found that empathy is innate in most humans. Other brain research suggests that altruism is a brain impulse and that empathy is the basis of morality. Then there is the generally agreed upon theory of personality of the self-theorists: if given a safe, accepting environment, every person has the potential to live a constructive, healthy life, which is good for himself and his community. At this stage in the progression of human history, however, such a safe, accepting environment simply does not exist. There is no environment in the real world where an individual would not experience some manifestation of evil. Maybe the world doesn't have to be a perfectly safe and accepting environment. If so, where is the tipping point?

The Dalai Lama would add his voice to the chorus of those who do not see people as innately evil. Raised in a culture of compassion and nonviolence, he maintains an upbeat outlook on life and the future. He was asked, "How do you stay so optimistic and faithful when there is so much hate in the world?" The Dalai Lama responded: "I always look at any event from a wider angle. There's always some problem, some killing, some murder, some terrorist act or scandal everywhere, everyday. But if you think the whole world is like that, you're wrong. Out of 6 billion humans, the troublemakers are just a handful."[2]

From the Twos to the Teens

Born six days after the bombing of Pearl Harbor, many experiences from the "terrific twos" to the teens were an important part of my journey, contributing significantly to the shaping of my views about human nature. During World War II my Mom moved in with my paternal grandfather along with Aunt Gert (another daughter-in-law) and Aunt

Shirley (a daughter), while Dad, Uncle Phil and Uncle Frank served in the Armed Forces: Navy, Army and Coast Guard, respectively. I can remember getting up at night once in a while and going into the living room. Often I cried, wondering where my Dad was and why he wasn't home. Mom and the others in the house weren't always aware when it happened. When someone did wake up, I was always comforted and reassured that he would be coming home one day. About once every two months grandpa took us all out for a ride and dinner on Sunday. It was always fun until he lit up that big cigar on the way home. Then on came the radio and old time favorites like *The Lone Ranger, Amos and Andy, Sergeant Preston of the Yukon, The Green Hornet, Inner Sanctum* and *The Shadow*.

Raw emotion is stirred when confronted with a new awareness that you can't make any sense of cognitively or emotionally. On some level you process it as best you can, making up what you don't know so you can continue to cope in the world you have created for yourself. Sometimes what you make up is worse than what is. "What in the world is happening? How can this be?" If only I could have been shielded, protected and insulated from these terrible experiences and horrible truths that became a part of my awareness and my world. The moments that shatter the sense of safety and security in our lives, and change our reality are obviously different for each of us. The same holds true for the learning curve as it relates to evil, and the cognitive and emotional dimensions of coming to terms with a growing awareness of evil.

One of those early moments of learning for me came between 1949 and 1951. We were still living with my grandfather at the time, and he had brought home one of the early black and white TVs. One night shortly after its arrival, everyone was gathered in the living room to watch. I remember the experience vividly. My Aunt Hannah was visiting from California and we were watching a western. There was a gunfight, several of the cowboys got shot and I ran out of the room screaming. We had not been to any movies where there was killing, and at my stage of development I was not able to handle the idea of one human being killing another human being. That reality was too painful and too scary for me to comprehend and deal with. How could one person do that to another person? Dad came after me and tried to explain the cowboy was not really dead, he was just acting and it was all pretend. His best efforts were of no avail in convincing me to rejoin the others in the living room.

Another painful awareness about life and good and evil came several years later. Among the shows that Dad watched after I had gone to bed was Victory at Sea. On occasion he let me watch with him and that's when I asked questions about what was going on and what war was all about. He served on a destroyer in the Pacific. While I couldn't begin to spell them and had no idea where they were, I vividly remember the exotic sounding names of places like the Philippines, Guam, Tinian, Sipan, Eniwetok, Okinawa and Iwo Jima. As we watched Victory at Sea and he explained some of what it was about, I began to get the idea, that during a war people died and not everybody who went away to fight came home. Not everybody came home! Had I been lied to? I had just begun to scratch the surface of the reality and horrors of war, how two opposing groups of people both tried to win, and that sometimes meant killing hundreds and thousands of people on the other side.

Mom and Dad were saving for a down payment on a house and in 1951 we moved out of Grandpa's home on the far north side to our own home on the far south side. During the same time frame I was watching "Victory at Sea," the United States and the Union of Soviet Socialist Republics were tediously making their way through the diplomatic minefield of finding how to put the nuclear genie back into the bottle. We had not yet reached the stalemate of mutually assured destruction. This was the backdrop for yet another of those reality-shattering experiences that stirred raw emotion in the very depths of my being. Without being able to fully comprehend the enormity of the destruction, death, pain and suffering that would result from a nuclear war, I was very aware and very fearful once I learned that our neighborhood could be bombed. I found a bit of relief upon learning that if you made it to a bomb shelter you had a better chance to survive.

Just across the street from our home was William Bishop Owen School. One day we came out of school to find black and yellow signs designating the site as an air raid shelter; they became a constant reminder of a danger that thankfully I did not begin to comprehend. Learning to live with that constant awareness was something I never quite got used to or comfortable with. We also heard the regular testing of the air raid siren on the school roof and practiced getting under the desks. There was no escape from those constant reminders of nuclear war. I could see those signs from my bedroom window when I went to bed at night and in the morning as I opened the blinds. I worried a lot about being bombed. I had been assured once before that everything would be fine, when they really didn't know for sure. This time I didn't believe them.

Ironically, the school-yard was also a place of pure delight. It was the place we played baseball every possible moment. Since we lived just across the street, it was easy to run over whenever the guys gathered for a pick-up game. Baseball was an escape from the ominous and ever present reality of evil. You could lose yourself in the fun. This is where I learned that it didn't matter if you won or lost the baseball game. Just playing as hard as you could and putting your all into it was all that mattered; by so doing you found relief from the presence of those black and yellow signs on the center-field and right-field walls. In my early years I was never able to understand how people could be so brutal, so savage and so inhuman. Sadly, I do now.

The End of My Innocence

There was no longer any possibility of a return to a place of innocence; it was not an option. For me there was no escape to an earlier time, when the world was experienced as much friendlier, much safer and much less threatening. *Please, please, let it not be so!* My perception of reality was almost too painful to bear. *Please tell me I'm wrong. Please tell me this isn't the way it is.* I wanted so very much for the world to be different from the way I was seeing it. It was the end of innocence.

Starting to read newspapers and studying history in school confirmed my new perception of the world. One experience and awareness after another served to multiply the reality of the depravity of human nature. About that time I began to understand what was probably the greatest evil in the history of what I increasingly viewed as a dark world: Adolph Hitler and Nazi Germany.

"Upon his very first entrance into the House of Commons as Britain's new Prime Minister on May 13, 1940, Winston Churchill only received a lukewarm reception from the assembly, while at his side, outgoing Prime Minister Neville Chamberlain was heartily cheered. Churchill then made this brief statement, which became one of the greatest calls-to-arms ever uttered. It came at the beginning of World War II when the armies of Adolf Hitler were roaring across Europe, seemingly unstoppable, conquering country after country for Nazi Germany, and when the survival of Britain itself seemed quite uncertain."

(We) are in the preliminary phase of one of the greatest battles in history.

I say to the House as I said to ministers who have joined this government, I have nothing to offer but blood, toil, tears and sweat We have before us an ordeal of the most grievous kind. We have before us many, many months of struggle and suffering.

You ask, what is our policy? I say it is to wage war by land, sea and air. War with all our might and with all the strength God has given us, and to wage war against a monstrous tyranny never surpassed in the dark and lamentable catalogue of human crime. This is our policy.

You ask, what is our aim? I can answer in one word. It is victory. Victory at all costs—Victory in spite of all terrors—Victory, however long and hard the road may be, for without victory there is no survival.[3]

"The systematic annihilation of millions of men, women and children in extermination camps makes the Holocaust one of the most horrifying events in human history."[4] The early mass executions were too messy and too visible for the German high command, so a "neater" and more efficient method had to be found. Rudolph Hess, commandant of the extermination camp at Auschwitz-Birkenau describes the solution. "The two large crematoria, Nos. I and II, were built during the winter of 1942-1943. . . . They each . . . could cremate c. 2,000 corpses within twenty-four hours. . . . Crematoria I and II both had underground undressing and gassing rooms which could be completely ventilated. The corpses were brought up to the ovens on the floor above by lift. The gas chambers could hold about 3,000 people."[5] That masses of humanity, 6,000,000 people, could be subjected to death camps, gas chambers and crematoria is a horror we can hardly imagine. An afternoon at The Holocaust Museum in Washington D.C. was one of the most difficult experiences in my life; the emotional distress was painful almost beyond belief.

While we were there, it went into lock-down and we were not allowed to leave. Given where we were and understanding why it might have been a terrorist target, there were some anxious moments. It turned out there was a disturbance outside of the entrance. The incident served to greatly accelerate the learning curve that day. It was clear that our experience of anxiety and fear was only an infinitesimal hint of what the Jews went through. It is so very hard to imagine the darkness that could result in some within the human family treating others in such a manner. For me some healing came from the pages of Victor Frankel's *The Courage to Be*.

While Nazi Germany under Hitler may have been "a monstrous tyranny never surpassed," history is indeed a "dark and lamentable catalogue of human crime." During my brief pilgrimage down the long road of history, here are some of the horrors I remember. In addition to Hitler we have had to find a way to try to come to terms with the likes of Rwanda, Chechnya, the "killing fields" of Cambodia, the Halabja poison gas massacre of more than 5,000 Kurds by Saddam Hussein, the 1995 Oklahoma City bombing of the Murrah Federal Building that claimed 168 lives and injured more than 680, the terrorist attack on September 11, 2001, Libya and Syria.

Cool Customers in Control during the Cold War

Graduating from high school in 1959, we were dropped off on the threshold of one of the most tumultuous decades in the history of our nation, the years that shaped and molded the lives of a generation. This was just one more period in the record of human history when evil was so evident in the hearts and lives of people—and I would hold in all of our hearts and lives.

From 1945-1991, the term "Cold War" was descriptive of the relationship between the Soviet Union and their eastern European satellites, on the one hand, and the western world led by the United States on the other. Periodically there were incidents that led to dangerously elevated levels of tension which easily could have led to a nuclear war. The Cuban Missile Crisis (1992) was the one that had the greatest potential to become a calamity that could have ended civilization as we know it.

From October 22 until October 28, 1962, it was as if time moved in super slow motion. I was a student at Concordia Senior College in Ft. Wayne, Indiana, where I began my studies in preparation for becoming a pastor. If we had not had some very cool customers at the helm of the Ship of State, time might have stopped completely. The CIA had obtained photographs showing the Soviets were shipping nuclear missiles to Cuba. While explaining the situation in a speech to the nation President Kennedy noted the U.S. boycott on trade, but made no mention of the secret campaign of economic and military sabotage code-named Operation Mongoose carried out by the CIA under Kennedy's orders for the previous ten months.

> (The Cuban Missile Crisis was) supposed to have been the moment when the nuclear age proved viable. Apocalypse was, after all, averted. Kennedy resisted the counsel that would have bombed the missile sites or invaded Cuba; his precision was vindicated by Khrushchev's decision to withdraw his missiles. When the chips

were down, the superpowers wised up. But the hindsight is pat, a luxury. Another ending was possible, the ending of all endings, and then we would not be alive, most likely. . . .

    Kennedy gave his 'quarantine' (better called by a less diplomatic term, blockade) speech on Monday night, October 22, 1962. For six days . . . (until) the news was broadcast that Khrushchev was backing down, the country lived out the awe and truculence and simmering near-panic always implicit in the thermonuclear age. At colleges in New England, some students piled into their cars and took off for Canada until further notice.[6]

Offered the chance, I wonder if I would have joined them. It wasn't that far from Ft. Wayne to Detroit to Windsor, Ontario, or straight north through Michigan and across the Mackinac Bridge. Either route would lead into the vast expanse of central Canada.

    Three years later I made that journey. However, the circumstances were so very different. It was a carefree time of joy and happiness. After being married in Wausau, Wisconsin, we traveled through Chicago to Detroit, into Canada at Windsor and on to Niagara Falls for a traditional honeymoon. Then it was back west through Canada to the beauty and peace of Mackinac Island. Yet the irony did not escape me and there were moments when other thoughts simply overwhelmed my awareness. As I was driving through Canada with my new bride sleeping on my shoulder, reflecting on the stark contrast between the two possible scenarios for a journey through Canada was extremely unsettling. For obvious reasons I didn't share those thoughts and reflections with Karen. The events of October 1962 stirred emotion in the very depths of my being, including memories of those yellow and black signs.

Race and Rage

Coming out of a final exam for a religion class at Ft. Wayne on November 2, 1963 we learned someone had tried to assassinate President Kennedy. When the announcement came that he had died, shock and disbelief, followed by grief and sadness gripped the nation. Lyndon Johnson was sworn in as President and guided the process that led to the passage of the Civil Rights Act of 1964, which was supposed to guarantee blacks the right to vote and access to public accommodations.

The civil rights movement had been gaining momentum for some time. Growing up on the south side of Chicago, you were immersed in racism. I remember what it was like when my Mom and Grandma took me to Wrigley Field for the first time. The Cubs were playing the Dodgers. Roy Campanella had joined Jackie Robinson. The game was fun. The sideshow wasn't. Even as a young boy growing up in an environment and community where racial prejudice was rampant, deep down inside I just knew it wasn't right to call them *schwartze* (the black ones) or the "n" word. I didn't yet understand why the founding fathers made the accommodation recognizing the legitimacy of slavery.

When I was a catcher on the baseball team at Luther High School South in Chicago, my Dad was able to get me a Roy Campanella catchers' glove through a friend at the Wilson Sporting Goods factory. It is just like the one in the museum in the new Yankee Stadium. I still have the glove and all of the conflicting emotions that come along with it, both the happy and the sad memories of a time that left me conflicted and confused. For me it was a troubling juxtaposition of baseball and race. It may not have been like that for anyone else, but it was like that was for me. It was my memory and my experience. It is a part of what shaped me and who I am.

Our third son, Matt, was born in Springfield, Illinois, where we lived from 1975-1985. During those years I came to much more fully appreciate Lincoln's conviction and strength of character during the Civil War. 486,000 men died in the Union and Confederate armies as they fought for the soul of a nation. Of the many Springfield experiences that contributed to somber reflection about the history of our nation, two were especially powerful. The first was a dramatic presentation of "Your Obedient Servant, A. Lincoln" at the outdoor theatre in New Salem, where during the final act you found yourself right in the middle of a battle between the Union Army on the stage and across the front, and the Confederate Army charging up from the rear. The second was a very special candle light event at the Old State Capitol, where we heard Lincoln's "House Divided" speech delivered by an impersonator from the very podium from which it was first spoken. The war that was fought and the blood shed to free African Americans from the yoke of slavery and to acknowledge them as brothers and sisters in the human family is still a work in progress. Even though we have a black president, we're still not anywhere near the end of the journey.

It was 1955 when Rosa Parks was arrested for refusing to give up her seat and move to the back of the bus. The feelings that were eating away at the pride and dignity of the black community for years began to surface. A bus boycott was organized; it ended in 1956 after the buses had been integrated. But the floodgates of pent-up emotion opened up and poured out. Black churches were bombed, little girls were killed, and dogs and fire-hoses were used to break-up demonstrations. Race riots broke out. The eyes of many Americans were opened by the response of the authorities. Many more began to understand—to get it.

Lutheran pastors do a one year internship (vicarage) before being ordained, usually during the third of our four years at the seminary. In 1967 I was assigned to Calvary, Lincoln Park, Michigan, in the downriver area south of Detroit. While we were there, race riots broke out. It gets your attention when you hear gunfire from your apartment. You learn a whole lot more about the rage that led to looting and burning. Large caliber military artillery was used by the National Guard to help restore order. It shakes you to your very foundation when you see the holes from artillery shells in the walls of buildings in the metropolitan area where you live right here in the USA, and put pictures of those walls and the armored vehicles in your family album. What happened in Detroit and the 1967 race riots throughout our country, together with the historically significant events of the next 12 months, changed me forever. It was a period of intense internal emotion—a giant step in the formation of who I am and what I am about.

4,700 US Army Paratroopers and 8,000 National Guardsmen were called in to restore order in Detroit. 43 people died. What was happening that caused riots to erupt? Was this was a microcosm of all of the battles in all of the wars that have been fought throughout history, and the millions of brave people who have died throughout history. Is this what it comes down to? Differences get resolved by people killing people. Sadly, given our human nature, that is exactly what happens.

Vietnam and the Loss of America's Innocence

The United States had become involved in Vietnam as a consequence of decisions made in our strategic interest during the height of the cold war. The fear was that if South Vietnam was lost to the communists, then Cambodia, Laos, Thailand, Burma, Indonesia and other countries in Southeast Asia would fall like dominoes. Acting within the framework of the domino theory Presidents Eisenhower, Kennedy and Johnson made decisions that resulted in significantly increased involvement and entanglement in a guerilla war.

Initially a majority of Americans supported our involvement. However, the fighting escalated, more and more troops were sent, casualties mounted and the reassurances of victory by President Johnson did not materialize. As the war dragged on and the numbers of dead and wounded continued to rise, support for our involvement was increasingly called into question. Many Americans were having second thoughts. Protests that began mostly with young people soon included people of all ages. In January 1968 at the start of Vietnamese new year, known as Tet, the Communists launched attacks in 30 major cities shattering any illusion that we were winning the war. "The country went into shock. . . . A nation that commits itself to myth is traumatized when reality breaks through. . . ."[7]

The dominos now fell quickly in a way that was never intended. Opposition to the war increased even further. Walter Cronkite, an iconic national voice and a part of our collective conscience flew to Vietnam to assess the situation for himself. On a CBS special report broadcast on February 27, he said "that the only 'realistic, if unsatisfactory' conclusion was that 'we are mired in a stalemate' and that 'the only rational way out' was 'to negotiate not as victors, but as an honorable people who lived up to their pledge to defend democracy and did the best they could.' . . . When Cronkite spoke, 'the shock waves rolled through government.'"[8]

"1968"

Little did anyone know that the Tet offensive and Cronkite's heart-to-heart with the nation were just the beginning of what would be one of the most tumultuous years in American history. On March 28 President Johnson announced that he would not seek another term. Robert Kennedy, now a candidate for president, responded by saying the Tet offensive "has shattered any illusion with which we have concealed our true circumstances, even from ourselves."[9] Deep feelings were again stirred by two more shocking events that occurred shortly thereafter. Dr. Martin Luther King Jr. was assassinated while standing on the balcony of a Memphis motel on April 4. The country erupted into riots in about 80 cities. A friend of the black community and candidate for president, Robert Kennedy, was shot and killed while campaigning in Los Angeles on June 5.

1968 was a tumultuous year for our nation. It was the same in my personal world. I was flooded with even more emotion and was in no position to even begin to process all that was swirling around in my life and in the country. There is always so much excitement in anticipation of "Call Day," when candidates at the seminary receive their assignments to serve in ministry. Dr. King had been assassinated a few weeks before our class gathered in worship for the announcement of calls on May 1. May 24 was graduation from Concordia Seminary, St. Louis. On June 5, Robert Kennedy was assassinated. I was ordained on June 9 at Ashburn Lutheran, my home congregation on the south side of Chicago. On July 7, I was installed as pastor of St. Paul's Lutheran Church, Shobonier, Illinois.

October 18-29, 1962	Cuban Missile Crisis
November 2, 1963	President John F. Kennedy Assassinated in Dallas
August 7, 1965	Married Karen Otto at Trinity Lutheran in Wausau, WI
July 23-27, 1967	Race Riots broke out while on vicarage in Detroit
January 1968*	North Vietnam begins Tet Offensive
February 27, 1968*	Walter Cronkite reports to the nation on Vietnam
April 4, 1968*	Assassination of Dr. Martin Luther King Jr. in Memphis
May 1, 1968*	Call Day – Received first ministry assignment
May 24, 1968*	Graduation at Concordia Seminary, St. Louis
June 5, 1968*	Assassination of Robert Kennedy in Los Angeles
June 9, 1968*	Ordination into the Ministry at Ashburn Lutheran, Chicago
July 7, 1968*	Installation at St. Paul Lutheran, Shobonier, Illinois
August 26-29, 1968*	Violence at Democratic National Convention in Chicago
October 4, 1969	Our son Scott was born in Vandalia, IL
May 4, 1970	4 students killed by Ohio National Guards at Kent State U.
May 18 & June 17, 1972	Watergate burglaries
November 2, 1972	Our son Tim was born in Peoria, IL
August 9, 1974	As a consequence of Watergate President Nixon resigns in the face of almost certain impeachment
April 30, 1975	US leaves Vietnam after 16 yrs, 68,000 dead; a Chinook-46 picks up the US Ambassador and the last 11 marines from the roof of the US embassy in Saigon
June 13, 1977	Our son Matt was born in Springfield, IL

In some ways it was like I was living in two worlds, and in one of them I felt very much alone. While my wife had a sense of how I was trying to deal with the flood of conflicting emotion, I chose to share only part of it with her as she was going through enough adjustments of her own: leaving behind the colleagues on her teaching staff, her friends from the sem scattering all over the country, a church six miles from a town of 400, only two of the roads leading in were oiled, a 60+ year old parsonage, enough mice that we kept a tally of the hunt, two outhouses for the facilities at church, a pig farm 100 yards east of the parsonage (thankfully the prevailing westerlys blew the smell of farmers' gold away from us most of the time) and no air conditioning in a part of south-central Illinois known as Little Egypt.

Most of the folks in my life— family, relatives, the members of St. Paul's—seemed strangely oblivious to the turmoil swirling around us as a nation. Perhaps we were all in shock. And they certainly had no way of knowing the turmoil I was going through in my life. Thankfully, the quiet life in rural Shobonier allowed time for prayer, reading and study as I assumed my pastoral duties, and for reflection on all that was happening in a world that seemed so far removed from the consciousness of our parishioners.

Some in the congregation had a hard time understanding why we had to travel the 100 miles back into St. Louis to spend a day once a month. Karen appreciated being able to keep the same hairdresser she went to when we lived there. While waiting I enjoyed being able to get to the seminary library and bookstore. Afterwards we went to Famous-Barr for a great baked onion soup and sandwich and some shopping—mostly looking. Then it was off to the fantastic and free St. Louis Zoo. Often we stayed for a Cardinals game, a Blues hockey game or a musical at the outdoor Saint Louis Municipal Opera in Forest Park. Even though it can get hot and muggy during the summer, we loved St. Louis: Forest Park, the Zoo, franchises for all four professional sports, the Muny, Grant's Farm and a first class paper—the St. Louis Post Dispatch. With a couple of cold Buds even the heat didn't seem so bad. Back at St. Paul it would be easy to detach from all that was going on in the world around us.

The Gateway Arch and Museum of Westward Expansion were being built while I was still at the seminary. We watched on TV as they installed the top piece that connected both legs. Perhaps its completion was a timely personal metaphor for the gateway to a whole new world, as I was reflecting on and learning about a whole set of new experiences. I prayed and struggled to be able to get my arms around my new world and make some sense out of it. The journey through the '60s was like rafting down a wild river—with class 4 rapids in 1967 and class 5 in 1968.

The folks at St. Paul were wonderful people. They received us warmly, welcomed us into their lives and kept us in their prayers and in their hearts. It was my responsibility as their pastor to listen to them and to speak the forgiving and healing Word of a loving God in a way that connected with them in their world. It certainly would not have been appropriate to drag them into mine. One of my two worlds remained a very lonely place. In the peace and quiet of the farm fields in central Illinois, I tried to begin to make sense of all of the hatred, brutality and killing

"Listening" to the corn grow that summer and watching the planting of the winter wheat in the fall did not slow the pace of all that was happening in our country and the world, and certainly did not insulate me from those events. One of my worlds, the one that seemed to have left St. Paul behind, was a very dark and evil place. Little did I know then that there were many very dark and evil places right there in the lives of the folks at St. Paul. My seminary education did not prepare me for those who came to a young and inexperienced pastor straight out of the seminary to lay at the foot of the cross the dark corners and secret places in their lives.

Fortunately, I was speechless, and therefore didn't respond too quickly with simplistic solutions or pat answers. I learned by experience that anything I might say would have been shallow and almost meaningless before they had a chance to bare their souls, to share the depth of feeling, emotion, darkness, pain, shame and guilt they were carrying. When it was clear that they were exhausted and broken, had confessed their sins and were desperately in need of the comforting assurance of forgiveness, that Word was spoken in the name of the Father and of the Son and of the Holy Spirit. It is our sacred privilege as clergy to assure the troubled and burdened that there is no sin so big or so bad that it can't be forgiven. In Jesus Christ, there is nothing that can separate us from the love of God.

We were just starting to settle in at St. Paul's when The Democratic National Convention was held at the International Amphitheatre in Chicago from August 26-29, 1968. The nation's attention was riveted to the confrontation between anti-war protestors and Mayor Richard J. Daley. In April 1970, President Nixon announced that he had sent troops into Cambodia on a search and destroy mission for Vietcong bases. The news of the widening of the war led to protests, sit-ins and the occupation of buildings on university campuses, and led to the killing of four student protesters at Kent State University by the Ohio National Guard. Two student protestors were also killed by police at Jackson State College in Mississippi. The antiwar movement began to decline, as did the will of the people of our nation to prosecute the war.

Life was so much less complicated back in 1962 when it was clear that the Lord was calling me into the ministry. In just six short years, my life had been changed forever. You couldn't find a better place to begin to try to cope than within the "friendly confines" of ministry in a rural congregation. Through it all there would be no compromising of faithfulness in my calling to bring the Word of God to bear on the struggles, pain, grief, loss, doubts, spiritual searching and guilt (we Lutherans are experts when it comes to guilt) of the members of the congregations I would serve as under-shepherd. There would also be no returning to a life that was insulated from what was happening in the world in which we as God's people are called to serve. For me it was a time of considerable prayer and reflection, about the issues themselves and the interface between those issues and the living out of our Christian lives. Our nation was going through an identity crisis. I was going through an identity crisis. On top of that our national church body was going through a gut wrenching identity crisis.

This Is Who We Are

While history is complicated and nuanced, what is clear is the capacity of human nature to act out in ways that are truly evil. Misinformation and distortion form the basis of the propaganda used to manipulate and motivate, as the identified enemy is vilified and the masses whipped into a frenzy that seeks revenge. These are powerful dynamics which lead to outcomes that are barbaric, uncivilized and inhuman: injustice, enslavement, torture, killing and ethnic cleansing. Man's inhumanity to man is one of the tragic storylines of history. Yet, this is who we are.

Documentation of mass graves and killing fields fill many of the darkest chapters. Genocides chronicle ethnic tragedies that are beyond belief. Hearing about massacres in the news is so sickening that you don't feel like eating. Mere mention of Babi Yar, Auschwitz and Treblinka, Dachau and Buchenwald, Bosnia and Kosovo, Rwanda and Burundi, Sudan and Ethiopia, and Cambodia and Sri Lanka trigger images of atrocities so unthinkable that we have developed unconscious strategies to make it possible to repress them from consciousness, thereby insulating ourselves from a pain too overwhelming to bear.

Going back to the 1389 Battle of Kosovo and the defeat of Serbian Prince Lazar at the hands of the Ottoman Turks, the history of the Balkans has been complicated. More recently a long history of war and conflict has deteriorated into massacres of people whose only crime is their ethnicity. Some of the killing even occurred in areas that had been designated by the U.N. as "safe havens." According to the U.N.'s chief war crimes prosecutor Carla Del Ponte and her aides, NATO estimates of 10,000 Bosnian Muslims killed "might yet be born out."[10] During three years of ethnic cleansing under the leadership of Slobodan Milosevic, also known as the "butcher of Belgrade," somewhere between 5,000 and 10,000 ethnic Albanians were killed.

A year later a "U.N. tribunal indicted Bosnian Serb political leader Radovan Karadzic and military commander Ratko Mladic . . . on new charges of genocide and crimes against humanity for their roles in the atrocities committed after Serb troops overran the U.N. 'safe area' of Srebrenica in July (1995)"[11]

"Judge Fouad Riad said evidence submitted by chief prosecutor Richard Goldstone depicted 'scenes of unimaginable savagery: thousands of men executed and buried in mass graves, hundreds of men buried alive, men and women mutilated and slaughtered, children killed before their mother's eyes. . . . These are truly scenes from hell, written on the darkest pages of human history.'"[12]

What happened during the Holocaust and the Bosnian Serb assault on Srebrenica, as well as in Rwanda and Darfur is chilling. The horror of mass murder is inhumane. But we can't deny reality, as painful as it is. We try and try to comprehend how our human nature could be capable of atrocities like these.

Ethnic cleansing, "exterminating categories of human beings – this is a distinctively human activity. . . .Christopher Browning of Pacific Lutheran University . . . says mass murder and the ubiquity of cruelty suggests the need to seek explanations in 'those universal aspects of human nature that transcend the cognition and culture of ordinary Germans.' . . . Today, April 16, is the Day of remembrance for Holocaust victims and survivors. Since 1945 the theme of remembrance ceremonies has been 'Never again.' But again Europe is sifting skulls from the earth over mass graves, this time of Muslims, victims of . . . what? Ordinary Serbs?"[13] We continue to see evidence of the depravity of human nature.

In just 100 days from April through July 1994 an estimated 500,000 to 800,000 minority Tutsis were shot, hacked and clubbed to death in Rwanda by majority Hutus. Reading multiple accounts of the atrocities is so heartbreaking, so sad and so tragic that is easy to seek out a way, any way, to insulate yourself from so many accounts of man's inhumanity to man. One powerful and compelling incident reported by Thomas Friedman is indicative of so many others.

Nothing quite compares you for the beauty of Kibuye. The tiny Rwandan village is nestled on a terraced hillside overlooking Lake Kivu, the high volcanic lake in the heart of central Africa.

There are streams and waterfalls coursing through the hills. Not far from here, among the cloud-shrouded volcanoes, Dian Fosse researched 'Gorillas in the Mist.' On a promontory jutting into the lake is a large Catholic church built of stone, surrounded by tall banana trees.

And that is where the beauty stops.

Because just behind the church there is a deep hole and down in it are five members of Physicians for Human Rights, exhuming a mass grave – one of dozens that scar the Rwandan landscape from the fever of genocide that broke out here in April 1964.

Thousands of Tutsi and moderate Hutu villagers had come to the church, thinking that this was God's house and that it would protect them from the rampaging Hutu extremists. It did not. They were slaughtered between the pews, hacked to death with machetes in the reflection of the stained-glass windows, and then buried beneath the banana trees. . . . Their bodies have long since decomposed, but relatives can sometimes identify family members from clothing fragments of the skeletons.

Some of the bones speak for themselves, like the pair of hands that were sliced in a straight line across the knuckles. The victim must have been holding up his hands, trying to shield his face, when a machete was brought down on him with enormous force. Some 4,000 people were murdered in this spot alone—500,000 altogether in Rwanda.[14]

In yet another tragic period of human savagery one can't understate the plight of the Darfur region of western Sudan. "The State Department reckons that in the last two years, 60,000 to 160,000 people have been murdered. Other informed estimates put the death toll as high as 400,000. Whatever the exact number is, it was sufficiently horrific as to cause then-Secretary of State Colin Powell to identify it as 'genocide' last fall."[15] "Secretary of State Colin Powell, speaking to raise pressure on Sudan to stop the atrocities in the region of Darfur, declared Thursday for the first time that the killings, rapes and destruction that have forced 1.5 million people from their homes amounted to genocide and should be treated as such by the United Nations."[16]

As the evidence mounted over the years, there was no alternative other than to recognize the depravity of human nature. I suppose we have the choice of whether or not we want to live in reality or escape from it into a self-created and therefore psychotic world where one is insulated from these realities. Those who choose to live in the real world try to balance the ledger: Gandhi, Mother Teresa, M.L. King Jr., and the Dalai Lama on the one side, while Stalin, Hitler, Bin Laden and Pol Pot are on the other. *Time* described this tension as an "Historic Duality— The Altruistic (and) The Atrocious."[17]

"War at any time is a total collapse of civilization and is ultimately a terribly dehumanizing event."[18] Somehow to me you can't avoid the sense that the cumulative weight of the Holocaust, the "Killing Fields," Bosnia, Rwanda, Darfur and all the wars throughout history are overwhelming evidence of man's inhumanity to man. How can human beings do these things to other human beings? It was on a porch swing during the peace and quiet of a central Illinois summer that I prayed and pondered and tried to make sense of all the cruelty, brutality and inhumanity.

The root causes, be they political, economic or ethnic, serve the interests of the perpetrators, who are often manipulated by the propaganda of their leaders—propaganda which has taken on a life of its own and become a chapter in the story of what they consider to be a factual and reliable account of the history of their people. The myth that is manufactured becomes truth. Convinced of the rightness of your cause, you are ready to defend your rights, correct past injustices and take revenge for past abuse, even if it involves killing and cruel, inhuman behavior.

The world, as I have come to know it, leaves me with clear sense that whatever conceptual model one uses to describe the origins of evil, there is no doubt that evil infects our whole being and influences who we are and what we are about. This has been my experience, and the reality and presence of evil in all of us is consistent with all of it. "Are people born wicked? Or do they have Wickedness thrust upon them?" Whichever is consistent with your belief system or organizing principle, evil is very real—a disease that infects every fiber of our entire being.

The study and discussion of evil is the thread that runs through the interwoven fabric of literature, psychology, philosophy and religion. A powerful description of human nature as well a summary of my own journey is found in William Golding's *Lord of the Flies*. In the notes that followed the book Golding shares his reflections. "After this (the pig's head is cut off and impaled on a stick) occurs the most deeply symbolic incident in the book, the 'interview' of Simon, an embryo mystic, with the head. The head seems to be saying, to Simon's heightened perceptions, that 'everything was bad business. . . . The half shut eyes were dim with infinite cynicism of adult life.' Simon fights with all his feeble power against the message of the head, against the 'ancient, inescapable recognition,' the recognition of human capacities for evil and the superficial nature of human moral systems. It is the knowledge of the end of innocence, for which Ralph is to weep at the close of the book."[19] Gradually, over the years it all came together – this is what human nature is really like. This is who we are. This is who I am.

I weep often, sobbing deeply when reflecting on the loss of my own innocence and the capacity of human nature to do evil, to act in ways that are brutal, cruel and inhuman. I weep for my grandchildren and all children who one day come to the awareness of the end of innocence in their lives. My heart breaks for the children of Rwanda and Darfur.

Well, Where Does Evil Come From?

Where does "wicked" come from? Volumes have been written about the nature of man. It is a theological-philosophical-anthropological issue that has been studied and debated since the beginning of time, together with the accompanying foundational questions. Where did I come from? Why am I here? What is life all about? I will not attempt a comprehensive discussion of that issue. I will simply and honestly share the beliefs and the presuppositions, conceptual framework and convictions which shape my thinking and the choices I have to make about how to live my life. I hope you will find them helpful as you sort through all of this and make choices about how you are going to live your life.

My sense is that we have a corrupt human nature, one that is inclined to do evil instead of good. Our hearts are inclined toward evil. Evil and wickedness flow out of us from within. Evil is the very core and essence of our being. This view stands in stark contrast to the belief that, "basically, we're good people." But are we really being honest when we claim the moral high ground that is occupied by acceptable standards of ethics, morals and values? Are we deluded or is this reality? Have we become spin masters of our own moral character? The spin is believed and takes on a life of its own. It becomes truth. Perhaps we have to believe our delusion, because the alternative view of what people are really like is simply too painful to assimilate into our conscious awareness.

The global theme of good versus evil is usually understood in terms of a tension. We believe in good and evil and we would like to think we choose the good. We believe in right and wrong and we like to believe we choose the right. We all have our monsters, but most of us do a pretty good job of keeping them on a leash. To what degree do love and reason bring out the good in us? At this point in the development of my thesis all that is necessary is to note that we do indeed live in this tension.

My understanding of evil is consistent with what I believe the Bible teaches. The concept was introduced to me back in seventh and eight grades. However, it was years before I began to grasp the fullness of what the total depravity of human nature was all about. One could say that what I was taught influenced my views about human behavior, and that I have conceptualized history in a way that supports Lutheran doctrine. There is no way for me to prove otherwise. Again, I want to acknowledge upfront that these are my convictions, and the sermons nobody wants to hear are those that suggest the reality and presence of evil in all of us, and that our evil rears its ugly head and makes its presence known in every aspect of our lives. It makes itself known in our thoughts, words and deeds. All I can say is that this view has been confirmed by all I have observed and experienced. Acknowledging this truth about ourselves is an essential first step in changing the way we do things in our lives so as to be able to better serve the interests of others. Nevertheless, whatever our thoughts about the origins of evil, there is indeed this reality called evil that defines our lives. One can make the case that human nature isn't all darkness and certainly point to numerous examples of the better parts of ourselves—our better angels; this issue is the focus of Chapter 12.

What Evil Looks Like in Our Lives

What evil looks like in our lives is a much easier question to answer. "Homo Selfishness" was the headline of one article. For me that was a new way of describing human nature, and it hit the nail on the head. Better known descriptions of our nature include "the survival of the fittest" and "every man for himself." "Looking out for #1" is another. My **thesis** is that **we have this innate tendency to look out not just for the needs of ourselves and our own, but also for our wants, at the expense of the unmet needs of others**. We experience a powerful internal tension between lives that are:

**self-centered,
self-seeking and
self-serving,**
on the one hand, and
**self-giving,
self-sacrificing and
selfless,**

on the other. This gets to the heart and core of what human nature is really like, of what our human nature is all about. It includes everything that is implied when we use the terms "self-interest" and "greed."

C. S. Lewis provides a summary statement for human nature that can be helpful.

> The moment you have a self at all, there is the possibility of putting yourself first—wanting to be the centre—wanting to be God, in fact. That was the sin of Satan: and that was the sin he taught the human race. . . . What Satan put into the heads of our remote ancestors was the idea that they could "be like Gods"— . . . be their own masters—invent some sort of happiness for themselves outside God, apart from God. And out of that hopeless attempt has come nearly all that we call human history – money, poverty, ambition, war, prostitution, classes, empires, slavery—the long terrible story of man trying to find something other than God to make him happy.[20] . . . Now what was the sort of "hole" man had got himself into? He had tried to set up on his own, to behave as if he belonged to himself. In other words fallen man is simply not an imperfect creature who needs improvement: he is a rebel.[21]

The notion that, "basically, we're good people," that we're not all that bad, just doesn't cut it. If it were true, we wouldn't need the 10 commandments, constitutions or laws. Thomas Hobbes *Leviathan* (1651) offered an excellent statement that summarizes the understanding of how the nature of man interfaces with the need for government. As he saw it we are not guided by reason and morals but by animalistic instincts and a ruthless struggle for self-preservation. To keep from destroying each other people contracted with a commonwealth called "that great Leviathan . . . to which we owe our peace and defense." People need government to enforce the laws they contract to and agree upon, to guarantee their freedom, to ensure the protection of their rights and to maintain order. Without that contract, self-interest and greed would lead to competition and chaos.

The underlying reason we need laws and law enforcement is that, bottom line, as individuals we function on the basis of self-interest. That's reality. The system of laws we call government serves to control our baser instincts and foster the common good. We are not by nature altruistic. We need laws to protect ourselves from the reality of "every man for himself" and "the survival of the fittest." You see, we look out not just for the needs of ourselves and our own, but also for our wants at the expense of the unmet needs of others.

The chasm that separates self-interest and altruism in our lives is both wide and deep. You don't have to scratch very much, dig very deep or look very far to find the truth about what we're really like. We are out of touch with reality, living in a never-never-land that doesn't exist. It is difficult to argue that human nature is driven by anything other than self interest.

Certainly, we have to take care of ourselves first or we would be in no position to help others. So it comes down to a conversation about finding a consensus as to what constitutes needs and when we cross over into the realm of wants. It seems to me that common sense would tell us when something feels more like a want than a need. At some point we have to address this issue of needs and wants. For now recognizing the reality of evil and its manifestations as self-interest and greed is sufficient.

You may be of the opinion that I have not given a balanced presentation of human nature, choosing instead to select examples that describe it at its worst. Therefore the discussion continues by taking a look at what's going on in our daily lives—the decisions we make and the actions we take. We'll consider what at first glance appears to be less extreme, more civilized manifestations of what I have called the unthinkable darkness and evil in our lives. It is time to begin our soul-searching and reflecting on what we're really like; this will be the task of the next four chapters.

Chapter 3
The History of American Greed: from the "Robber Barons" thru 2007

"Unless you become more watchful in your states and check the spirit of monopoly and the thirst for privileges you will in the end find that . . . the control over your dearest interests has passed into the hands of these corporations." Andrew Jackson

"You trample on the poor and force him to give you grain. Therefore, though you have built stone mansions, you will not live in them; though you have planted lush vineyards, you will not drink their wine. For I know how many are your offenses and how great your sins. You oppress the righteous and take bribes and you deprive the poor of justice in the courts" (Amos 5:11, 12).

My Opening Argument: The Evidence against Them Is Overwhelming

Chapters 3 and 4 include many examples for the purpose of emphasis. These were not isolated instances. They were deeply established patterns of behavior that happened again and again and again over a long period of time. When you see greed and self-interest surface repeatedly as fraud, deception and dishonesty, you finally begin to wonder. The intent is to make it difficult, if not impossible, to avoid seeing what these people were really like, so that you are unable to minimize or marginalize their behavior and how widespread it is. When you hear example after example and become aware of the sheer number of people involved and the seriousness of their offenses, the cumulative weight gets heavier and heavier and you begin to buckle under the load of reality. It finally starts to sink in. You get it! You understand. The cumulative record is overwhelming. You can't spin the facts enough to deny the truth and validity of their message.

While most people know something about the fallout from the self-interest and greed prevalent in the industrial and finance communities, my concern is that many may not have realized that these practices are so widespread. Using example after example helps you to understand that these things do indeed happen all the time. It is standard operating procedure for these folks. It is just their way of life. We need to hear these examples as if they were the constant pounding of a jack-hammer. The repeated abuses of the system are like pulling up to a stoplight when the vehicle next to you has one of those ultra-loud sound systems where the continuous boom of the base has been amplified to the point where you really get aggravated. This is how I hope you feel each time you hear another example of corruption and fraud. I want people to finally say, "Enough is enough! I get it! I see what you're trying to say." Then in Chapters 5 and 6 I intend to make the connection as to how their behavior is also descriptive of us and draw the conclusion that we also have the same tendency to look out not just for needs of ourselves and our own, but also for our wants at the expense of the unmet needs of others, many of whom are suffering and living in misery and pain.

If I didn't make my point with enough emphasis and impact, I was afraid the reader would not feel the full weight of the argument I am trying to make about what *our* human nature is really like—that these guys are not good persons, that they are not nice guys and neither are we. It is only when you see the pattern repeated over and over again that you begin to get an idea of just how ruthless these guys were. They didn't care who got hurt or who was left behind. They didn't care about the damage they left in their wake, as long as they made a profit. Ethics, morals and values were not in their vocabulary. I felt that it was only by overstating the case, that there might be a chance of getting you to see my point. The result could also be experienced by the reader as overload. You could get bogged down and lose interest. But I hope you will be patient and follow along; you may find it quite rewarding.

Also, while there are many who know something about the unethical, dishonest and fraudulent behavior on Wall Street, my hunch is that the overwhelming majority do not have an in-depth understanding of what happened. They or someone they knew experienced the fallout in terms of a pink slip or foreclosure notice, but they are not well enough informed to be able to connect the dots. Given my convictions about the importance of the message, I chose to err on the side of caution in deciding how much foundational information and explanation were needed.

Additionally, after reviewing the vast amount of material written about the subjects of Chapters 3 and 4, and the complexity of the subject, I decided to rely heavily on source material. Quotes were carefully selected and woven together to tell a story, a story that has more credibility and is more compelling given the status and expertise of the writers. It is my hope that the story that follows will convey the magnitude of the greed and self-interest characteristic of industrialists and financiers, and how their unethical, immoral and illegal behavior had a devastating negative impact on the lives of so many others.

"*The Gilded Age:*" A Book for All Seasons

While we were living in Springfield, Illinois a new Public Affairs Center opened at what was then called Sangamon State University. What a terrific addition for the community. The inaugural performance was Hal Holbrook doing *Mark Twain Tonight*. It was a classic.

Twain's perceptiveness in seeing through the hypocrisy in business, the church and our national ethic is a gift that just keeps giving, in contrast to the industrialists and those on Wall Street who just keep taking. All who have read *Huckleberry Finn* remember the moment when he refuses to go against his conscience and does what he believes is right. He chooses not to turn in "Miss Watson's Jim," a runaway slave. He resisted the culture's attempt to influence his conscience in a way that the folks mentioned in this chapter have not.

One of the subjects of Twain's musing on American life was "the excesses of the era of greed. . . ."[22] His first novel was *The Gilded Age*, which he co-wrote with Charles Dudley Warner. The term "Gilded Age" came to describe the graft, materialism and corruption in the public arena from the end of Reconstruction in 1877 until the turn of the century.

The history of American greed from the "Robber Barons" of the "Gilded Age" thru 2007 vividly demonstrates what people have always been like. The fraud, corruption and moral decay of this period are manifestations of the evil that is evident in every age. It is my contention that the root of their behavior lies deep in our "wicked" human nature.

We are and always have been preoccupied with ourselves. We see ourselves as the center of our world—in competition with all others around us.

The "Robber Barons"

There is no question that nineteenth century titans—Carnegie, Rockefeller and Morgan—set the stage for the empire builders of the twentieth century. The importance of their contribution to the progress of the economic and industrial growth of our nation cannot be overlooked. However, we cannot wink at their notorious character and reputation. They "lived in booming, anarchic times and thrived on them. The Gilded Age was a turbulent period of unfettered capitalism and unfathomable wealth . . . —an environment free of income tax, meddling regulators, and other curbs on the animal spirits of freewheeling entrepreneurs."[23]

> Three men—Andrew Carnegie, John D. Rockefeller and J. Pierpont Morgan—personified . . . all the greed, guile and enterprise of the age. . . .
>
> . . . (When) Rockefeller (1839-1937) . . . co-founded Standard in 1870, the oil fields of western Pennsylvania—the heart of the new industry—were in a chaotic state as gluts dragged down prices below production costs.
>
> . . . Never the curmudgeon of myth . . . (it) is certainly true that he was not the least bit squeamish, about tough tactics. He colluded with railroads to gain preferential freight rates, secretly owned rivals, bribed state legislators and engaged in industrial espionage. . . . (He) rolled up one refining center after another until his control was absolute. . . . At the same time, he was a devout Baptist with a ministerial air, who professed to have no less a business expert than the Lord on his side.
>
> Rockefeller believed in a new economic order that he dubbed 'cooperation;' President Theodore Roosevelt and his trustbusters had another word for it—monopoly—and the Lord proved no help to Rockefeller against T.R. Rockefeller's tough tactics forced America to define the limits of corporate behavior. Since Rockefeller managed to figure out every conceivable anticompetitive practice,

the authors of the Sherman Antitrust Act in 1890 simply had to study his career to draw up a reform agenda.[24]

In the end, Rockefeller amassed a fortune that beggared description. When his net worth peaked at $900 million in 1913, it was equivalent to more than 2% of the gross national product; such a share would today be worth $190 billion, or nearly three times as much as Bill Gates' wealth.[25]

At age 23 Carnegie (1835-1919) made a small fortune as head of the Pittsburgh division of the Pennsylvania Railroad.

When he was 33, the rich young man lectured himself that his continued pursuit of wealth "must degrade me beyond hope of recovery." Yet he couldn't abandon the money chase. . . . His steel furnished the sinews of America's (railroads,) burgeoning towns and factories.

. . . If Carnegie fancied himself the friend of the workingman, he had to face the ultimate comeuppance in 1892 when his associate Henry Clay Frick brutally suppressed striking workers in Homestead, Pa., in the bloodiest clash in U.S. Labor history.

After selling his empire to J.P. Morgan in 1901 . . . Carnegie devoted himself to good deeds. A prodigious philanthropist, he created 2,800 free libraries worldwide. "The man who dies rich dies disgraced," he declared bluntly. Like Rockefeller, Carnegie endowed large corporate foundations. . . . At his death he had disbursed almost his entire $350 million fortune.

If Rockefeller and Carnegie built the industrial age, Morgan (1837-1913) financed it.

. . . (By) the 1890's he controlled one-sixth of America's railway system.

Like Rockefeller, Morgan scorned competition as wasteful and ran afoul of federal trustbusters. . . .

(The) scale on which Rockefeller, Carnegie and Morgan operated was unprecedented, paving the way for a world of global companies and capital flows. And their money built a platform for philanthropy that has grown every bit as much as their corporations.[26]

Their lives constituted a fascinating and contradictory mix. No matter how much they are credited with spearheading the economic and industrial development of our nation, there was a price to pay in terms of compromising ethics, morals and values, and the countless people crushed by their ruthlessness.

Decade of the Deal

Times change; people don't. During the 1980s we had a replay of what took place in the 1880s and the era of the "robber barons." The difference is that there were more laws and regulations in place and the authorities had become far more effective in their efforts to sniff out and prosecute abuses. And prosecute they did. The self-interest and greed of the 1980s resulted in one case of massive fraud after another. Headlines captured the essence of what was happening:

"A Game of Greed"[27],

"Junk-bond King Deposed"[28],

"Greed Decade's Debt May Burden the '90s"[29],

"Junking an Ugly Era of Greed"[30],

"Pigs Always Get Slaughtered"[31], and

"Wall Street: A Greed Apart"[32].

The last article provides a great summary of the 80's that is brief and to the point.

    In financial circles leveraged buy-outs were the hot item of the '80s. Corporate raiders have become infamous: Carl Icahn, T. Boone Pickens, Paul Bilzerian and Canadian Robert Campeau. They made money by manipulating financial instruments, using somebody else's money to leverage a buyout and stripping the company of valuable assets. Drexel Burnham Lambert supplied the money in the form of junk bonds.

    The man of the decade and the face of Drexel Burnham was Michael Milken. He was a studious Main Street kid from the suburbs who went to Wharton School, where he wrote a paper that supported the thesis that junk bonds could be good investments. After graduation he signed on with Drexel Burnham for $25,000 a year. Using junk bonds sold by Milken and other Wall Street firms, raiders targeted large companies that were valued well below what they were really worth. By 1987, Milken had amassed more than $550 million. In 1987, Drexel was indicted for securities fraud. In 1989, it pleaded guilty to several counts, was fined $650 million and as part of the settlement was required to fire Milken. By 1990, Drexel Burnham had to file for bankruptcy. Milken also faced a 98-count fraud and racketeering indictment. In the process of the "bigs" playing the "game," a whole lot of money was lost in the retirement accounts and pensions of the "average Joe."

> You've already heard a lot about these Wall Street weasels. There was "*The Predators' Ball,*" the 1988 book on Michael Milkenomics and the junk bond empire at Drexel-Burnham. There was "*Barbarians at the Gate,*" the 1990 page turner about the RJR Nabisco takeover. There have been scores of magazine covers and newspaper spreads moralizing over the Greed Decade. . . .
>
> Do we really need another account of these little piggies who went to the market and pillaged it? James B. Stewart's *Den of Thieves* . . . suggests we might. Here is the definitive narrative of the men who rigged Wall Street in the 80's, and the federal prosecutors who brought them to putative justice. . . . "Den of Thieves" is the interlocking stories of Dennis Levine, Martin Siegel, Ivan Boesky and Michael Milken— . . . whose insider-trading ring made millions and shattered any pretense of market integrity.
>
> . . . (It's) certainly the first time one reporter has laid out the scandal in such detail. What's most compelling, though, is the overpowering case the book marshals against Milken. Lavine comes across as an oaf, Boesky a loon, Siegel a neurotic. But Milken emerges as the embodiment of evil.[33]

While a plea deal resulted in the dropping of the racketeering charges against him, Milken did plead guilty to 6 counts of fraud, was fined $600,000 million and given a 10 year prison sentence. There are those who believe he got off too light. "Considering all the damage he did to stockholders, taxpayers and the public's confidence in the stock market, Milken is getting off easy."[34]

Sweet Deal Makes Lots of Dough:

Granddaddy of All
Deals Goes Down in My Old Neighborhood

"The biggest takeover battle in history raises questions about greed, debt and the well-being of American industry."[35] This article caught my attention because it was about the company that made those wonderful cookies in a factory about two miles from home, and a smell we inhaled hundreds of times, especially strong whenever we would take the Kedzie Avenue bus right past the Nabisco plant.

> The very best at the leveraged buyout was Henry Kravis, who snatched "RJR from the company's chief executive, Ross Johnson."[36] This was "the ultimate deal: the 1988 buyout of RJR Nabisco, which Kohlberg Kravis Roberts, headed by Henry Kravis, acquired for $25 billion. The battle for RJR combined all the excesses of the era, pitting Milken and Kravis against Cohen and Johnson, the RJR chairman who stood to make more than $100 million by winning the fight. The victorious Kravis walked off with $75 million in fees alone as part of his prize."[37]

The Savings and Loan
(S & L) Crisis

Milken at Drexel Burnham and the other investment firms that sold junk bonds were also significant factors in the savings and loan disaster. Charles Keating was the symbol of misconduct for the S&L crisis. In 1979 the Securities and Exchange Commission claimed that he and a partner committed fraud by diverting company assets to their own personal use. Keating signed a consent decree in which he admitted no wrongdoing, and promised not to do it again.

In 1990 he was charged with violations of California's securities laws by misrepresenting the nature of the high-risk junk bonds issued by Lincoln Savings and Loan Association. The catch was that the bonds were not covered by federal deposit insurance, and the institution's investments in real estate, junk bonds, went south. The bonds became worthless and small investors lost their savings. The fraud and racketeering charges against him were thrown out in 1996 after he had served 4 ½ years of a 12 ½ year sentence, but not the $1.5 billion civil judgment. The bond holders were able to collect about 74 cents for every dollar they invested. As for you and I, the taxpayers, Keating's misdeeds cost us $2.5 billion.

By 2020, the American taxpayer will have to pay a cleanup bill for the entire S&L industry that could exceed $500 billion.[38]

After serving in the Navy as a fighter pilot Keating "emerged in public life in the late 1950s as a vigorous opponent of pornography, a campaign he continued for three decades. President . . . Nixon appointed him in 1970 to the Federal Commission on Obscenity and Pornography."[39] Keating, however, was unable to recognize the ethical and moral implications of his financial misdeeds. The civil judgments against Keating were no less obscene than the causes he opposed so vigorously for three decades. The irony of the juxtaposition of both examples of the darkness of human nature is powerful.

The obscenity involved in pornography and greed is deeply rooted in human flesh. Both capture the depravity of human nature in their attempt to exploit others for personal gain. All of his efforts to protect people from the evils of pornography were compromised when he left average folks trying to pay off their own homes with a $2.5 billion tax bill. However well intentioned some of his efforts may have been, his character and reputation have been tarnished forever.

The Keating Five and Then Some

While Keating is the poster child for the S & L scandal, the list of those complicit in the disaster includes a who's who of government leaders, including five senators investigated by the Senate Ethics Committee. All accepted large campaign contributions and were his advocates in dealing with federal regulators. Only Alan Cranston was cited for major ethics violations. Senators Reigle and DeConcini were said to have given the appearance of a conflict of interest, while Senators Glenn and McCain were said to have exercised poor judgment.

A magazine article provided a thorough compilation of those it called "Villains of the S&L Crisis" together with an explanation of their involvement.[40]

- Reagan factotum James Baker – Scandal exploded on his watch

- Former Federal Home Loan Bank Board (FHLBB) chief Jay Janis – Lowered S&L capital standards

- Utah Senator Jake Garn – Promoted riskier S&L activities

- Texas Representative Jim Wright – Protected S&L's in the House
- Florida's Claude Pepper – House gatekeeper on S&L bills
- Former FHLBB head Edwin Gray – First downplayed the danger
- Wisconsin's William Proxmire – Stopped reforms in the Senate
- California's Tony Coello – Netted huge S&L contributions
- Ex-FHLBB chief Richard Pratt – Helped loosen government rules
- California Assemblyman Pat Nolan – Lifted all limits on state thrifts
- Economist Alan Greenspan – Thumb's up for Keating's S&L
- Texas Republican Steve Bartlett – '87 law propped up shaky S&L's
- Budget official Constance Horner – Kept number of examiners down
- Democrat Fernand St. Germain – S&L's best friend in the House
- Californian Allan Cranston – S&L's best friend in the Senate
- S&L boss Charles Keating – Stuck taxpayers for $2.5 billion
- Deregulator Donald Regan – Didn't foresee the crooks
- Office of Management and Budget boss David Stockman – cut regulators' budget
- FHLBB Chairman M. Danny Wall – Crisis? What crisis?

Some of those involved expressed regret about how the S&L crisis came down. With reference to the Garn-St. Germain bill (1982) Texas Democrat Jim Wright said it was a "'grotesque error', and says of the scandal: 'I'm ashamed. I wish I had seen it coming and organized to stop it from happening. But I didn't.'"[41] Garn himself concedes that part of the legislation was a major mistake. "Officials at the U.S. League of Savings Institutions, which supported the rules changes, now rue them. 'We thought we were dealing with the traditional people we had always dealt with. . . .' Donald Regan, too, says he has learned that there is an 'avaricious, greedy, criminal element' in all industries. If he had known then what he knows now, would he have favored so much deregulation? 'The answer is no.'" He was naïve and got religion too late. He underestimated the degree to which people are greedy and operate on the basis of self-centered, self-serving, self-seeking principles.

"Tales of Greed, Lawlessness, (and) Loss Turn Business Pages into Tabloids"[42]

Time goes on. Years are grouped into decades. Decades get stacked in piles of ten, and centuries pass. Many things change. Human nature does not. 2002 witnessed the collapse of a virtual "Who's Who" in the echelons of big business who were involved in shady deals of all sorts. The litany of names is familiar: Ken Lay, Jeff Skilling and Andrew Fastow at Enron; Dennis Kozlowski at Tyco; Bernie Ebbers at WorldCom; Sam Waksal at ImClone; Richard Scrushy at HealthSouth; and John Riga at Adelphia. When in Dallas, I remember driving by Enron and the crooked "E"—what irony.

Ken Lay and Jeff Skilling became the poster boys for business-accounting scandals. In the summer of 2001 Sherron Watkins, a kid from the middle class who always had a flair for the numbers, summed it up.

> The numbers didn't add up. A pair of letters she wrote to Chairman Ken Lay exposed top officials—perhaps including Lay himself—who for months had been trying to hide a mountain of debt, and started a chain reaction of events that brought down the company. Watkin's letters along with thousands of other documents are now in the hands of congressional and criminal investigators who are probing how Enron, its pet-rock auditors at Andersen and a host of other supporting actors allowed the country's seventh largest company to suddenly go bankrupt in December. "I am incredibly nervous that we will implode in a wave of accounting scandals," Watkin's wrote of Enron's financial health. "I have heard one manager level employee ... say, ... 'We're such a crooked company.'"
>
> Maybe you can only glimpse the soul of a company when it breaks open right before your eyes. But we know now, thanks to Watkins, that Enron hid billions of dollars in debts and operating losses inside private partnerships and dizzyingly complex accounting schemes that were intended to pump up the buzz about the company and support its inflated stock

price. We also learned last week that executives at Andersen, the accounting giant that enabled Enron's every move, fretted about the arrangement but saw the chance to double their fees if they just kept their heads down.

. . . As all these characters tell their self-serving stories, the fall of Enron is the most revealing sort of failure. It is a failure of the old-fashioned idea that auditors, directors and stock analysts are supposed to put the interests of shareholders above their own thirst for fees. It is a failure of government: having greased nearly every campaigner's palm in Washington, Enron worked overtime to keep the regulators from looking too closely at a balance sheet gone bad. . . . (The) last people to learn of the looming reckoning were going to be millions of Enron shareholders.[43]

In the process Enron hoodwinked the IRS. Outside advisors who colluded with Enron received $88 million. "Enron and its advisors conspired to mine the tax codes for tax schemes. They ensured that no one—particularly the IRS—would ever discover what they were up to," Max Baucus (Senator from Montana) said. . . . By using advice from sophisticated attorneys, investment bankers and accountants, "corporations like Enron have an inherent advantage over the IRS. . . ." The company's tax department became a profit center with its own yearly revenue targets. . . . "Enron's failure in December 2001 destroyed the retirement savings of thousands of employees and hurt individual investors and pension funds nationwide."[44]

The documents had been shredded and the handwriting was on the wall. The headline of one article read, "Andersen's Descent into Greed Leaves Integrity Behind."[45] "As many as 80 people who worked at Arthur Andersen's Houston office were involved in the destruction of documents related to Enron. . . ."[46] It wasn't long before "(a) federal grand jury indicted Arthur Andersen, one of the country's Big Five accounting firms on obstruction of justice charges Thursday for shredding tons of sensitive Enron documents last fall. . . . The indictment charges that Andersen . . . 'did knowingly, intentionally and corruptly persuade' employees to 'alter, destroy, mutilate and conceal' documents related to Andersen's audit of the fallen energy giant."[47] "Arthur Andersen so wanted to please mega-client Enron that it was willing to bend the rules. Not just the rules, the laws. And not just bend them, break them . . . by shredding documents federal investigators were seeking. Faced with a conviction for obstruction of justice, Arthur Andersen had no choice but to liquidate. You might say it was the only way to account for its actions."[48]

The Settling of Accounts

Ken Lay, former chairman and CEO of **Enron**, and Jeff Skilling, former CEO and COO went on trial in 2006. The jury rendered its verdict on May 25, 2006. Sentencing took place on October 23, 2006.

> Lay was convicted of all six counts of securities and wire fraud for which he had been tried, and could have faced a total of up to 45 years in prison; however, he died of a heart attack on July 5, 2006, prior, to sentencing. Accordingly, the judge vacated Lay's conviction on October 17, 2006, since he died before he was sentenced and before all appeals could be exhausted.[49]
>
> Skilling was convicted on 19 of 28 counts of securities fraud and wire fraud and acquitted on the remaining nine, including charges of insider trading. He was sentenced to 24 years, 4 months in prison, and cannot be released before serving less than 20 years, 4 months. In addition, he must pay $630 million to the government, which includes a $180 million fine.[50]

On May 8, 2013 he reached a plea deal in which 10 years was taken off his term (possible release in 2018 instead of 2028) in exchange for his forfeiture of $40 million to be used for restitution for victims of Enron's fraud and an agreement to end all appeals of his 2006 conviction. The revised sentence would still be more than twice any other defendant in one of the most notorious corporate frauds in U.S. history. Ex-**Enron** CFO Andrew Fastow was sentenced to six years in prison for his role in the collapse.

In June 2005 Dennis Kozlowski, the former chairman and CEO of **Tyco International** and his top lieutenant CFO Mark Swartz were convicted of 22 counts of fraud, conspiracy and grand larceny and faced prison sentences of eight to 25 years. He looted his company of $150 million, and "reaping $430 million more by covertly selling company shares while artificially inflating the value of the stock."[51] When visiting my brother in Portsmouth, New Hampshire I saw the palatial estate that Kozlowski was building, and wondered how many folk had been hurt in order to pay for it. He is the guy who bought the now infamous $6,000 shower curtain and threw a $2 million party for his wife that Tyco partly funded.

"Bernard J. Ebbers, the founder and former chief executive of **WorldCom**, was sentenced to 25 years in prison for his role in an $11 billion accounting fraud that brought down the telecommunications company in 2002."[52] Sam Waksal ex-CEO of **ImClone** was sentenced to seven years for insider trading. Richard Scrushy, former **HealthSouth** CEO, was acquitted of federal charges of massive accounting fraud that sent the rehabilitation chain into bankruptcy. However, he was convicted on civil charges brought by HealthSouth shareholders and ordered to pay shareholders $2.9 billion. He is serving a nearly seven year sentence for a 2006 conviction in a separate state government bribery case. "John Rigas (founder and former CEO), who turned a $300 investment a half-century ago into cable TV behemoth **Adelphia Communications Corp.**, was sentenced to 15 years in prison Monday for his role in the looting and debt-hiding scandal that pummeled the company in bankruptcy. Rigas' son Timothy, 49, who like his father was convicted last year of bank fraud, securities fraud and conspiracy, was sentenced to 20 years in prison."[53]

Not in the Mutual Fund Industry – No Way!

Yep—and it happened to us right here in the village where we live. We moved to Menomonee Falls, Wisconsin in 1985. It has been a great place to live and to raise our children. When my mother went to heaven, my sister, brother and I each received a share of her small estate. Karen and I thought what better place to safely invest it than in a local fund with a solid national reputation, and a CEO who had breakfast in a local restaurant. Dick Strong was a pillar of the community.

> If investors learned one thing this year (2003), it's that even the most trustworthy companies aren't above suspicion. . . . (When) New York Attorney General Eliot Spitzer leveled charges of trading improprieties at mutual funds, investors really were stunned. The mutual fund industry was supposed to be different. It was supposed to give the small investor the same treatment as the swells. Some funds, however, sold out their own investors for a few big clients.[54]
>
> . . . But the new wave of middle class investors ran squarely into the time-honored Wall Street tradition of sticking it

to the little guy. The retail investor, as opposed to the big institutional investors, has always been lowest on the food chain for advice, information and service. Big institutional accounts normally get Wall Street's best research, information and fastest execution. And despite the flood of money from small accounts, Wall Street wasn't able to overcome tradition. When the bull market ended in March 2000, the scandals started to unfold, and many of them hit small investors the hardest.

Merrill Lynch agreed to pay a $100 million penalty in May 2002 to settle allegations that its brokerage advice to retail investors was tainted by conflicts of interest.

. . . But the mutual fund trading scandal showed just how callous Wall Street could be. Some fund companies allowed large clients to make rapid, in-and-out trades in the funds. That's not illegal. But the same fund companies clearly stated in their prospectuses that they wouldn't tolerate rapid-fire trading. Making exceptions for big clients is illegal. And some companies also let clients buy shares at the 4 p.m. closing price after 4 p.m., and that is illegal.

The scandal has touched big name companies like Janus Capital, Strong Financial, Invesco, Alliance Capital, Putnam Investments, Federated investments and MFS. Lawrence Lasser, the lavishly paid head of Putnam, has resigned in the wake of the scandal. Richard Strong, founder of Strong Financial, has stepped down too.[55]

"You are not going to believe this," I told my wife. "Strong Funds is involved in the mutual fund scandal. They apparently took advantage of us too." It happened right here in our own community with our local investment firm. We were included in a class action lawsuit and received several small settlements.

The fund-trading scandal marked a new low for Wall Street, even worse than the pump-and-dump tactics employed in the mania for initial public stock offerings of the late 90's. "It's hard to feel sorry for some people who bought some stupid dot-com stock," says Joe Nocera, a longtime observer of the financial world and whose book *A Piece of the Action*, captured the middle-class embrace of Wall Street. After all, Wall Street had always preyed on naïve speculators.

Funds were supposed to be better. "Mutual funds were supposed to be the honorable alternative—they would let you give your money to a professional, who would manage it well on your behalf," Nocera says. That just wasn't the case, says Massachusetts Secretary of State William Galvin, who uncovered market timing by Putnam portfolio managers this fall. "The funds said, 'We are all in this together. You can trust our competence,'" Galvin says. "What they delivered was deceit and underperformance." . . . Investor reaction ranges from disappointment, to deep cynicism.[56]

An honest small fund director's report about abuses made individual investors feel like the game is rigged. Big sophisticated investors were gaming the system. A Securities and Exchange commission review found that 50 percent of the funds had made special arrangements for market timing, "rapid, short-term trading that . . . drives up costs for other investors—and late trading, the illegal practice of allowing investors to trade after hours using outdated prices. . . . "(Eliot) Spitzer says that an alert board of directors can easily detect market timing using public information about the fund's trading volume, and would never allow fund executives to trade their own funds against the interest of shareholders, as the chairman of Strong Funds is accused of doing."[57]

Rapacious

"'Greed is not a bad thing,' (Ivan) Boesky said in 1985. 'Everybody should be a little greedy . . . You shouldn't feel guilty.'"[58] Milken's indictment and conviction on federal fraud charges resulted in Boesky's plea deal with the government relative to the charges filed against him for running a stock trading scheme that relied on insider information. He named Drexel and Milken as collaborators in his schemes. Ivan Boesky was imprisoned for his illegal use of inside information. It doesn't seem to be a coincidence how it all turned out for Boesky, Keating and Milken. A little greed seems to lead to a little more and on down a road that can get you in a whole heap of trouble.

Earlier in the chapter I used a quote that included the word "rapacious."[59] It was also used in the subtitle of an article about the "Robber Barons"[60] Unpacking its meaning provides a fitting summary of this chapter. The term describes an unscrupulous person who is excessively grasping and inclined to seize or extort what is coveted. The smart, the strong and the cunning live by preying on the weak, the vulnerable, and the unconnected. Rapacious is descriptive of how the dark side of human nature operates on the basis of greed and self-interest. The purpose of this chapter was to expose the greed and rapaciousness rampant in business.

The rapacious are a complicated breed. They hardly seem moved by the possibility of another meltdown in our economy, or the world economy, or all of the people who will be hurt. The vultures continue to circle, waiting to prey on their next victim. Less than two months before its collapse bankrupt Drexel Burnham Lambert began giving out $260 million in 1989 bonuses to employees. The whole Drexel episode was not humanity's finest hour. But, truth is, that is the nature of the beast. What was the editor of *Newsweek* smoking when the headline on the cover of the Jan 4, 1988 issue was approved: "THE 80's ARE OVER - Greed goes out of style." Really! I don't think so!

Hopefully, all of the examples make it extremely difficult to avoid the truth about what these people are like. Hopefully, they make it extremely difficult to be able to minimize and marginalize the point and just blow it off. The next chapter will continue the same strategy, the only difference being that the examples have just happened in the last few years. They are so recent that we are still experiencing the economic consequences and still trying to get the economy back on track. Again, I want the examples of greed and self-interest to reach the point of overload, where you can't avoid drawing the conclusion that we have a tendency to look out not just for needs of our own, but also for our wants at the expense of the unmet needs of others.

Chapter 4
Close Call: The Near Economic Meltdown of 2008

"Unless somebody can find a way to change human nature, we will have more crises." Alan Greenspan

"Therefore everyone who hears these words of mine and puts them into practice is like a wise man who built his house on the rock. The rain came, the streams rose, and the winds blew and beat against that house; yet it did not fall, because it had its foundation on the rock. But everyone who hears these words of mine and does not put them into practice is like a foolish man who built his house on sand. The rain came, the streams rose, and the winds blew and beat against that house, and it fell with a great crash" (Matthew 7:24-27).

Not More Evil, Just More Visible

One more point needs to be added to the discussion at the beginning of Chapter 3. Most would agree that those referred to in this chapter are sleazy at best. Nevertheless, it is most certainly not my intention to vilify them in any way; this will be perfectly clear when you get to Chapter 5. While they are shady characters, it is not my intent to pick on them or single them out for having a unique set of character traits.

It is our familiarity with them because of their involvement in well known recent events that suggested their inclusion as the vehicle for getting my point across. Since what they did is still so fresh in our minds, it made them excellent examples. I chose them only because they were able to help make my case and validate my thesis. As in the last chapter, however, it was my intent to pile example on top of example to the point where you feel the full weight of the argument. I wanted to set the table with emphasis and an exclamation point, so that when the thesis is applied to us, it has maximum impact. When we get included in the mix of those described as greedy and selfish, I want to make sure we get it. The folks noted in this chapter are no more evil than the rest of us; they just happen to live lives that are more visible.

The Fundamentals of Our Economy are Strong

Both the financial community and the government had a role to play in bringing our economy and the world economy to the brink of a collapse of catastrophic proportions. Homebuyers, loan companies, Wall Street firms, CEOs, ratings agencies, regulators, Congress, the executive branch and insurance companies were all responsible. However, in terms of the relative weight of their impact, the investment bankers bear the biggest share of responsibility. The failure of the checks and balances in the system simply set the table. When the economy went into a downward spiral, it was average people working hard to make a living and provide for their families who were hurt the most. They lost good jobs, received foreclosure notices on their homes and depleted their savings. Why should we have expected anything different?

During the early years of the new millennium there were signs of economic uncertainty. Feeling uneasy, I paid attention to what was going on and remember hearing President George W. Bush repeatedly reassure us that the fundamentals of our economy were strong. "Trust us, said the voices of Washington. First, the Bush Administration: Trust us! … We have surpluses as far as the eye can see. … The economy is fundamentally strong, and more tax cuts will make it stronger. And we can save social security by letting you invest in the markets."[61] If the president said the fundamentals were sound, that was good enough for me.

Federal Reserve Chairman Alan Greenspan echoed similar sentiments, saying, "the U.S. economic recovery remains solidly on track despite the recent sharp drop in stock prices. … The fundamentals are in place for a return to sustained healthy growth."[62] I don't believe they lied nor had any intent to deceive. They were honestly convinced of the truth of their message.

It blows my mind that the president and his economic advisors, including the Fed chairman, didn't get it. It is astounding to think that they didn't understand the dangers inherent in the dynamics of their economic policy. A crisis that threatened our whole economic system and standard of living was on the horizon, and they didn't see it coming—that is frightening. The same is true for investment counselors, financial advisors and fund managers, whose clients lost 35-50 percent of the value of their portfolios when the bottom fell out; they never saw it coming either. By 2011, "Nine in 10 of the popular retirement plans are at least back to where they were in October 2007, the peak of the stock market."[63] For those who expected it to take longer, that was good news. The reality is that investors lost four years of growth plus earnings. It could have been worse, but it wouldn't have had to happen at all except for the greed and self-interest on Wall Street. President Bush signed off on a $700 billion dollar bailout.

Then the Unthinkable Happened

First-time home buyers and those who had wanted to upgrade were thrilled with their homes. It wasn't paid for, but they were able to enjoy it every day. Most couldn't believe it was really theirs. Never in their wildest dreams did they think they could own a home like this. It all happened in a red hot housing market where large loans became available to folks who never thought they could get them. But if they were careful and everything went right, they could do it; and if they couldn't quite make it, they could always sell for a profit in an appreciating market.

Then the bottom dropped out of the economy and peoples' plans for the future quickly faded. There wasn't much they could save. They didn't understand what was happening. They didn't understand that the economic stability of the whole country was threatened. There were a whole lot of people who had lost their jobs—often multiple wage earners in the same house. When they could no longer make the payments and went to sell their homes, they found out that the price had crashed and they couldn't even sell it for enough to pay off the mortgage. Foreclosure loomed as a possibility. They were devastated.

How could this happen? This chapter is my take on the answer to those questions. Those who lost their homes were understandably focused on the pressing, immediate needs of their family. The bigger picture was that our whole economy was in a very precarious position—we had come within a whisker of total economic meltdown.

After the collapse of Lehman Bros. in 2008, Federal Reserve Chairman Ben Bernanke, Treasury Secretary Henry Paulson and New York Fed president Timothy Geithner stood on the brink of catastrophe. Their decision not to bail out Lehman set off a near panic among investors and lenders worldwide. In response, the government implemented a $700 billion bailout and has since adopted a series of rescue measures that put U.S. taxpayers on the hook for a potential $14 trillion, author Barry Ritholtz says.[64]

While the health of both our economy and the world economy hung in the balance, and though the issues had an exponentially larger potential for disaster, the underlying dynamics were the same. What happened was that yet again we had an economic replay that reflected self-interest and greed. We shouldn't be surprised. The difference was that this time a whole lot more people got hurt and the fallout had the potential to be catastrophic.

When you hear a good old fashioned home mortgage described in the context of mortgage based securities called credit-default options (CDOs), which are sold on the subprime mortgage market and secured with credit default-swaps (CDSs), you know you're playing in somebody else's ballpark and by somebody else's rules. All you can do is trust that they know what they are doing, that they are serving your best interest, that the government is keeping a watchful eye on their business practices and that everything will be all-right. It wasn't. Wall St. behaved recklessly, government regulators missed the warning signals and taxpayers picked up the tab.

Here is a condensed version of the story of the collapse of the subprime mortgage market, and the domino effect that led to cataclysmic upheaval in our financial markets. *House of Cards: A Tale of Hubris and Wretched Excess on Wall Street* is one of many intriguing and helpful accounts of what was behind the near meltdown of the economy. It happens to be about the demise of Bear Stearns due to its huge position in toxic mortgage based securities. "Toxic" debt was dressed up to appear more secure than it actually was. How could they take such enormous risks? There had been a huge change in the legal structure of Wall Street partnerships

> ... from shared-liability partnerships to corporate structures that spread the liability from the partners according to their capital contributions to shareholders based on their ownership.... (Firm) employees – no longer technically referred to as partners – were

encouraged by their bosses to use their new shareholder's capital to take vastly more risk than ever before. The men running Wall Street knew full well that any liability for their risk- once born by their partners –now fell to nameless, faceless shareholders. . . . The holy grail of investment banking became increasing short-term profits and short-term bonuses at the expense of the long term health of the firm and its shareholders.[65]

Since they were playing with other peoples' money, caution was thrown to the wind. This is the reason for all the metaphors about Wall Street gambling with somebody else's money.

Housing Bubble Bursts

In October 2004 Fed Chairman Alan Greenspan observed "that although 'pockets of severe stress within the household sector . . . remain a concern,' the likelihood of 'housing price bubbles' appeared small."[66] In 1993, President Clinton used HUD to implement his agenda to increase home ownership among minorities, and encouraged the relaxation of their standards for loan qualification. The Clinton Administration had made changes to the Community Reinvestment Act of 1977 that facilitated the securitization of subprime loans. The first securitization of $385 million was underwritten in part by Bear Stearns. "(President Clinton) oversaw an era of great prosperity—and deregulation."[67] Due to the changes, the housing market added 1.5 million new homeowners. "From the mid-1990's," (Dennis) Sewell wrote, "(banks) began to abandon their formerly rigorous lending criteria."[68]

This is what led to the growth of the subprime mortgage market. The term "subprime" refers to the credit quality of borrowers who have weak credit histories and therefore a greater risk of default than prime borrowers. In order to compensate for the additional risk, subprime borrowers are offered higher interest rates and less favorable terms. Prime borrowers are those with high credit ratings and low debt, and are therefore less likely to default.

Enter the investment bankers. "Hedge funds played an important role in the shift to sloppy mortgage lending, and (John) Devaney was one of the cheerleaders. By buying up mortgage loans, Devaney and other hedgies earned a fat return for a while, which encouraged mortgage outfits to make ever sketchier loans."[69] With housing prices continuing to rise rapidly, more and more money was lent to those who would have difficulty keeping up with the payments if there was a downturn in the economy. More iffy mortgages were approved. "Mortgages were offered with only three percent deposit requirements, and eventually with no deposit requirement at all. The mortgage banks fell over one another to provide loans to low-income households and especially minority customers."[70]

Henry Cisneros, Clinton's Secretary of Housing and Urban Development from 1993 to 1997 was quoted in *The New York Times* in October 2008 as saying, ". . . people 'who should not have been homeowners' had been lured by 'unscrupulous participants— bankers, brokers, secondary market people. . . .'"[71] Small cracks in the system began to appear. But "there was simply too much money to be made as the housing bubble continued to inflate for any of the participants— not only at Bear Stearns, but also across Wall Street—to stop and take notice.'"[72]

> Three days later (February 24, 2007) the *Wall Street Journal* interviewed Lewis Ranieri, the godfather of the mortgage-backed security and the pioneer trader of them when he was at Salomon Brothers from the 1960's until . . . 1987. . . . The growing problem was that 40 percent of the subprime borrowers in 2006 were not required to produce pay stubs or other proof of net worth . . . and lenders were relying more and more on computer models to estimate the value of homes. "We're not really sure what the guy's income is and . . . we're not sure what the home is worth," Ranieri said. "So you can understand why some of us became a little nervous. . . ." The *Journal* made it clear that "Mr. Ranieri isn't predicting Armageddon. Some of the riskier new types of mortgages will probably perform 'horribly' in terms of defaults, leading to loses for some investors. But, he says, the 'vast majority' of mortgages outstanding are based on sounder lending principles and should be fine."[73]

CDOs—"Financial Weapons of Mass Destruction"

The next turn in the downward spiral that led to the near collapse of our economy could only happen on Wall Street. This time, however, even many of the Wall Street wizards didn't understand the financial instruments they were using. "It is tempting to blame the whole political-industrial complex, starting with whoever had the bad idea of lending $750,000 to someone making $17,000 a year; the regulators who said that was O.K. and the politicians who encouraged them; the financial geniuses who rolled up all of those mistakes into a big ball of bad loans, chopped them up and sold them; and above all the presiding executives who got performance bonuses whether they performed or not – buying and selling things whose value they could not possibly know, . . . unleashing on the markets what Warren Buffet called 'financial weapons of mass destruction.'"[74] When you bundle prime and subprime mortgages together and use the bundles as collateral for bonds, you create the potential for a gigantic problem—which is exactly what happened. When the economy began to cool, the snowball started rolling downhill, picking up mass with every turn.

We're there a whole bunch of folks who borrowed more than they could afford? Sure. If their home loan applications would have been reviewed using traditional standards, many would have been rejected. Most of us depend on the "experts" to tell us when our dreams exceed our means. I clearly remember when we were told that our financial position was such that our chances of getting the loan we needed were "skinny." My wife would probably need a job before we could get the loan. If the bank where we went to get the loan approved our application even though we couldn't afford it, we would have assumed that they were the experts and knew what they were doing. Surely they would know whether we could afford to make the payments. We would have gone ahead and signed, as did many other folks. As long as the bank is willing to loan the money, why not sign? The people who borrowed more than they could afford aren't the real culprits. They are not the big players. If they were the only problem, our economy would have never reached the brink of collapse.

>Potential home buyers went to brokers like Ameriquest Mortgage.

>(Hudson) takes us on a tour of the financial carnival tent pitched by subprime factories like Ameriquest. The place was characterized by sleazy lending pitches and fraudulent techniques. . . . The book zeroes in on the relationship Ameriquest had with Lehman Brothers—the biggest subprime enabler. Ameriquest and its related companies packaged more than $170 billion in subprime loans into mortgage-bond deals. Lehman went bust.[75]

This turn in the spiral involves "the bigs" who handled the buying and selling of those bundles or packages of shaky mortgages; this was the core of the problem. As just noted, brokers like Ameriquest sold bundles of prime and subprime mortgages to banks that used them as collateral for bonds they were selling. Then multiplying the danger many times over, investment banks bundled those bonds into high sounding financial instruments called collateralized debt obligations (CDOs), then turned around and sold the CDOs. CDOs are also known as derivatives—investments that derive their value from the collateral that guarantees their worth, which in this case were bundles of bonds backed by a lethal blend of prime and subprime mortgages.

To provide a steady supply of CDOs to sell, Merrill Lynch loaded up on $41 billion worth of bonds. "Firms (even borrowed) to load up on CDOs and real estate. Lehman Brothers was leveraged more than 30 to 1."[76] Then folks with home loans they couldn't afford began to default, and tried to sell. Housing values declined, as supply exceeded demand. The mortgages that were the collateral for the bonds bundled into CDOs lost value. The investment banks that held the bonds as collateral lost huge amounts of money and didn't have sufficient cash reserves to cover the losses; they began to collapse, which caused our whole financial system to come tumbling down like a "House of Cards."

CDSs

Understanding the financial transactions involved in the subprime housing crisis requires that we are also aware that there was a second investment strategy that involved credit-default swaps (CDSs). As part of President Clinton's goal of increasing home ownership, he "ushered out the Glass-Steagall Act and signed the Commodities Futures Modernization Act, which exempted CDSs from regulation."[77] "Before the meltdown, few people had ever heard of credit-default swaps (CDSs). They are insurance contracts—or, if you prefer, wagers—that a company will pay its debt. **As a founding member of AIG's** (American International Group) **financial products unit, (Joe) Cassano knew them cold.** In good times, AIG's massive CDS-issuance business minted money by essentially writing insurance against a financial Katrina (an insurance policy against a bond default). . . . Those contracts were at the heart of AIG's downfall."[78] AIG sold insurance policies (CDSs) to protect investors from failures, and when homeowners defaulted on their mortgages in large numbers, the American taxpayer had to pay off the policy. "As Bernanke explained recently, 'AIG exploited a huge gap in the regulatory system. There was no oversight of the Financial Products Division. This was a hedge fund, basically, that was attached to a large and stable insurance company.'"[79] In essence, AIG drove a semi through the exemption and made huge profits from selling CDSs and then needed a $150 billion loan from American taxpayers to stay afloat.

The reason it was necessary to bailout AIG is because it is so big and so connected in the global financial community that its failure would cause a chain reaction of enormous proportions.

The Greatest Trade Ever: The Behind-the-Scenes Story of How John Paulson Defied Wall Street and Made Financial History by Gregory Zuckerman explains an important corollary to the second strategy. "(A) renegade hedge fund manager outwitted the mortgage-market cognoscenti, betting the market was headed for a major fall, a bet that earned more than $15 billion for his firm."[80] "(A) few professional investors foresaw the collapse of the subprime mortgage market and then pocketed millions from their big bets. . . . Each of the people profiled in the book, *The Big Short* by Michael Lewis, saw the bubble through a different lens. . . . Each found ways to short the market and make enormous bets that the bonds would crater. . . ."[81] Isn't it fascinating how a few folks saw what was coming while most of the big players didn't."

Lewis spreads the blame for the financial meltdown:

- Bond Raters Standard and Poor's and Moody's rate subprime bonds incorrectly, magically turning BBBs into AAAs.

- Lax accounting rules let mortgage companies assume their loans would be repaid.

- The Securities and Exchange Commission ignored inflated valuations of ... CDOs.

- Wall Street firms were clueless about the immensity of the subprime woes. 'They didn't know their own balance sheets,' Eiseman (one of the professional investors who foresaw the collapse and made billions) says.

- Insurer AIG ... didn't believe home prices could fall across the country simultaneously.[82]

What Happened to the System Safeguards?

Diversification

"Mortgages used to be the stars of finance. Home loans, after all, have a lot going for them: The vast majority of people, even today, make their mortgage payment on time. What's more, mortgage bonds are made up of thousands of home loans, giving them safety through diversity. So how did these bonds become so toxic that they've poisoned banks and threatened the entire economy?"[83] When CDOs were bundled they became a mix of prime and subprime loans. When home buyers began to default on their loans in large numbers, the bonds for which they were collateral also defaulted, as did the CDOs in which they were bundled. The point is that the mortgage bonds that the CDOs used as collateral contained both prime and subprime loans that were commingled, and couldn't be sorted out. When the economy tanked the whole package became a toxic asset.

It was like a chain reaction accident in the fog. Because there was a layering of financial instruments, people did not know that the collateral was compromised and toxic, and therefore didn't recognize the high risk that accompanied their investment. "People also began to realize that, as (Paul) Friedman described, 'one of the bedrock concepts of the whole securitization model, diversification'—the theory that a broad pool of borrowers provided inherent protection from price declines and defaults—'was fundamentally flawed. In fact, when we had declines around the country it became obvious that if you had a big pool of borrowers who had identical characteristics you really didn't have any diversification at all.'"[84]

Ratings Agencies Fail to Accomplish their Primary Purpose

Today a small club of bond ratings agencies, led by Moody's, Standard and Poor's and Fitch, wields enormous power, sending investors scrambling simply by changing the ratings that the firms assign. . . . [85] As it relates to the near total economic collapse, they put quality AA and AAA ratings on risky CDOs, giving investors the confidence needed to buy what were virtually worthless pieces of paper. Their "business model morphed from one in which investors paid for the ratings to one in which the bond issuers did. That generated more revenue, but also created a massive conflict of interest, often cited in the current mortgage mess. . . . SEC head Mary Schapiro is now signaling that the ratings system might need to be changed further, particularly who pays for the ratings."[86]

A probe of the three investor's services raised significant questions about the reliability and integrity of ratings assigned to mortgage based securities.

In his September 2007 congressional testimony, Kyle Bass, the managing partner of Hayman Capital who once worked at Bear Stearns, accurately defined the problem. "Unfortunately the relationship between the bond issuers (Wall Street investment banks) and the [ratings agencies] presents a fundamental conflict of interest because the [ratings agencies] are dependent on the issuers for their revenues.... The bond issuers, as sellers of risk, have an incentive to see that the risk they are selling is priced as cheaply as possible—in the marketplace this means obtaining as high a rating as possible—because once they sell the bonds they are relieved of any risk burden. It is this incentive, and the fact that they work closely with, and provide payment to, the [ratings agencies] that places into question the objectivity of the ratings provided by the [ratings agencies]. The ultimate holders of the risk, the buyers of these bonds, have the most at stake in accurately pricing the risk, but instead rely on the ratings bought and paid for by the sellers."[87]

Without those ratings most of the CDOs would have come under much closer scrutiny by the buyer. The ratings agencies bear considerable responsibility, as their failure was foundational to the collapse of the economy. A trusted and essential part of our financial system failed to exercise one of the safeguards that sound the warning about questionable investments. There are obvious concerns that honest ratings are trumped by the desire to make a bigger profit. Self-interest in the form of greed wins out once again.

Here is one account of the role played by Moody's.

> As the housing market collapsed in late 2007, Moody's Investors Service, whose investment ratings were widely trusted, responded by purging analysts and executives who warned of trouble....
>
> A McClatchy investigation has found that Moody's punished executives who questioned why the company was risking its reputation by putting its profits ahead of providing trustworthy ratings for investment offerings.
>
> ... It also stacked its compliance department with people who awarded the highest ratings to pools of mortgages that soon were downgraded to junk. Such products have another name now: "toxic assets."

The Securities and Exchange Commission issued a blistering report on how profit motives had undermined the integrity of ratings at Moody's and its main competitors at Fitch Ratings and Standard & Poor's, in July 2008.

Moody's disputes every allegation against it. "Moody's has rigorous standards in place to protect the integrity of the ratings from commercial considerations. . . ." But insiders say that wasn't true before the financial meltdown. . . . "The story at Moody's doesn't start in 2007; it starts in 2000," said Mark Froeba, a Harvard educated lawyer and senior vice president who joined Moody's structured finance group in 1997."

"This was a systemic and aggressive strategy to replace a culture that was very conservative, an accuracy-and-quality oriented (culture), a getting-the-rating-right culture, with a culture that was . . . less likely to assign a rating that was tougher than our competition," Froeba said.

After Froeba and others raised concerns that the methodology Moody's was using to rate investment offerings allowed the firm's profit interest to trump honest ratings, he and nine other outspoken critics in his group were 'downsized' in December 2007.[88]

A reviewer for *All the Devils Are Here: The Hidden History of the Financial Crisis* by Bethany McLean and Joe Noceera sums it up. "Moody's ... CEO Brian Clarkson, fouled a proud corporate culture by whoring ratings for earnings"[89]

Where Was the Regulatory Oversight?

While the issue of regulation is discussed in terms of whether it is beneficial or harmful to business, a subject to which I'll return in Chapter 10, it is also one of the contributing factors in the economic collapse of 2008.

The Securities and Exchange Commission was created during the Depression to bolster confidence in financial markets and root out fraud. But under former chairman Christopher Cox, the agency was less than aggressive. . . . The man who should have played a major role in sounding the alarm about – and perhaps preventing – America's financial meltdown now stands accused by critics of being asleep on the job. . . . Long an evangelist for deregulation, the affable 56-year-old conservative former California Congressman took a custodial approach to a job that called for muscular leadership. The mismatch between Cox and the world he was meant to police became such an embarrassment to the Republican Party that GOP candidate John McCain publicly called for the firing of the SEC boss. . . . [90]

Cox said his agency lacked authority to limit the massive leveraging that led to the financial collapse.

"In truth, the SEC had plenty of power to rein in risky behavior by such investment banks as Lehman Brothers and Merrill Lynch, but chose not to."[91] Henry Paulson provides a summary that makes the point. "There's so much that needs to be done, so much work. . . . Some people want to say there is too little regulation. It's not that. It's just outdated, outmoded and ineffective. The architecture was put in place in a different era, and it hasn't kept pace with the evolving financial markets."[92]

When It Doesn't Add Up, Find the "x" Factor that Solves the Equation

Some on Wall Street and in the insurance business didn't really understand the financial products they were selling. They simply kept on doing their job knowing they were making a lot of money. That is scary! "Many policymakers and way too many bank CEO's had not the foggiest idea of what was going on. Those who did lacked the strength or vision to call off the party."[93] Others did understand and kept selling anyway, knowing there was a significant risk to individual investors and homebuyers.

The excesses of the financial sector of the economy were like a plague, a time of unbridled greed and speculation. Some have called Wall Street the world's biggest casinos—the only difference being that they were playing with somebody else's money. Since there would be no consequences, they could place bets even though the risks were enormous and the outcomes potentially disastrous.

The issues involving the buying and selling of financial products like CDOs and CDSs are complex. We trust our bankers and financial advisors, assuming they "understand" and will work in our best interest. But as workers, homebuyers, 401(K) investors and retirees, we have been burned once too often: the Robber Barons, junk bonds, the S&L crisis, corporate accounting scandals, mutual fund fraud and then the housing bubble and the collapse of Wall Street investment firms. Greed never goes out of style! Greed is the "x" factor that solves the equation. The financial misdeeds involved were systemic, something akin to corrupt human nature. The outcomes were compounded by the ineffectiveness of the regulations established by legislators, who are compromised by the special interests who contribute to their election campaigns.

When Alan Greenspan speaks, everybody listens, and at a congressional hearing he said some things that not only addressed financial issues, but also the character of the people who made the decisions.

> Greenspan called the banking and housing chaos a "once-in-a-century credit tsunami" that led to a breakdown in how the free market system functions. (The global economic crisis) left him—an unabashed free-market advocate—in a "state of shocked disbelief." The long time Fed chief acknowledged that he had made a "mistake" in believing that banks operating in their self-interest would be sufficient to protect their shareholders and the equity in their institutions. Greenspan called it "a flaw in the model that I perceived is the critical functioning structure that determines how the world works." (He added that) he was "partially" wrong in opposing regulation of derivatives and acknowledged that financial institutions didn't protect shareholders and investments as well as he expected.[94]

When reporting on the same hearing, another reporter put it this way: "The maestro admitted... that he has 'made a mistake in presuming' that financial firms could regulate themselves."[95] A few months later Greenspan is quoted as saying "Unless somebody can find a way to change human nature, we will have more crises."[96] But it took some time for him to "get religion"—so to speak.

Back in 2002 before the Senate Banking Committee Greenspan shared a message that sounds very much like what he shared before the same Congressional Committee in 2008. A common thread runs through what happened in the late 1990's and what happened in 2008. "'Infectious greed' caused corporate abuses, Greenspan says. 'Infectious greed.' The man who gave us 'irrational exuberance' is back, with a phrase that sums up the late 1990's even better than that one did."[97]

It doesn't take much to figure out that many of those in the banking industry were pretty sleazy. Greenspan said it more forcefully and with greater clarity.

"An infectious greed seemed to grip much of our business community.... The incentives created by poorly designed stock options 'overcame the good judgment of too many corporate managers. . . . It is not that humans have become any more greedy than in generations past. It is that the avenues to express greed had grown so enormously." Stock options meant that executives could get rich if they faked profits, and fake them they did. ...Greenspan was eager to denounce the excesses of the last decade.[98]

What an incredible admission! We are self-centered, self-serving, greedy people, who will maximize the exercise of those traits whenever the opportunity presents itself.

Here is a more complete statement of what he shared before the Senate Banking Committee in 2002, six years before the collapse of 2008.

"Why did corporate governance checks and balances that served us well in the past break down?" he asked. At root were the soaring stock prices "in the latter part of the 1990's that arguably engendered an out-sized increase in opportunities for avarice. An infectious greed seemed to grip much of our business community. Our historical guardians of financial information were overwhelmed'" he said.

"In recent years shareholders and potential investors would have been protected from widespread misinformation if any one of the many bulwarks safeguarding appropriate corporate evaluations had held," the Fed chairman said, adding, "In too many cases none did."

"Lawyers, internal and external, auditors, corporate boards, Wall Street security analysts, ratings agencies and large institutional holders of stock all failed for one reason or another to detect and blow the whistle on those who breached the level of trust essential to well-functioning markets," he said. . . . "Most of all he blamed corporate executives for the wave of scandals. "I was wrong," Greenspan said, in thinking that government and regulatory agencies would be enough to keep CEO's honest.[99]

While the economic dynamics at work in the late 1990s and 2008 were different, he had a chance to get religion in the sense of becoming much more aware of the realities of human nature back in 2002. He must not have been paying attention to the sermon.

Greenspan's successor at the Fed, Ben Bernanke, came to services regularly to be sure he wouldn't be led astray. He paid attention and included greed as one of his presuppositions. "He knows that the economy is awful, that 10% unemployment is just too high, that Wall Street bankers are greedy ingrates, that Main Street still hurts."[100] "If left to the desires of their heart, they will take it all and run. It has always been that way."[101]

The titles of some of the key books covering the period give us insight into their view of the nature of man:

Bailout Nation: How Greed and Easy Money Corrupted Wall Street and Shook the World Economy by Barry Ritholtz,

The Sellout: How Three Decades of Wall Street Greed and Government Mismanagement Destroyed the Global Financial System by Charles Gasparino,

Morgan Was Corrupted by Wall Street Greed and Unleashed a Catastrophe by Gillen Tett, and

House of Cards: A Tale of Hubris and Wretched Excess on Wall Street by William Cohan.

In most accounts of the period Wall Street investment bankers seem to be pictured as vultures of the first order, feeding off the dead meat of foreclosed homes. Sure the homebuyer purchased irresponsibly and bears responsibility, as do the mortgage brokers and bankers who approved loans for those who didn't have a credit history that was good enough to indicate that the loan would be a sound investment. It also seems as if the alphas in the packs of lending wolves were the investment banks that packaged these loans, resold them and brought down the whole financial system. Those responsible for the financial meltdown made decisions that affected millions of people, not just one household.

Furthermore, they made decisions about those funds with little risk to themselves. Remember, when investment banks changed from partnerships to publicly traded corporations that invest other peoples money, there was a whole lot less personal risk when making investments that could either lose a bundle or bring in significant additional income for their clients. But whatever the outcome, it didn't matter to the banker. Just making the transaction would generate fees that would translate into huge salaries and bonuses. They had everything to gain and nothing to lose by going to the "casino" and taking risks by making huge bets with investor money on derivatives called CDOs. Yet, nobody thinks they did anything illegal or even morally wrong.

> This is the year the sheen came off capitalism—when the "stupid" in the cliché phrase "it's the economy, stupid" came to very clearly refer to those captains of finance who, using blind greed as a propellant, steered the global economy into the shoals. . . .There is enough blame to go around for this financial crisis. Top prize goes to the architects of the crisis—those who bundled and sold mortgages, destined for foreclosures, as sound instruments.[102]

While the problems leading to the meltdown were systemic, investment bankers rationalized their behavior within the context of that systemic dysfunction. It began with a systemic flaw in the home mortgage industry, where Countrywide popularized the approval of exotic mortgages to iffy borrowers. Then the ratings agencies were willing to put AA and AAA ratings on risky mortgages packaged in bundles. Investment banks bought the bonds with the iffy mortgages as collateral, even when it was clear that the risk of default was considerable. The investment banks were systemically irresponsible in re-packaging bundles of bonds and re-selling them as CDOs for a fee, even though they knew the investment was a bad risk. Insurance companies like AIG were systemically flawed in insuring high risk loans with CDSs and made their commissions. Regulations were systemically weakened. The political system that passed the regulations has been bought for a long time. So nobody does anything wrong. Nobody does anything illegal. They never do. The problem was with the system and what "they" were doing stayed within the boundaries of the system.

Then some have the nerve to say that it was all our fault, that none of this would have happened if we hadn't been so greedy and bought houses we couldn't afford. Blaming the collapse of the housing market on greedy home buyers is the biggest pile of crap I have ever heard. Yes, some lied on their home loan applications. Some lied about their employment record. Some lied about how much they earn. Some lied about their assets and liabilities. Some wanted to make huge profits in an appreciating market and borrowed more than they could afford. All of this is true. Yet, even if the consumer is a greedy idiot, it was the mortgage brokers who approved the loans and the bankers who took the enormous investment risks. While our greed could lead to disaster in our personal finances, it hurt nobody but us. It was the banks that took on enough toxic debt to almost sink both our economy and the world economy. The fallout from the homeowner's decisions was limited, whereas the fallout from buying, bundling and reselling toxic assets was nearly catastrophic.

The impact of the decisions and actions of investment bankers is so much more far reaching than the impact of homebuyer decisions, as to be in another universe. It is a stretch, to put in the kindest possible way, ludicrous and self-serving, to put it more realistically, to see any comparison in terms of the relative weights given to the responsibility for individual decisions that contributed to the economic collapse. The mortgage brokers and bankers who approved the individual home loans and bundled them into bonds, and the Wall Street firms that bundled the bonds into CDOs are supposed to know what they are doing. It is their business. Their attempt to scapegoat the little guy is putting a spin on the dynamic that is outrageous, perhaps intended to deflect blame as part of making a case to Congress that regulatory reform isn't needed.

> Two years ago, as the nation's mortgage market crumbled and credit seized up, the federal government took over the largest purchasers of mortgages- Fannie Mae and Freddie Mac, which were sinking under the weight of deep losses and investor distrust. Since then these wards of the state have cost taxpayers $150 billion, and the Congressional Budget Office says the bill may be as high as $389 billion by the time all is said and done. We don't join the critics who claim that Fannie (Mae) and Freddie (Mack) were largely responsible for the housing crisis. That explanation is simplistic and simply wrong. . . . The culprit was greed all around—including in the halls of Congress.[103]

The Blind Leading the Blind

The culprit was greed all around—on every level of an interconnected, over-leveraged, dysfunctional financial system, where irresponsible decision making was routine. The outcome was near catastrophic damage done to our economy, more specifically to homebuyers, 401(k) investors trying to be responsible by saving for their retirement, retirees using conservative strategies and those who lost their jobs when the economy tanked. This is just so tragic and so sad. The history of finance and banking and the stories of the Robber Barons and Wall Street are well known. The numbers are so astronomical when measured by Main Street standards that we can't even begin to comprehend the magnitude of the greed. Their management decisions can affect the economy of our country and all of the hard working folk trying to make a living. If it wasn't for the damage done to our economy, especially the "average Joe," there would be a temptation to laugh instead of cry. Their greed caught up with them. It's just that they brought the whole economy down with them.

> The lack of regulation has morphed Wall Street into a place that regularly trades against our economy. It's our jobs vs. their bonuses on every trade. And if you think Wall Street is going to protect your interests, then I've got a AAA-rated, subprime-mortgage-based CDO to sell you.[104]

Greed was exacerbated by flat out incompetence. Two of the biggest private-equity firms found themselves in deep trouble because they didn't realize the risks they were taking. AIG apparently didn't understand the risks involved in selling CDSs. "The likes of Citi owned AAA-rated mortgage securities they thought were as safe as Treasury securities. But since the ratings agencies screwed up royally by not analyzing the securities properly. . . . Citi et.al. got whacked."[105] They, too, apparently had no clue they were taking risks beyond those they usually had to deal with and could manage.

> Don't forget, too, that a fair number of Wall Streeters got wiped out because their wealth was tied to their firm's stock price. They weren't the only ones who didn't understand what they were doing. Dick Fuld, the former CEO of Lehman, had shares and options worth about $1 billion at their peak. He got less than $1 million after he sold them when the stock went bankrupt. . . . James Cayne, CEO at the defunct Bear Stearns, was in a similar situation. If Fuld and Cayne had known that their firms were as badly at risk as they proved to be, don't you think they'd have sold as much stock a they could before their firms imploded? . . . The CEOs didn't understand the fine print. These firms collapsed out of ignorance fueled by avarice—a particularly toxic combination.[106]

Do These Folks Have a Pulse?

The very same evening the revision of this chapter from a rough draft to a first draft was completed there was a report in the news that Greg Smith, a vice-president at Goldman Sachs, resigned and wrote a scathing article in the New York Times that was critical of their corporate culture. It was an eye-opener. While Goldman would no doubt put its own spin on the musings of a disgruntled employee, after a while you have to begin to wonder how often Wall Street takes advantage of their clients. Listening to "Up With Chris Hays,"[107] a lady on the panel said that here is a guy (Greg Smith) who said out loud what Wall Street insiders know, and the rest of us suspect but can't prove, namely, that given the opportunity, Wall Street "will rip your face off." Ouch!

"Former Federal Reserve Chairman Paul Voelker, 84, whose "Volcker rule" (one of the Federal Governments regulatory measures being considered in response to Wall Street's involvement in the Great Recession of 2008) would limit banks like New York-based Goldman Sachs from making bets with their own money, called Smith's article 'a radical, strong piece."[108] It makes you think twice about dealing not only with Goldman Sachs, but with everybody on Wall Street.

The issue surfaced again close to home in Menomonee Falls at Wells Fargo, the investment bank that bought out The Strong Funds. We considered keeping our investments there. After all they were a big firm with a long history and a good reputation.

> Wells Fargo and Co. will pay more than $6.5 million to resolve Security and Exchange Commission claims that a brokerage unit and former employee sold complex securities without disclosing risks to investors.
>
> (They) sold asset-backed commercial paper structured with mortgage-backed securities and collateralized debt obligations to municipalities, non-profits and other customers during 2007....
>
> "Broker-dealers must do their homework before recommending complex investments to their customers,' Elaine C. Greenberg, chief of the SEC Enforcement Division's Municipal securities and Public Pensions Unit, said in the agency's statement. 'Municipalities and other non-profit institutions were harmed because Wells Fargo abdicated its fundamental responsibility as a broker to have a reasonable basis (doing enough research on the products it sold) for its investment recommendations to customers."
>
> Wells Fargo, which resolved the SEC's claims without admitting or denying wrongdoing, will pay . . . a $6.5 million fine. . . .[109]

On October 22, 2012 Savannah Guthrie, assisted by Mara Schiavocampo, did a "Today"(NBC) show segment on Greg Smith, questioning him about his years at Goldman Sachs and his new book—*Why I left Goldman Sachs - A Wall Street Story.*

GUTHRIE. Back in spring a vice-president of Goldman Sachs shook up the financial world with an op-ed, *Why I'm leaving Goldman Sachs,* in the New York Times that laid out why he was leaving his mid-level position, claiming there was a culture of excess and utter disrespect for clients.

SCHIAVOCAMPO. That New York Times piece was utterly explosive. . . . It was the op-ed heard around the financial world. In March Greg Smith, a Goldman Sachs vice-president, publicly resigned after 12 years with the investment bank in a New York Times op-ed, writing "the environment now is as toxic and destructive as I have ever seen it." Saying investors openly spoke about ripping their clients off, sometimes referring to them as Muppets, and claiming that the big banks had learned nothing from the financial meltdown of 2008.

JIM CRAMER (Host of CNBC show—"Mad Money"). This piece is true. It is shocking that nothing's changed. . . . These people helped bring down the world.

SCHIAVOCAMPO. . . . .Smith (argued that) Wall Street today is as unscrupulous as it has ever been. . . . Smith said the word "Muppet" was widely used, writing, "being a Muppet meant being an idiot, a fool, manipulated by someone else. . . ." Goldman has contested the claim, saying (Smith) was just plain wrong. Writing in a statement to NBC News: "Mr. Smith's op-ed portrayed a firm that is unrecognizable to us."

GUTHRIE. What in your mind crossed the line at Goldman?

SMITH. Banks should be in the position of capitalism and making money. But capitalism doesn't need to come with unethical behavior.

GUTHRIE. What is the most egregious example of what you call unethical behavior that you personally witnessed?

SMITH. This idea of teachers' retirement funds (or) . . . pension funds (coming) to a firm like Goldman or Morgan Stanley, and they're saying, "Give us a good idea." These firms are overcharging these people. . . . This directly affects people. When a teachers' retirement plan in Virginia or Alabama is paying the bank an extra $2 million, that affects people and I think that it is unacceptable. . . . A teachers pension fund gets tricked into a product they don't understand. . . . Our clients are being ripped off. I think it is pretty well known on Wall Street that getting an unsophisticated client to trade a very sophisticated product is a way to make money very quickly.

The overwhelming majority of us simply don't understand high risk investments, hedge funds and the futures market. We trust our financial advisors. While those types of investments can produce higher returns, they carry considerable additional risk. As Smith indicated, the same is true for retirement plans and other forms of investment trusts.

What Smith is saying is hard to prove. The big players in the world of finance are as slippery as greased pigs. They are really hard to grab and hold on to, hard to pin down, hard to corner, adept at finding a way to elude a "firm" grasp. Wiggling wildly if need be, and squealing loudly, they slither away with the cover of their lawyers and accountants. These big corporations are more powerful than we can imagine. It is almost as if they are "untouchable."

It sounds like a broken record. The behavior of those on Wall Street has been stuck in the groove of greed and self-interest expressed as unethical, immoral and fraudulent behavior for years. The culture of corporate greed remains ever present. The situation has gotten so out of control now that the goal of regulation and law enforcement is reestablishing a level playing field even for well to do investors who can't compete in the majors with the big boys. Isn't it ironic that now even those in the upper class need to be protected from the greed and avarice of those higher up on the food chain. And just where does that leave the rest of us? We get some help from the government, the only entity with enough reach and muscle to even try to get its arms around the problem.

Preet Bharara, U.S. Attorney for the Southern District of New York leads what is referred to as the third wave of Wall Street prosecutions. Rudy Giuliani led the first and nailed Michael Milken. Eliot Spitzer was the "star" of the second, and is linked to Bharara in that both addressed the unfairness of insider trading.

> Spitzer's spotlight helped prompt new regulations that forced the large financial firms to divest themselves of some in-house research capabilities to prevent collusion between research-chasing analysts and their stock-peddling colleagues. The idea was to strip the big brokerage firms of their access to inside info and give access to all investors. Instead, the activity was essentially outsourced to people who left the firms to set up their own research organizations . . . which then sold the information back to the Wall Street firms. Expert networks . . .

got good at penetrating corporations and connecting traders on the outside with corporate operatives on the inside who had useful information to sell."[110]

Using warrants to legally wiretap, Bharara uncovered evidence of the illegal trading of inside information. Primary Global Research's James Fleishman was sentenced "to 30 months in prison, but is appealing."[111] Raj Rajaratnam is in jail on charges involving securities fraud and conspiracy, while appealing his 11 year sentence.[112] "Bharaha has also charged Mckinsey & Co. CEO Rajat Gupta—like him a first generation immigrant from India who made it in the U.S.—with securities fraud."[113] "Gupta . . . was sentenced to two years in prison and fined $5 million on his securities fraud conviction in an insider-trading case."[114]

Gupta's dealings stemmed from his relationship with . . . Raj Rajaratnam. The one-time billionaire hedge fund boss controlled up to $7 billion in accounts. Prosecutors described how Gupta raced to telephone Rajaratnam with stock tips sometimes only minutes after getting them from board conference calls, helping Rajaratnam make more than $11 million in illegal profits for him and his investors.[115]

On the same page of the same paper there was another update on the fallout from the collapse of the mortgage market.

The latest federal lawsuit over alleged mortgage fraud paints an unflattering picture of the doomed lender: Executives at Countrywide Financial urged workers to churn out loans, accepted fudged applications and tried to hide ballooning defaults.

. . .The prosecutor, Preet Bharara, said he was seeking more that $1 billion, but the suit could recover much more in damages. Bharara described Countrywide's practices as "spectacularly brazen in scope."

. . .Countrywide was a dominant force in mortgage lending, but was also known for approving exotic, even risky loans. By 2007, as the subprime mortgages collapsed, Countrywide was anxious for revenue. The lawsuit alleged that the company loosened its standard for making loans while telling Fanny Mae and Freddy Mac, which were buying loans from Countrywide, that standards were getting tighter. To churn out more loans, Bharara said, Countrywide introduced a program that eliminated checks meant to ensure that mortgages were being made to borrowers who could afford them. . . . It also said that bonuses were awarded solely on the basis of the number of loans that an employee could generate, not on their quality.

The process led to "widespread falsification" of mortgage data, Bharara charged. And when Countrywide executives became aware of the dangerously high number of borrowers defaulting, it hid the problem.[116]

We get a sense that these folks do not have a conscience. You wonder if they even have a pulse. If they don't have any feelings for those hurt by their actions, you wonder whether they're even "alive." It is almost as if they have become one with their inanimate technology, programmed to function in a reality where humans play a subservient role in their high tech strategies for accumulating wealth. It appears as if they simply exist in a psychotic world where there aren't any internal controls that can differentiate between the moral and the immoral, the ethical and unethical and the legal and the illegal. They function within the framework of some sort of otherworldly grey-area of reality from where with little if any resistance they slide into the realm of darkness. Whether you call it a game, competition or blood sport, they are out to win, and take no prisoners along the way. It is what they do. It is who they are. It is so tragic. They have "traded" life and love for leaked insider information and leverage.

If this seems unduly harsh, I'll do my best to be fair in describing the rest of us in equally disparaging terms. I'm going to do just that in Chapter 5, where I'll make the case for describing all of us as being in essence no different than they are. If those on Wall Street are all self-centered, self-seeking and self serving, and share a propensity for greed and self-interest, so are we. Such is the nature of the beast.

While reading about Bharara I ran across an unanticipated connection to my thesis.

Bharara developed a first-generation immigrant's passion for the American way of government. In his first week at Harvard, he engaged in a now famous all night argument with another newcomer, Viet Dinh, who later became a powerful lawyer in the George W. Bush administration and an author of the Patriot Act. Dinh argued that the framers of the Constitution believed men's hearts were evil, while Bharara insisted they thought they were good.[117]

I would be naïve to think that I could win a debate against Bharara. But I sure would like to know the arguments he used to make his case.

Chapter 5
"They" is "We"

"In a nation that was proud of hard work, strong families, close-knit communities, and our faith in God, too many of us now tend to worship self-indulgence and consumption. Human identity is no longer defined by what one does, but by what one owns. But we've discovered that owning things and consuming things does not satisfy our longing for meaning. . . ."
Jimmy Carter

"Do not judge, or you too will be judged. For in the same way you judge others, you too will be judged, and with the measure you use, it will be measured to you. Why do you look at the speck of sawdust in your brother's eye, and pay no attention to the plank in your own eye? How can you say to your brother, 'Let me take the speck out of your eye,' when all the time there is a plank in your own eye? You hypocrite, first take the plank out of your own eye, and then you will see clearly to remove the speck from your brother's eye" (Matthew 7:1-5).

"Who Stole' the Cookie from the Cookie Jar?"

We did a lot of singing during the nineteen years and 290,000 miles we drove our '79 Chevy station wagon. As long as we had a young child, we included a little song where they could join-in and play along.

"Tim stole' the cookie from the cookie jar?" "Who, me?" "Yah, you!" "Couldn't be." "Then who?" "Daddy stole' the cookie from the cookie jar!" "Who, me?" "Yah, you!" "Couldn't be." "Then who?" "Matt stole the cookie from the cookie jar!" "Who, me?" "Yah, you!" "Couldn't be." "Then who?"

And so it went, always shifting the blame to somebody else. "They" did it. It's always the unidentified, but usually implied, "they" who is responsible for doing, saying or deciding something that we think is wrong, dumb or stupid.

"They" were the ones who got us into this financial mess. "They" were the ones who saw an opportunity to make some big bucks, and made decisions that border on the unethical and illegal, even when it put a whole lot of people at risk. "They" didn't so much as blink an eye before taking full advantage of the situation. "They" were the ones who brought the economy to the brink of collapse. All "they" cared about were their commissions and bonuses. It is the Wall Street investment bankers who with their financial wizardry are the crooks and the bad guys. It's all their fault.

But what would we have done if we were in their shoes? Would we have made the same choices? I'm sorry to have to let you in on a dirty little secret. Truth be known—"They" is "We." We are just as bad as they are. We are all villains! We are all vultures! "Who, me?" "Yah, you!" "Couldn't be." This chapter is an explanation of how I understand the connection between us and the calculating, hard-hearted vultures. Making this connection is foundational to the core of my thesis. "They" is "We," and none of us are good persons.

I have to admit it though, the investment bankers sure did a number on the little guy. It seems like it is always the little guy who gets taken advantage of, and who in the end loses the most. The little guy always seems to get the shaft at the hands of the rich and powerful. Sleaze balls and scum bags doesn't even begin to describe those in the financial community whose behavior caused so much harm to so many, while they got rich.

However, if we are going to describe the players in finance and business in this way, then I would also suggest that we are just like them, that "They" is "We." While it certainly appears that the executives at some Wall Street investment banks bear most of the responsibility for the near economic meltdown of 2008, the truth is that in terms of ethics, morals and values, we are no better than they are. We need to be lumped together and identified with the rich. Our choices and decisions also impact the little guy- the suffering, starving millions living in squalor with little sense of dignity or hope.

We know first hand what it's like to experience the fallout from the decisions of those who conducted their business without any concern for how it affected the average guy and the little guy. Now let's be fair and apply that same principle in the evaluation of our behavior. We too don't care about the fallout from the decisions we make. And, in the same way, it is the little guy who usually gets hurt. We need to be numbered among those who make decisions that do a number on the little guy. We too make choices and decisions that demonstrate that we are totally oblivious to the plight of others. This is exactly what I mean when I say that "They" is "We."

Why spend two chapters describing the self-interest and greed of industrialists, business leaders and the players in Wall Street firms? "Enough already! We get the point! Heads they win; tails we lose!" The CDOs tanked, but they still received their commissions and bonuses. We lost our jobs, our incomes, our houses, and our retirement plans and savings accounts took a big hit. Then at the end of the downward spiral of the chain of events that led to the near collapse, we find out that some of them had even stacked the deck, and turned our losses into even more gain for themselves. Goldman Sachs used CDSs illegally. They allegedly had a hand in selecting the bonds that were packaged into the CDOs they sold. Knowing the bonds were packed with toxic assets, they "bet" that the CDOs would fail by buying CDSs to insure themselves against any losses. They marketed the CDOs to clients as sound investments, received commissions for the sale, and then received even more income from the insurance policies they sold on the CDOs they knew were toxic and had a high probability of failing. Selling investments that had a high probability of failure is unconscionable; wanting to make even more by betting on their failure is an example of greed run wild.

These guys on Wall Street are animals. They are vultures. They are the bishops and knights with their castles, while we are the pawns, who end up footing-the-bill for their grand schemes. This is what these guys are really like. Calling them shysters is a compliment. Alan Greenspan totally underestimated their capacity for recklessness in the interest of greed and gain. Once he finally did get it, he probably understated what they are really like when he described them as being consumed by "infectious greed." Why belabor the point? Why be so nasty? It is only when we consider the cumulative record of the misdeeds and distorted ethics, morals and values of investment bankers that makes us want to puke, that you will fully grasp what I'm getting at when I say that we are no different — that we are just like them. While we remain cloaked in respectability, and give the appearance of being something we are not. The truth is "They" is "We."

Look, I'm not interested in singling out the Wall Street crowd. I'm not interested in judging, blaming and criticizing them. I'm not interested in pointing the finger at them. The end game is not to convince you that they are a sorry bunch who don't care about anyone, who don't care who they use, who don't care who they hurt, and who pay little if any attention to ethics, morals and values. I'm not interested in pointing out those who are the very epitome of self-interest and greed and making them symbols of evil.

Rather, I want to make it perfectly clear what I mean when I compare them to us and, and assert that deep down we are no different than they are. The purpose is to make it perfectly clear that we are not decent people who have occasional lapses of character, make relatively minor incursions into the realm of what is immoral and unethical and demonstrate a level of greed and self-interest that is inconsequential. Rather, my point is that we are just like them, that deep down in our human nature we are all the same, that we are all rotten to the core. We are all alike! "They" is "We!" I'm suggesting that if we had been in their shoes, many of us would have done the same thing. I'm suggesting that given the frame of reference of the current circumstances our lives, we all do the equivalent of the same thing. Our lives are characterized by the relentless pursuit for more. While we haven't sold any toxic CDOs or bought any CDSs as a hedge against expected losses, greed and self-interest run wild in all of our lives. While evaluating our options, we don't consider the needs of the weak, the vulnerable, the forgotten and the dying. We too have made choices and decisions that demonstrate we are oblivious to the plight of others. This is another glimpse at what is meant when I say that "They" is "We."

As painful as it might be, we just have to take an honest look at ourselves. We have to find out who we really are and what we are really about. It is a journey that leads to the awareness that we are indeed no different than the investment bankers. They just play in bigger sandboxes than we do. The differences are a matter of scale and degree, not essence. The indicators of what their human nature is like are just more visible and out there. Everyone can see their human nature for what it is. But bottom line—we are just like them. If given the opportunity, Main Street people do the same thing as Wall Street people. While our circumstances may be more modest than theirs, we are just as self-centered, self-serving, self-seeking and greedy as they are. At best we are civilized. At worst we are barbarians. That's just the way it is. That's the way "they" are. And that's the way "we" are. If you're going to talk about the bundling of toxic assets, you have to talk about how we have to be bundled together with those I have described as being the epitome of evil. I'm saying that for all practical purposes and with the exception of those closest to us, we don't care about anyone. We too don't care about the fallout from the decisions we make. Sadly—no, tragically—we don't care who we use and who we hurt.

When confronted with this image of ourselves, we respond with shock and stunned silence. "Wait a minute. What did you say? What in the world are you talking about? You must have misspoken. You didn't mean that, did you? We're not all like that!" I did say it, and I did mean it. We're all like that. When I shared these thoughts with someone close to me, his response was direct and to the point: "Everybody? All the time?" The answer is "yes" and "yes." We need to be honest and own the truth—no airbrushing, no touch-ups, no photo-shopping.

Finally you get it. Finally it sinks in. Finally you understand what I'm trying to say. Finally you're getting a clear picture of how I see human nature. You may not agree, but you do understand. Driven by greed and self-interest these guys were ruthless. They were corrupt, mean, cold, calculating and heartless. They were poster boys for evil. They took advantage of people every chance they had, every time there was an opportunity to make another buck for themselves. They didn't care how many broken families and broken lives they left in their wake. They did it again and again. They were evil and so are we.

In the previous two chapters I used many examples to drive home the point of how unfavorably I view them. When I said that we are just like they are, I wanted to be sure to get your attention and make sure you understood. There can be no mistaking how I see people. Our behavior is reprehensible. Our ethics, morals and values are bankrupt. We are just as greedy and self-centered as they are. We are just like them. And just like them we behave badly again and again, each and every day. We are no different than they are. This is how I view human nature. "They" is "We."

This book is an attempt to shine some light into the darkness of our being, and this chapter gets to the heart of the matter. In my belief system we lack an awareness of the truth that we are not the kind, caring, compassionate people we think. We don't see it that way at all. Maybe we don't want to see it. Not seeing it serves to insulate us from the pain, suffering and misery of others, and allows us to pursue our goals, hopes and dreams

The remainder of this chapter will provide further explanation. And, would you believe, we are still getting warmed up when it comes to hearing the sermons nobody likes, the ones that expose us for who we really are?

Can You Handle the Truth?

We all need to take inventory and do some soul searching. We all need to go through a process of self-examination to see if we are as caring and compassionate, as committed to serving and meeting the needs of others as we think we are. My sense is that most of us are content with who we are and what we are about, that we are content with the way we are living our lives. Perhaps we haven't been challenged to examine the presuppositions and assumptions, the ethics, morals and values on the basis of which we have established our beliefs, and which guide our behavior.

My hunch is that we don't even come close to taking inventory and being honest in seeing ourselves as we really are. Therefore, my intent is to encourage in-depth soul-searching, and to suggest some guidelines for such a process. Is there anything to my contention that we are all greedy, self-seeking, self-serving folk who look out not just for the needs of our own, but also for their wants, at the expense of the unmet needs of others? You have to wonder if investment bankers care about anything other than their own compensation. In the same way I wonder if we care about anything other than our own needs and wants or about what goes on in our own little world. If the phrase "our own little world" has a bite to it, it is supposed to.

We know that some CEOs and business leaders have engaged in behavior which if not illegal, is ethically and morally questionable at best. They were most certainly reckless and irresponsible. Now consider that "48% of workers admit to unethical or illegal acts. . . .

> A major study . . . finds that ethical and legal lapses are common at all levels of the American workforce. The study shows that the violations are so rampant that if you aren't stealing company property, leaking company secrets or lying to customers and supervisors, odds are the worker next to you is.
>
> Nearly half, 48%, of U.S. workers admit to taking unethical or illegal actions. . . . These include one or more from a list of 25 actions, including cheating on an expense account, discriminating against co-workers, paying or accepting kickbacks, secretly forging signatures, trading sex for sales and looking the other way when environmental laws are violated.
>
> . . . Constant ethical violations have made workers so callous that deception passes for good salesmanship. . . . "If someone

can talk me into buying and $8,000 copier rather than one that sells for $4,200, they're going to get a pat on the back. I see that as unethical if all I need is the $4,200 model."

. . . Retail stores lose more to employee theft than to shoplifting. . . . Entry-level restaurant and fast food employees confidentially admit to stealing an average of $239 a year in cash and merchandise. . . .

The federal government successfully sues for more than $100 million a year, mostly from defense contractors and hospitals and doctors that over-bill. . . . [118]

These folks are typical. We are clueless when it comes to understanding what our human nature is really like and how it is reflected in our behavior.

This article gives us a window into just one area of our lives. My sense is that this behavior is also descriptive of what our ethics, morals and values are like in all aspects of our lives. Corruption, consumption, vanity and greed are words that describe all of us. So, how can we expect a higher standard of behavior from investment bankers than we expect of ourselves? We experience a constant internal tug-of-war going on between the ethical and the unethical, the moral and the immoral. President George H. W. Bush spoke of 1,000 points of light, George W. Bush championed Compassionate Conservatism and Bill Clinton's motivational phrase was, "We can do better than that." The truth is that we operate out of a posture of greed and self-interest. All we care about is what is happening in our own lives. As long as we are free to pursue our goals, and hopes and our dreams, we're quite content, thank you. What's happening around us just doesn't concern us all that much. It's every man for himself—survival of the fittest.

We need to be honest with ourselves. We need to go through a process of self-examination to see if our ethical and moral standards are anywhere near as noble as we have assumed. Let's look honestly at ourselves and not pretend to be something we're not. Once we have a better sense of what we're really like, we can begin to consider whether we want to continue to flow with the current in the river of tradition that has been our life, or whether we want to fight against that powerful current and make some changes.

If only it could be true that we weren't just like the Wall Street crowd. If only it could be true that we weren't self-centered people looking out not just for the needs of our own, but also for our wants, at the expense of the unmet needs of others. The naked self-interest and greed of the sleazy characters noted in the previous chapters is nothing short of despicable. Too many of the small-fry were hurt and hurt badly. We learned of our misfortune when we lost our jobs, received our foreclosure notices and opened the statements for savings and retirement accounts that had lost much of their value. It leaves us with a really bad taste in our mouth.

However, we start to sputter, cough and choke when challenged to consider the possibility that we are no better. If we try to deny what we are really like, however, just who do we think we are kidding—nobody but ourselves. To suggest otherwise would be doing a grave disservice. It is not just them. It's all of us. The dynamic I'm describing is descriptive of all of us. We are different only in that the decisions they make and the choices they have made involve a whole lot more dollars and affect a whole lot more people than our decisions and choices do. When they get caught with their hands in the cookie jar, it makes the front pages. When we do it, most of the time nobody even finds out. They are made to look like the villains. We are able to maintain a masquerade of decency. They are big time; we are small time. Otherwise we are very much alike. Only a thin veneer of respectability hides the greed and self-interest that run to the very core of our being and define who we are. Accepting the truth about ourselves is a bitter pill to swallow. However, it is not until we see and own the truth about ourselves that there is any chance to change and be different.

Maybe you want to embark on a journey of self-examination and self-discovery, and maybe you don't. Maybe it is too scary to make the journey, as you don't want to risk finding out that maybe you're not the good person you would like to think you are. Maybe you prefer to remain blissfully ignorant in your current "reality," even if it is a self-constructed conceptual framework designed to insulate you from a painful truth.

For those who are willing to take the risk of heading on down the road of soul-searching and self-discovery, uncertainty looms over every hill and around every curve. We will touch all of the hot-buttons that trigger whatever feelings of insecurity and inadequacy we may have. We will be confronted with ambiguity. We will have to deal with the intense anxiety felt when we encounter threats to our self-image and sense of self-worth.

In order to facilitate the process of soul-searching and self-discovery, I have identified five benchmarks against which our views, beliefs and convictions can be measured and assessed. The five issues are indifference, rationalization, the American Dream, charity and sins of omission. As we reflect on where we stand with respect to each issue, we will gain significant insight and self-awareness with respect to what we're really like. We will be compelled to be more truthful and honest in assessing and seeing who we really are. If a pattern begins to emerge with respect to where you stand on these issues, it may become much more difficult to avoid facing the truth about yourself.

So we are going to make a number of important stops on the journey to greater self-awareness. At each stop we need to take time for soul-searching and reflection. While we may begin the journey with fear and trepidation, it also holds the promise of being extremely enlightening and rewarding.

Indifference

At the first stop we need to ask whether or not we are indifferent. Our self-examination begins with reflection on a George Bernard Shaw quote. **"The worst sin toward our fellow creatures is not to hate them, but to be indifferent to them, that is the essence of inhumanity."**[119] Wow! When I heard those words for the first time, it was like a laser piercing the darkness and opening a new window into my soul. All we want is to be left alone so we can provide for our families, live respectable lives, and enjoy a little of the good life. For the most part, we prefer to remain comfortably insulated from the pain, misery and suffering that are all around us. *Basically, we're good people. Leave us alone. Don't bother us.*

Columnist and syndicated talk show host Dr. Laura also nailed it. She describes the essence of who we are in a way that makes it difficult to evade the truth about our nature. "Regard for one's own welfare, advantage and best interests, in competition with others, is part of our survival instinct. Survival requires that you and yours have the resources you need to sustain yourselves. . . . **Defying selfishness is a stretch and a strain. It means you have to imagine that others are as important as you are. On what basis could strangers be seen as important as me and mine?"**[120] Wow! Here was yet another new window into my soul. Two more windows were open and more fresh air was circulating throughout the house. We learn a lot about ourselves when we have to decide where to draw the line that separates responsibility for our own family and indifference to the needs of others. It is at the point where our needs and the needs of our own are satisfied that the choices get tougher; this is when Shaw becomes so relevant as he creates an ethical dilemma of titanic proportion. The issue of where to draw the line between needs and wants will be addressed in Chapter 8.

As long as we are financially stable and enjoy some of the trappings of the good life and the American Dream, we settle into a comfort zone where we are quite content. The needs of others living in want, suffering and misery rarely appear on our list of priorities, let alone at or near the top. Most of the time they aren't even on our radar. The truth is that we could care less! How can I say that, you ask? The answer is exactly what this book is about. The old adage, "Out of sight, out of mind," is a perfect description of our attitude. "Indifference" is our middle name. Certainly strangers aren't as important as me and my family!

Rationalization

As we continue our soul-searching on the journey to greater self-awareness, we make the second stop at a place where we are offered the opportunity to rationalize and justify our decisions about the competing choices between the needs and wants of our own, and the needs of others. We can rationalize just about anything. It has always been that way. Furthermore, we can always find those who will agree with our view and support our choices. We all have a way of compartmentalizing issues in order to make sense of the world and of life. We could call it our world view, our organizing principle or our belief system. Within the context of our world view, I have suggested two options that are consistent with my thesis: the survival of the fittest and every man for himself. "Looking out for #1" is another way of saying the same thing. My thesis is that we look out not just for the needs of our own, but also for their wants at the expense of the unmet needs of others. There is this powerful tension between lives that are self-centered, self-seeking and self-serving, on the one hand, and self-giving, self-sacrificing and selfless, on the other. It is within the context of this tension that we decide how much responsibility we have to care for those who are not our own.

The capacity of the human spirit to rationalize just about anything simply amazes me — it is astonishing. In the political arena it's known as spin. In this process we all seek to justify or rationalize our principles, decisions and behavior. We all like to think that, "basically, we're good people." Most of us see ourselves as generous people. We frame our beliefs and behaviors in ways that others would deem appropriate and acceptable. What I'm suggesting is that we need to go back and revisit the issues that have placed us in tension, and do some honest soul-searching to determine how it is that we have resolved it. We need to try to identify where through rationalization we have made compromises. My view is that in most of our lives we don't even begin to come close to realizing our capacity for being able to help those in need, as we have developed rationalizations that undermine our sensitivities and our principles. Frankly, it seems to me that our understanding of what it means to be kind, caring and compassionate is far less than noble.

The American Dream

Examining our understanding of the American Dream and asking how much of the dream we are entitled to will give us further insight into whether we are as ethical and moral as we think we are; this is the third stop on the journey to greater self-awareness. Being able to claim our part of the American Dream remains very much a part of the national psyche. President Obama in the State of the Union Address on January 26, 2011 once again described key elements of the dream that we have come to believe is a part of our birthright. They include,

> . . . opportunities for a better life that we pass on to our children,
> . . . a job that pays the bills, a chance to get ahead.
>
> We may have our differences in policy, but we all believe in the rights enshrined in our Constitution. We may have our different opinions, but we believe in the same promise that says this is a place where you can make it if you try. We may have different backgrounds, but we believe in the same dream that says this is a country where anything is possible. No matter who you are. No matter where you come from."
>
> That dream is why I stand before you tonight. That dream is why a working class kid from Scranton (V.P. Joe Biden) can sit behind me. That dream is why someone who began by sweeping the floors of his father's Cincinnati bar (Speaker of the House John Boehner) can preside as Speaker of the House in the greatest nation on earth.
>
> I'm not sure how we'll reach that better place beyond the horizon, but I know we'll get there.

Since 2008 we have experienced a period of economic turmoil and crisis during which the American Dream has been going through a downward adjustment on the way to establishing a lower baseline— a new normal. Given some tweaking of the dream, many still believe in its viability, and hold on to the hopes and aspirations that have always been a part of what it means to live in America. A downsized version of the dream is still out there.

We are so fortunate and so blessed to live in America with its ideals of life, liberty and the pursuit of happiness—a country that has enriched our lives and the lives of so many who have gone before us. Even a downsized version to the American Dream holds the promise of a comfortable lifestyle, upward mobility as we climb the ladder of success, wanting to enjoy "the good life," and wanting our kids to be better off than we were, having every opportunity to succeed if they are willing to work hard. It begins with a job and the hope that there will be raises. Its centerpiece is owning your own home. It includes the opportunity to earn enough to educate our kids and start saving for retirement. For many this is what the good life is all about. They are happy with modest increases in their material status, seeing their children do a little better than they did, quietly socking a little bit away, retiring and having enough saved to do some of things they've always wanted. If only we can find a way to work together and create the opportunity for that vision to become reality for all our citizens. People from all over the world still long to come to our shores and to share in our wonderful dream.

In the context of this chapter, what is critically important is how the concept of the American Dream relates to our conversation. I would suggest that there is more to life and that you are only truly happy when you are able to use who you are and what you have for the benefit of others. Nuts! You knew there had to be a catch. Back to the sermon, to the serious issues, the stuff that asks you to ponder and pray. Along the way there are choices to make. There is the temptation of materialism, which leads to the primacy of things over people. There is the temptation to buy into the rampant consumerism encouraged by the masters of marketing. Pope John Paul II said that he was "worried that the affluent West was turning consumerism into a religion and ignoring its Christian roots. This is a question that all people, if they are honest with themselves, cannot help but ask. . . .   Have not money, the thirst for possessions, (and) power . . . diverted man from his true destiny?"[121]

There is the occasional hint that Americans want their dream to incorporate the needs of others as well as environmental concerns.

> The American Dream, once exclusively an economic goal in which Americans sought better material lives for themselves and their children, is changing to embrace a belief that the dream must also include attention to social needs and environmental protection, according to a new survey.

> The public opinion poll . . . found that 66 percent . . . believe that economic development can be achieved together with environmental protection and health and happiness.
>
> . . . According to a report on the survey, "the challenge becomes how can we, as a nation, afford to 'have it all:' A job that contributes to the welfare of society and a lot of money; Inner peace and a swimming pool; Economic growth and a cleaner environment"[122]

But a glimpse is all we get. Dealing with how we can "have it all" becomes a political discussion, and does not fall within the purview of my thesis or my purpose in writing. My intent is to focus on decisions we make as individuals and families, given the vision of the American Dream. As individuals, how do we describe our view of and relationship with the American Dream? How can I do right by my wife and kids, while not forgetting about the welfare of others?

Providing for those in my household is my responsibility, the right thing to do, a noble thing to do. Yet, we live in this moral and ethical tension. We have to ask whether or not it is being cold and cruel, insensitive and indifferent, when somebody else's kid is starving to death, and we do nothing about it, even though we could? It is the right thing to do to make sure my kids have a decent place to live. But how nice does it have to be when the toilet drains right down the street in front of another kid's house, and we could have done something about it? Is it cruel and inhuman when somebody else's kid contracted malaria, dysentery or AIDS through no fault of their own, and our family could have done something to help, but didn't? Within the context of our own economic realities and the choices we make while in pursuit of the American Dream, do we even bother to ask how our decisions impact others? It is as we make decisions within the framework and circumstances of our lives that we have to ask whether or not we are any different than Wall Street investment bankers?

Would you believe we are still just warming up when it comes to the sermons nobody wants to hear?

While we may not be guilty of crass materialism, we still cherish a middle class lifestyle within which we remain largely indifferent to the needs and well being of others. We want to remain cloaked in the mantle of respectability. Under our system of government we are free to determine for ourselves the balance between our pursuit of the American Dream, and our concern for the well being of others.

Given the context of our own economic realities and the choices open to us in pursuit of The American Dream, each of us has to ask how our decisions impact others, and whether we are really any different than Wall Street investment bankers. We measure ourselves by others in our society, rather than by a higher standard of morality, decency and respectability. We measure ourselves by the norms of our culture, rather than by higher standards of caring, compassion and kindness. We have become comfortable with our lifestyle, and have lost a sense of indignation about the serious injustices and inequities of our time.

The truth is "They" is "We." It's not just the investment bankers on Wall Street; it's all of us. They don't care about those who get hurt by their decisions, and neither do we; this is the guiding principle I'm using as the basis for my belief that "They" is "We." We are just like them in that we do not care about those hurt by our decisions when other options are available to us and we could have chosen to do something that takes the well-being of others into consideration. It is in the exercise and application of this principle where we can clearly see that we are no different than they are. They don't care about who gets hurt by their decisions and neither do we. "They" is "We."

Charity

Reflecting on our charitable giving and volunteer service is another window into our moral and ethical health and wellness, and the fourth stop on our journey to self-awareness. We would do well to ask ourselves a series of questions. What is our motivation for charitable giving and service? How concerned are we about those living in poverty, about the unfortunate, about the disadvantaged and about the vulnerable? By what standard do we measure how compassionate and generous we are? Given our potential, exactly how are we doing with our contributions to church and/or charity? Have we ever kept a log of our volunteer hours in order to be able to evaluate the amount of time we spend volunteering?

First, we need to get a handle on charitable giving patterns in our country. This first set of statistics from a Gallup survey goes back a few years. However, they are consistent with more recent figures.

> The study of 2,775 American households, described as the first of its kind, showed that among those making charitable contributions, households with incomes below $10,000 gave an average of 2.8% of their incomes while those making $75,000 to $100,000 gave 1.7%.

... "Many people thought they were very generous.... But for the first time, this study shows they were not that generous at all."

... The study demonstrated the contrast between "heart-warming generosity and bone-chilling selfishness."

"It is the poor and struggling who generally lead the way.... Most of the people who have made it financially don't give a damn."

... The survey showed that only 9% of households gave 5% or more of their average incomes to charity in 1987, and those who volunteered their time came mainly from the lower end of the income scale.

... According to the survey, those who gave only to religious groups contributed 2% of their incomes to charity, while those who gave only to non-religious groups contributed 0.9% of their incomes.

... Those who contributed to both religious and non-religious groups gave an average of $380 in 1987 to non-religious groups while those who gave only to non-religious organizations gave and average of $352. The average contribution to religious organizations of those who gave to both religious and non-religious groups was $796, a total of $1,176.

... Twenty-nine percent of the households surveyed made no charitable contributions in1987.

Of the households that did give to charity (religious and non-religious), the average contribution was $790. The average share of income contributed was 1.9%.

Gifts by 19% of the households represented 70% of total contributions. Those households which contributed 2% or more of their incomes had an average household income of $34,220. Households that contributed less that 2% of their incomes had an average income of $39,060.[123]

The numbers from a few years later tend to confirm the same giving trends. "The percent of household income given to charity declined from 2 percent to 1.7 percent between 1989 and 1993. About half of the 'charity' goes to churches and other religious institutions, and much of the rest goes to colleges, the arts and ... hospitals."[124] A 2003 study of charitable giving found that households contributed $1,872 each.[125] The average of total household contributions was $2,213 in 2011 with the median being $870.[126] "(A 2009 article reported that) those households with an income of $158,388 gave $3,326 (2.1 percent)."[127]

If you're looking for excuses not too give, there are plenty of them. Mismanagement is one. Or, examples of mismanagement could serve as a reminder to do our due-diligence and investigate how much of each contributed dollar is used for administrative overhead and how much goes directly to meet the need. Another excuse is the stories in the media about how some foreign governments have done little to invest contributions in local industries and development projects which could create food self-sufficiency or provide an alternative to farming. Instead, they spend vast sums on weapons of war. Then there are those corrupt foreign leaders who skim and divert some of the charitable aid into secret numbered accounts at banks in Switzerland and the Caymans. The net result is that donors cut off support. The question is whether these issues become an excuse not to give, or a time for re-allocating those dollars to charities in which we have confidence that our contributions will be put to good use. If we want to, we can always find an excuse not to give. While most of us do give, my sense is that reflective of self-centered hearts that are not very compassionate or caring, our giving does not begin to approach an amount that could be considered generous. We have this perception of ourselves as being a whole lot more charitable than I believe the facts indicate. The truth is that we're indifferent, insensitive, pursuers of the American Dream who rationalize and justify the amount we contribute to church and charity.

One of the "Letters" from the readers of *Time* expresses the kind of soul-searching that I am encouraging.

> Your report on the desperate Rwandan refugees, 'Cry the Forsaken Country,' brought tears to my eyes. It made me feel selfish. I'm worried about paying my bills on time and about getting tickets to a special event, while the people of Rwanda are fighting to stay alive. They are walking among the diseased, dying and dead and worrying about getting a cup of fresh water. Children are lying next to their dead mothers, scared, hungry and alone.[128]

The headline for a column by Philip Chard made the need perfectly clear: "World's children beg for your attention."

Christmas is for Children, many say.

Most of us cherish the little ones who inhabit our lives. We want the best for them. But as (individuals), we have forsaken many of the world's youth, and the consequences are horrific.

"Fact: Approximately 5 million children die each year of hunger, either starving to death outright or perishing from the ill effects of malnutrition. The loss of life is equal to about four Sept. 11 attacks every day of the year.

A recent UNICEF study tells us that almost half the planets children are growing up hungry and unhealthy. This tragedy isn't caused by the absence of resources. It's caused by the absence of our collective passion and will.

World food production is sufficient to feed the millions who are starving. Consider that, in 2000, the number of overweight people worldwide (about 1.2 billion) equaled the number who are hungry and malnourished, a quarter of whom are children.

There are problems we can't solve, but hunger isn't one of them. Doing so requires that we live the family values (the human family) that we so righteously profess.

And it is entirely do-able.

. . . Fact: About half the planet's workers, or about 1.4 billion people, earn less than two dollars a day, and over 170 million are children. Most child laborers forgo school (their best hope for a better life) to help feed their families.

. . . This Christmas, do more than pray for peace on earth, good will to all. For the sake of our children, help make it happen.[129]

Chard's comment about "the family values (the human family) that we so righteously profess," seems to call into question the commonly held notion that we are a generous people. My sense is that Chard is "right-on." Our perception of how generous we are does not even come close to mirroring reality.

Volunteers also make huge contributions to charity.

Independent Sector, a Washington research and lobbying group, commissioned a Gallup pole to plumb the depths of our charity:

What do we give, and why, and who does the giving, and how much? It turns out that almost half of all American adults offer their time to a cause, an astounding figure even allowing for the number of people who lie to pollsters. And most are giving more time than ever. These are commitments, not gestures. The average volunteer offers nearly five hours a week, for a total of 19.5 billion hours in 1987—the equal, roughly, of 10 million full-time employees. There is something infectious about mercy.[130]

From September 2009 through September 2010 26.3 percent of Americans over the age of 16 volunteered through or for an organization.[131] The actual number of volunteers was 62,790,000, and the median number of hours served was 52.[132] 63.400,000 people volunteered in 2009 with a 26.8 percent volunteer rate. The 2009 figures represent 8.1 billion hours of service worth the equivalent of approximately $169 billion dollars.[133]

Stories and statistics used to be a source of great encouragement. What volunteers are doing is commendable and in some cases exemplary, and a blessing to each and every person who is served and helped. Past presidents George H.W. Bush, Jimmy Carter, Bill Clinton and George W. Bush all feel strongly about volunteerism and have devoted time and energy to encourage it. What volunteers are doing in our country is fantastic, awesome, magnificent.

Again, however, at the risk of sounding like the *The Grinch Who Stole Christmas*, we have just scratched the surface of our potential as volunteers. The "Me" generation is not dying, not by a long-shot. While those who aren't volunteering at all need to get involved, those of us who are already involved could do so much more.

We are a self-centered, self-serving, self-seeking bunch, who have a whole lot more to learn about being self-sacrificing, self-giving and selfless. We give and help, but my sense is that we have hardly begun to come anywhere near realizing our full potential as donors or volunteers. This is who we are. How I wish it were different!

Sins of Omission

At the fifth stop on our journey to self-awareness, we find another way to further the process of reflection and self-examination; here we consider the Christian distinction between sins of comission and sins of omission. Making this distinction gives a more complete picture of our self-centeredness in a way we don't usually consider, namely, by considering what we could have done but didn't. A sin of commission is when we do those things that God's Word teaches us not to do. A sin of omission is when we fail to do what is commanded. This is the final stop on the journey.

We have this favorable impression of ourselves. It is not my intent to diminish the importance of being a kind, loving, sensitive, understanding spouse or being a parent who spends time with your children or being a decent person and helping others where you can. It is what is left undone that is of critical importance. Just how much more could we do for the poor and the suffering and the less fortunate.

Love, care and concern for others are compromised by our self-centeredness expressed by providing not just for the needs of our own, but also for their wants, at the expense of the unmet needs of others. We've had our chances to do something about human need, pain, suffering and misery and we've dropped the ball. To the degree that this is an issue for each of us, we contribute to evil and suffering through sins of omission.

The opportunities for charitable giving are everywhere. The specific choices about where to give and how much to give are ours. By the world's standards we are very wealthy people. We are living the good life and have the world by the tail. The national household average of 2 percent giving to charity seems like such a pittance. We are stingy tightwads who really don't care all that much about those in need. Seems to me I just heard that it costs about $194 for a family of four to go to a major league ball game (only $176 here in Milwaukee). Within the framework of sins of omission the failure to contribute generously in effect becomes a contribution to evil and suffering. "They" is "We."

Cutting a Deal to Sell Our Souls

My sense is that we are self-centered, self-serving, self-seeking, indifferent, insensitive, pursuers of the American Dream, who rationalize and justify the meaning we attach to how much we contribute and the amount of time we serve and help as volunteers. Our greed is thinly disguised by token contributions to church and charity, and minimal contributions to needs resulting from natural disasters and human tragedy. "'Natural disasters', (Mitch) Snyder (a voice for the homeless) says, 'do not call into question our values and our lifestyle. Homelessness does.' . . . Two urges are at odds. . . . One implies charity and generosity. The other says to hell with community, create your own niche. The negative side has become dominant. But the other side nags at us.'"[134] We are just charitable enough to salve our consciences. We don't give sacrificially or volunteer all that much.

An underlying assumption of this chapter is that most Americans are wealthy when compared with most people in the world. We are rich by an accident of birth.

Therefore we have to ask ourselves the hard question: have we used the freedom, security and safety of this great nation as the launching pad for a life of service to others? How do we choose to use our freedom? It doesn't appear to me as if we have responded very well to the opportunities for service that our freedom affords. We have an inflated sense of our goodness and an inflated sense of our moral standing.

It is certainly understandable that within the context of our culture we get caught up in pursuing the American Dream, wanting our kids to have the clothes and communication devices that most kids have and working long hours to buy, upgrade or remodel our home. But what about those born in countries and communities where life is so different from what it is for us. There are pressing unmet needs in the lives of people everywhere. And, we need to be reminded of these needs again and again. Sadly, even multiple reminders have little effect, let alone change hearts. The truth is that we would like to limit our awareness to what is going on within the relative comfort and contentment of our immediate surroundings. We don't want be reminded of all the tragedy, war, famine, pain and suffering in the world. That stuff is too troubling, too unsettling and too ugly. It agitates and challenges. "Forget that! We have our own little life to live."

Again, it is not my intent to be judgmental or critical; that is not my role. I have enough of my own stuff to deal with as it relates to all of this. However, it certainly is my intent to raise the visibility of the issue in a way that forces us to make conscious choices and decisions about whether we want to continue to live in the strong current of the river of culture and lifestyle in pursuit of the American Dream, or whether we want to make some changes. We need to realize that we have been influenced, hoodwinked, or seduced into choosing the lifestyle of our consumer culture, which has become accepted as the norm, and in the process have created a bubble that allows us to insulate ourselves from the pain and suffering of others. It happens to all of us. This is the way most of us live, until our ethics, morals and values are called into question. It is almost as if we have been mesmerized by a pre-hypnotic cultural suggestion. I'm suggesting that the cultural norms for goodness, ethics, morals and values are totally inadequate.

If anyone threatens to prick the bubble of the reality we have created for ourselves, we hit the ceiling. We fiercely resist that which threatens our world view and lifestyle, not to mention our self-image. We have to find a way to push it back out of our awareness. If we allow it to become a part of our awareness, we have to go through the painful process of acknowledging that we have been deceived, snookered and hoodwinked into believing that, "basically, we're good people." If we don't fight to keep it out of our awareness, we are compelled to ask whether or not we have rationalized and justified our worldview and lifestyle and in the process have become insulated from and indifferent to the reality of all of the pain, misery and suffering that are out there.

Once we experience this powerful tension, we either have to repress and deny these issues, or continue the process of soul-searching and self-examination. My intent is to try to surface these issues, to try to help you understand how our worldview and lifestyle have developed and to try to encourage the attachment of greater significance to continuing on down the road of self-awareness.

Near the end of the 1980s, *USA Today* ran a cover story: "'Narcissism' loses out in the USA's crises." The front page graphic was titled, "The '80s: Decade of Excess," and the lead pullout was "'decade of the '90s will emerge as a decade when people began to care.'" It described the '80s as "years of excess," when we were "greedy" and "gluttonous." "Oozing out of the 'Me Decade,' instant, total gratification anchored itself in the social lexicon. Our favorite new board game was, aptly, Trivial Pursuit. 'The '80s above all was a decade where everybody was reaching out to grab everything they could,' said Michael Marsden, a popular culture professor at Bowling Green State. . . .In late 1987, in the movie *Wall Street*, Gorden Gekko told us 'greed is good.' By then we knew better. (Oh! Really!) . . .The number of homeless people triples to 3 million, say the activists. The government's figure was 350,000. 'The decade of the 90s will emerge as a decade when people begin to care,' Marsden says."[135] I don't think so!

It is simply wishful thinking to believe that we will begin to care more now than in the past. I'm not at all optimistic that much of anything will change. "They" is "We." But I wanted to at least try to start a conversation for those who are interested. I wanted to preach in a way that encouraged self-examination and made the congregation squirm uncomfortably in their pews. I was aware that this strategy would probably trigger defense mechanisms, which would go into overdrive—justifying and rationalizing and making excuses. We find a way to repress and deny challenging issues which are brought into our awareness—this issue is ultra-challenging.

I find no delight in getting under people's skin. It is not fun to intentionally try to get people angry and upset. There is way too much suffering in the world to be playing games with these issues. However, my sense is that unless we face the truth about ourselves as people who look out not just for the needs of our own, but also for their wants at the expense of the unmet needs of others, there is no hope that anything will ever change. There would be cause for celebration if people would begin a journey down the path of being more caring and compassionate.

I'm asking that we examine our ethics, morals and values, which leads to the discovery of what's really important to us. Powerful forces pull both ways, threatening to tear us apart. Are we truly caring and compassionate, or have we cut a deal and sold our souls for what has been marketed and extolled as the good life, the American Dream? We all have to come to terms with the truth about ourselves, or find a way to insulate and protect ourselves from the pain of that truth. A part of that truth is that "They" is "We."

"They" is "We." This is the way it has always been and this is the way it will always be. In Tom Brokaw's March 2010 CNBC special on the "Boomers" there was an admission that we may have been too self-centered, too self-absorbed, even narcissistic. He expresses the hope that the "boomers can give back a little bit." A "little bit" says it pretty well. Sadly, I don't expect much more from any generation.

Providing for our families is our first priority. However, we must have conversations about how our household views the needs of others, and how we are going to reach out and care for those in need. Are we going to do it through volunteer service and/or by contributing to charities that can go where we can't go and do what we can't do. If the family doesn't buy in, you certainly shouldn't make unilateral decisions about the allocation of family resources. Just make sure to take the time to nurture family relationships and conversation, and then decide how you want to use your own personal time in service and where to contribute your fair share of the family budget. We usually don't have these conversations in our households and end up doing little if anything when it comes to charity. By omission we contribute to the pain and suffering of many.

If you really want to, there are all sorts of places where volunteers are needed in your community. There are a number that have tasks that you would be comfortable doing, and others for which you could be trained. But there is something that each of us can do. Then there are the needs of church and charity to which we can contribute. Identify the spiritual and charitable needs that are meaningful to you and about which you feel a strong sense of commitment. The following are just a sample of the thousands of possibilities that are out there where you can contribute and/or volunteer:

> Your church or place of worship;
> The charities of your denomination or religion;
> Soup kitchens, rescue missions, and shelters;
> Habitat for Humanity;
> The United Way;
> The American Red Cross;
> The Salvation Army;
> CARE;
> Oxfam America;
> UNICEF;
> Children's Fund International;
> Many hospitals, like St. Jude Children's Research Hospital;
> Heart funds;
> Cancer funds; and,
> all other health issue funds.

There is so much more that we could be doing to help and support, and it just isn't happening. I wish I could be more positive, hopeful and optimistic that this trend will change. But I can't!

You choose the need; just give and give generously. Sadly, our failure to give speaks volumes about who we are and about human nature. If nobody ever put it to you this way before, that's one thing. If you have heard the message before in terms of living a life of compassion versus a life where you are entitled to your fair share of the good life, then it may be an indication that you are like the rest of us—hard-hearted, uncaring, insensitive, indifferent or all of the above. That is straight from the shoulder and pretty blunt. It may be stated more emphatically than you have ever heard it before. As they say these days, "It is what it is." We look out not just for the needs of our own, but also for their wants at the expense of the unmet needs of others. There is this powerful tension between lives that are self-centered, self-seeking, and self-serving, on the one hand, and self-giving, self-sacrificing, and selfless, on the other. It is within the context of this tension that we choose how we are going to relate to those other than our own. In Chapter 10 we will be even more specific about our expectations relative to the American Dream and our perception of ourselves as, "basically, good people."

Here is an invocation I gave at the gathering of the Illinois Association of Community Action Agencies back on May 24, 1978 in Springfield, Illinois. It's my prayer for all of us as we struggle to see ever more clearly who we are, what we are like, what we are about.

> Almighty Father, We praise you for the wonderful world you have created for us and thank you for another day to enjoy it. For most of us it's been a good day to be alive. But for so many others in the communities from which we come, it hasn't. They woke up this morning to face the same overwhelming problems and burdens they have been struggling with and suffering through all their lives. Some are barely able to meet their basic needs. Others can't even do that. Many of them are bitter, angry and resentful.
>
> Father, you created them to celebrate life in your world, but for too many it's been a life of torment, poverty, and deprivation since they were born. They have been demeaned as second class citizens in their own country. It is so easy for we who live the good life to forget them, even though we are employed in the jobs where we, more than anyone else should be aware of their suffering and hardship. Forgive us for forgetting them too often.
>
> Forgive us for being so wrapped up in our own lives. Forgive us for giving a higher priority to our personal wishes, goals, hopes and dreams, than to the much more modest hopes and dreams of those who only want to live in dignity as human beings.
>
> May this dinner strengthen us and may the program and the evening inspire us to continue our efforts through community action to bring about those changes which will give all the opportunity to live in dignity and realize the full potential with which they were endowed by you as their creator.
>
> Thanks especially for those who remarkably remain positive, hopeful and cheerful in challenging and difficult circumstances; they are special gifts of encouragement to us. Thank you for the privilege of letting us be your instruments in addressing their

most pressing, yet modest needs, and trying to bring more joy into their lives. In Jesus Name. Amen

There is a heart breaking story about a woman named Mariana Martinez. She lived in a one room house with her husband, mother and three daughters. The headline and leader went like this: "**On $3 a day.**" "The roofs over their heads are made of tin: the walls, scrap metal and cardboard. The floors were dirt. The food: rice, beans, no meat. What does work at Nicaragua's garment factories buy? Basic survival."

Not one of us would trade our lives for hers'. However, the story, a tough one to read, ends on a little bit of a happy note. "Mariana and Elvio rarely leave the village except to work. The family has one day together each week—Sunday—and she says they take simple pleasure in that."[136] There are millions of Marianas in our world, and many more millions who would gladly exchange places with Marina in a heartbeat, because her situation is much better than what they have. We can't change the world. We can't save the world. We can try to do our part to reach out to more of those who need us.

Most of those on Wall Street have a lifestyle of excess. Truth be told – so do most of the rest of us. Most Americans who live on Main Street have more than enough to be comfortable and enjoy life. As for all the money lost by the average Joe and Jane in retirement accounts, lost jobs and foreclosed homes, the Wall Street crowd could care less. We're no different. We too continue to enjoy a comfortable lifestyle while millions are starving. We don't seem to care very much about those in great need, struggling just to retain some semblance of human dignity. "Half the world's people live on less than $2 a day and a billion people on less than $1 a day...."[137] Sadly, I don't expect an awareness of that fact to make much—if any—difference in our lives. We just don't care. Our indifference betrays our inhumanity. Soul-searching reveals indifference, rationalization and sins of omission, and confirms what I am suggesting. "They" is "We."

This sermon is a challenge to do some soul-searching and to struggle with becoming more caring and compassionate, a tough *row to hoe* for folks living in a society characterized by consumerism and materialism. Giving away most of what we have and offering huge chunks of available time in service to others is not our vision of the good life. We bristle when it is even suggested. We give evidence of a hardness of heart that has not been broken.

Chapter 6
Christians and the Calculus of Indifference

"Steaming from that pit, a vapor rose
Over the banks, crusting them with a slime
That sickened my eyes and hammered at my nose.

That chasm sinks so deep we could not sight
Its bottom anywhere until we climbed
Along the rock arch to its greatest height.

Once there, I peered down; and I saw long lines
Of people in a river of excrement
that seemed the overflow of the world's latrines.

I saw among the felons of that pit
One wraith who might or might not have been tonsured—
one could not tell, he was so smeared with shit." Dante Alighieri

From the parable of "The Good Samaritan" – "On one occasion an expert in the law stood up. 'Teacher,' he said, 'what must I do to inherit eternal life?' 'What is written in the law,' he replied. 'How do you read it?' He answered: 'Love the Lord your God with all your heart and with all your soul and with all our strength and with all your mind, and, Love your neighbor as yourself.' You have answered correctly,' Jesus replied. 'Do this and you will live.' But he wanted to justify himself, so he asked Jesus. 'And who is my neighbor?' "In reply Jesus said: 'A man was going down from Jerusalem to Jericho, when he fell into the hands of robbers. They stripped him of his clothes, beat him and went away, leaving him half dead. A priest happened to be going down the same road, and when he saw the man, he passed by on the other side. So too, a Levite, when he came to the place and saw him, passed by on the other side. But a Samarian, as he traveled, came where the man was; and when he saw him, he took pity on him. He went to him and bandaged his wounds, pouring on oil and wine. Then he put the man on his own donkey, took him to an inn and took care of him. The next day he took out two silver coins and gave them to the innkeeper. 'Look after him'he said, "and when I return, I will reimburse you for any extra expense you may have"' (Luke 10:25-35).

Hypocrisy as a Function of Evil

In terms of being self-serving, greedy and indifferent, we could call Wall Street investment bankers sleaze balls and scum bags and describe the rest of us rascals, scoundrels and scallywags. But what about Christians? How do they measure up? In the calculus of indifference Christians are culpable by an exponentially larger factor. Ouch! These are harsh words to describe folks who have a rather favorable impression of themselves. I am most definitely suggesting that Christians represent the essence of self-interest and greed, the epitome of what it means to be grasping, self-centered and self-serving. It would be easy for Christians to dismiss my opinion as that of a wing-nut, and tune out the rest of the sermon. While the words will bite and bite hard, my prayer is that you will hang in there and continue to follow along. You just may be blessed.

Jesus also had some hard words to say to those who considered themselves to be religious. In the parable of "The Good Samaritan" it was the religious leader and lay assistant who walked right past the man who had been badly beaten. To drive home the point that their religion had lost its very meaning and purpose, he compares them to a person they would consider to be an undesirable half-breed—a hated Samaritan. Samaritans were not recognized as full-fledged members of the house of Israel. Today we Christians are the members of the religious establishment, the clergy and lay-assistants who pass by on the other side. How is it that we are the worst offenders? The answer is what this chapter is all about.

Including a discussion of why Christians should be different is necessary because so many in our culture aren't familiar with Christian teaching. In recent years fewer children have gone to Sunday School or church, and, therefore, today many adults lack even a minimal understanding of Christian teaching. Therefore, there is little chance they would understand what is meant by the statement that in the calculus of indifference, Christians are culpable by an exponentially larger factor.

My father had a saying about those who would get themselves in trouble, but had a knack for finding a way to wiggle out of it: "They could fall into a shithouse and come out smelling like a rose." That's us. Time after time we fall far short of God's expectations, and time after time he forgives us and washes us clean. We Christians have more reason than anyone else to be self-sacrificing, self-giving and selfless, and yet are not all that different from everybody else. How does one get across a painful truth that desperately needs to be surfaced in a way that doesn't hurt and offend? How do you preach the sermons nobody wants to hear without the congregation tuning out, or possibly asking you to leave. There is no way to sugarcoat painful truth. If I am failing in my attempt to avoid being judgmental and critical, please forgive my limitations and ineptitude. That is certainly not my intent. The words of the hymn apply to me too, "Chief of Sinners, Though I Be."

Suggesting that those who represent themselves as the religious in-crowd have distorted God's teaching to suit their own purposes is nothing new. Jesus spoke exactly the same way to the religious establishment in his day. "You hypocrites! Isaiah was right when he prophesied about you: 'These people honor me with their lips, but their heart is far from me. They worship me in vain; their teachings are but rules taught by men'" (Matt. 15:7-9). "Then Jesus said to the crowds and to his disciples: 'The teachers of the law and the Pharisees sit in Moses seat. So you must obey them and do everything they tell you. But do not do what they do, for they do not practice what they preach'" (Matt. 23:1-3). "Woe to you, teachers of the law and Pharisees, you hypocrites! You are like whitewashed tombs, which look beautiful on the outside but on the inside are full of dead men's bones and everything unclean. In the same way, on the outside you appear to people as righteous but on the inside you are full of hypocrisy and wickedness" (Matt. 23:27-28). The parallel today is saying to those of us who consider ourselves to be good Christians that we are not the generous, charitable, compassionate people we think we are. While we have more reason than anyone to be kind, caring and loving and charitable, our lives aren't noticeably different from the general population.

"Divine Comedy" No Laughing Matter

When we moved into our first parsonage in the summer of 1968, the house had indoor plumbing, but there was still an outhouse. We kept it there as a conversation piece, and named it "The Honey Dump." It also served as "Plan B" should the well run dry, which it did that very first summer. Since the church had no indoor plumbing, there were operational "his" and "hers" outhouses. The one room school did have a new bathroom.

The block long "town" consisted of the church, parsonage, school, teacherage, sawmill, two occupied residences, one that was abandoned and a pig farm that was about 100 yards east of our home—thankfully our winds were the prevailing westerlys most of the time. However, when the wind blew from the east or on those calm, hot, sultry days in a part of south-central Illinois known as "Little Egypt," the smell was considerable. The second spring we went into town to buy an air conditioner from the appliance store, whose owner was also the undertaker. He said he would give us a real good deal— because if we put one in our window, he would sell a whole lot more. We lived in what many preachers call a goldfish bow—that's a house right next to the church where your members and the whole community can watch your every move. Anyway, the air conditioner helped a lot with the smell since we could keep the windows closed.

Now what in the world does all this have to do with the very serious issue of folks caring about the suffering and disadvantaged that live in squalor, finding it difficult if not impossible to retain a sense of dignity, while all of us live rather comfortably. The folks in our congregation were like most Christians: good citizens, neighborly, with a reasonable standard and practice of ethics, morals and values. Suggest to them that they might not be the good Christians and the good people they think they are and they are likely to be hoppin' mad. They wouldn't take to that suggestion very kindly. Well, that is my dilemma, and the solution to the calculus problem, namely, to try to find a way to get we Christians to see ourselves as we really are.

Christians have far more reason than anyone else to be different. We believe in a Savior who as a suffering servant died on a cross in our place, as our substitute. On that cross he endured the punishment we deserve because of our sins. Instead, all are offered forgiveness and eternal life in heaven. Our Savior then calls us to respond by showing our love for all he has done for us by loving others in his Name. As I see it, however, we don't live our lives in a way that is noticeably different from others, even though we say we believe in him as the one who died to save us. As Americans we are rich by the world's standards. We are free to decide how we want to spend our money. When it comes to using our resources in ways that reflect self-interest or using them for the benefit of others in need, Christians are not all that different from everybody else. You would expect us to be different, but we are not. I wish I saw it differently, but you have to call it the way you see it. Our failure to make a difference, even though we have more reason than anyone else to be different, makes us the worst of the worst—the scum of the earth.

Something in my reading years ago grabbed my attention in a way that was like getting hit up-aside the head with a 2X4. I went back and reread several passages from Dante's Inferno that I thought might be an answer to prayer in helping to get we Christians to see ourselves as we really are, and to indelibly fix it in our awareness. Without a doubt Dante's words would help. When I retired from St. John's, West Bend, the congregation gave us a monetary gift that covered the cost of a European tour—8 countries in 22 days. It was a fantastic experience—seeing and experiencing even more than we had hoped for: getting a feel for old Europe, seeing almost all of the well known places and an enjoying a thoroughly delightful journey through the history of the arts. Visiting Florence I couldn't help but reconnect with memories of Dante and *The Divine Comedy*, especially the *"Inferno."*

Dante's vision of the *"Inferno"* or hell is a realm of the dead who rejected spiritual values. They exhibit beast-like cruelty and depravity, violence and a corrupted intellect that seeks to defraud and take advantage of others. Now you think this would make investment bankers nervous. Truth be told—it should make all of us real nervous, especially we Christians. We should be even more uncomfortable, because we are the ones who have reason to live differently, but don't. As we begin our "journey through hell," we are the ones who ought to feel very apprehensive. With Dante and Virgil we pass the gates of hell and immediately began to hear cries of anguish.

"This excerpt is taken from Canto 18 of the *"Inferno,"* in which Dante and Virgil visit the 18th circle of hell, which is divided into ten trenches containing the souls of people who had committed malicious frauds upon their fellow human beings."[138]

> We had already come to where the walk
> crosses the second bank, from which it lifts
> another arch, spanning from rock to rock.
>
> Here we heard people whine in the next chasm,
> And knock and thump themselves with open palms,
> And blubber through their snouts as if in a spasm.
>
> Steaming from that pit, a vapor rose
> Over the banks, crusting them with a slime
> That sickened my eyes and hammered at my nose.

That chasm sinks so deep we could not sight
Its bottom anywhere until we climbed
along the rock arch to its greatest height.

Once there, I peered down; and I saw long lines
Of people in a river of excrement
that seemed the overflow of the world's latrines.

I saw among the felons of that pit
One wraith who might or might not have been tonsured-
one could not tell, he was so smeared with shit.[139]

Both ordinary folk and clergy (the tonsured) were "smeared with shit . . . in a river of excrement that seemed the overflow of the world's latrines." If anybody deserves this, we Christians do. We have been promised forgiveness and given the assurance of everlasting life in heaven, and yet it doesn't seem to make much of a difference in the way we live.

Exposing Our Self-Deception

In sermons and the Christian media we make a really big deal out of the decline in ethics, morals and values in our country. We condemn the evil we see flourishing all around us and the erosion of traditional values. We talk a lot about "them there sinners out there." We are quick to be critical and judgmental of the moral quagmire that is our culture.

Here is another take on this situation. I wonder if that kind of preaching and teaching distracts Christians from the primary mission of the Church, reaching the lost for Christ. It sidetracks us and drains resources and energy from what we should be doing. In addition, using that perspective as a theme in our preaching and teaching comes across to the culture as hypocritical. They hear our words. They hear us lament the sad state of affairs in the moral decay around us. However, they notice little if any difference in the way we live as compared to other decent, hard working, law abiding folk.

If there is truth about our culture that must be spoken, then that same truth spoken to Christians is devastating to our sense of who we think we are. We are deluded. We are mistaken. We misunderstand the full message of the Scriptures and the call to discipleship, the call to be faithful followers of Christ. We come so far short of the standard he has set for us that we are hardly recognizable to him as his people. If there is a scathing indictment of our culture, it needs to be multiplied exponentially for Christians. While we give the appearance of respectability, the truth is that it cloaks a measure of ingratitude that is beyond comprehension, and for most of us conceals a life that looks nothing like what God had in mind when he called us to be his children and invites us to be his disciples.

We all have a way of making sense out of the world and life. As noted earlier it could be described as a conceptual framework, organizing principle or belief system. For Christians the foundation and structure is provided by what the Bible teaches. We let the Scriptures define ethics, morals and values like love, compassion, caring, sharing, decency, freedom and justice. Within our belief system our perception is that, "basically, we're good people." My intent is also to encourage Christians to do some serious soul searching, take an honest look at ourselves and see if we are indeed the good, kind, generous, loving, caring folk we think we are.

If anyone deserves the punishment so pungently described by Dante, it is we Christians. This would seem to be a very reasonable, fair consequence for our self-centeredness. We rationalize, reframe and reconstruct reality the way we want it to be, rather than seeing life the way God sees it and living life his way. The use of the word "chasm" is most appropriate to describe just how big the difference is between how see ourselves and how God sees us, between how we behave and how we think we behave. God sees us one way and we see ourselves totally differently. We fail to see just how much misery could be alleviated and how much suffering could be relieved, if only we were more concerned about the unmet needs of others. This chapter will seek to explain and develop this train of thought much more completely.

Looking into my own heart and my own life and the hearts and lives of Christians in light of the heart rending plight of so many in our world, I am appalled that we have so often stood silently by and done nothing. When the conversation is about looking out not just for the needs of our own, but also for their wants at the expense of the unmet needs of others, what I see in the lives of Christians doesn't look much different from what I see in others. We are just as greedy, self-centered, self-serving and self-seeking as everybody else. Pastor John Kieschnick, who has been helpful to many of us on our journey of spiritual growth, says: "We aren't basically good people, who need just a few more pep talks to help us realize how good we are. We are helpless, hopeless sinners, far away from God and with no possible way of earning his love, forgiveness and acceptance."[140] Then He sent His Son.

Why Christians Should be Different

Now we move from a description of what we Christians are like to an in-depth discussion of the reasons we should be different. Indeed, Christians have more reason and motivation to be different than anyone else. We should be the cream of the crop when it comes to ethics, morals and values. It is here that we gain insight as to why harsh words such as those of Dante are reserved for Christians.

We believe that what transforms us is the fantastic realization of the self-giving, self-sacrificing, selfless love for us shown by Jesus death on the cross for us. All motivation for living a life of love and service is rooted in "a deep, rich, awe-filled gratitude that the God of the universe, who needed nothing and no one, stooped to express his love in a way that obliterated the barrier of sin that separated us from him"[141] Yet, we hold back and keep our distance from God. There is dark sin in our life. Our past haunts us. What if everybody in our life knew? Therefore, we need to hear that there is no sin so bad, so terrible, that God won't forgive us. ". . . The bad news is that we do sin daily. The good news is that God forgives freely."[142] This is the essence of the reason we eagerly seek to serve him, to dedicate our lives to him.

The Gospel is the good news that we are forgiven and saved through the innocent suffering and death of our Lord Jesus Christ, and his rising from the grave on Easter morning. Hebrews 12:2 puts it this way: "Let us fix our eyes on Jesus, the author and perfecter of our faith, who for the joy set before him endured the cross, scorning its shame, and sat down at the right hand of the throne of God." Or, in the words of John 3:16 that we cherish, "For God so loved the world that he gave his one and only son that whoever believes in him shall not perish but have eternal life."

We matter to God. We are important to God. So after convicting us of our sin, God speaks to us in his Word and let's us know that he loves us so much that he sent his Son to endure the cross for us, that in the shed blood of his Son we are forgiven, and in his resurrection guaranteed eternal life. We are awe stuck by the depth of his love and compassion. We experience the overwhelming joy and gratitude of the great exchange, where we bring him all the dirt and filth of the sin in our lives and he exchanges it for a white blanket of forgiveness. As we are cleansed of our sinful, self-centered, self-serving lives by the self-giving, self-sacrificing, selfless love of Christ who gave his all for us, he becomes our model for living. Empowered by the Spirit we give our all for him, follow his example, and live self-giving, self-sacrificing, selfless lives of service.

We are overwhelmed with a love and gratitude that shapes every aspect of our lives. This is what transforms us and moves us to live a life totally devoted to the one who died for us. All we do is lived out as a response to what he has done for us. "The more we are overwhelmed by the grace of God, the more we'll want to represent him every moment of every day, in every endeavor of our lives. And we'll want our purposes to line up with his purposes."[143] We as Christians have more reasons than anyone for living exemplary lives of selfless service and sacrifice. We as Christians have more reasons than anyone for caring for "the least of these" (Matt.25:31-46) whenever and wherever we can.

You would expect us to be different? We have all the reason in the world to be different. We have been forgiven and assured of eternal life in heaven—that should be all the reason in the world to be different. Our mission is to share the Gospel of God's love for us in Jesus Christ with the world so all can find comfort in the forgiveness of their sin and the promise of heaven. You would think that our beliefs would make a difference in our lives. I just don't see it. We don't even give sacrificially to support our mission and outreach efforts to tell others about our Jesus, let alone seek to meet the tragedy of human need all around us. Wow! You can't tell the difference between Christians and everyone else. We blend in very nicely with those around us. We have accommodated ourselves to our culture.

There are many more reasons why you might expect us to be different, and they are all built on the foundation of the Gospel. The sermon song is finished. The sermon begins. Expectant faces look toward the preacher.

- A single mother sighs, praying that her children will let her make it through the sermon, and maybe even to listen to part of it.

- An older man in failing health turns up his hearing aid. Frustrated and angry with diminishing strength and energy, he's searches to make sense of his losses. He feels like he's no use to anybody—that he's just in the way.

- A high school sophomore listens with an MTV conditioned attention span.

- A discouraged business owner is experiencing a severe decline in sales.

- A Bible class teacher dealing with a major moral failure clings to faith by a fingernail.

- A married couple, sitting together in the pew, but hardly speaking at home, hope for renewal of lost affection.

- A frustrated parent of an angry teen looks for guidance and confidence.

- A widow's eyes fill with tears as her hand touches the empty seat beside her.

- A cancer patient needs a reason to suffer through the next series of chemo treatments.

- Her mate is desperate for the strength to persevere.

- A contractor, competing with kickbacks and cheats, wonders if his ethics are antiquated.

- A nurse exhausted from a twelve-hour shift hopes for renewal.

- A lonely soul hopes for connection with others.

- New Christians listen, eager to grow in the faith.

- Longtime members hope for revival from spiritual lethargy.

- Debaters want a convincing argument.

- Tired volunteers long for a lift.

- Frazzled staff seek a shot in the arm.

- Leadership Board members seek guidance and vision.

- Those down in the dumps need to be uplifted.

- The confused seek wisdom.

- The troubled seek peace.

- The mad seek release.

- The sad seek encouragement.

The preacher begins. For three sentences everyone listens intently, wondering, "Is there a word from God for me today?" Who dares to rise and preach in the face of such expectation? Who can meet such a multiplicity of need? Only God can. God speaks through the preacher's faltering words, stiff outlines and familiar clichés. God speaks through his words, his tears, his personality, his humor, his gestures and his spirit. God uses unworthy vessels to anoint hearts, lift spirits, relieve pain and enlighten understanding. The power in preaching is not the preacher. It is God. God speaking through a man gives a beautiful gift in a plain brown wrapper. God has a word for us. Shhhhh. Listen.[144]

God's people gather for worship in expectation, and he does not disappoint. He gives beautiful gifts. The preacher brings the words of hope and promise found in His Word. "I lift up my eyes to the hills—where does my help come from? My help comes from the LORD, the Maker of heaven and earth" (Ps. 121:1, 2). "Humble yourselves, therefore, under God's mighty hand, that he may lift you up in due time. Cast all your anxiety on him because he cares for you. And the God of all grace, who called you to his eternal glory in Christ, after you have suffered a little while, will himself restore you and make you strong, firm and steadfast. To him is the power for ever and ever" (1 Pet. 5:6-7, 10- 11). "Come to me, all you who are weary and burdened, and I will give you rest" (Matt. 11:28). The pastor shares words of comfort and reassurance.

The preacher shares that God will bring healing and peace out of trouble and sadness for those who in faith belong to Christ. He shares that anything which causes sorrow is something the Savior will use to bring blessing—something he will use to serve his glory and our good. Romans 5:3-5 teaches us that sorrows draw us closer to him. "We also rejoice in our sufferings, because we know that suffering produces perseverance; perseverance, character; and character, hope. And hope does not disappoint us, because God has poured out his love into our hearts by the Holy Spirit." But there is one thing sorrow can never do. It can never, ever separate us from God's love. "For I am convinced that neither death nor life, neither angels nor demons, neither the present nor the future, nor any powers, neither height nor depth, nor anything else in all creation, will be able to separate us from the love of God that is in Christ Jesus our Lord" (Rom. 8:38- 39). God keeps his promises to watch over us even and especially in our sorrows.

Now you understand why Christians should be different. In the Bible God speaks to us when we need so very much to hear a word of forgiveness, when we are experiencing illness or injury, when we are grieving the loss of a loved one or when we are having trials and troubles in our relationships.

- He has stood at the door of our lives and knocked even though our lives have all kinds of bad stuff (sins) that we really didn't want him to see. But he comes anyway, he looks all around. He sees what's in the dark corners and secret places in our lives, and still he forgives. This is what the Gospel is about (John 3:16). This is what the parable of the Prodigal Son is all about, or more accurately, the parable of The Forgiving Father.

- He has cleaned up our messes.

- He has helped us to recover from a serious illness or injury.

- He has strengthened and sustained us through troubled times.

- He has been there to encourage and support us through our trials and heartaches.

- He has been there to help smooth things out when the going gets rough.

- He has walked with us in times of grief, and helped us to find a little more healing and peace each day.

- He has relieved our suffering, and given us the strength needed to make it through the day.

But What Happens After the Messes Are Cleaned Up?

Therefore, if there is a case to be made against those who are self-serving and self-centered, the strongest, most compelling case could be made against us. Why? Because if we believe what we say we believe, we have the most compelling reason to live self-giving, self-sacrificing, selfless, dedicated, committed lives of service. We have the best reason, the best motivation to be caring, kind, loving and charitable. Once we have come to know the heart of God, once we begin to grasp the enormity of his love for us, it ought to make all the difference in the world and others ought to be able to see the difference in our lives.

Then what follows in Christian teaching doesn't follow in practice, namely, how our overwhelming joy and gratitude transforms us into people who want to express our love by living lives totally dedicated to his service, living lives that honor our Savior. This is the part of the message that gets tuned out. His call to live lives of loving service gets shuffled off to the side together with the very real and often desperate needs of others. Martin Luther speaks to this issue.

> . . . Those who know and accept the child Jesus not only give honor to God but treat their fellow men . . . with peaceable demeanor, glad to help . . . any man. They are free from envy and wrangling, for the Christian way is quiet and friendly in peace and brotherly love where each gladly does the best he can for another.[145]

Roland Bainton adds this perspective.

> Once again Luther's critics arise to inquire whether if a man in the end has no standing with God he should make the effort to be good. Luther's answer is that morality must be grounded somewhere else than in self-help and the quest for reward.

> . . . The righteousness of the sinner is no fiction. It must and it will produce good works, but they can never be good if done for their own sake. They must spring from the fount of the new man. 'Good works do not make a man good, but a good man does good works.' Luther variously described the ground of goodness. Sometimes he would say that all morality is gratitude. It is the irrepressible expression of thankfulness for food and raiment, for earth and sky, for the inestimable gift of redemption. Again morality is the fruit of the spirit dwelling in the heart of the Christian. Or morality is the behavior becoming the nature of one united with Christ. . . .[146]

Again, here are Luther's words.

> The apostle Paul said, 'Let this mind be in you which was also in Christ Jesus, who being on equality with God, emptied himself, talking the form of a servant, and becoming obedient unto death.' Paul means that when Christ was fully in the form of God, abounding in all things, so that He had no need of any work or any suffering to be saved, was not puffed up, did not arrogate to himself power, but rather in suffering, working, enduring and dying made himself like other men. . . . All this he did to serve us. When God in his sheer mercy and without any merit of mine has given me such unspeakable riches, shall I not then freely, joyously, wholeheartedly, unprompted do everything I know will please him? I give myself as a sort of Christ to my neighbor as Christ gave himself for me.

Bainton summarizes it this way: "This is the word which ought to be placarded as the epitome of Luther's ethic, that a Christian must be a Christ to his neighbor."[147]

We ought to be so overjoyed that one would expect us to completely surrender, to offer ourselves ready for a life of loving service, commitment, and dedication. While we are so blessed to have a Father who loves and forgives us, our lives don't change much at all. This is astounding! Of all the indictments that could be handed down, the case against us Christians is the strongest of all. The evidence is overwhelming. We should be the most grateful people of all and our lives should show it, but they don't. If anyone has a reason to be self-giving, self-sacrificing, selfless, dedicated, committed, we do. We have more reason than anybody else to be different. We have the best reason, the most motivation to be caring and charitable, but we're not.

So what do we do after he forgives all the bad stuff? What do we do after he has always been there to support, sustain, strengthen, encourage and lift us up during times of sickness and suffering? What happens when all of the messes are cleaned up? What do we do once we have received healing and peace in relationships. We are eager to receive all of the above, but still, we don't change. We are very comfortable with the lifestyle to which we have become accustomed. We don't want to be inconvenienced. We want to be able to continue the pursuit of our own goals, hopes and dreams. Jesus' teachings about love and helping those in need are so far down our list of priorities as to be irrelevant. For most Christians being a faithful follower of Jesus is little more than an afterthought in their daily routine.

God has something very important to say to the broken, the grieving, the troubled, the distressed and those whose lives are a mess. What does God have to say when with his help the messes have been cleaned up, the broken have been restored, the grieving are comforted and the troubled and distressed find healing and peace? There is more to say! There is a word from God that needs to be spoken.

After there has been a time for healing and we have taken the time to give thanks and sing our praises, the preacher needs to remind them that it's time to rejoin the congregation in service. It's time to once again become full partners in helping the congregation to carry out its mission and vision. What needs to follow is teaching and preaching that calls out a response to all that our loving and merciful God has done for us. After the messes have been cleaned up, our people need to be reminded again of their call to self-giving, self-sacrificing, selfless lives of service, showing their love for him by dedicating themselves to loving and serving one another in his name.

After the messes are cleaned up, there is a powerful temptation for those who have been so richly blessed to resume the life they were living before the crisis, one that doesn't look much different than most people in our society. We don't seem to change all that much. There may be some movement, but nothing dramatic or transformational.

Kieschnick says, "People are watching us to see if our commitment to Christ makes any difference in how we live. . . . I'm convinced that most people aren't looking for perfection. They're looking for honesty, integrity and authenticity. They want to see if our actions match our words."[148] We are also quick to acknowledge that any progress we may make toward living out the Biblical model for a faithful follower of Christ happens only with God's help.

I believe that the model of what a faithful follower of Christ looks like has something to offer to all of us. It is well worth our consideration as the model we choose as our baseline standard for the process of reflection, soul-searching and self-examination necessary to answer the question as to whether or not we are good persons. The next chapter describes that Biblical model.

Chapter 7
With Basin and Towel

"Ask not what your country can do for you, but what you can do for your country." John Kennedy

"Whoever wants to be great among you must be your servant, and who ever wants to be first must be your slave—just as the Son of Man did not come to be served, but to serve, and to give his life as a ransom for many" (Matthew 20:25-28).

Needed: A Higher Standard for What It Means To Be a "Good Person"

The truth is that we have gutted the essence of what it means to be "a good person. If being "a good person" is meant to imply that we are kind, caring, compassionate and generous, then using that phase to describe us is totally misleading and inappropriate. Our ethics, morals, and values have been nearly emptied of significance and stripped of meaning. What's shocking is that we weren't even aware that it had happened. We missed it. I did too. We are so much a part of the world around us and so into our culture that we aren't even aware anymore of what it means to be a truly "good" person. A purer and more accurate understanding of the term was crowded out of cultural norms long ago, and has been absent for a long time.

Mankind has progressed to an advanced stage of civilization, and shows some degree of common decency. There may be fleeting glimpses of kindness and compassion, brief moments when we are caring and nice. Certainly there are times when give each other a little bit of help. Then we take this gigantic leap to a place where we have convinced ourselves that we're really doing pretty good. The truth is that we are doing barely enough to maintain our image and give the appearance of being a "good person." My sense is that our lives are a moral desert, an ethical wasteland.

Our protestations to the contrary, we are not "good" persons by any reasonable standard; describing ourselves as "good" is stretch. Connecting the dots does not lead to that conclusion. We use our financial resources for our wants as well as our needs. When compared to our potential, our charitable contributions and volunteer efforts are minimal at best. The question for this chapter is whether we are willing to re-evaluate our current level of commitment to help and care for others, and whether we are willing to change our lifestyle, reorder our priorities and make sacrifices in order to do more.

The intent of this chapter is to help with the task of developing a higher standard for what it means to be a "good" person, and then integrating it into our worldview and lifestyle. The Christian concept of discipleship is offered here as the baseline standard for evaluating whether "Basically, We're Good People" or not. This model is the one with which I am most familiar as a Lutheran Christian pastor—one that I consider exceptional and worthy of consideration. Whether we realize it or not, we all have a standard, by which we evaluate ourselves—a yardstick by which we measure ourselves. Whether the standard is that of our culture or a religious, moral or ethical tradition, it is very important for us to be aware of it. Only then are we in a position to consciously decide whether or not we will continue to use that standard or adopt a new one.

Humble Servants

We don't want to be inconvenienced, let alone asked to make a radical transformation in our lifestyle. We don't want to submit to God's will for our lives and live in a manner that is consistent with what we claim to believe. Yet that is exactly what Christians are called to do; that is exactly what "discipleship" is all about. Oops, there I go again, using religious shorthand, which is just one more reason people don't understand and therefore don't like sermons. It is really tough to get the point of the sermon when we use those code words; discipleship is one of them. A disciple is the word used to describe a faithful follower of Jesus Christ. "Discipleship" is another of those words that has lost much of its original meaning in terms of how it used today. The Scriptural understanding is so very different from the way in which we use it as descriptive of the Christian life.

The previous chapter was about why Christians ought to be different. This chapter is about what that difference looks like, in terms of what discipleship looks like—what a life of discipleship is all about. The insights of James Boyce, Presbyterian pastor, writer and editor, offer an inviting and helpful introduction to the subject.

> The parable of the Good Samaritan is probably the most irrelevant part of Jesus teaching so far as the lives of most Americans are concerned. Many Americans are excessively materialistic and thus view life as for their own benefit rather than as a sphere in which they can serve.
>
> . . . It is not what others can do for us, but what we can do for others that matters. Our model is the Lord Jesus Christ, who on the night of his arrest demonstrated a servant's attitude by clothing himself with a towel and stooping to wash his disciples' feet.[149]

Foot washing was provided as a courtesy by the host at a time when getting your hot, tired, dusty, dirty feet washed was really appreciated, even more than getting a foot massage or pedicure. This washing was usually done by a servant. On this occasion there was no servant, and not one of Jesus disciples stepped-up to volunteer. During the meal Jesus got up and took off his outer garment, wrapped a towel around his waist, poured water into a basin and began the menial task of washing their feet.

"When he had finished washing their feet, he put on his clothes and returned to his place. 'Do you understand what I have done for you?' he asked them. 'You call me teacher and Lord, and rightly so, for that is what I am. Now that I, your Lord and teacher, have washed your feet, you also should wash one another's feet. I have set you an example that you should do as I have done for you. I tell you the truth; no servant is greater than his master'" (John 13:1-17). It was a lesson in humility and selfless service that was soon to be given its ultimate expression when Jesus died on the cross as their suffering servant. After he rose from the dead just a few days later, it began to make so much more sense. Based on his selfless, sacrificial love for us, he calls us to a life of humble, loving, selfless service. In essence, that is what being a disciple is all about.

God's Description of the Good Life: Discipleship

Discipleship is something that happens in the lives of Christians as we come to and are moved by the ever increasing awareness that we are richly blessed. So exactly what do disciples look like and how are they different? Living Christianity, not just confessing it, is more than being a fairly regular attending member of a church who lives pretty much like everybody else during the week. As disciples we want Jesus to be the Lord of our life, not just the Savior of our soul. Discipleship is the spiritual equivalent of Obsessive-Compulsive Disorder. As it relates to being disciples, we are called to become obsessive-compulsives in yielding ourselves in complete surrender to Christ. It is an eager, willing, joyful surrender. The call of God in the Scriptures is a call to obedience, willing obedience, not something you have to do, not a life into which you are carried kicking and screaming. It is an obedience that is humbly submissive—something you want to do. Discipleship is a way of life consumed with a passion to praise and honor the Jesus we love, as we show our love for him by loving and serving others in his name.

Discipleship is being a faithful follower of the Jesus who loved us enough to suffer and die on a cross in our place, as our substitute, taking the punishment for all of our sins. He is our King, the one who we want to sit on the throne of our lives. As God's children, knowing what he has done for us, we don't want to do anything that would dirty his name or harm his reputation. We bear the name Christian. Everything we now do we do because we want the name of God to be honored. We want to live in a way that does not tarnish God's good name, empty it of significance or treat it as if it were irrelevant. For the Christian, living to honor God's name becomes a natural thing, a natural expression of our life. It is who we are. It is what we are. It is what living the Christian life is all about.

When others look at us, they need to see God. They need to get an idea of what God is like. We wear the brand and carry the reputation of the parent company. God's intention is for people to look at us, and then praise and magnify his name because of what they see in us. God's name is to be lifted up in our lives, so the rest of the world will come to know what a fantastic, loving God we have.

Discipleship and Prayer

It is in the context of discipleship that we that we gain a more scripturally based understanding of prayer. The ACTS model, an acronym for the fifth book of the New Testament, is a simple yet helpful guide for daily prayer; it is a reminder to include the elements of adoration, confession, thanksgiving and supplication. Supplication is shorthand for bringing our requests to God. Most folks have a mistaken notion of what prayer is about. We visualize God as this celestial vending machine: we put in our needs and concerns and then expectantly wait for him to pop out the answer we are looking for.

The Scriptures make it clear that when we pray for physical needs, we are always to include a qualifier, something like "according to your will," "if it is your will" or "nevertheless, not my will but yours be done." God wants us to bring all of our concerns and needs to him (health, employment, peace, etc.) and He promises to hear us and answer our prayers in a way that is intended for our good and his glory. Certainly we pray, asking him to intervene on our behalf and to help bring about the outcome we desire, fully believing he can do it. The reason we always add a qualifier is that we don't know whether from an eternal perspective what we are asking is best for us.

As we become mature disciples, there is a change in our understanding of our prayer. At that point prayer is no longer only about asking God to get on the same page with us, but asking him to help us get on the same page with him. We are no longer asking him to help work things out so that our plans, our hopes, our goals and dreams are realized. Rather we asking for the spiritual insight needed to walk with Him and accomplish his will. It's not about our plans, hopes, goal and dreams; it is about how God acts through his people to accomplish his plans. We no longer ask him to get with our program, but we pray that he will help us to get with his program. While it is not what people want to hear, prayer is not about asking for God's help in carrying out our agenda, but for him to guide us so we can help carry out his agenda. We pray that our purposes will line up with his purposes. As disciples we are called to be radically different. How we approach prayer is one way of getting an idea of what this difference looks like.

The Pastor's Biggest Challenge

It is in the process of carrying out the task of nurturing a congregation in the lifelong process of growing and maturing as disciples where the pastor finds his greatest challenge. Once your people come to know God's comfort, healing and peace, you pray fervently that they will respond with lives of joyful obedience and loving service. You pray so very hard that God would use you as his chosen vessel to be the catalyst, the spark, and the igniter for his people as they grow and mature spiritually and become more faithful in their life of discipleship. The pastor prays and works using the power of the Holy Spirit at work through Word and sacrament to transform peoples' lives so they seek to walk daily with the Lord and to develop a close personal relationship with him. The pastor is God's spokesman, in a "plain brown wrapper."

A pastor prays that his people will no longer conform themselves to the world's thinking and the world's ways, but rather find in Jesus their purpose for living—their reason for being. The pastor prays that his people will be led to understand that living the life you want to live, having your own plans, hopes, goals and dreams and then asking God to get with the program and help make it happen will only lead to emptiness and disillusionment. This pastor prays that God would use him to share the Word, and in so doing release the very power that can transform lives.

At this point seven years into my retirement I'm more excited about life than I've ever been. I'm more excited about the future than I've ever been. I'm more excited about the opportunities for the whole Church to be about the mission we were given by Jesus than I've ever been. I'm not looking forward to kicking back and just taking it easy. No way! I am more passionate than ever about continuing to serve, rejoice and celebrate the fullness of a life of discipleship.

I graduated from Lutheran High South in Chicago in 1959, and was shaped by the sixties, those years of hope occasionally interrupted by days of rage intended to crush those who felt strongly about righting the wrongs they saw in the world around them and who sought to express their convictions through non-violent action. In a spiritual sense I still have that Man of La Mancha passion personified by Don Quixote on a quest to right the wrongs of this world in pursuit of a heavenly cause. Deep down I'm an idealist and a dreamer in pursuit of the primary mission of the Church: making disciples of the un-churched and the de-churched, and living in the way described in John 13:34-35: "A new command I give you:

Love one another. As I have loved you, so you must love one another. By this all men will know that you are my disciples, if you love one another." I have a burning passion for souls and a burning passion to care for those Jesus called "the least of these:" the disadvantaged, the underdog, the rag-a-muffins, those suffering injustice, the poorest of the poor.

Christian discipleship is not a Sunday thing; it is a 24/7 thing. Christian discipleship is a way of life, not just a Sunday ritual. Discipleship is selling out for Christ! Discipleship is a life of joyful, willing obedience. Discipleship is a commitment to live according to God's plan, rather than your own. Discipleship is maturing from being a half-hearted and lukewarm Christian into one that is passionate and dynamic. Discipleship is finding the joy in living that comes when you are humbly and joyfully obedient to a loving Lord and Savior. More and more of our brothers and sisters in the faith are growing in faith and committed to a life of discipleship where:

- Jesus is the center of our lives;

- Jesus gives meaning and purpose to our lives;

- He is our reason for being;

- He is our everything;

- He gave his all for us, and in response we seek to give our all back to him in service.

After Sunday worship an unbelieving friend one of our members brought to church said, "If I believed what the pastor said, and what you say you believe, my life would be transformed, and everybody around me would know about it." Amen! Mature Christians are passionate about being disciples, faithful followers of Christ, totally committed to living their lives for him. All of this may sound like a foreign language, even to some Christians. Others understand, but are nowhere near that level of commitment on their faith journey.

Here are some of the more powerful passages that inform a life of discipleship.

- "Then Jesus said to his disciples, "If anyone would come after me, he must deny himself and take up his cross and follow me. For whoever wants to save his life will lose it, but whoever loses his life for me will find it" (Matt. 16:24-25).

- "'Love the Lord your God with all your heart and with all your soul and with all you mind.' This is the first and greatest commandment. And the second is like it: 'Love your neighbor as yourself'" (Matt. 22:37-40).

- "'Lord, when did we see you hungry and feed you, or thirsty and give you something to drink? When did we see you a stranger and invite you in, or needing clothes and clothe you? When did we see you sick or in prison and go to visit you?' The King will reply, 'I tell you the truth, whatever you did for one of the least of these brothers of mine, you did for me'" (Matt. 25:37-40; Revised Standard Version).

- "Dear friends, since God so loved us, we also ought to love one another" (1 John 4:11).

Again, inspiring Christian writer John Kieschnick has some great insights that add to the fullness of the description of what the life of a disciple looks like.

> We say we want to "be more like Jesus," but what does that mean? Certainly, one of the main characteristics of Jesus was his servant's heart. In Matthew's Gospel Jesus explained the upside down nature of authority and service in God's kingdom: "Jesus called them together and said, 'You know that the rulers of the Gentiles Lord it over them, and their high officials exercise authority over them. Not so with you. Instead, whoever wants to be great among you must be your servant, and whoever wants to be first must be your slave – just as the Son of Man did not come to be served, but to serve, and to give his life as a ransom for many'" (Matt. 20:25-28).
>
> Jesus is the ultimate servant. If we want to be like him, we'll learn to serve with a dynamic blend of gladness and passion, and we'll find the role where we can be most effective in building his kingdom. When our hearts are full of God's grace (Oops, we have to define another one of those theological buzz words), the free and undeserved gift of God's love and forgiveness in Jesus Christ, and we see him using us to change lives, we experience genuine delight.
>
> . . . Paul wrote often about his passion for serving Christ, and made it crystal clear that the source of his motivation was the incredible grace of God. In his second letter to the believers in Corinth, he explained, "For Christ's love compels us, because we are convinced that one died for all, and therefore all died.

And he died for all, that those who live should no longer live for themselves but him who died for them and was raised again" (2 Cor. 5:14-15). He made choices everyday to live wholeheartedly for Jesus Christ for the single, compelling reason that he was overwhelmed by Christ's sacrifice for him. Nothing else came close. Throughout his letters, we find Paul referring to the awe-inspiring grace of God as his foundation and source of joy and strength.

> The same grace that motivated Paul to love and serve Jesus Christ is the grace that motivates you and me—it's no different. As you and I are overwhelmed with God's love, forgiveness and purpose for our lives we'll do everything to please him and expand his kingdom. We won't need to be prodded or cajoled. Nothing can hold us back! When we see needs, we'll dive in to meet those needs.[150]

Once we know that God has put us in the world for a purpose, and we are moved by compassion to follow him, we live with a sacrificial mentality and have no regrets. We are ready to substitute God's agenda for our own. We no longer live for ourselves, we live our lives as a thanks and praise response for the shed blood of Christ.

My experience as a pastor is that as long as you describe discipleship in broad strokes and general terms, people can discount and marginalize the message to fit their idea of what Christianity, discipleship and church membership look like. When presented in general terms, many simply don't grasp what a walk with the Lord is all about. Immature Christians rationalize and justify the validity of their own compromised version of discipleship, which allows them to avoid making a total commitment to a life of loving service. The vast majority of Christians just don't get it when discipleship is explained in terms of Jesus being the center of our lives, the one who gives meaning and purpose to our lives or the one who is our everything. Consequently, most do not dedicate themselves to serving the Lord with all their being. A life of willing and complete obedience simply does not follow. When sermons are the generic version that don't include specifics, most of the time not much happens. Lives are not transformed and we come no where near measuring up to a Biblical standard. We can't assume that Christians understand the radical call to discipleship and service that is set forth in the Scriptures. However, whenever the foreign language of discipleship gets translated into plain English, people get their backs up. It is when you get concrete and specific that folks think that you are unrealistic and out of touch. This is the pastor's biggest challenge.

We hear the beautiful Gospel message that as Christians living in a close personal relationship with Jesus, we are forgiven for all of our sins, even for not being totally committed to serving the disadvantaged, the starving, the suffering and the poorest of the poor. We are forgiven, but it doesn't seem to make any difference. We go on living lives that look pretty much the same as before and pretty much the same as everybody else. Most Christians either have not been clearly taught the radical call of the Gospel to total commitment and dedication, or have found a way of reinterpreting, redefining and reframing what the Scriptures teach to meet their needs, to fit their own personal beliefs about Christianity or to be compatible with a way of living the Christian life that does not in any way inconvenience them or get in the way of the pursuit of their own goals and hopes and dreams.

Our beliefs make it clear that the most important thing is that there ought to be an urgency to be about an all out effort to share the Gospel so more people will believe and fewer will be lost for all eternity. Our lives simply do not reflect that urgency. There is no sense that we need to be putting forth a maximum effort every day. John 9:4 says, "We must work the work of him who sent us while it is day; for night cometh when no man can work." We know the story. There should be an urgency to tell others about our Jesus. I just don't see it.

What happens? Where does our spiritual journey get derailed? Americans have developed what might be called an affluent state of mind. We have been shaped by the promise of opportunity in a land of plenty. Christians get caught up in this mindset and are just as powerfully influenced by it as everybody else. Living the American way of life in pursuit of the American Dream is a very appealing temptation for Christians living in our culture. Then we hear the words of Matthew 6:24, "You cannot serve both God and money." That triggers spiritual warfare as we struggle with the excesses of materialism, pleasure, comfort and leisure.

Getting Derailed on the Journey to Becoming a Disciple

Americans have been raised to take for granted the validity and morality of the pursuit of the good life, and we Christians share many more sentiments with our culture, than with the teachings of the Bible. We live in a culture devoted to the celebration of at least a middle-class life-style. We have been deceived and blinded into thinking that even for Christians there is nothing wrong with that attitude. Our society is organized around the "pursuit of happiness." Within the framework of the freedom we are blessed with as a nation, you would think that Christians would define those words differently than most citizens, namely, that we are free to choose to use our freedom in service to others. We don't! The upper class has their large homes, investments, classy cars and like the feel of first class. We're no different. The toys that most Christians have are just less expensive: pick-ups, boats, campers, snowmobiles and if you live in Wisconsin, a place "up north."

In order to give clarity to this discussion, it will be necessary to provide lots of specifics. The differences between a Christian ethic and the ethics, morals and values of our culture are much greater than most of us think—perhaps I should say, greater than most of us have been taught in our churches. For now, I want to begin a discussion of the stewardship of our financial resources and our time, the really hot topics that aggravate, irritate and annoy immature Christians. These are the sermon topics that are right at the top of the list when it comes to sermons nobody likes. This section will just be a taste of what will be the focus of the next chapter.

How many times have we heard, "All they ever talk about is money." Again, we love those comforting and reassuring sermons, but we don't want hear the call to discipleship that inconveniences us, and gets in the way of our goals, hopes and dreams. The Biblical concept of stewardship is that of being the manager of property that belongs to another. All that we have comes from God. He is the owner of all things, and he asks us to manage the portion that he has entrusted to our care for awhile. We don't give a portion of what is ours to God. It all belongs to him. Our contributions are part of the management of what he has entrusted to our care. Our motivation for giving is rooted and grounded in his selfless and sacrificial love shown for us on the cross. Our giving is a sacrificial response to all that he has done for us.

In the church it is often suggested that we follow the Old Testament practice of giving 10 percent of our income to the Lord. Surfacing this issue in congregations usually meets with considerable resistance. One of the first indications that members are perturbed usually comes in the form of the question, "Do you mean 10 percent of the net or of the gross?" Yet, even this question doesn't come close to the heart of the issue. Tithing is not the operative principle that informs the giving of New Testament Christians, and is not the goal in our life as Christian stewards. Rather it is just one important milestone along the road to complete surrender as faithful followers. Sacrificial giving can mean giving much more that 10 percent.

A pastor with whom I served as associate had a member who was contacted by the IRS. It wasn't because they wanted to do an audit in which he had to produce documentation to verify the amount he deducted. Rather, he had deducted more than the 50 percent of his adjusted gross that the IRS allows for contributions. He was very grateful for the Lord's sacrifice for him, and it showed in his response. Most of us are still in the process of maturing spiritually, often resisting total dedication and commitment. Others have been transformed and give sacrificially. A stewardship brochure that was recently distributed in our congregation concluded with these thoughts. "God's Word encourages us to be generous. 'And God is able to make all grace abound in you, so that at all things and in all times, having all that you need, you will abound in every good work' (2 Cor. 9:8). Through His gift of faith, God transforms us from selfish people who hoard our blessings to generous people who give freely. Only God is capable of removing the hindrance of selfishness to our giving."[151]

Another indication that Christians are still in the process of being transformed is that they are needs-givers rather than sacrificial givers. Here are just two of the nuances to the issue of "needs giving." First, we will support bricks and mortar. Folks will give to a building program. It is far less difficult to raise funds for an organ, to renovate and redecorate the church or to add an education wing or fellowship hall, than it is to support evangelism, mission and Christian charity. Second, the idea that we give out of the abundance of our blessing means that we are not just motivated to help meet the budget and make a pledge to the building program. Rather, each year Christians have to decide what amount would be a sacrificial offering and cheerfully give all of it, even when that amount exceeds what we are giving to support the operating fund and the building program of our home congregation. We give to the Lord, not to a need. We exercise our judgment in managing the resources that he has entrusted to our care, deciding how much to give and how much of the total should be allocated to operating budget, capital needs, mission and charity. Motivating people to grow and mature and become sacrificial givers is a challenge. And it is through the hearing of God's Word that we learn about and come to believe in all that he has done for us, that is our motivation.

The Christian stewardship of our resources reflected in our spending priorities betrays a pious veneer. How do we get off thinking we are upstanding church members when people are homeless, living in poverty, malnourished and starving while we live in excessive comfort.

As we respond to all he has done for us and seek to live as his disciples, he helps us keep things in perspective, he tries to remind us what is really important, recognizing that we are conflicted and by nature resist his will. He teaches that life is "more important than food, and the body more important than clothes"(Matt. 6:25-33). When we become preoccupied with accumulating things, this pursuit becomes our reason for being and devalues our existence.

For Christians and non-Christians alike there is an ongoing tension between being self-centered, self-serving and self-seeking, on the one hand, and self-sacrificing, self-giving, selfless on the other. Our inclination is to remain indifferent; that's just human nature. Remember that line from George Bernard Shaw: "The worst sin toward our fellow creatures is not to hate them, but to be indifferent to them. That is the essence of inhumanity." Given the context of our consumer oriented culture every one of us can fall into that trap. Are we concerned about the homeless, the stranger and the outcast? Have we been advocates for the weak and the powerless, or have we allowed injustice to have its way?

Knowing myself, there can be no illusion of Christian perfection, except when realized in the grand and glorious pronouncement of God in Christ: "Arise, your sins are forgiven." We Christians remain human beings and as such we are vulnerable and can be "got at" somewhere, sometime, somehow. The truth is it happens everywhere, in every way and all the time. We have accommodated ourselves to and become very comfortable with a worldview and lifestyle that is consistent with the American Dream. We have more reason than anyone else to be different, yet we have managed to adapt and fit in quite nicely with the society around us. We are glad to receive that part of the Christian message that meets our needs, and then take cover in our culture when we want to marginalize and disregard the life of a disciple, which we consider just too fanatical. We want to revise the Biblical understanding of God's teaching so that it fits with our agenda. Our sinful human nature operates on the basis of naked self-interest and greed. It is not just some mortgage brokers and investment bankers who operated that way; that's the way we operate too. Perhaps now the reader can more fully grasp why the imagery of being covered in excrement is so appropriate.

A comment like, "all they ever do is ask for money," is an indicator of Christian immaturity. Mature Christians who are grateful for all Christ has done are not offended or upset by stewardship sermons that focus on our returning to the Lord a portion of what he has entrusted to our care. One of the senior pastors with whom I served at St. John's, Dan Kelm, had a neat insight for sermons about financial stewardship using the phrase, "It's not supposed to hurt there." In the course of going to the doctor for a regular checkup he pushes against you. You wince and he says "It's not supposed to hurt there." So it is, when the subject of Christian giving comes up and some Christians cry out in agony. But it's not supposed to hurt there. It's not supposed to hurt once you grasp Christ's self-giving, self-sacrificing, selfless service to us on the cross, and you receive forgiveness of sins and the assurance of eternal life in heaven. "It's not supposed to hurt there."

We need to have the same conversation about the stewardship of time. There are thousands ways to enjoy rest and recreation. All were intended as wonderful blessings from God, who also rested on the seventh day. All can be wholesome activities. But Christian stewardship requires keeping our use of time in the proper balance. When we have honored our commitments as husbands, wives, parents and providers, then Christians are called to use their talents and abilities in volunteer service in church and community.

If you bowl or play baseball twice a week, play computer games for five hours a week, go hunting or fishing once a month, in addition to watching a couple of hours of television and spending a couple of hours on the internet each week, yet spent little if any time in volunteer service, it reflects a lack of love for and commitment to our Lord. It is clear that your life as a disciple is way out of balance. This brief description of the stewardship of time is sufficient to make the point for now. There will be a much more complete discussion of this issue in the next chapter.

We prefer a watered-down Christian ethic, a compromised Christianity. We see ourselves as good citizens, who want a Christianity that helps to smooth out the rough times in our lives as we enjoy the freedoms afforded by our Constitution in this great nation. We want a Christianity that doesn't inconvenience us in any way, that doesn't conflict with our agenda, that doesn't get in the way of the pursuit of our own hopes and goals and dreams, a Christianity that doesn't cramp our style. We give and serve just enough to be able to convince ourselves that we are kind, caring, charitable people, even though we don't serve all that much or give sacrificially.

A Scaled-Down Discipleship that Fits
Our Preconceived Ideas

My intent and hope is to challenge you to consider the difference between the values of our consumer-driven, materialistic, pleasure-oriented culture, on the one hand, and the life of a self-giving, self-sacrificing, selfless servant, on the other. Kieschnick again captures the essence of this point. "We need to be careful that we don't read our own values and ideas into the Bible. I love the cartoon I saw years ago of a little girl peeking into a room where her brother was reading the Bible. The boy told her, 'Don't bug me sis. I'm trying to find some verses to support my preconceived ideas!'"[152] Many pick and choose the ideas they want to include in their belief system, and dismiss the teachings they don't want to include. We have defined for ourselves what it means to be a good person and what living a good life is all about. Rather than measure ourselves by a high standard of ethics, morals and values that has been established centuries ago and stood the test of time, we use a weak, watered-down version that reflects the views of the consumer-driven, materialistic culture in which we live. In the process we have convinced ourselves that we are fine, decent, upstanding people who do enough of the right things to make it possible to say, "I'm a good person."

This is what all of us are like, some to a greater degree and some to a lesser. Given the opportunity and given their individual circumstances, people make self-centered, self-serving decisions. The only difference is that some folks make decisions that are of greater magnitude and are thus are more visible only because they have more.

The same dynamic is operative for Christians. The Christian ethic is a very high standard. While we ought to feel very uncomfortable in the presence of a holy God, we just don't have that sense about ourselves. We have this picture, this concept, that we are kind, decent, good people, who while sinners, aren't all that bad. We don't have the foggiest notion that we are evil, hard-hearted and uncaring. We are clueless! As long as we hang on to an image of ourselves as people of faith who are walking with the Lord, we are participants in a massive cover-up. God's standard is very different from the reality of what we are like. As a result, who suffers? Who gets hurt? Not us. We are forgiven. Those in need are the ones who continue to suffer, and will continue to suffer until we become aware of how far we miss the mark in loving, caring Christian service. Bonhoeffer is spot on in what God thinks about all this. "God will not be separated from our brother: he wants no honor for himself so long as our brother is dishonored"[153]

Most Christians see themselves as decent, good people, who leave the world for an hour on Sunday morning to go to church to be assured that their sins are forgiven and that they will go to heaven. Cheap grace is gladly and willingly taking all the goodies that God offers without the follow through that would in the eyes of the world help validate what we say we believe. What is holding us back? What is getting in the way? The answers lead to a discussion of human nature. What are we in our essence? What are we really like? What makes us tick? Most would say that, "basically we're good people;" we're not all that bad. Yet, after we leave worship on Sunday it's back to business as usual. When we follow this pattern, we take advantage of God's goodness, love and forgiveness. We take him for granted. We use him. We dishonor him.

"The central Christian belief is that Christ's death has somehow put us right with God and given us a fresh start."[154] "In the same way a Christian is not a man who never goes wrong, but a man who is able to repent and pick himself up and begin over again after each stumble...."[155] Our problem is that we take advantage of God's willingness to forgive. We know the drill. We know just how to game the system so we end up being forgiven. We play fast and loose with God's goodness and grace. We walk a fine line that borders on contempt. Spiritually, we are hanging on by a thread. We grieve God so very, very much.

We are indeed hypocrites who give the appearance of holiness. Behind the external face of respectability is a person who looks out not just for the needs of their own, but also for their wants, at the expense of the unmet needs of others. We deceive no one but ourselves. We believe that we are good Christians, good people. We just don't realize how far short of the mark we come in responding to God's call to live out the Biblical model of discipleship. For many years I have struggled with and been deeply troubled by the tentative, wishy-washy, lukewarm response of Christians to God's love for us in Jesus Christ. Within the context of our own belief system, it is just so clear that we aren't living the life of obedience to which we are called by the Gospel.

Even after becoming a believer, the Apostle Paul wrote, "For the good that I would, I do not; but the evil which I would not, that I do" (Rom. 7:19). Paul still had his old nature. Only now, Christ had entered his heart and he was in a constant process of being transformed. That is the way it works. We know that Jesus Christ has died for us and we want him to change us more and more all the time. No longer do we defend our selfishness and our cold-heartedness toward others. We confess it and ask for God's help in following Christ's example and becoming more like him. This is a radical, ongoing transformation that is never complete.

> Scripture teaches that we cannot not sin, that our natural human condition, apart from God's grace and the faith He creates is a life separate from and hostile to God. In this state we pursue only self-preservation, self-gratification and self-exaltation. In his vivid words Martin Luther described it as having a heart "curved in on itself." As such we are unable to live in obedience

to God's command to love Him with all of our heart, soul, mind and strength, and to love our neighbors as ourselves. The Holy Spirit, working through that holy but unattainable expectation, brings us to cry, "If we say we have no sin, we deceive ourselves, and the truth is not in us" (I John 1:8 English Standard Version). This is being honest about the reality of our condition, and leads to repentance.[156]

> Now what was the sort of 'hole' man had got himself into? He had tried to set up on his own, to behave as if he belonged to himself. In other words fallen man is simply not an imperfect creature who needs improvement: he is a rebel who must lay down his arms. Laying down your arms, surrendering, saying you are sorry, realizing you have been on the wrong track and getting ready to start life over again from the ground floor – that is the only way out of a "hole." This process of surrender . . . is what Christians call repentance. Now repentance is no fun at all. It is something much harder than merely eating humble pie. It means unlearning all the self-conceit and self-will that we have been training ourselves into for thousands of years. It means killing a part of yourself, undergoing a kind of death. . . . But the same badness which makes us need it, makes us unable to do it. Can we do it if God helps us? Yes, but what do we mean when we talk of God helping us? We mean God putting into us a bit of Himself, so to speak. He lends us a little of his reasoning powers and that is how we think: He puts a little of His love into us and that is how we love one another.[157]

I am most definitely suggesting that we are not the generous, charitable, giving, compassionate people we think we are, and that while Christians have far more reason than anyone to be charitable toward those in need, we are not living our lives in ways that are noticeably different than everybody else. People have to accept the truth about themselves before any significant change is possible.

To say that God disapproves of us, is disappointed with us and is disillusioned by our timid, lukewarm, less than whole-hearted response to his whole-hearted, sacrificial love for us is a gross understatement. To say that God is offended is to barely scratch the surface when trying to express the intensity of what he is feeling. As I read the Scriptures, we forgiven believers fall so far short of what God's standard of the transformed life looks like that it must grieve him beyond measure. While we think pretty highly of ourselves, that's not what God thinks of us. He has to be so hurt by forgiven believers who fall so far short of his will, whose life of obedience and surrender in most cases only vaguely resembles the life of discipleship described in the Scriptures. He has to be deeply saddened. He must sob and weep. It has to break his heart.

He gave his Son to die for us, and in the Good Friday account, the governor's soldiers mocked him, spit on him and hit him on the head again and again with the staff they had given him (Matt. 27:27-31). In effect, we do the same thing every time we stray from the path of discipleship, choosing rather to live life within the context of a personal religion that we have created for ourselves, a religion that does not call for surrender and sacrifice. Every time we stray, we spit on God again, and give him another slap in the face.

In the context of that part of the service where we confess our sins, some have suggested that we might feel awkward and uncomfortable in the presence of God. That doesn't begin to capture how God really feels. He is appalled with us. We have this sense that we are kind, decent, good people, who while being sinners who do some bad things, could by no means be considered evil, uncaring, mean, cruel and heartless. Untold damage is done by allowing us to maintain the image of ourselves as people of faith who are walking with the Lord, when by God's standard that is so far from the truth. Believers don't get it; they don't see the contradiction in what they claim to believe and how it is lived out in their lives.

How does all of this relate to my thesis? We Christians have the task of representing and reflecting our loving God. This is the church's mission. What kind of representatives are we if Monday through Saturday our lives don't look all that different from others in our culture. If we are just as greedy, self-serving and self-centered as everybody else, then what difference does it make whether we're Christian or not? Why would anyone want to join the family of faith? If we are a people who claim to be forgiven by a loving God, then it stands to reason that this would make a difference in our lives. But who's kidding who, there isn't much of a difference, if any at all. The common denominator for all of us, Christians included, is that we're greedy, selfish, self-centered, self-serving people who look out for ourselves and our own at the expense of the unmet needs of others.

When we disregard Scripture and pick and choose what we like and don't like out of the preaching we hear, we are playing God. It takes a lot of audacity when we decide for ourselves what we will accept and what we will not accept, whether we will be obedient and surrender to following God's will and live lives of dedicated service or not. If we don't like all of what we are hearing from the pulpit, we tune out what we don't like, and accept what we do. Somehow we feel we have the freedom and the right to disregard or reject what we don't want. We create our own concept of God and formulate our own belief system, one that is consistent with what we want God to be like. The level of obedience, commitment and surrender connected with our own personal belief system is generally consistent with a minimum of inconvenience, let alone sacrifice. Our claim to be Christians followed up by a life that lacks conviction and passion about walking with the Lord becomes a stumbling block for those who we would hope to lead to the Lord, wanting them to find the love, joy, peace, forgiveness and eternal life that we have found in him. Our lukewarm commitment to Christ clearly suggests that we Christians are by nature self-centered, self-serving folks, just like everybody else.

One Sunday at St. Johns, West Bend, our Senior Pastor, Jeff Dorth, observed that when challenged by the pastors to live a life of faith as a dedicated disciple, when called to a life of obedience based on God's Word, many in the family of faith respond, "He didn't really mean that! No way! Nobody can live that way. We'll just fly under the radar and keep doing things the way we want." We eagerly receive the news that we have a Father who loves and forgives us, but don't we don't want him to stick his nose into our business. Many have this attitude that you don't have to listen to what the pastor says. They feel they have the right to take it or leave it, the right to live their life any way they want, even if God's Word teaches something different. The result is that during the week many make lifestyle choices that are in conflict with what they hear on Sunday. All of us are asked to surrender our will to his purposes— and not just on Sunday, but Monday through Saturday.

We have reasons that far exceed any other motivation to be passionately, totally, completely, and selflessly committed to the mission of sharing the Gospel. Yet, our response is minimal at best. However, when it comes to being greedy, self-serving and self-centered, there is no difference between us and everybody else. As it relates to ethics, morals, values and sacrificial giving to church and charity, there might be some difference, but not much. We fall so far short of our calling to live in a way that reflects a loving God that we become a stumbling block for those who are considering Christianity.

During the confession we say the words, but from the results in terms of change in our lives, it seems like we say those words without conviction and a sense of their gravity. We confess a few moral lapses, a little bad language, some impure thoughts and losing our cool in relationships with those nearest and dearest to us—all good stuff. But rarely is there acknowledgement of the pervasiveness of our sinfulness reflected by the lack of willing obedience as faithful disciples. We minimize our sinfulness. We look at ourselves and think we're not all that bad. God looks at us and sees a vast wasteland of darkness.

We hear that Jesus is the Lord of our lives, not just the Savior of our souls, that he is to be first in our lives, that we are to put him before everything else, but it just doesn't happen. My sense is that we have not made the connection between being "disobedient" and going our own way, on the one hand, and the call to follow him as faithful disciples, on the other. What we have left is a watered-down, compromised version of what discipleship and obedience are all about. We Christians just don't get it. We all see ourselves doing enough of the right things. We join in the chorus of those who say, "I'm a good person."

On a recent Sunday morning the concerns about a lack of passionate discipleship hit me it really hard. The songs, the liturgy and the Scripture readings were especially uplifting. They were joyful, comforting and inspiring, touching so many of the right themes:

- that Christ is our hope and strong deliverer,

- that he is the defender of the weak and comforts those in need,

- that he will lift us up on wings like eagles,

- that the wounded are made whole, and

- the captives are set free and forgiven.

If you were hoping for inspiration, comfort and assurance, it was all there. But somehow we just don't get it when it comes to the discipleship part. The response falls flat. Even when the service is joyful and uplifting, the passion to have him as the Lord of our life does not carry over once we walk out of worship. I left the church flooded with emotion, reflecting on what it had to say about this chapter.

It was all there for me—everything I needed. I'm sure I wasn't the only one. We begin the service in expectation, and whatever our needs, we are not disappointed. But as the recipients of such abundant blessing, we are called to a life of discipleship and to do all we can to meet the unmet needs of others. We just don't get that part. We just don't get it. We have little if any sense just how far we have strayed from the path he has set for us. We are blessed beyond measure, but come up short in living out his will for our lives. We just want the God who heals, comforts, strengthens, lifts- up, encourages, forgives our moral lapses and cleans up our messes.

The Operative Principles: Self-Denial and Loving Service

Bottom line, we are the sermons nobody likes. When others see and hear the sermons we Christians preach by how we live our lives, they get turned off. They look at how we live and they don't want anything to do with Christianity. But oh how I see so much more potential for the guilt ridden, God-fearin', hymn singin', pot-luck lovin' folks in my own denomination, The Lutheran Church-Missouri Synod, and all other Christians as well.

While this book is not a call to the asceticism of St. Francis of Assisi, it is in a very real sense a model that is definitely in the same ballpark, one that with revision could be very helpful for those who choose the path of discipleship. One of the ladies in our small group home Bible study at St. John's said: "You want us to become little Mother Teresas, don't you?" While we are only spiritual midgets compared to Mother Teresa, the lady in our group heard what I was saying. She was on the right track. She was on the track that I believe will bring joy, satisfaction, meaning and purpose for all of us.

Many point to Mother Teresa as exceptional and as an exception to the rule. The implication is that there is no way you can expect us to be like her. But why should Mother Teresa be an exception? Given our circumstances, we could apply the same guiding principles in our lives as she did in hers.' Even the rich and successful among us could live like Mother Teresa or St. Francis. "But you can't expect us to be like them! That is too idealistic! You're out of touch with reality. You're a dreamer." Implicit in the assertion is that we have a right to more. But, is it our birthright and are we entitled to more? Couldn't we all live an existence characterized by frugality and simplicity. Isn't it a higher and more noble purpose to choose a life-style of self-denial motivated by a concern for and a desire to be better positioned to meet the needs of our brothers and sisters in the human family. This leads us all the way back to our reflections on human nature. Are we self-centered, self-serving and self seeking, or self-giving, self-sacrificing and selfless?

We get out of bed in the morning concerned about our job, about how we are going to pay the bills, about the quality of the education our children will receive that day, about the tension in our marriage or about the rebelliousness of our teenager. These are very real issues. However, at the same time, we need to be concerned about those in our country and throughout the world who are malnourished, refugees displaced by civil wars and regional conflicts, parents with sick children who have no access to basic health care and the homeless. Our personal challenges do not absolve us from our responsibility to also love and care for others. Our personal circumstances are not sufficient grounds to justify a special dispensation that frees us from our responsibility to care for the poor and disadvantaged or others who are troubled and burdened. We seek out and welcome the help of others as we act responsibly in trying to deal with our concerns, and we try to be there for others who need us. This is what discipleship is about. This is what living with basin and towel at the ready is all about. I offer it to you as a model that can serve as the baseline for evaluating how we're doing when we say, "I'm a good person."

Sacrificial living and sacrificial giving in our time can hardly be compared to the hardships born by the aesthetics. We need to carefully reflect on the standards and guidelines that are appropriate for us in this time and in this place. I am most definitely advocating a lifestyle based on the principles of self-denial and loving service that I view as essential for those on the journey of spiritual maturity. There is no way any of us can say, "I'm a good person." All of us continue to resist owning the truth about ourselves, especially we Christians, who in the calculus of indifference are more culpable than others by an exponentially larger factor.

An appropriate way to close this chapter is by noting two additional Scripture passages that are descriptive of a life of discipleship.

- "For Christ's love compels us, because we are convinced that one died for all, and therefore all died. And he died for all that all who live should no long live for themselves, but for him who died for them and was raised again" (2 Cor. 5:14-15).

- **"But if any one has the world's goods and sees his brother in need, yet closes his heart against him, how does God's love abide in him (1 John 3:17)?**

Traveling down the road of life with "basin and towel" in hand and a purse ready to open in order to help care for those beaten and left for dead is not standard operating procedure for us. Therefore, this chapter was intended to help with the task of developing a higher standard for what it means to be a good person, and then adapt and integrate that standard into our lifestyle. The next chapter gets into detailed specifics that further clarify this standard in a way that make it impossible to miss the point.

Chapter 8
The Sermons Nobody Wants to Hear

"How many times can a man turn his head, and pretend that he just doesn't see. The answer, my friend, is blowin' in the wind. The answer is blowin' in the wind." Bob Dylan

"I appeal to you therefore, brethren, by the mercies of God, to present your bodies as a living sacrifice, holy and acceptable to God, which is your spiritual worship. Do not be conformed to this world but be transformed by the renewal of your mind, that you may prove what is the will of God, what is good and acceptable and perfect" (Romans 12:1-2; RSV).

Then Why Preach Them at All?

The purpose of this discussion of the stewardship of our financial resources and our time is to surface issues that we would prefer not be brought into our awareness. "I don't want to even think about the possibility that I've adopted a minimal standard for evaluating whether or not I'm a good person. After all, the standard I use fits comfortably with the lifestyle I've have chosen. I don't want anybody upsetting me by suggesting that I give and serve just enough to convince myself that I'm kind, caring and charitable. So, please, don't get into specifics about how I manage my financial resources and use my time. I plead with you- don't do it. I might get upset and find another church and another preacher—a preacher who 'understands.'"

We prefer the sermons about comfort, healing and forgiveness, and about God's promises to sustain, support and encourage. And God indeed blesses us with all of that. Yet, he wants to bless us with so much more. However, the path to being able to receive all of his blessing can be painful. It includes the necessity of hearing the sermons we don't like, the ones that are heavy on the specifics, where it is much more likely you will get nailed.

Sorry about that! I'm not being sarcastic. I really mean it! I don't get any sadistic pleasure from preaching the sermons that nobody wants to hear. I don't enjoy getting under people's skin. If there were another way to do it, I would. Then why write this book? First, I hope that all who read it will find more of the fullness of life's meaning and purpose, together with all of the joy it brings. Second, a transformation in your life will mean that through you many more of the unfortunate and destitute who are overwhelmed, overburdened, starving, suffering, abandoned and living in misery will receive at least a little more help, healing, relief and peace.

Chapter 8 is the story of preachers who have chosen to go ahead and speak the truth in love. Chapter 9 is the story of those who accommodate their message to the wishes of the congregation—the preachers who bail and compromise the truth.

"Preach Preacher, Preach!"

On a chilly Sunday evening in late winter I joined "Gone Fishin," one of our praise bands at St. John's, to lead worship at the Oshkosh Correctional Center. It was the second time we were going there. The first time we were surprised when 150 inmates showed up at the first service and another 100 for the second. Most seemed to be from Baptist and Pentecostal backgrounds, so it just made sense to use a contemporary worship style and the music with which they were familiar, rather than our more traditional and formal Lutheran liturgy and worship. The service began with a choir of inmates singing a rousing, energetic spiritual that was clearly one of their favorites. Our praise band tried to capture the moment and maintain the momentum, and they were awesome.

While preparing the message, my prayer was to be able to share the Word in a way that both convicted (no pun intended) and healed. Without mincing words I spoke directly to their situation and their need. My prayerful reflection in preparation led me to take a risk. I didn't know how a message that would challenge and confront would be received. It could easily have been the kind of sermon they did not want to hear, and would not be well received. Careful to introduce the are suggesting. "Preach preacher, preach," they would shout, but to somebody else. Amen! The sermons nobody wants to hear are the ones that call us to a life of discipleship and challenge us to a life of Christian maturity.

Stewardship

Stewardship is managing resources that belong to another. Christians recognize that our time, talents (gifts or abilities) and treasure all belong to God. It is our responsibility to manage them for him. I'm going to identify three reasons why Christians get upset when the sermon is about stewardship. First, when joining a church, many are not required to even take a basic course that summarizes Christian teaching, including an explanation of discipleship. Consequently, their spiritual growth continues on a slow track and many remain immature. If they had taken a basic course they would understand that what we call "giving" is more accurately described as returning to Him a portion of what was his in the first place. Second, we've just assumed that what we have is ours. We've worked hard for it. We've earned it. We deserve it. Third, living in a consumer-driven culture, we feel we are entitled to our fair share of the good life. Our justifications and rationalizations make it possible to at least temporarily maintain our views. Then along comes the preacher sharing a word from God about stewardship that hits our stewardship hot-button and we get upset. But after awhile, we get more and more immune to them. We are increasingly able to discount the importance of preaching and teaching about stewardship. The intended message rolls off like the proverbial water off a duck's back. Therefore, when Christians hear sermons about the stewardship of time and financial resources, about volunteering and giving, not much happens. I've tried to describe my perception of the landscape that is out there.

It doesn't seem that there has been much change in the response patterns of Christians and non-Christians for a long time. I wondered why. My sense is that an important part of it is that most of the stewardship sermons I've heard, and what I have been taught and read about charitable giving lacks specificity. I believe that it will be very helpful to engage in a conversation that adds the specifics to the principles and guidelines. In the process it will be impossible to avoid some really touchy subjects. We'll start with a discussion of the stewardship of our financial resources, and then consider the issue of how much time we spend as volunteers.

Distinguishing between Needs and Wants

Christian stewardship of our financial resources compels us to make a distinction between needs and wants. The thesis of this book is that we look out not just for the needs of ourselves and our own, but also for their wants at the expense of the unmet needs of others. This statement implies that we can distinguish between needs and wants. This is it! Finally! This is what we have been waiting for—right? This is when we really get specific. This is where it can get ugly. This is where we really get nailed, as the specifics make it impossible to miss the point. This is where we have to speak the truth and confront that which Christians want to avoid more than anything else.

We Christians try everything in our power to avoid the truth that we are indeed miserable sinners. Yet, we need to hear the unvarnished truth and be convicted of our sin. Without an awareness of the full extent of our sinfulness, Christ's suffering and dying on the cross is emptied of significance and we can't fully appreciate the joy found in being forgiven. It was our sins that made his death necessary. The painful reality is that we have to get specific about our sinfulness in the context of how well we discern the difference between needs and wants. These are exactly the kinds of sermons that Christians don't like and don't want to hear. They are not the sermons where your hearers enthusiastically respond, "Preach preacher, preach."

Those who are not Christians also have to make the same choices about needs and wants in the context of the unmet needs of others. They have to make those choices based on their own philosophy of life, organizing principle, world-view or belief system. Using the word "sermon" as a metaphor for the messages and teachings of cultural gurus, teachers of self-help strategies, sages, and philosophers, as well as religious leaders— there are sermons that we really don't like and really don't want to hear.

Kieschnick has some great insights about sermons that address the issue of giving.

> People act strangely when pastors talk about giving. If we preach on the cross, the glory of God, or almost any other topic, Baptists say, "Amen, brother!" Charismatics stand up, raise their hands, and shout, "Hallelujah!" And Lutherans exhibit their usual emotional outburst of a feint smile and a slight nod. When we talk about giving, though, many people take personal offense and treat us like we're pushy used car salesmen.[158]

... The habit of giving generously and cheerfully is both a response to the grace of God and a reminder of God's gracious provision in our lives. People who give have an authentic faith and those who are learning to give are growing in their authenticity.

... We give out of hearts that overflow with gratitude for God's great grace. If we've experienced even a taste of his love, forgiveness and strength, we won't grouse about giving. Instead we'll be thrilled to participate with God in his great work.[159]

... The concept that everything in the universe was created by God and is owned by him shatters our self-absorption. Those things we treasure so much aren't ours at all. They are God's, and he's just loaned them to us for a while. We are stewards of the riches, resources, and possessions he has entrusted to us. ...

Grasping the fact that God owns it all helps me open my hand and present to him all that he has given me. I tell him, "Here, Lord. All this is yours. What do you want me to do with it?" That prayer is a far cry from daydreaming all day about more and bigger stuff! And knowing that God owns it all helps me when I'm shopping because I realize that many of the things I buy, I just don't need at all. That money could be used much more powerfully in other ways.[160]

The excerpts from the article that follows provide a point of departure for getting into a broader understanding of the specifics of the differences between needs and wants. "Harvard's Coles senses a turning from the success cult among many college students. 'Right now there are almost 1,000 [Harvard] students doing volunteer work with the elderly, or as tutors with children,' Coles points out. He regards this as a hopeful sign of 'decency, compassion and sensitivity to others. ...' Some graduate students in professional schools, on the other hand, still seem preoccupied with their personal ambitions."[161]

The article ". . . lays bare the marrow of the problem, namely, the nature of people's wants. If Americans wish to strike a truer ethical balance, they may need to re-examine the values that society so seductively parades before them: a top job, political power, . . . a penthouse or lakefront spread, a killing on the market. The real challenge would then become a redefinition of wants so that they serve society as well as self. ..."[162] It also touches on many of the key issues related to my thesis and provides a framework for a discussion that includes all the key issues: the importance of decency, compassion and sensitivity; personal ambition; self-interest; a redefinition of wants. The next step will be to take this framework and apply it first to Christians, and then everyone else.

The vision of the American Dream tugs at all of us:

1. homes (furniture, appliances, remodeling, square feet of living space);
2. vehicles (price and options on cars, vans, SUV's, pick-ups);
3. electronics (smart phones, computers, iPads, flat screen TVs and music systems);
4. recreation, leisure and entertainment (boats, snowmobiles, campers, motor homes, vacation homes, country clubs, fitness clubs and season tickets for sports or the arts); and
5. a retirement where we can do some of things we've always wanted.

All of these are blessings intended for our enjoyment. There is nothing inherently evil or immoral with any of them. The challenge is to define the difference between needs and wants and to maintain a balance in the context of our consumer-driven, materialistic culture. Maintaining that balance is tough given that our decision making as consumers reflects sophisticated marketing techniques used to manipulate and influence our choices. We don't think about how rich we are in part because we have been brainwashed into thinking that the accumulation of all this stuff is our birthright, and in part because the essence of the promise of America is the opportunity to pursue the American Dream. In the process it is easy to lose our moral compass and the ability to distinguish between needs and wants.

Who decides what is a need and what is a want? The Christian ethic provides an excellent structure that can be used to guide the process of seeking an answer. Therefore, I will discuss needs and wants from a Christian perspective, remembering all that Christ has done for us, the many brothers and sisters in the human family who are in desperate need, the very comfortable lives we live and the cautions that the Bible gives about being too attached to material things. "No servant can serve two masters. Either he will hate the one and love the other, or he will be devoted to one and despise the other. You cannot serve both God and Money" (Luke 16:13). I would also submit that these Christian principles offer significant potential benefit when generalized and applied by the entire population.

Jesus' love for us guides us as we make specific decisions and conscious choices in the process of putting together a budget. The very first line item for Christians is the amount for church and charity. For years, setting aside a tithe has been suggested as reflecting Biblical teaching. Tithing is a big challenge for those with small household incomes.

A New Testament understanding of Christian stewardship, however, suggests that tithing is simply an important milestone on the journey to spiritual maturity. For Christians, the spiritual struggle is to move toward giving a double tithe, or even thirty percent or more of your income. At the same time the attraction of the American Dream keeps tugging on us. As stewards, choose we must.

Looking at the other line items in the budget, how much will we allocate for lodging: home, apartment, furniture, appliances, remodeling, square feet of living space, second home or time share? While no one can define the difference between needs and wants for your situation, Jesus' love guides us as we make the specific decisions and conscious choices necessary to establish specific amounts for each line item. Certainly *having it all* simply does not reflect the self-giving, self-sacrificing, selfless love of Christ for us. Comparing ourselves to others in our culture who have more just doesn't cut it as a measure that is reasonable and fair. Their decisions are between them and God, and we dare not judge them. How easy it is to justify and rationalize our decisions about spending by comparing ourselves to others—even to Christians who have not yet matured as stewards. Then how much is appropriate when making decisions about living space? We make that decision in response to all that our Lord Jesus has done for us.

It certainly isn't all cut and dried. There may be those who want to enjoy a nicer home or a vacation home, but are committed to including all or most of the proceeds from that home as a charitable gift in their estate plan. Our stewardship plan is a complex process that can include many variables and contingencies. As we are moved by God's love for us as shown by his sending Jesus to be our Savior, we develop an overarching stewardship plan based on sacrifice in order to be able to give generously to the unmet needs of others.

Another line item is for vehicles and transportation. The range of choices goes from basic, economic transportation to luxury and class. How nice of a car do you need? How many options are enough? When Christians buy a vehicle without consideration of the self-sacrificing love of Christ for us, the needs of others and where it fits in to our total stewardship plan, the decision is unacceptable. Most Christians don't agonize over this. Why should we? Maybe you can give witness and be an inspiration to others. Maybe you find great enjoyment in having an antique car, a '50s or '60s muscle car, Corvette, pick-up or convertible. Having one isn't just ok; it is something God intended for your enjoyment, something that can be accounted for within the big picture of your total annual budget and lifelong stewardship plan. However, we do need to think about these things within the context of our total stewardship plan. We are probably not giving sacrificially if we have a really nice home, a great vehicle, a fishing boat package, season tickets for our favorite football team and two weeks in a time share. *Having it all does not reflect the self-giving, self-sacrificing, selfless love of Christ for us.* Then how much is appropriate when making decisions about living space, vehicles and entertainment? We make that decision in response to all that our Lord Jesus has done for us. "I appeal to you therefore, brethren, by the mercies of God to present your bodies as a living sacrifice, holy and acceptable to God, which is your spiritual worship. Do not be conformed to this world, but be transformed by the renewal of your mind. . . " (Rom. 12:1-2; RSV).

When you look at the snapshot of the American Dream, we Christians have hundreds of thousands of choices to make about how to manage all that God has entrusted to our care. The materialism of the consumer-driven economy in which we live wants us to think that if we work hard and earn it, we deserve it. It is not easy to be a faithful Christian steward in our culture.

You're beginning to get the message. At all income levels we have choices to make. Living at or near the poverty line and barely making ends meet is not easy. You see so many in our nation who have so much more. Single moms and many households with both parents working don't have it easy. Many are struggling and may never be able to buy their own home. For those in our country with smaller incomes, the spiritual struggle is looking around, seeing folks who have so much more than we do, and yet trying to be generous. Those of us on easy street simply don't appreciate all of our possessions, and want to have more of the luxuries enjoyed by others. It is one thing to commit to sacrificial giving, if it means that you can barely afford the payment on your modest home. It is another to commit to being a sacrificial giver, if it means you have to choose between a larger mortgage payment needed to buy a bigger house or have enough to take a nice vacation every year. The choices are different for all of us who live in a country where all but a very few of us are rich compared to the average standard of living in the rest of the world.

For those of us who have children, there is another issue that is layered on top of those already noted. We need another line item for the education of our children. With a college education getting as expensive as it is today, our budget has to be stretched even further. Surely we can compromise sacrificial giving during those years when we incur considerable expense for education. I would suggest that our children are especially blessed when as a household we all make the sacrifices necessary to be able to supplement what the student can earn, and keep the amount of student loans to a minimum. Those in a position to send their children to college or a university have given their children a great start in life and after graduation can reallocate that line item as an annual addition to what they are already giving to church and charity as sacrificial stewards, or increase the charitable portion of their estate plan. What an appropriate thank-offering for the blessing of being able to provide your children a good education.

We need another line item for the grouping of issues related to retirement. Who knows when someone will have to go into assisted living, need nursing care or even the specialized care needed for Alzheimer's or dementia? Should we purchase long term care insurance? What about vacations, travel and leisure? We may want to make a significant contribution to meeting the needs of others, but don't want to give so much away that it jeopardizes the care plan for our golden years. Long term care insurance is very expensive. However, if long-term care needs have been met without using all of the resources set aside for that purpose, you can make provision in your estate plan to distribute the unused funds to church and charity. For those of us who have our own savings plan instead of a long-term care policy, it may mean that we maintain our current contribution level at 10 or 15 percent, rather than 20 or 25 percent. If we are blessed in a way that we don't need all of the savings set aside for long-term care, then we can similarly designate in our estate plan that the unused funds be distributed to church and charity according to our wishes.

We all need an estate plan that directs the distribution of assets that remain after we have gone to heaven. Who inherits what's left after care needs are met? Are you going to leave most of your estate to the children or relatives? Who in the world is going to criticize you for leaving your estate as an inheritance for your children? Through them you can be a blessing by providing educational funds for future generations. But where do gifts to church and charity fit into our estate plan? I am most definitely raising the issue as to whether or not for Christians there are ethical considerations reflecting Biblical principles that need to be taken into account when making decisions about the distribution of our estate. Again, we need to ask whether we are looking out not just for the needs of our own, but also for their wants at the expense of the unmet needs of others.

Unless there are special needs and circumstances, after you have provided for family and given your children an education, you have to ask how leaving your children a significant portion of your estate fits into your calling as a Christian steward who has a responsibility to continue to manage the blessings entrusted to your care even after you are in heaven by giving directives as to the distribution of any remaining assets. This is an issue with which we all have to wrestle. For Christians, finding the balance is informed and guided by a loving God who sent his Son to be our Savior, a Son who lived the self-giving, self-sacrificing, selfless life of a servant. All he did for us is the touchtone and key that guides us in our decision making about what we decide are needs and what we decide are wants, and how much of what remains in our estate we will to return to him at the end.

Making financial decisions is something we are called to struggle with as his disciples. At one point I saw the gray area between faithfulness and unfaithfulness as being quite broad; not any longer. Grey areas conveniently allow too much wiggle room where we can rationalize and justify choices that clearly ignore the call to discipleship based on the sacrificial love of Christ, who asks us to show our love for him by caring for the brother in need.

We all have to ask how this plays out in the decisions and choices we make. Can we judge another's decisions? No. Can we identify that point where someone has so much stuff that they have crossed the line from needs to wants? Not always. However, common sense tells us when we and others are not living the life of a disciple. Do those of us with means need to shoulder more of the burden for the weak and vulnerable? Specifically, if we claim to be believers in Jesus we do need to consider Biblical teaching that those with material possessions have the responsibility to help a brother in need. We are not just to "love in word or in speech but in deed and in truth" (I John 3:18; RSV).

Let's look at a suggested framework for a family budget.

1. Church and Charity
2. Food
3. Clothing
4. Housing (mortgage, rent and utilities)
5. Health Insurance
6. Education
7. Vehicle
8. Retirement Plan
9. Electronic Technology

10. Recreation and Entertainment
11. Estate Plan (including gifts to children, relatives and charity)

We are blessed abundantly and have many choices to make as we set our priorities. The choice to have a larger home for your family may mean that you choose lower priced, basic vehicles. Spending more on clothes or electronics, may mean you spend less on recreation and entertainment. If you love to travel or spend weekends and vacations in your camper or at your second home, you may make much more modest choices when it comes to your primary residence, vehicles, electronics, clothing and other recreation and entertainment. The same could be true if your family's priority is to have a great boat for fishing and water skiing, a country club membership or motor home; however, it certainly seems inconsistent with the Christian ethic to want to spend significant additional dollars in other categories. The Scriptures call us to live modestly and give generously. It is a struggle to sacrifice and deny yourselves, when you don't see others making similar sacrifices. The materialism and consumer mentality of our culture is both pervasive and contradictory to the Christian ethic.

Just because we are richly blessed in terms of having the income and resources needed to have lots of material things and be involved in all kinds of recreation, travel and entertainment doesn't mean we are entitled to have it all. Rather it means that God has given us the privilege of being a part of upper management in the stewardship of what is his. Being successful simply means that we will continue to live modestly, even as God positions us to be able to designate how significant amounts of our resources can be used to help the brother in need. You now have a much better idea of the issues we need to consider when evaluating how you are doing as a steward. Hopefully, you have been given enough food for thought and prayer to address the question as to whether you are looking out not just for the needs of your own, but also for their wants at the expense of the unmet needs of others.

Listen to Kieschnick again.

> Have you ever seen pictures of starving people in a Third World country and thought, "How sad. Too bad we can't do much of anything about it"? But is it true that we're helpless to meet that need? A fascinating article about John and Sylvia Ronsvalles, the founders of *Empty Tomb, Inc.* in Champaign, Illinois, tracked consumption and giving patterns of Americans and American Christians in light of desperate needs around the world. In "The State of Church Giving Through 2003," the Ronsvalles assert,

"If members of historically Christian congregations in the U.S. had given at the 10% level in 2003, there would have been an additional $156 billion available. The potential impact of this money is seen in the need statistics that could be addressed in Jesus name: $5 billion could stop the majority of 29,000 deaths a day around the globe among children under five, most of whom are dying from preventable poverty conditions; $7 billion could provide basic education for the world's children...." I find these statistics to be staggering, don't you? And especially so in light of Jesus' comments that "inasmuch as you have done it for the least of these my brothers, you have done it for me."

Too often, we excuse our selfishness and blind our eyes from the needs of others. We think, "Hey, I deserve everything I've got.... Or "I've worked hard for my money. I'm sure not going to give it away!" Or "Hey, it's their problem not my problem. Let them work for what they need. I've got enough to worry about."[163]

You and I are incredibly wealthy. "Well, no," some of us might be tempted to say, "I don't have a boat like Frank, or a new car like Janice, or a big house like the Marshalls." If we compare ourselves with the next level (or two or three levels) up the economic ladder, we'll always feel disappointed and sorry for ourselves. . . . Middle-class Americans enjoy a standard of living that would be the envy of the wealthiest people in the world only a couple of generations ago, and the envy of most of the world today. If you're going to compare, look through the eyes of gratitude and truth, not envy and demands.[164]

It comes down to everyday decisions about the cars and houses we buy, how much we spend eating out and the amount we spend on electronics, clothes, entertainment and travel. These are conversations we need to have with God in prayer and with the other members of our household. More often than not, sermons that indicate the need for decision making based on these principles are sermons that people don't want to hear. Suggesting the need to reflect on such decisions based on a higher standard of ethics, morals and values can stir righteous indignation, even downright hostility. But who cares? I can just disregard those parts of the sermon I don't agree with. My prayer is that the hearers moved by the Holy Spirit would see the light go on and want to learn more, and that the response would be, "Preach preacher, preach."

Bottom line, it is imperative that we have a conversation about finding a reasonable consensus as to what constitutes our needs, and when do we cross over into the realm of wants? It seems to me that common sense tells us when something feels more like a want than a need. This is a conversation that needs to be had. It begins with recognizing the reality of evil and its manifestation as self-interest and greed. Once evil takes hold and greed and self-interest get their foot in the door, they want to do more than drop by for a visit. They want to move in, take over and rearrange the furniture. If we're honest with ourselves, we'll admit they already have. It is tough to own the truth that deep down we are rotten to the core, that the essence of our being is self-interest and greed personified. Acknowledging that truth about ourselves is almost too painful to bear. It hurts so much to admit that we are motivated by naked self-interest that we have to repress and deny it. We bury that reality really deep. What we want to believe is that, "basically, we're good people" who take care of our own.

There is a difference between living lives that are self-sacrificing, self-giving, and selfless over against lives that are self-centered, self-serving and self-seeking. In contrast to Christ looking out for us and putting our needs before his own, we look out not just for the needs of our own, but also for their wants, at the expense of the unmet needs others. This sermon asks us to do some soul searching relative to how much we really care about the unmet needs of others. We are constantly challenged to make lifestyle choices that are in conflict with what we hear in church on Sundays. We are so used to a life full of all sorts of stuff. Some haven't yet learned that you don't have to have all that stuff to be happy.

We've come to believe that we are entitled to our fair share of the American Dream. When the preacher starts sticking his nose in where we don't think it belongs, we don't like it one bit. We don't want a religion that asks us to do some reflection and soul-searching about whether or not our belief that "basically, we're good people" is really true. We aren't all that excited about a religion that teaches sacrifice and self-denial. The preacher has no right to make us feel guilty. These are the sermons nobody likes. The more specifics that are added, the less we like them.

The Pitfalls of Needs Giving

There is an implicit danger in the pattern of charitable giving known as *needs giving*. *Needs giving* is putting ten or twenty bucks into the Salvation Army kettles several times during the Christmas season, contributing $50 or $100 to help Lawrence O'Donnell provide "Desks for Africa" or participating in a community fundraiser to help purchase a specially equipped van for a middle-class family overwhelmed with expenses incurred caring for a child born with severe disabilities. While doing much good, making your contributions in this way can "contribute" to a false and inflated sense of what we're really like.

Don't misunderstand me. These and the hundreds of other needs just like them are great causes, and it is fantastic that we step up the way we do. So many meaningful needs are being met. It is a wonderful blessing to those in need when our hearts are touched and we are moved to respond by making a contribution.

We pull together as neighbors, as communities and as a nation when there is a crisis. We give following natural disasters like floods, tornadoes, wildfires and earthquakes, or local tragedies like house fires or mine explosions. We give to special funds for those who can't afford the expensive medical treatment needed following accidents or for the treatment of a rare disease. Some contribute to food pantries, rescue missions and shelters for battered women and the homeless.

What I'm asking is that you take time to review and evaluate how much you give. Do you have a budget that designates a specified percentage for annual giving to church and charity? This is different than just random giving when your heart is touched by something like Katrina, the earthquake in Haiti, the tsunami in Banda Ache or the tornado destruction in Tuscaloosa or Joplin. There is a pitfall when standard operating procedure for us is to give only when touched and moved by a natural disaster or emergency; as this pattern of giving may not reflect much depth of caring and compassion.

Providing assistance in times of need is important and a tremendous blessing to those who receive it. Yet, in the process we may deceive ourselves into thinking that now we have done our fair share, that we have done our part and that we have given back. We begin to believe that we are more generous than is actually the case. The danger is that giving to veterans on Poppy Day, buying Girl Scout cookies and giving $25, $50 or even $100 here and there during the year can salve our conscience, get rid of most of our guilt and make it possible to see ourselves as, basically good people. *Needs giving* can lead to the illusion that you are kinder, more caring and more compassionate than would be indicated by comparison with any realistic standard.

Needs givers are those who do not have a household budget that includes an annual giving plan with a specific percentage designated for church and/or charity. The result is that while their charitable contributions help so very much, they usually involve little if any sacrifice. It is a whole lot different when you adopt a household budget with a line item that includes an emergency fund. If the total amount designated for natural disasters and local tragedies isn't all needed in one year, the balance can be carried over as an addition to next year's emergency fund or distributed immediately to a religious or charitable need that is already on your list of favorite designated recipients. You're getting a sense that I want to emphasize the importance of going about this process with intention. Charitable giving isn't just the practice of giving when we are touched and moved by the need. Rather it is recognizing the magnitude of the need that is out there, in the context of our tendency to look out not just for the needs of ourselves and our own, but also for our wants, at the expense of the unmet needs of others. What is important is whether or not the sum total of our giving reflects a sacrificial gift.

Managing the Use of Time

The stewardship of our time is another touchy subject, maybe not as touchy as money, but it gets our attention. My concerns are the same. Namely, we come nowhere near the point of realizing our full potential in setting aside time for volunteer service. Even those who do volunteer have not given much thought to evaluating our volunteer efforts using our potential as the baseline. In order to do a self-assessment we have to bring some measure of specificity and preciseness to the discussion. It helps to keep a log and chart our use of time by category. While this may seem tedious and unnecessary, it is the only way to accurately evaluate how well we are doing. Most of us only have a general idea how we're doing, which usually leads to an inflated perception of our "goodness."

Primary Responsibilities and Activities

Worship – in church and devotions at home

Relationship commitments as spouses and parents

Employment

Education

Exercise: working out, walking, biking, swimming

Time with friends and relatives

Volunteer Service

Recreation, Leisure and Entertainment

We could name hundreds of wholesome and enjoyable activities, all of which are wonderful gifts of God. We do need time for "rest and re-creation:"

- travel;

- sewing, knitting, quilting, ceramics, etc.;

- gardening;

- playing cards;

- reading;

- listening to music;

- outdoor recreation: baseball, golf, tennis;

- indoor recreation: bowling and basketball;

- computer and phone: surfing the net, social media, games;

watching TV; and

going to movies, concerts and sporting events.

Why do Christians want to use their time wisely? They want to take care of the primary responsibilities God has given them, have some time for rest, recreation and renewal, and then allocate as much time as possible for volunteer service. Logging and charting use of time by category gives us a picture of how we use our time that can be quite revealing. The point is that you have to find the proper balance. As with the stewardship of financial resources, we also have to make choices when it comes to recreation, leisure and entertainment.

Again, once we have fulfilled the primary responsibilities we have committed to in relationships as spouse, parent and/or provider, then as Christians we are called to use our talents, gifts and abilities for volunteer activities in church and/or community. We just have to find the balance between time needed for R & R and the time we set aside for volunteer service. It would seem that if you spend two hours a day watching TV, two hours a day on your computer, play dart-ball or basketball one evening a week and then go fishing on the weekend, with no time set aside for volunteer service, that the stewardship of your time that week is way out of balance. If your typical daily routine includes spending two hours reading, an hour in the garden and two hours watching TV with little if any time set aside for volunteer service each week, then the stewardship of your time is way out of balance. If you spend Sunday watching your favorite football team, an hour or two watching TV two or three more times a week and play golf on the weekend, with only an hour or two a month set aside for volunteer service, then the stewardship of your time is way out of balance. Spending an hour a day in the garden, a couple of hours watching TV, and two or three hours a day quilting or doing ceramics, and a half hour a day reading the paper, with only an hour or two set aside for volunteer service each month, then the stewardship of your time is way out of balance.

We do need to stop and think about it. Logging and charting the use of your time to see where you fall on the continuum that indicates more or less Christian maturity can be very helpful. It is absolutely essential that we make a conscious and intentional effort to evaluate and monitor the use of our time. When measured by our potential, we need to get a sense of how much time we take for ourselves, and how much time we make for meeting the needs of others.

Time for TV, or on your computer or iPad, enjoying Facebook and tweeting, recreational activities like rock climbing, hiking, working out or baseball, your hobby, reading, fishing and hunting are all wonderful blessings that afford opportunity for relaxation and fitness, rest and renewal. However, use of free time in these ways becomes problematic when they get out of balance with how much time we spend as volunteers. It is important to maintain a balance in your life, and not spend 10 hours a week enjoying a hobby or reading, ten hours watching TV, eight hours on your computer or iPad or playing video games, and then just one hour a week as a volunteer.

The allocation of time can be balanced out over a year to accommodate a vacation, a week's fishing trip to Canada or deer hunting. Some activities are more time intensive during certain seasons. You can compensate by putting in more volunteer hours during the other months of the year. Again, the point is to recognize the importance of going about this process with intention.

Special Circumstances

Being a Single Parent

Having a Special Needs Child

Caring for Aging Parents

Time Consuming Commute to Work

Illness and Disability

Working Two Jobs:

> living at poverty line—barely able to make it, or

> helping to put the kids through college.

Retirees need time for R & R too, including activities like chatting and "holding court" in the morning over coffee and breakfast at the local café or "burger-biggie." But the bunch that gathers for coffee and conversation can also set aside time for caring and kindness. The same goes for those who gather at their local community center for a noon meal. Retirees also need to chart the use of their time. Seniors can also participate in the service opportunities at their church or in their community. They are not just there to be served, but also to help and serve others to the degree that it's physically possible. They may want to contact local nursing homes or the nearest VA hospital or veterans home, and find out if there are any residents who don't get many visitors. Retirement is not just about kicking back, taking it easy and doing all of the things you have always wanted to do. My sense is that many retirees feel that they have worked hard all their life, and are entitled to kick back and just enjoy life. Common sense informs retirees as they evaluate whether they are self-giving, self-sacrificing and selfless, or self-centered, self-seeking and self-serving.

I have a good friend who is retired and in good health. Since Katrina he has regularly volunteered to join teams from his church affiliated with Samaritan's Purse. They go on location to help in response to the many natural disasters we have experienced these past years. He is a talented carpenter and together with other guys who have that gift, they help with the clean-up and repairs. He is now a team leader who has returned to the gulf coast many times. He could afford to hire someone to go in his place, but he chooses to do it himself, remains active in his local congregation and generously supports their ministry.

There are so many ways in which we use the time designated for recreation, leisure and entertainment—our *free time*. When we add up such activities and compare the total to how much time we spend volunteering to serve and help others, the results for most of us are revealing. So what is an appropriate response? For Christians, it would seem like the minimum for volunteers could easily be 20 to 40 hours per month. Of course, it depends on your circumstances. Some are able to do more. Some have their hands full of responsibility already: caring for a child with special needs, a grandchild or an aging parent. They simply don't have as much time available to volunteer as others do and may only be able to serve four or five hours a month. Look, I have no right to evaluate or judge whether what someone is doing is enough. All I know is that those who love Jesus because of all he has done for them are cheerfully eager and ready to serve whenever and wherever they can.

A Challenging Summary of Stewardship Issues

The purpose of the discussion of the stewardship of financial resources and time is intended to surface issues that some of us may not think about or pray about nearly enough, and which we would prefer not be brought into our awareness. We would rather the sermon be about comfort, healing and forgiveness, about God's promises to sustain, support and encourage. The sermons we don't like are ones that are heavy on the specifics, as that's when it is much more likely that we will get nailed. This sermon is based on the premise that we don't realize all the ways we spend money until we see it written down, and we don't know where the time goes until we keep a log and chart the ways we use it. When we see both our budget and a chart of our use of time written down in black and white, it can be a real eye opener and get very uncomfortable. We feel like we are entitled to spend our money and use our time any way we want. Well, we are indeed free to make those choices. Whether we're entitled to or not is a whole different question. Certainly, Christians are called to a high standard of obedience in response to all that God has done for us in Christ.

Every once in a while you hear Americans referred to as the most generous people on Earth. While we may be the most generous by comparison, even that is not saying much. If human beings are a bunch of greedy, self-centered, self-serving misers, then we may simply be the most generous of the bunch.

This is true for middle-class Americans who have a nice home, two vehicles, maybe a pick-up truck or recreational vehicle, a boat, a snowmobile or a camper. We are living pretty high on the hog. All the while we remain indifferent to the plight of those who are burdened and struggling in misery and need. In Bible times it was the orphans, the widows and the poor, which is the equivalent of the suffering, the starving, the rejected, the unwanted and the forgotten of our day. The way most people relate to others in need in our country and all over the world may not change, but you can. You can be different. Just because others are convinced that their current lifestyle is one of high ethical and moral standard, it doesn't mean that it's true, or that it justifies our living the same way. Their mantra is, "We've worked hard for it! We've earned it! We deserve it." While what they say may be technically true, they forget that they were blessed to be born in the USA—not Somalia.

Most of us see ourselves as decent, neighborly, law abiding citizens who believe that, "basically, we're good people." Maybe we're civilized and decent, but thinking that we are good is at best a delusion. Most of us don't come close to being kind, caring and compassionate. How can we be so calloused as to think we can spend our time and money any way we want, when there are so many in our world who are starving and in desperate need, and whose modest hope is to live in safety and dignity? If we don't say it, we act like it is every man for himself. If we don't admit it, we act as if our organizing principle is the survival of the fittest. The truth is we are self-centered, self-serving, self-seeking folk who look out not just for the needs, but also for the wants of ourselves and our own at the expense of the unmet needs of others. This is the kind of sermon nobody likes. The response of the hearer on a good day might be something like, "Lighten up, preacher! What are you, one of those religious fanatics'?"

Maybe I am, depending on how you define it. I'm not advocating that we all become monks and nuns. I'm not advocating that like the aesthetics we give away all of our possessions. But I am most certainly saying that we have a whole lot to learn about living frugally and modestly. I am saying that most households need to begin a radical transformation in the ethics, morals and values that determine our lifestyle. I am saying that God wants us to use all of his gifts with an eye on his kingdom. And being a part of his kingdom involves behavior that many would label fanatic. We consider others as being as important as ourselves. We who have the world's goods do not close our hearts to those in need. We eagerly desire to approach what it means to sacrifice. We want our behavior to resemble that of an ethical and moral obsessive-compulsive disorder. While we may not give away all of our possessions, we will not hang on to more than we need. These are the sermons nobody wants to hear.

Others may laugh at those of us who give and serve sacrificially, and desire to do even more. They may think we are suckers. But we see ourselves as being indifferent, uncaring, cruel and inhuman, unless and until we adopt a self-giving, self-sacrificing, selfless lifestyle, reflected in the stewardship of our time, talents and treasure. We are the ones who shout, "Preach preacher, preach." We want to be challenged by God's Word and strengthened by that Word to pursue a life of Christian maturity. We want to be able to spiritually discern the difference between needs and wants. Yet, for most of us, our charitable giving is only a fraction of what it could be and our volunteer efforts do not come near realizing our potential. And we really don't want to hear one more sermon about it.

Chapter 9
The Sermons Nobody Wants to Preach

"But the call to follow Jesus in the narrow way was hardly ever heard."
Dietrich Bonhoeffer

"When they saw the courage of Peter and John and realized they were unschooled, ordinary men, they were astonished and they took note that these men had been with Jesus. . . . Then they called them in . . . and commanded them not to speak or teach at all in the name of Jesus. . . . After further threats they let them go. . . . Now, Lord, consider their threats and enable your servants (Peter and John) to speak your word with great boldness" (Acts 4:13,18,21 and 29).

Bonhoeffer's reference is to a passage from "The Sermon on the Mount" in Matthew 7: 13-14: "Enter through the narrow gate. For wide is the gate and broad is the road that leads to destruction, and many enter through it. But small is the gate and narrow the road that leads to life, and only a few find it." The application was to preachers whose sermons lacked boldness, clarity and conviction. Hanged by Nazi SS Black Guards in April 1945, he deserves the authority and respect worthy of one who was martyred for his faithfulness and his passion, for speaking and acting with great boldness.

No Fire in the Belly

It caught me off guard a number of years ago when a well known lay leader in the Milwaukee area told me that we young preachers didn't have any fire in our belly, like the old-timer's did. He was referring to the "hell, fire and brimstone" sermons of an earlier era. However, with all of the fervor and energy that characterized many of the sermons of old, my concern about today's preaching was also true of the old-timers. Is today's preaching about discipleship too generic? Has our teaching and preaching about discipleship lacked specificity? Is "the call to follow Jesus in the narrow way …ever heard. . . . What (has) happened to all those warnings of Luther's against preaching the gospel in such a manner as to make men rest secure in their ungodly living?"[165] Bonhoeffer speaks about preachers and preaching from the position of honor and reverence due one who in every sense of the word was a disciple and churchman. He was a man on fire in speaking up for the Lord Jesus, whom he dearly loved. By contrast it is with the humility of a mediocre preacher with no standing, who has great respect and admiration for his colleagues in the ministry that I try to write a chapter about what I see as a significant flaw in our preaching. I proceed humbly, and with great hesitation, reservation and caution.

I also proceed with great hesitation for another reason. The Eighth Commandment teaches that we are to explain everything in the kindest possible way. When studying this commandment way back in confirmation class, I learned another version of the meaning that included the words, "put the best construction on everything." It is my hope and prayer to honor the Eighth Commandment while writing.

My sense is that preachers today do not have a lot of fire in their belly. An encounter with the risen Christ transformed timid, fearful Peter. This was the disciple who during Jesus trial denied knowing him three times—and yet he became a man of courage who spoke boldly of Christ, even in the face of threats and imminent danger. Throughout the Church we need a similar transformation.

You go to church to listen to what God has to say to you that day through the liturgy, Scripture readings and sermon. You go to listen to what God is saying to you through the proclamation of the preacher based on a portion of Scripture. I have always tried especially hard not to evaluate or critique preaching. Nevertheless, after much prayer, and while I'm very uncomfortable doing so, it seems necessary. The pastors in the congregations where we have been members, the pastors with whom I have been privileged to serve and our current pastors are the ones I have listened to most. We get along great and I anticipate some great conversation about all of this. Over the years I have also listened to the sermons of many others and have read hundreds more in the books of sermon resources available to us. My comments and observations reflect an evaluation of the cumulative record of my experience of all the sermons I have heard and read over the years.

For me there is a characteristic that transcends how personable and dynamic the preacher, the length of the sermon or whether the preacher reads too much of it. The defining issue for me is the preacher's willingness to include the totality of all that God wants to say to us. Forgiveness, support, comfort and encouragement come to us as a free gift through God's absolutely fantastic and unfathomable love for us in Christ. There is one more element, however, that needs to be added to the list—the one that is most often left out in the totality of the balanced spiritual diet with which God wants to feed us. The element that gets short-changed is the proclamation of the full meaning of the call to discipleship, including specific examples of what a life of discipleship looks like. These are the sermons nobody wants to preach.

Just yesterday, while in the process of working on this chapter, we were in service as visitors in another congregation. A friend was retiring and being recognized for his years of faithful service. The pastor did a great job of leading the liturgy, and his sermon was extremely well prepared and engaging. I wish I had his gifts. My deep sadness was that while the sermon set the table for a powerful call to surrender and commitment as disciples, when the main course was served, he waffled. It was watered down, bland and lacked a call to Christian commitment and service—a huge disappointment. I've known the guy who was retiring for years and he was an exemplary disciple. The preacher squandered a fantastic opportunity to describe the surrender, commitment and dedication characteristic of faithful followers of Christ and a call and challenge to live that life with God's help, as the servant we were recognizing had done. It was one of those weak, generic calls to discipleship that I have heard so often. Why wasn't there more of a challenge to those present? What am I missing?

We visited with some of their members both before and after the service, and they were dedicated and faithful people. Yet my sense is that due to a lack of being challenged, they have not yet come close to realizing their full potential as disciples. Oh how I have prayed that I am wrong, asking for forgiveness for my judgmental and critical thoughts—violations of the Eighth Commandment. I look forward to any correction and chastisement I may need from my fellow pastors, and stand ready (kneel is more like it) to repent and ask for forgiveness.

Sermons with Specifics Have More Wallop

When you reflect on my thesis expressed in general terms, then add the specifics, those general statements take on a whole lot more meaning. All of a sudden the same sermon gets very personal and packs quite a wallop. It sounds different when you hear the call to have Jesus as Lord of your life and not just the Savior of your soul. When commitment and surrender in your role as a steward of time and financial resources are explained in plain English, obedience to Jesus as Lord of your life means so much more. Moving from a generic presentation to one that is quite specific gives the same sermon a dramatically different meaning. When you hear a call to discipleship that involves denying yourself, taking up your cross and following him, without mincing words when it comes to the specifics of the application, it means so much more than the generic version you usually hear.

Now that you have a much clearer understanding of what the call to discipleship is all about, you have a much better idea why it is that one would hope we Christians would live life with a sacrificial mentality. Yet, we continue to substitute our agenda for God's, and to pursue our goals, hopes and dreams rather than his. It's not that the generic version doesn't effect change. It can and does. It just makes it so much harder. It's almost like we're trying to put obstacles in the path of our hearers. Some do figure it out for themselves and are deeply moved. However, when the preacher makes the application in clear and unequivocal language, the effect is multiplied many times over. The hearer can much more easily dismiss the generic. Again, it's like Bonhoeffer said: "What (has) happened to all those warnings of Luther's against preaching the gospel in such a manner as to make men rest secure in their ungodly living?"[166]

Pastors also know that many in their flock are troubled, and how much they are looking forward to Sunday and a message that offers comfort, forgiveness, encouragement and peace. Pastors know the members who are hurting, and whose lives are a mess. Pastors hurt with them, cry with them and pray for them more than their people will ever know. Pastors know the kind of sermons their people want to hear. And God's Word does not disappoint; it speaks powerfully to all of this. God's Word offers forgiveness for their sins, brings relief from their pain and calms the storms and troubled waters in their lives. God's Word brings comfort to those who are grieving and overwhelmed by sadness and loss, and restores to wholeness what has been broken. God's Word gives guidance on how to clean up the messes we have made. Pastors know what kind of sermons their people want to hear. The messages of comfort and encouragement mean so much to those who are distressed and overwhelmed by what is happening in their lives. God's Word is a powerful message of the hope and promise that are ours in Jesus Christ.

At the same time, remember, preachers have a calling from God to comfort the afflicted and afflict the comfortable. Pastors know that their members don't even like the generic, watered-down version of stewardship sermons. They respond to stewardship sermons that get specific, as they would to cleanser in a bathtub. Stewardship sermons that get specific make it harder to go through the spiritual gymnastics necessary to maintain the image that, basically, you're a good Christian and a good person.

Our seven year old grandson Bryan swings a pretty mean bat and expresses what can only be described as pure delight each time he hits the ball so hard that it "nails" Grandpa, whose reactions are too slow to either catch it or duck out of the way. Actually Bryan embraces all of life with that same joy, enthusiasm and energy, and is a pure delight to have around. In case you didn't know, even a Wiffle Ball leaves quite a welt. The frequency of getting nailed is directly correlated to when Grandpa backs up a few steps before making the next pitch—especially important now that we're using a hard ball. Believe me—preachers take absolutely no delight in nailing their parishioners.

However, it is our calling to be sure the message is proclaimed to our hearers in a way that makes it perfectly clear that they have been sinful (self-centered, self-serving and self-seeking), and doesn't let them wiggle off the hook or duck out of the way of the truth. They get nailed, and that is the preacher's intent. Parishioners keep backing farther and farther away. They keep resisting. But the preacher keeps nailing them, even when they get to the big leagues with the pitcher's mound at a distance of 60 feet 6 inches from home plate. When we're addressing spiritual issues, we're no longer in Little League, or even high school or college ball. We're not even playing in the minors. We're playing with the big boys; we are addressing major league issues about the meaning of life. If the preacher is faithful to his calling, those of us who are hearers are going to continue to get nailed. When we get nailed spiritually, we tend to back away a little. We fortify our defenses even further in order to avoid the pain involved in facing the truth about what we're really like. Just in case you didn't know it, preachers are preaching to themselves first and foremost. Hmm! Maybe that's why we avoid preaching the sermons nobody wants to hear.

Preachers do not get a mischievous little glint in their eyes or derive any sadistic pleasure when they nail their hearers. We nail them because we love them and care about them very much. We want so very much for them to discover the overwhelming joy and pure delight that comes with the insight and awareness of realizing just how far we have strayed from the path of discipleship and just how much we have been forgiven. The message of forgiveness brings along with it release from the burden of sin and guilt, an unspeakable joy and a calming peace. I have lived a self-centered, self-serving, self-seeking life where I have looked out not just for the needs, but also for the wants of myself and my own at the expense of the unmet needs of others, and yet forgiveness is mine in Jesus. I keep trying to get my arms around the breadth of God's love for me, but I just can't. It is more than I can comprehend. I am overcome with indescribable joy and gratitude.

Most folks don't think of themselves as all that bad and don't want to be called out as sinners. Ironically, preachers really don't want to preach about sin either. They may dabble in preaching generically about our being sinners. But they hesitate when it comes time to spell out the specifics. Now I have to be careful as I'm again bordering on being judgmental, critical and blaming. However, it seems clear to me that the pervasiveness of sin in our lives tends to be grossly understated. Sin contaminates every fiber of our very being. We are a spiritual mess. We hear some generalizations about sin, but we're way too gentle and timid in exposing what people are really like. On Sunday we assure the flock of forgiveness and send them on their way with a little spanking, rather than the unvarnished truth. We repeatedly miss the opportunity for another stinging indictment that compels serious spiritual soul searching and leads to even greater appreciation of God's love and forgiveness and a response that gives evidence of an increase in commitment and surrender.

All too often our hearers leave the service and continue on living their lives pretty much like they did before they came to the service, lives that don't look all that different from everybody else. Oh, maybe their language isn't as coarse and vulgar as some. Maybe they avoid gross immorality. Yet, when it comes to being self-sacrificing, self-giving and selfless in their service to others, they aren't much different than the general population.

Parishioners don't like it one bit when challenged to face the truth about themselves—what they're really like. It's painful to see ourselves as we are: no masks, no illusions, no rationalizations. Members don't like to have to do any soul-searching about human nature and whether they themselves are altruistic or egocentric. How dare you suggest that I'm not a good person! How could you even entertain the thought that I'm not a good Christian? However, this is exactly what happens when the sermon is a clarion call to the life of joyful obedience described in the Scriptures. But that is only one of the two essential parts of the sermon. The second part is that Christ "sold out" for us when he died on the cross so that our sins are forgiven. The Gospel message is what compels us to "sell out" for Christ, knowing that he "sold out" for us. We find in him our reason for being, loving and serving.

Go Along and Get Along

I already shared the story of our visit to a congregation in Steeler country, where the pastor was a prophetic voice calling for a discipleship of surrender and sacrifice. This is not the kind of message that most of our people want to hear. Most Christians would prefer sermons about Jesus as the shepherd who comforts and cares for them, about Jesus as the sacrifice who died on the cross for our sins.

My wife's comment that day was, "That was one of our kind of sermons." At the time I was serving at St. John's Lutheran in West Bend, Wisconsin. The Senior Pastor had a heart for the Lord and a passion to give his all in service. Dan was an inspiration to me. His previous call was to serve as a missionary in Bulgaria just after the "iron curtain" and the Berlin Wall came down. Yet, Christians continued to experience oppression under the government that remained in place. With four children under the age of five, including a four month old baby, he and Rachel embarked on a journey to serve in a ministry where the lifestyle was much more primitive than ours. I accepted the call to serve the people at St. John's as his Associate primarily because of his vision and his passion, and because I knew he had a heart for the Lord that didn't quit.

He wanted our sermons to be a balance of what people want to hear and what they need to hear. He set the tone and vision of how we needed to challenge our people to a life of discipleship, faithfulness and service. They were the kind of sermons that made people very uncomfortable, because they called for a level of commitment and dedication that is way beyond that which most people are looking for when they become church members. Yet, I am convinced that our sermons also didn't include enough of the specifics, and therefore compromised the challenge of a prophetic call to discipleship. Our lack of specificity muted the impact. We did begin to include a clearer picture of a radical call to discipleship in the ministry plan, for the assimilation of new members. I can't wait until he reads this to see what he has to say about it. It could be another of those great conversations we used to have, candidly sharing our views and challenging each other.

Earlier in my ministry I served at Trinity, Peoria as Associate to Jerry Freudenberg, a faithful, caring pastor and friend. From early on the centerpiece of Jerry's sermons was that "God is to love." Later he coined the term "TIGLTYTY"—Trust in God's love to you and through you. We balanced each other quite well as my sermons were already tending thematically toward a more radical call to commitment and surrender as dedicated disciples. Looking back, however, my preaching in Peoria lacked the specificity needed to make them more effective.

Just a few years ago we did a round robin with neighboring congregations during the six Wednesdays of Lent. Each pastor prepared just one mid-week sermon and then preached it in their own congregation and five others. This is a huge time saver for preachers, as we had to prepare only one mid-week sermon instead of having to prepare two sermons a week for six weeks. It also gave our members opportunity to hear neighboring pastors preach the Gospel using different styles, constructs and language. "Gospel" is religious shorthand for "good news"—the good news that our sins are forgiven through Christ's suffering and dying on Good Friday's cross, and his rising from the grave on Easter morning to validate his victory over sin, death and the devil. Perhaps one of the other pastors in the area would frame the Gospel message in a way that would get through to some more effectively than their own pastor.

Preaching one week during a round robin at a neighboring church someone made a rather direct comment as he was leaving. He said, "That was a little heavy. You dropped quite a load on us for being a guest preacher at a Wednesday evening Lenten service." The sermon was one of those prophetic calls to a self-giving, self-sacrificing, selfless life of commitment and service, in response to the Gospel. "It was one of our kind of sermons." He knew what I was driving at. He heard. He understood. The power of the Holy Spirit was working through the Word in his life, or else he wouldn't have said anything other than a polite, "Good evening, Pastor."

On occasion there was a temptation to use the same dynamic for selfish purposes. The time to "nail 'em'" real good was on those rare Sundays when the Raiders had a game that was being televised with a noon kickoff in the Midwest, and I was in a hurry to get home for the game. We didn't have the technology to record our favorite programs back then. There was a good chance that if I preached about commitment and surrender together with a call to radical discipleship, that the greetings at the door would be brief. Nobody wanted to engage you in conversation about those sermons—thankfully, there were exceptions. On the days when there was a clear call to discipleship, there were also those present who I knew were hurting, and came to God's house seeking comfort, encouragement and hope. I would include their concerns in the prayers, and take time to visit with them afterwards.

The Spiritual "Sweet-Spot"

Timidity and a lack of specificity in preaching have been going on for centuries. The difference is that now we live in an affluent society, where average people have the potential to acquire so much more; and therefore, the specifics have the potential to have a much broader impact. After World War II American clergy were excited just to have so many folks in church. My sense is that they lost their focus on being prophetic in setting forth the vision of a discipleship of surrender, sacrifice and commitment taught in the Scriptures. Congregations were growing, offerings were increasing, Sunday Schools were full and everyone was happy. We had found the spiritual "sweet-spot."

It seems to me that the consequence was that parishioners were not challenged by Scriptural teaching about what discipleship is all about. As a result most Christians in mainline denominations like ours didn't radiate the dedication and zeal of disciples who loved their Lord for all he had done for them. The clergy were content, and so were the parishioners. It is very interesting to note, however, that a surprising number of members of mainline denominations were discouraged by the lack of vitality and passion. They began to seek out Christian congregations where members were more vibrant and alive, congregations where people were passionate about living out their faith in ministry and service. My sense is that this was a major factor in the decline of mainline denominations and the simultaneous growth of non-denominational congregations. Clergy in mainline denominations either didn't recognize this dynamic and see it as a wake-up call, or didn't know what to do. The laity that remained had no clue that they weren't living the life of passionate, dedicated disciples. A conversation like this would have been like speaking a foreign language to them. These were concepts with which they simply were not familiar. They were under the impression that they were good Christians.

Today the challenge for the clergy is that we have all—laity and clergy—been seduced by the good life that has become the cultural norm. Our preaching strategy exacerbates the problem in that we consciously choose to allow our members to remain insulated from the full impact of the call to discipleship. We cut our members too much slack, allowing them to be way too comfortable on a journey where they could be so much more faithful and find so much more joy and peace in lives of loving service.

As noted, when you shift from generic to specific, the same sermon packs a lot more wallop. Just what does a walk with the Lord look like? Just what does a life of obedience and surrender and loving service look like? It all begins with the celebration of the forgiveness of sin that is ours in Christ, and the assurance that where there is forgiveness, there is also life and salvation. The dynamic goes something like this. *We are sinners. Our self-centered human nature influences us to walk down a very different path than God would have us to follow. We bring our sins to God in confession, pleading for forgiveness. For the sake of Jesus who suffered and died on the cross— in our place, as our substitute, taking on himself the punishment our sins deserve—God exchanges our sins and in return gives us forgiveness. We respond freely, eagerly and willingly in grateful devotion with lives of obedience, surrender, commitment and service.*

We Christians are all on a spiritual journey. We are on the way, a work in progress. Sincere Christians who face the truth about themselves realize, as they reflect on the specifics, just how much they fall short of living out God's plan for their lives. They also know they are forgiven for getting sidetracked by an affluent, materialistic, consumer-driven culture and feel compelled to change by God's mercy and readiness to always forgive. Moved and strengthened by the Holy Spirit, we are ready to renew our efforts to be faithful. The call of God in the Scriptures is a call to obedience, willing obedience, not something you have to do, not a life where you comply out of fear that there will be hell to pay if you don't. Because we have been forgiven by the saving work of Jesus Christ, it is an obedience that is humbly submissive; it is something we want to do. We have received this fantastic, free and undeserved gift. And yet we aren't living lives of sacrificial service to God by loving and serving others, and we certainly don't like being challenged to do so by sermons that address the specifics.

It is likely that a huge majority of Christians today have never been shown the full and complete picture of what it means to be a disciple. We had no way of knowing what discipleship is all about unless we figured it out for ourselves by hearing the Word read in services or by reading the Bible at home. Timidity among the clergy results in a Christianity that compromises the teaching of what it means to live lives of obedience and surrender. It is perfectly understandable that by default Christians learn a diluted, watered down, compromised version of Christianity and the call to discipleship. Somewhere along the road to Christian maturity an unvarnished, uncompromised understanding of discipleship has to be taught. Somewhere along the road to Christian maturity folks have to learn what being a disciple is all about.

A Little Spanking

We go to church wanting the spiritual equivalent of a little spanking. Remember when you were a little kid and did something wrong, you waited for your parents to find out and give you a good scolding and a few pats on the butt. Then everything was ok again. You didn't have to worry any more about your parents finding out or what your punishment might be. Spiritually, we also like to get nailed just a little, with a generic, watered down sermon that tells us we're sinners. But, please, don't get carried away and make a really big deal out of it. We like to have our behavior framed in the context of relatively minor moral and ethical incursions into sin.

Then in the Sunday sermon we get our little spanking, get the punishment we deserve, and everything is ok again in our relationship with God; we're tight. It is interesting to note that the proverbial "hell, fire and brimstone" sermons served the same purpose; this is why some actually look forward to one every now and then. We sinners sit there and take our punishment. These pats on the butt don't sting much. Even when spoken in a soft, calm easy manner, sermons that teach the fullness of what is involved in the call to discipleship using specific examples, hurt a whole lot more than "hell, fire and brimstone." We are exposed as being self centered, and we don't like it. The preacher has closed the loopholes and eliminated the ambiguity that would allow wiggle-room, and we don't like it. There is no denying it, and we don't like it. There is no hiding, and we don't like it.

"Preacher, don't imply that I'm wicked, that I have the tendency to look out not just for the needs of myself and my own, but also for our wants at the expense of the unmet needs of those who are suffering and in desperate need." This is a touchy subject, and the responses can get real dicey for the preacher. "You can preach all the hell, fire and damnation you want. You can give us a good tongue lashing for our misdeeds and dalliances on the fringes of immorality. But don't you dare go for the jugular by suggesting that we are numbered among the wicked. Just don't go there." Members really get ticked off at the sermons that nail them, making a direct connection between their thoughts, attitudes and behaviors, and the realm of wickedness and ungodly living.

There is no way to carry out this prophetic role without triggering a maximum defensive response. You can't say it in a way that is gentle, non-judgmental and non-critical enough to avoid hitting their hot button. You try to meet people where they are by indicating that it is perfectly understandable why, given the influence of our culture, they have the outlook on life that they do. The reality is your hearers won't like it no matter how tactfully and sensitively you try and say it. They know themselves only too well, and they know exactly what you're talking about, and they don't want you to go there because it hurts.

"You can point out that at times I drink too much. You can say that I don't understand my wife and haven't been nearly as good of a husband as I could be. You can point out that I haven't spent enough time with my kids. And I need to be reminded that I spend too much time with the guys, bowling, playing baseball and fishing. But don't you dare tell me that I'm not caring, kind and charitable, or even suggest that I need to do some soul-searching about whether or not I'm a good person. Now you're getting too close, and you're way out of line."

Preachers are far too adept at accommodating the expectations of the flock, choosing to avoid the specifics that would nail grandpa and everybody else. The members line up in the pews to get their little spanking for having a few sinful thoughts, saying a few bad words and doing a few bad things. When the stewardship of time, talents and treasure is mentioned, we are gently chastised as being lukewarm. Preachers are far too timid. We don't set the bar nearly high enough. By omitting the specifics we implicitly give permission for a bland brand of Christianity that lacks commitment, boldness and fire. We lack a truly prophetic voice.

Look, we preachers know only too well what kind of sermons people want to hear and what kind they don't. We know exactly the kinds of sermons they like, and exactly the kind they don't. We know the kind of sermons that will elicit the "Fine sermon, Reverend," as people leave worship, and those that draw little if any response. It's no secret. Our people prefer a comfortable Christianity that does not inconvenience, and that does not get in the way of the pursuit of their goals, and hopes and dreams. They don't want to hear a prophetic word that gets really specific and threatens the comfortable life to which we have become accustomed. Sadly, we preachers sell out and compromise the truth and put our blessing upon what they perceive to be a good Christian life.

However, once we have been led in faith to know and see our hearts for what they are, self-centered, self-serving and motivated by self-interest, and in faith realize that Jesus also knows us inside out, sees us for what we are, and still loves us and forgives us, it is life transforming. It's like flipping the "on" switch. Now we want to be challenged and to learn what Christian discipleship, selling out for Christ and being totally devoted to Christ are all about.

In our walk with the Lord, we worship together as congregations at least once a week. In worship, we are nurtured spiritually and challenged by what the Scriptures teach through the lessons read and the sermon. We are challenged to a life of surrender and obedience on a continuum of discipleship that it is hardly recognizable within the context of the convenient belief system we have created for ourselves, a belief system that focuses on having our needs met and the pursuit of our own goals and dreams. My sense is that what we need to hear from the pulpit is that measuring Christianity on a scale of 1(immature) to 100 (fully mature), most of us can be found somewhere between level 24 and level 44. Oops! That seems harsh! Not really! It is probably being too kind. The actual numbers are probably between 14 and 34.

Bottom line – most Christians certainly don't live the life of a dedicated disciple. The temptation and pull of our materialistic culture is one part of the explanation. If the clergy do not give us a clear picture of what being a faithful follower of Christ looks like, the magnetic attraction of cultural influence is quite effective. The Gospel message framed in general terms and lacking specificity allows all kinds of loopholes and opportunities to rationalize and justify our perception that, "basically, we're good people." Without a doubt our timidity as preachers is a significant factor in accounting for the chasm that exists between the Scriptural model of discipleship, and how we live it out in our lives. The sermons we preach aren't that helpful to our people as they try to resist the temptations of our culture. By not proclaiming the full truth of God's Word, we allow them to perpetuate an illusion. All they get is a little pat on the butt. It doesn't hurt much. They hardly even notice it, and that's just the way they like it.

Totally Innocuous – Not the Least Bit Challenging

We learn from the Bible that faithful believers find favor in the eyes of God because of the forgiveness of sins freely offered to us through Christ's suffering and dying on the cross in our place, as our substitute, and are assured of eternal life in heaven. The rest of the story usually gets short-changed. It is at this point that the rest of the story is almost always omitted, namely, how the overwhelming joy and gratitude for forgiveness and eternal life transforms us into people who want to express our love and gratitude by living lives totally dedicated to his service, lives that honor our Savior. This last part is often minimized and understated. Not wanting to rock the boat, preachers shy away from the sermons people don't want to hear.

Others are afraid that we will give folks the impression that living lives of dedicated service and good works are the way we earn God's favor and the right to go to heaven. We don't do good works to get to heaven; we do good works because we have already been given the gift of heaven. We don't do good works in order to be saved. We live lives of dedicated, loving service because we have already been saved through the suffering and death of Jesus Christ. What part of the teaching about good works are we afraid people won't understand? We never have to worry whether we are good enough or have done enough to earn our way to heaven. We aren't and we don't.

When you preach in a way that a fourth grader can understand it, clarifying and amplifying the theme by adding the specifics, the sermon is packed with meaning. It sounds different when you hear the message that Jesus wants to be Lord of your life, not just the Savior of your soul. When you hear a call to discipleship that involves denying ourselves, taking up our crosses and following him, it means so much more than it did before. This preacher prays fervently that Christians will continue to grow in their spiritual maturity, continually moving toward a life lived with a sacrificial mentality. I just don't see it happening. I so very much want to see it. People continue to substitute their agenda for God's, and preachers are reluctant to call them on it.

Catholic Bishop Thomas J. Gumbleton echoes the same dynamic is a slightly different context.

> Few Catholics have poured over their bishops' lengthy pastorals on peace, justice and the economy. Now the nation's bishops have approved a more accessible version they hope will attract the average lay person.
>
> The bishops, in the 14-page document, call on every Catholic to promote human life and dignity and defend the poor in everyday choices.
>
> . . . The bishops' justice document is their most direct in making "the call for the ordinary believers to shape their lives in light of the search for justice. . . ."

But a critic and longtime social activist, auxiliary Bishop Thomas J. Gumbleton of Detroit, said the document doesn't go far enough.

"It's totally innocuous, not the least bit challenging," Gumbleton said. "It very mildly says that we should do something about simplifying our lifestyle. **But if you really want to challenge people, tell them they don't have a right to what is beyond their needs when others lack the barest necessities.**"[167]

Amen, brother! Now that was a call to discipleship. It expresses my sentiments exactly. That was "one of our kind of sermons." I agonized over preaching the sermons that challenged God's people to reach yet another level of spiritual maturity. How this pastor prayed that in joyful obedience the congregation inspired and motivated by the Holy Spirit would respond to the love of God shown in Jesus Christ. You want so much for your flock to find purpose and meaning in their lives, to find the joy and peace that comes with lives of humble and faithful service. Then you remember that you're only the "plain brown wrapper." You remind yourself that it is only the Holy Spirit working through the Word that can touch, empower and transform lives. Just speak that Word clearly and without apology, letting the Word convict the sinner, lead him to repent and turn his life around. But I'd better do it clearly without waffling, trying my best not to allow them any wiggle-room.

Sermons the Clergy Don't Want to Preach

For the most part, those who are not Christians don't see the differences they would expect to see in our lives based on what we claim to believe about a loving, accepting, self-sacrificing God who died on the cross in our place that we might have forgiveness and eternal life. The world does not see us as humble, forgiving servants who seek to meet need wherever we find it. Part of the reason non-Christians resent our efforts to evangelize is because it is readily apparent that we are spiritually and morally bankrupt. From their perspective, "We've got a lot of nerve." Because of this we as Christians stand under the strongest and most comprehensive indictment served against any of the self-seeking, self-centered and self-serving members in the human family. The Christ-like life, so beautiful to behold, is rarely found. Others "hear" the sermons we preach through our lives, note the obvious inconsistencies and are turned off. They look at how we live and they don't want anything to do with Christianity. Bottom line, we are the sermons that nobody likes. Yet, it is precisely those sermons that ask for more commitment and sacrifice that are not to the liking of rank and file Christians. And, the clergy seem all too willing to compromise principle and oblige the wishes of their members. We are the sermons non-Christians don't want to hear in large part because of the sermons we clergy do not want to preach.

There are several things I would humbly ask non-Christians observing us to consider. As just noted, the first is that most Christians have not been challenged by their spiritual leaders to a life of discipleship, a life of self-giving, self-sacrificing, selfless sacrifice and service that demonstrates our love for God in the way we love and serve our neighbor. Preachers don't like to preach sermons like these as part of the process of spiritual nurture that results in a growing and maturing into a life of discipleship. We have preached that which is innocuous and not the least bit challenging. Using the phrase "the least bit" might be overstating the case just a bit, but not much. Our proclamation of God's truth is so diluted and compromised that our hearers are cushioned, if not totally insulated, from the full impact of God's Word.

Second, we Christians are a work in progress. We are still in the process of being transformed. It might help if there were only some way that we could rightly divide those who are more mature in the faith from those who are not. Perhaps we have to limit membership in the visible church to those who are more deeply committed as demonstrated by a life of faithful service. Others would be welcome to come to services, participate in Bible study and serve alongside of us, where the Holy Spirit can work in them through the Word while they are still on a journey that will lead to Christian maturity. You would have to establish specific criteria for membership, which could be difficult—but is not impossible—to implement.

This is not to say that those who do not meet the criteria for membership are not Christians. Only God knows that. There is no intent to convey any sense that we can or should judge others. Rather, the intent is to find a way to get people's attention by conveying the message that the life of discipleship to which Jesus calls us is so very different from what most Christians think it is as to be hardly recognizable. We may also need to consider the idea for the benefit of non-Christians. They need to know that the behavior of most Christians is not representative of what Jesus taught. It is not representative of disciples who have a close, personal relationship with Jesus and walk daily with him. By so doing we would identify those they would label as hypocrites, those whose behavior is a stumbling block to Christianity. At the same time, by not perpetuating minimum standards for church membership, we would avoid the danger of giving so many Christians a false sense of spiritual security. Some congregations have adopted variations of this practice already.

Prophetic preaching that exposes members for who and what they are is not appreciated, not what people want to hear and often rejected. Again, we in the clergy know the sermons people don't like and don't want to hear. We know our people consider these sermons to be unrealistic, radical and even fanatical. We know they will become uncomfortable, defensive and angry and find ways to rationalize and justify not living according to God's will as it is taught in the Scriptures. We know they have their own ideas about the kind of religion they want. We know they pick and choose the teachings of Scripture they like and blend them into their own personal brand of Christianity, rather than being faithful to the scriptural call to discipleship. We have to preach all of this in a culture that surrounds them with a totally different reality. The attraction of the lifestyle to which we have become accustomed has the effect of sabotaging the call to commitment and surrender. The preacher is called to speak God's prophetic word in his time and place. It isn't easy. It isn't popular. These are sermons nobody wants to preach.

When you preach a challenging sermon and one of the faithful says, "I sure wish so-and-so was here for that sermon," or "There are a lot of folks who needed to hear that," you try not to show you are discouraged and sad. Rather, you assess the faith-life of each person, meet them where they are and continue to pray for guidance on how to help them grow. They need to be engaged, nurtured and fed at the level where they are on the journey to Christian maturity. They need to be led to the next levels of discipleship, challenged to a daily walk with the Lord and helped to develop a close personal relationship with him.

When we are not challenged to a life of commitment, dedication and faithful service characteristic of a mature faith, and we are not living that way, the world notices. They notice when are relating to others within and without the family of faith in ways that lack compassion, caring, understanding, reasonableness, thoughtfulness, consideration and respect. They observe and they wonder why. It is not hard to figure out why the world sees us as self-righteous, judgmental, critical and intolerant, rather than humble servants meeting needs wherever they are found. They don't see us practicing what we preach. And for this we stand under the strongest possible indictment.

We as pastors aren't being faithful to our call when we understate the meaning of discipleship. If discipleship is not taught as a self-giving, self-sacrificing and selfless life of service to our Lord, we compromise the truth. The heart of the matter is that we don't set the bar for discipleship anywhere near high enough, anywhere near the level where members are challenged to sell out for Christ and become totally devoted to him. By omission we give permission for a watered down, wishy-washy, lukewarm brand of Christianity that lacks conviction, boldness and passion. Since Christians can be found all along the continuum of maturity, we need to have a plan that picks people up at all levels of maturity, and inspired by God's saving love, invites them to grow into higher levels of surrender, obedience, commitment and service.

The clergy know the score. It's no secret. Rather than take up the challenge, the vast majority capitulate and find a niche where they can mind their own business and be comfortable. Why beat your head against a wall? Why wear yourself out trying? Why get depressed? All you have to do is lead worship each week, visit the sick and shut-in and be there for the baptisms, weddings, funerals. Don't get frustrated or burn yourself out preaching and teaching a vision opposed by the majority.

The preachers who are still faithful, devoted and passionate keep preaching and teaching messages that address the core values and organizing principles of our lives, the beliefs to which we are willing to commit ourselves and the convictions that inform our decisions and motivate us to act. These messages have to challenge us to look deep into our hearts and find out what it is that we believe life is really all about and how we respond when moved by the Holy Spirit. Somewhere in the congregation's ministry plan the call to discipleship has to be taught and emphasized. Somewhere along the road to Christian maturity folks have to learn what being a disciple is all about. People need to be challenged to sell out for Christ and totally dedicate their lives to him. Once I own that my heart is self-centered and self-serving and influences me to make decisions and choices based on self-interest, and yet my Lord Jesus Christ sees me just as I am, knows me like a book and still loves me and forgives me and doesn't give up on me, that assurance is transforming and life-changing.

Again, preachers know what their people want to hear. We also know what God calls us to do as his prophetic voice. If we as clergy fail to challenge people with the sermons and teachings they don't want to hear, we become responsible for the lack of passion and commitment we see among the laity. When we compromise or water-down what it means to be a disciple, then we assume partial responsibility for the lack of passion and commitment we see among our flock. Preaching sermons people don't want to hear is not popular, but that is a huge part of our job description. Allowing people to remain comfortable with the notion that while there are some shortcomings in their walk with the Lord that, basically, they're good people, does them a disservice. Confession is meaningless without specificity. We need to discuss the stewardship of our time, abilities and treasure in great detail, using concrete examples. Confession is meaningless until we are convicted by our track record that at the core we are self-centered, self-serving folks who look out not just for the needs, but also for the wants of ourselves and our own at the expense of the unmet needs of others.

All along the way on our journey through life, God wants us to bring our problems, our issues and our messes to him. He wants us to bring our pain and hurt and brokenness to him. But what happens after brokenness ends in reconciliation and the pain is relieved? When we are restored and made whole once again, it is easy to return to life as usual, to get back into our old routines and to live our self-centered, self-serving lives; this is so tragic and so sad. Preachers have to bring this to our attention even though we don't want to hear it. They need to challenge us to express our gratitude by living lives of surrender, obedience and loving service to him, as we seek to get on the same page with him and accomplish his agenda.

Sadly, most Christians have a mistaken impression of what they are really like. We perceive ourselves as neighborly, caring, charitable people who are upstanding citizens with a reasonably high standard of ethics, morals and values. My whole point is while we think that image describes us, we don't even come close to being at that level. Only a few even come close to living up to the Biblical standard.

Our ability to repress, deny, rationalize or justify the perception we have of ourselves makes it possible to paint a much rosier picture than is consistent with what the Scriptures teach. We are unable to see that we are lukewarm, hesitant to totally surrender to the Lord and half-hearted in our commitment. Buried beneath several layers of deception is the truth that deep down, human nature is evil, self-centered and self serving. Given the inspiration and motivation of the Holy Spirit, and the Christian freedom we enjoy, we can become loving servants and sacrificial, first fruits givers. We do, however, need to be made aware that we are not as generous, caring, compassionate and charitable as we think we are. When measured by the Biblical standard, we don't even come close. Our rationalizations simply do not cut it. There is immense suffering in our world. There is so much poverty and need. We are indifferent to it. "How many times can a man turn his head, and pretend that he just doesn't see. The answer my friend, is blowin' in the wind. The answer is blowin' in the wind." These are the sermons nobody wants to preach.

The Connection between the Sermons People Like and the Ones They Don't

God has something very important to say to the broken, the grieving, the troubled, the distressed and those whose lives are a mess. But what does the he have to say when the broken have been restored, the grieving are comforted and the troubled and distressed again find healing and peace? What does God have to say when with his help the messes have been cleaned up? There is more to say! There is a word from God that needs to be spoken.

When people have worked through their issues, when there has been a time for healing and when we have taken the time to rejoice and praise God, they need to rejoin the congregation in service, and once again become full partners in helping the congregation to carry out its vision and mission. What needs to follow is teaching that calls out a response to all that our loving and merciful God has done for us. After the messes have been cleaned up, our people need to be reminded again of their call to self-giving, self-sacrificing, selfless lives of service, showing their love for him by dedicating themselves to loving and serving one another in his name. After the messes have been cleaned up there needs to be a prophetic call to radical discipleship, and all that entails in terms of time, abilities and treasure.

After the messes are cleaned up, there is a powerful temptation for those who have been so richly blessed with healing and peace to resume the life they were living before the crisis, one that doesn't look much different than most people in our society. The similarity between sermons people want to hear and the ones they don't want to hear is that when God's Word comforts, heals, strengthens, uplifts, encourages, renews and blesses, we are still slow to respond in grateful devotion by living lives of selfless, loving service. We don't seem to change all that much. There may be some movement, but nothing dramatic or transformational.

"Tell It Like It Is"

We, as Americans, have this perception of ourselves that is far from the truth. What we're really like bears little resemblance to our self image. Most of us see ourselves as decent, generous, charitable, caring, neighborly, law abiding citizens. We would describe ourselves as having a reasonable standard of ethics, morals and values. We think that, "basically we're good people." Most of us see it that way. My sense is that this perception is cultural mass delusion. We are not the charitable, generous people we think we are. Not even close. We are part of a humanity that is greedy and self-centered. We look out not just for the needs of our own, but also for their wants at the expense of the unmet needs of others.

Those of us who are so blessed that our kids have food, shelter and all of their other basic needs met are still not deeply moved and touched by the plight of parents who can't even provide the basics for their children and have to watch them die from hunger or disease. "How many times can a man turn his head, and pretend that he just doesn't see?" Are we totally indifferent? Don't we care? Are we so insulated from their pain that we can just go on with our lives without doing anything about it? Being hard-hearted and uncaring describes us to a "T." The heart of man is merciless.

We don't want to know about all of the tragedy, pain and suffering in the world. We would like to be able to limit our awareness of what's going on outside of the relative comfort, order and quiet of our own little worlds. We don't want to hear about the ravages of war and the barbaric and inhuman behavior that often accompanies it. We don't want to be reminded of drought and famine, hunger and starvation. We don't want to spend our days thinking about the millions suffering and dying from AIDS and other diseases. Those who garden, quilt, sew, read or do ceramics or woodwork see themselves as basically good people. Yet, there is a whole world of pain and suffering beyond the yard, craft room or workshop, and they hardly lift a finger to try to do something about it. It is one thing to be a decent person, a law abiding citizen, an upstanding member of the community and a good neighbor, and quite another to be a caring, compassionate servant of those in need.

You choose where you want to volunteer, but get involved helping and serving and strive to give generously of your time. There are countless adults and children who need you, like those at care facilities for the aging, veteran's homes and hospitals, big brother-big sister programs, after school tutoring and mentoring programs and adult group homes for the cognitively challenged. There are thousands of community and faith-based organizations just waiting for you to help; and, remember, we all have some talent or skill that can be such a blessing to one of these organizations.

Choose where you want to contribute, but give generously. Give to your local food pantry, rescue mission or homeless shelter. Give to your church, The United Way, the Red Cross or the Salvation Army. Giving no more than a pittance says something very clear about human nature. We are a sorry excuse for kindness, caring and compassion. We are a pitiful bunch. The truth is that we give just enough to salve our conscience and allow us to retreat into denial. If nobody ever put it to you this way before, that's one thing. But once someone has explained the vision to us, once we have heard the call to a life of compassionate service rather than a life where we feel we are entitled to our fair share of the good life, and still very little if anything changes, it indicates that we are hard-hearted, uncaring, insensitive and indifferent. Once you've had someone "Tell it like it is," you can no longer plead ignorance. This is the kind of sermon that nobody likes to hear.

We are not a charitable people with a reasonably high standard of ethics, morals and values. We delude, repress, deny, rationalize or justify the perception we have of ourselves. We paint a rosy picture of ourselves. The truth is that we bear little if any resemblance to people who are caring, compassionate and charitable. Am I missing something? It just seems we could do so much more when it comes to caring for those in need and seeking justice for the weak and vulnerable. We need to be about the task of educating ourselves about the crying needs of millions in our world.

> In an editorial in the New Your Times titled "The Gospel of Wealth", David Brooks recalls the economic excesses in America during the 1990s and points to a book by Rev. David Platt, *Radical: Taking Back Your Faith From the American Dream*.
>
> ... Platt calls on readers to cap their lifestyle. Live as if you made $50,000 a year, he suggests, and give everything else away. Take a year to surrender yourself. ... His book has struck a cord. His renunciation tome is selling like hotcakes. ... Leaders at places like the Southern Baptist Convention are calling on citizens to surrender the American dream.[168]

My prayer in the congregations I served was that members' lives would be transformed, a goal that never came close to being realized. Gradually I came to understand that my preaching of generic sermons that didn't include enough of the specifics hindered the process of spiritual growth. The Scriptures' call to surrender is so far from what can be seen in the lives of believers as to be hardly recognizable. The Scriptures' call to discipleship is a call that is so all inclusive that it becomes a stumbling block to those who would be followers of Christ. Saving faith exists all along a scale of 1(weak faith) to 100 (strong faith). Lukewarm Christians are walking on thin ice and taking a huge risk. When called to obedience and faithfulness as disciples and our response is minimal, we put ourselves in life-threatening spiritual danger. Our concept of walking with the Lord is a far cry from what the Scriptures teach. It is the prophetic calling of Christian preachers to surface this issue with all boldness and clarity. It is the calling of preachers to "Tell it like it is."

In a nutshell, here's my take on the situation. We have bought into our materialistic, consumer-driven culture's definition of "a good person." We think we are entitled to our fair share of the American Dream. Preachers have a prophetic role which includes the responsibility to address the issue of how we're doing as kind, loving, sacrificial servants. Yet, we preachers have adapted to cultural norms and allow the favorable impression we all have of ourselves go unchallenged. The truth is that we are nowhere near playing at major league levels of caring, concern and compassion translated into action that seeks to do something about the unmet needs of others. Most of us aren't even in the minors. Truth be told—we are "bush league" at best, Pee Wee League at worst. How does the preacher go about nurturing the flock through the Bible? Of course he will preach the comforting and encouraging messages that sustain, support and strengthen. He will preach about the call to discipleship in no uncertain terms, using unequivocal language and specific examples that stimulate soul-searching about God's calling to commitment, dedication and sacrifice. Preaching and teaching only what people want to hear without including what they need to hear makes us responsible for stunting their spiritual growth.

We Wiggle, We Waffle, We Waver

This was the title of a sermon I preached on February 2, 1997. The initial preparation of the sermon began on a Monday two weeks before the day it was delivered; that Monday happened to be Inauguration Day for Bill Clinton. Al Gore was his vice-president. While reflecting on the sermon, something Al Gore said during the acceptance speech he gave at the Democratic National Convention in 1991 came to mind. While he used the phrase "He waffled, he wiggled, he wavered" in a different context, I saw where it could be adapted to aptly describe the concept I was trying to convey in that sermon, and it aptly describes the point I want to make now.

Like the prophets of old, parish pastors of this day must speak the truth. They must not waffle on their responsibility to "tell it like it is." We must clearly teach what it means when God calls Christians to live lives of faithful discipleship. This is the kind of preaching that makes the hearer uneasy, and causes them to wiggle and squirm uncomfortably in the pew. It begins when the hearer is reminded that what we believe is of ultimate importance is reflected in how we use our time. God wants us to serve him by spending time with our spouse, children and parents. God wants us to make time for prayer, devotions and Bible study. God wants us to nurture our spiritual health by maintaining well-being in the physical and emotional dimensions of our spirituality. When any of the above get neglected because of how much time we spend bowling, watching TV, fishing, golfing or involved in a hobby, the influence of our culture causes us to wiggle, to waffle and to waver in our spiritual walk.

What we believe to be of ultimate importance is also reflected in how we manage and spend our financial resources. How we spend the dollars entrusted to our care is an issue in our relationship with God. The purchase of homes, vehicles, recreational vehicles, boats, snowmobiles, a place up north or a time-share clearly reflects our priorities. Our investments, retirement plan and estate plans all reflect our values. It gets uncomfortable. For us, driving a '79 Chevy station-wagon for twenty years, having three boys but not getting the snowmobiles and not eating out reflected our values. Bottom line—we need to examine the allocation of our resources to be sure our decisions reflect what we say we believe. We need to be sure that what we are doing is God-pleasing. We have to ask ourselves whether we've been influenced by culture and society or whether we are influencing culture and society. We have to ask ourselves whether the seductive power of the good-life has influenced us so much that we have become insensitive to the needs of others. The spiritual and physical needs of others are of unimaginable magnitude. How have we responded to those needs? All too often "We wiggle, We waffle, We waver"—we compromise what we say we believe.

If we are challenged by clear preaching and teaching about discipleship, and repeatedly reject the message, choosing instead a personal brand of Christianity that doesn't include a call for sacrifice and commitment, then we are skating on spiritual thin ice. We need God's help and strength in order to resist the alluring temptation of cultural standards and maintain an unflinching devotion to Him. We are influenced so much by our culture that we have a blind spot when it comes to self-interest, worldliness and materialism. We have to come to grips with the reality that faith can be corrupted by life-style, as well as immorality. The problem isn't out there somewhere. It is in our heart. It is how effectively we have been seduced by the alluring temptations that the world tells us are perfectly acceptable. Again and again, "We Wiggle, We Waffle, We Waver."

My hope and prayer is that the love and forgiveness of God will fill our hearts with such joy and gratitude that—moved by the Spirit—we freely and eagerly desire to walk down the path that Jesus would have us follow. We can't get enough of praising and thanking Him by loving and serving in His name, by doing all we can to meet the spiritual and physical needs of people everywhere. With our nature there is always the tendency "to wiggle, to waffle and to waver." But with God's strengthening and support, our desire is that it will happen less and less.

We Christians as a whole have given an absolutely horrible witness to what we believe. We need to get down off our moral soap boxes and start living transformed lives of loving service. We are not doing ourselves any favors. Unless we are out there every day serving the "least of these," the equivalent of the orphans and widows in Bible times, the hungry, the suffering, the starving, the rejected, the unwanted and the forgotten of our day, unless we are out there serving those who are living in misery, we squander the precious little moral authority we have left. But more than likely, we're not even interested in going down that path.

The preacher almost always sets the vision. It is we in the clergy who have to decide whether we are willing to preach the sermons our people don't like and don't want to hear. The vision for most congregations doesn't get very far beyond the "maintenance" mode. Yet, when the pastor's vision, preaching, teaching and leadership do challenge the flock to reach for a higher level of discipleship, the congregation usually comes nowhere near realizing their full potential. This is tough sledding for the clergy. They need our prayers and support.

Chapter 10
The Morality of Capitalism: There's Good News and There's Bad News

"By preferring the support of domestic to that of foreign industry, (the individual) intends only his own security; and by directing that industry in such a manner as its produce may be of the greatest value, he intends only his own gain, and he is in this, as in many other cases, led by an invisible hand to promote an end which was no part of his intention. . . . By pursuing his own interest he frequently promotes that of the society more effectually than when he really intends to promote it." Adam Smith

"But godliness with contentment is great gain. For we brought nothing into the world and we can take nothing out of it. But if we have food and clothing, we will be content with that. People who want to get rich fall into temptation and a trap and into many foolish and harmful desires that plunge men into ruin and destruction. For the love of money is the root of all kinds of evil" (I Timothy 6:6-10).

Will It Play in Peoria?

During 1973, I served as associate pastor at Trinity Lutheran in Peoria, Illinois, a ministry all about the "Good News" (John 3:16). Peoria is also corporate headquarters for Caterpillar; both would soon be going through some really tough times—business would drop sharply and home values would plummet. Now CAT has come back as a dynamic, thriving global corporation. I wonder how this book will play in Peoria?

1973 was also the year that "inflation adjusted mean earnings for men peaked"[169] The trend in earnings for men would be down hill from then on. As of 2011, 73 percent was also the number "of people (who) favor raising taxes on those with annual incomes of $1 million or more to help cut the deficit."[170] Capitalism hasn't always worked as well for the entire population. However, we are blessed to have a Constitution that provides the structure that allows us as a free people to have a spirited discussion about the economy and to make whatever adjustments are necessary.

Between July and October of 2011 I had to deal with four medical issues which involved sufficient discomfort to make it difficult to maintain focus and concentration for any length of time. Being away from my desk also afforded the opportunity for reflection on the chapters that I had written and on how to approach this one and the next—"The Morality of Government." The debt ceiling debate in Congress, Standard and Poor's downgrading of our credit rating, the nomination process for the Republican candidate for president, "Occupy Wall Street" and President Obama's job's plan were all in the news. From my perspective all of what was happening served to validate the views that formed the basis of these two chapters, as well as the premise for the whole book.

My reason for including this chapter is to address the issues of capitalism and free enterprise in the context of my thesis. Characterizing capitalism as either moral or immoral seems inadequate. It is more helpful for me to think of capitalism in terms of good news and bad news. While there is much about capitalism that is good, it also has painful deficiencies. It is vulnerable to manipulation and abuse by those motivated by greed, which leads to bad news for others.

Core Characteristics of Capitalism

The most influential proponent of *laissez-faire* (noninterference) economics was Adam Smith. Smith believed that left alone capitalism would be guided by an invisible hand that would create wealth and prosperity for everybody. Rather than a state controlled central economy that is supposed to benefit all citizens (socialism), Smith "stressed that the existence of the natural economic forces of supply and demand made it imperative that individuals should be free to pursue their own economic self-interest. In doing so all of society would ultimately benefit. Consequently, he argued that the state should in no way interrupt the free play of natural economic forces by government regulation."[171]

A number of prominent economists, beginning with Irving Fisher, took the position that financial markets know best how to make capitalism work. While Milton Friedman didn't believe the financial markets were perfect, he did think they were more rational than government. Some of Friedman's students used the term "efficient" to describe the U.S. stock market. Justin Fox noted the challenges to the core assumption of the rational market posed by the 1987 stock-market crash and the tech stock and real estate bubbles. He wrote an article that summarizes his view of capitalism. "The issue isn't whether financial markets are useful—they are—or whether the prices of stocks or bonds or collateralized debt obligations convey information—they do. There's also much to be said for the insight that is at the heart of efficient-market theory: markets are hard to outsmart. But when we give up second-guessing the market, we suspend our judgment. And without participants exercising judgment—applying research, heeding a broker's opinion—markets stand no chance of ever getting it right."[172] Convinced that markets don't always work perfectly, noted economist Joseph Stiglitz put the exclamation point on the issue of the deficiencies of the rational market model.

Ethical and Moral Considerations Inherent in Economic Systems

One can debate whether capitalism functions best when left alone to be guided by markets, or whether review and judgment are needed. However, what we can say with certainty is that the positives and negatives and the influence of good and evil in the operation of capitalism are brought into the system from the outside. They are not essential characteristics of any economic system.

Author and activist Sister Joan Chittister urged "people of faith to challenge world inequities. 'To suggest that business people are less spiritual than religious professionals,' she said, 'contradicts the Bible. . . . Where is the Christian leadership in the building of a new world view about the sinfulness of multinational structures that live off the backs of the poor?'"[173]

Also, here are a few comments by economist and historian of economic thought Robert Heilbroner about socialism from a perspective related to my purpose. "This is the ideal of Socialist Man—of man transformed from the competitive, acquisitive being that he is (and that he is encouraged to be) under all property-dominated, market-oriented systems, into the cooperative human being who finds fulfillment in unselfishness and who presumably can develop only in the benign environment of a propertyless, nonmarket social system."[174] Based on my thesis about the nature of man, you would expect me to ask of the proponents of socialism, "What have you been smoking?" Given the nature of man it just doesn't work that way.

Heilbroner then adds "whereas many of the problems that beset America undoubtedly have their roots in our capitalistic institutions, the fact that we have coped with them so inadequately is not a matter that can be blamed on capitalism as such."[175] "The point is clear: The original capitalist dispositions of the marketplace do not leave an irretrievable mark on their societies, but can be radically modified by taxes and transfers (benefits like Social Security, Medicare and Medicaid)."[176]

Capitalism itself is neutral. Within our Constitution and political system, it develops, morphs, and adapts in a way that reflects the values and will of the majority. The larger question is whether or not there is popular support for the idea that government should help the needy. Without the political will to do so, it simply won't happen. As I reflect on all this it just seems overwhelmingly evident that we continue to hold out the hope that we will realize our share of the American Dream, all the while remaining indifferent to others in desperate need. It's human nature. It's a dog-eat-dog world. It's all about the survival of the fittest. Sadly, it's every man for himself. Indifference to the desperate needs of other will continue.

To deny the tendencies of our basic nature is to distort reality. What we can do about it is another question completely. I just don't see much happening. The issue of whether the American character as defined by independence and personal responsibility will continue to be reflected in greed, selfishness and indifference or by a greater sense of altruism, community and being our brother's keeper when he is disadvantaged has been answered through more than 200 years of our history. Our ethic seems to be, *Perhaps I'll help a little if it doesn't cramp my style too much*. There is no reason to expect that it will be any different in the future. *After all, those who are unemployed and living in poverty are just plain lazy, could pull themselves up by their bootstraps if they wanted to and they think they are entitled to the benefits of a system that will take care of them if they choose not to work.*

Finding the balance between a system that fosters welfare dependency and one that offers incentives, encouragement and hope has always been a struggle. Capitalism as an economic system needs to be tweaked in order to function with fairness as it allows for independence, personal responsibility and ambition. I don't claim to know what is fair, what is right, and what is just. What I do believe is that the discussion is influenced by a human nature that moves us to look out not just for the needs of ourselves and our own, but also for our wants at the expense of unmet needs of the disadvantaged and desperate.

In an interesting article titled "Modern society ruining the meaning of life," Prince Charles, heir to the British throne, said "technological development 'has led to an indiscriminate consumerism' that feeds 'envy and greed and (divides) rich and poor within nations and between nations. . . . There is now, I think, a realization in many quarters that a search for alternatives is vital in the field of technological development to enable the economies of both the industrialized and Third World nations to evolve towards a convergence that is equitable and sustainable, not only in a world of limited land and material resources, but also in a world of greatly increased population'"[177]

Human Nature's Influence Permeates the Mechanisms that Govern Capitalism

A poll conducted January 19-21, 1987 found that "...76% saw a lack of ethics in businessmen as contributing to tumbling moral standards...."[178] The figure noted is part of an article sub-headed "At a time of moral disarray, America seeks to rebuild a structure of values."[179] Here is the magazine's description of the article. "Disclosures of hypocrisy and moral laxity infect leadership from Washington to Wall Street.... Do the transgressions represent a general shunning of values that Americans have always held dear, or are they merely a temporary blot brought about by the mindless materialism of the '80s?"[180] It seems to me the answer was given when the article referred to a values class taught by Harvard's Robert Coles. "During one class focused on F. Scott Fitzgerald's *The Last Tycoon*, Coles called out a cadence of four words from the book: 'Tolerance, kindness, forbearance, affection.' Then he asked, 'Can these lessons be taught? Should we teach them here? Will these qualities increase our nation's GNP?' One student thought not, arguing, 'It is difficult to say that human behavior is driven by anything other than self-interest.'"[181] These are my sentiments—exactly.

Grand pursuit: The Story of Economic Genius is a recent book by economist, journalist, professor and author Sylvia Nasar. Reviewer Rana Foroohar, assistant managing editor for *Time* magazine, says that Nasar "explains the history of economic genius."[182] Foroohar continues,

> The idea that humanity could turn tables on economic necessity—mastering rather than being enslaved by material circumstances—is so new that Jane Austin never entertained it.... (It) manages to put forward Nasar's entire thesis but also the great aspiration of modern economics: to lift up the majority of human beings living in squalor.
>
> Nasar ... would argue that economics has done a pretty good job of that, which is worth remembering in this post-financial-crisis era, when many economists seem to have lost their credibility, or at the very least their mojo. The laissez-faire, markets-know-best school of thought advanced by Milton Friedman, who gets his due in the book, has been proved faulty. But the Keynesian bailouts that the left hoped would get us out of this mess haven't worked so well either...."
>
> Still, as Nasar points out, economists ... must be doing something right, because 'the lives of nine-tenths of humanity have changed more in the century in which modern economics was born then in the 20 centuries before.' While more than a billion people still live in poverty, it's safe to say that a majority of humanity now enjoys levels of prosperity and choice—in food, living conditions and employment—undreamed of by the typical laborer in 19th century England, when Charles Dickens called for new and more generous economic thinking in *A Christmas Carol*."
>
> ... What hasn't changed is the key question: how to improve our material circumstances so that we can meet every other aspiration we might have. As we enter an era of rising inequality and income shifts that promises to be just as unsettling as the Industrial Revolution was, it is clear that economic genius is needed now more than ever.[183]

As I see it, however, no amount of economic genius can compensate for a human nature that is driven by self-interest.

Rather, selfishness and greed short-circuit the system. Author, psychiatrist and management consultant M. Scott Peck expresses my view.

> "Pure capitalism ... espouses the destiny of the individual even when it is at the expense of the relationship, the group, the collective, the society. Widows and orphans may starve, but this

should not prevent the individual entrepreneur from enjoying all the fruits of his or her individual initiative."[184]

Human Nature's Influence on Tax Policy

Tax policy is a prime example of how factors external to core capitalist theory exert a powerful influence on how the theory works out in practice. One view is to reduce taxes on the wealthy as those with resources (capital) will allocate them in a way that that will serve the greater good by creating more jobs; this is also referred to as the trickle down effect. In this view you don't want to increase taxes on the wealthy as their investments and spending will improve circumstances for all. President Reagan is the icon of this approach to economics. His "administration tried to cut taxes and boost defense spending at the same time. According to Reagan's true believers, the deficits were supposed to shrink as a result of the tax cut. By stimulating the economy's so-called supply-side, the cuts were expected to encourage work and investment so that Government revenues would actually rise rather than fall. Thus was born Reaganomics."[185]

"(His) proposed budget magic drew widespread skepticism, including George Bush's 'voodoo economics' charge during the 1980 presidential primaries. . . . (Also), one of the Administration's master strategists, Budget Director David Stockman, knew better. 'None of us really understands what's going on with all these numbers,' he confessed in a 1981 magazine article that rocked the White House. 'People are getting from A to B and it is not clear how they are getting there.'"[186]

PolitiFact Wisconsin reported Warren Buffet as saying,

> . . . very wealthy people like himself pay lower tax rates than the middle class, thanks to special tax categories for investment income.

> While the poor and middle class fight for us in Afghanistan, and while most Americans struggle to make ends meet, we mega-rich continue to get our extraordinary tax breaks.

> . . . Defenders say the lower tax rate (on investments) helps the economy because it rewards investors for risk-taking and entrepreneurship. They also argue that taxing this income amounts to double taxation because corporations pay taxes on their income before investors are paid dividends. We won't

settle the argument here, but there's no doubt that investors get lower tax rates on their income than workers."[187]

The inheritance or estate tax also has an impact on the system. One view usually refers to it as a "death tax" that undermines and penalizes those who own family farms and small businesses. The other view says "nothing is more un-American than an inherited elite that perpetuates itself."[188] The little guy suffers while the wealthy have more to leave to their children. Their children then have a leg up, an advantage, a running start on the next generation. "The richest families have the great dollar bulk of what are now taxable estates, and if they pass untouched, or lightly taxed, wealth and position in the U.S. will emerge as ever more inherited, not earned."[189] Whatever the merits of the arguments and whatever decisions are made, this is another external factor that impacts the functioning of pure capitalist theory.

Bailouts and Rescue Packages

The fundamental tenets of capitalism have at times been modified by bailouts and rescue and stimulus packages. "When big business gets into serious financial difficulty, they are not bashful about holding out the tin cup for public funds. Bailouts and other rescue operations are promoted in the name of saving jobs and protecting other public interests. . . . And sometimes government rescues are justifiable. Still, it's a lapse from classical capitalism."[190] "The welfare state—if that is what it must be called—is necessary to blunt the rough edges of capitalism and fill the void it leaves. No amount of gloating over the shortcomings of socialism will obscure that fact."[191]

One of the two biggest financial crises in our history occurred with near economic meltdown of 2008. Capitalism's internal market mechanisms proved inadequate to the task of averting disaster. A massive government intervention was necessary. "The government's epic intervention after Lehman's bankruptcy averted disaster. . . . A year ago, officials at the Treasury department and Federal Reserve didn't think letting Lehman go bankrupt would be a disaster. . . . (It)'s also clear that the authorities—then Treasury Secretary Hank Paulson, in particular—didn't want to intervene. The fed and treasury had taken a lot of flak for their earlier bailouts of Bear Stearns, Fannie Mae and Freddie Mac. It was time to let the market work."[192] Within days of Lehman's failure, it was apparent that the market wasn't up to the task.

. . . Early in the Great Depression, powerful voices at the Treasury and the Fed argued that financial crisis was a necessary corrective. "Liquidate labor, liquidate stocks, liquidate the farmers, liquidate the real estate," Treasury Secretary Andrew Mellon advised President Herbert Hoover. "It will purge the rottenness out of the system." This time around, after Lehman went under, no one at Treasury or at the Fed talked that way. Instead policymakers in the U.S. and overseas agreed that the panic had to be stopped at any cost. And it was, through a bailout that placed trillions of taxpayer dollars at risk. It was expensive, messy and unfair. But it worked. "I've abandoned free-market principles to save the free-market system" is how President George W. Bush described it last December."[193]

Presupposing the thesis presented in this work, human nature has hijacked the mechanisms and dynamics necessary for a fine tuned, smooth running capitalistic system. When you factor in tax policy, bailouts and rescue packages, you have a system that operates on the basis of principles that are self-serving and self-centered. You always have to factor in the hearts of people, who operate on the basis of self-interest, regardless the prevailing economic model. At best it is naïve and foolish to assume that those operating within the system are motivated by altruism. At worst it is delusional. We are all in it for ourselves.

Government Regulation - Not "Yes" or "No," but Current, Balanced and Effective

Let's go back to the source, and a commentary by Justin Fox that tries to figure out how Adam Smith would have addressed the issue of regulation.

You know Adam Smith for his "*invisible hand*'" the mysterious force that steers the selfish economic decisions of individuals that leave us all better off.

...Lately, though, the invisible hand has been getting slapped. The selfish economic decisions of home buyers, mortgage brokers, investment bankers and institutional investors over the past decade clearly did not leave us all better off. Did Smith have it wrong?

No, Smith did not have it wrong. It's just that some of his self-proclaimed disciples have given us a terribly incomplete picture of what he believed. . . . For Smith, the invisible hand was but one of an array of interesting social and economic forces worth thinking about.

Why did the invisible hand emerge as one idea from Smith's work that everybody remembers? Mainly because it's so simple and powerful. If the invisible hand of the market really can be relied on at all times and in all places to deliver the most prosperous and just society possible, then we'd be idiots not to get out of the way and let it work its magic.

. . . Fat chance. Most of the book *The Wealth of Nations* is an account of how we decide whether behavior is good or not. In Smith's telling, the most important factor is our sympathy for one another. "To restrain our selfish, and to indulge our benevolent affections, constitutes the perfection human nature," he writes.

. . . There are other whiplash moments in *The Wealth of Nations*. The Dominant theme running through the book is that self-interest and free, competitive markets can be powerful forces for prosperity and for good. But Smith also calls for regulation of interest rates and laws to protect workers from employers.

. . . Smith was also on to something that many free-market fans who pledge allegiance to him miss. . . . Markets don't exist free of societies and governments and regulators and customs and moral sentiments; they are entwined.

. . . Applying Smith's teachings to the modern world, then, is a much more complex and doubtful endeavor than it's usually made out to be. He certainly wouldn't have been opposed to every government intervention in the market.

. . . Asking "What would Adam Smith say?" is a lot easier than conclusively answering it. It's pretty clear, though, that he wouldn't just shout, 'Don't interfere with the invisible hand!' and leave it at that.[194]

Many in the financial industry take the position that regulation is stifling to the economy, and would like to dismantle most of the regulatory system. Anti-regulatory guru Philip Howard in *The Death of Common Sense* argues that we wouldn't need so many regulations if we just used some common sense. The catch is how you keep common sense from being influenced by self-interest and greed. Given my understanding of human nature, depending on the exercise of common sense to "deliver the most prosperous and just society possible" is unrealistic. Given all that has happened from the Gilded Age of the 1890s to the present, how can you simply trust business and industry to self-regulate in the interest of the public good? The financial industry is doing all it can to dismantle as much regulation as possible in order to generate more profits. What are the tradeoffs in terms of how less regulation affects Main Street?

> Washington *Post* columnist E.J. Dionne . . . argues that the Ginrich phase of American politics is neither conservative or revolutionary but instead reactionary, harking back to the Big Business Republicanism of the late 19th century. Ginrich is only the latest in a line of Republicans stretching back to Goldwater who have attacked government as the cause of the country's problems. Dismantling government they promise, will improve the economic well-being of all Americans and free the capitalist economy by reducing taxes and regulations, and free the capitalist economy to generate new wealth for everyone.[195]

In making the case for regulation Joe Klein, political columnist for TIME magazine, notes that President Obama proposed "a relatively modest reform of the financial system (that is) being chewed up by the . . . lobbyists of the banking industry. . . . (He) needs to make a direct assault on the greedheads who created the Ponzi economy and are now trying to gut his plan to make them do business honestly."[196]

The headline of a "*USA Today*" editorial used another metaphor involving money to describe what happened in the financial industry that caused the great recession and near economic collapse of the financial system in 2008. "Wean Wall Street Off Its Gambling Addictions: To Protect the Economy, Don't Let Big Banks Run In-House Casinos."

> Once upon a time Wall Street was about providing services to institutional clients. It helped them raise capital through lending and the underwriting of stocks and bonds. It helped them to manage their assets by advising them what to buy and what not to buy.
>
> These days Wall Street has come to resemble a vast and sophisticated gambling operation aimed at making fast profits and paying out fat bonuses. Its investment banks place bets with both their own money and that of clients. . . .

Getting the banking industry to at least partially revert to its former self is vital to prevent another meltdown. To that end, the Obama administration recently proposed prohibiting large banks that rely on government-backed deposits from running in-house hedge funds and private-equity arms.

This is not the be all and end all of banking reform, as large financial institutions can wreak havoc in many ways that don't involve betting their own money.

But the idea, which has been dubbed the 'Volcker Rule' after former Federal Reserve chairman Paul Volcker, is useful because behemoth banking institutions aren't just betting their money, but taxpayers' as well. That stems from the fact that they are so large that their collapse would mean economic calamity if they aren't bailed out again.

In today's plunderous financial culture, however, any effort to limit taxpayer exposure to risky bank behavior is seen only as a threat to profits and bonuses.

A once chastened financial industry has gone into full-court press in lobbying to portray this plan, along with a proposed consumer protection agency, as excessive regulation. According to the *Los Angeles Times*, banks spent $30 million to lobby in 2009, an increase of 12% from a year earlier.[197]

The 1999 repeal of the Glass-Steagall Act that prohibited commercial banks from taking excessive risks opened the door to abuse. The banks no longer had to restrict themselves to risking their own assets. In the period leading up to the collapse of 2008, they were placing risky bets with their client's money as well. The dynamics of the discussion involve a number of related issues: economic theory, businesses needing to make a profit, politics, and regulation. Human nature is a factor that impacts separately on all of these issues, as well as how the issues play out in relationship with one another; this relationship will be discussed further in Chapters 11 and 13.

Adam Smith's conceptual framework for capitalism is still the baseline for all economic discussion. Nevertheless, bottom line, Friedman, Keynes and Stiglitz, and as noted, even Smith himself, all believe that capitalism needs adjustments and interventions in order for capitalism to meet the needs of ever-changing economic conditions. Former Secretary of the Treasury Henry Paulson adds, "I believe in markets, but I don't believe you can have unregulated, unfettered markets. Since the beginning of time, they have been prone to excesses. The key thing is to make sure we have a regulatory system that can evolve with the markets."[198]

The degree to which external mechanisms are needed is open to debate. However, the introduction of the human factor into the equation always makes the tweaking of the fundamentals subject to self-interest and greed. This is just the way the world works. We have to accept it, get used to it, and find those ways to minimize its influence. We need to work at trying to find the right balance between free markets and too much regulation that works as well as possible in a world where all too often it's all about the survival of the fittest, while the weak and vulnerable are thrown under the bus. We all have the tendency to look our not just for the needs, but also for the wants of ourselves and our own at the expense of others.

An Insignificant, Replaceable Part in a Gigantic Economic Machine

Due to a combination of technological progress and globalization, we have witnessed a growing trend toward the marginalization of the worker. It began with the less educated, continued in the manufacturing sector, then spread to white collar workers and middle management. People who once considered themselves set for life on the assembly line, in the plant or in their cubicle, are painfully aware they may suddenly and unexpectedly find themselves out of a job. They hear words like right-sizing, downsizing, outsourcing or restructuring and they shudder.

Any evaluation of capitalism must also include an assessment of how its workers are treated. More and more they are treated like pawns, cogs or replaceable parts in the corporate big picture. They are caught in rightsizing and downsizing, as manufacturing plants move their operation to another region of the country or someplace else in the world where the cost of labor is cheaper. In a global economy where cheap labor abounds, there are always plenty of people ready and waiting for your job, and who will do it for much less pay. To get some jobs today you even have to sign a contract with a non-disclosure clause, meaning that if you are laid off, your employer doesn't have to give you a reason. Increasingly, it is every man for himself.

Some say American businesses care for their workers. It seems to me this was far more likely to be true years ago than it is today. "'Employers want loyal workers, but they aren't loyal in return. . . .' Many companies expect you to sacrifice your family life, your peace of mind, even your health in the name of success, but they don't reciprocate with any allegiance or commitment to you.'" As one manager told his employees, 'What you've done for this company in the past means nothing. Every day when you come to work, the contribution counter is reset to zero.' Some argue that this scenario is simply the new workplace reality, that competition is the name of the game, and that loyalty and fairness are anachronisms. Perhaps, but it is also true that the fundamental reason for a society to exist is to promote the welfare of its members. If the good of the few outweighs the good of the many, we'll all lose in the end."[199]

You hear many echoes of the same dynamic. There is an "erosion of loyalty between companies and employees, a sense that numbers now matter more than human beings: . . ."[200]

"Global Squeeze" by Richard Longworth adds some interesting insights into the devaluing of the American worker.

> The logic of global markets leads to more pressure on workers. . . . Millions of new workers appear on the world market every year, all hungry and ready to compete.
>
> "The overarching, anonymous world market . . . condemns increasingly large sections of mankind to superfluousness. . . . In the language of economics that means an enormous increasing supply of human beings is faced with a declining demand.
>
> . . . Everywhere, joblessness and instability have inched up from the working class to the middle class. . . .
>
> . . . This is the dehumanization of labor.
>
> . . . These jobs pay a wage. They keep bread on the table and gas in the tank. But by virtue of their "flexibility," they have little feeling of permanence or stability. Because of this the Americans who hold them feel little stability themselves and do not have the sense of the social compact, the shared responsibility between employer and employee, that underlay the postwar economy and created an American community based on work.[201]

Family therapist Augustus Napier sums it up nicely. "The dominant social metaphor for today . . . seems to be a free-market, corporate neo-Darwinism that worships the God of performance, promotes the survival of the smartest and richest, treats employees like replaceable parts in the corporate machine and views human vulnerability scornfully and patiently."[202]

There was a time when unions provided a needed balance to the powerful corporations. There was money to be made, and they were able to negotiate how to split the pot. First, it was the corporate world who overplayed their hand. To gain some leverage workers formed unions. Then the unions overplayed their hand. My sense is that both saw the handwriting on the wall in terms of the developments and mega-trends in our economy, but as long as there was money to be made they adapted to the changing landscape. With technological advancement and globalization, large budget deficits and the accumulation of huge debt, the whole economic playing field in the public and private sectors has now changed dramatically. Do we cut taxes or spending, or a combination of both? Do we limit union power or protect it? Do we advocate for or against the North American Free Trade Agreement? There are all kinds of questions. We are in the midst of the struggle to find the answers.

Under-girding the system is the corporate mantra: how much can this employee make for me. They don't really care about the employee. "Even if big gains lie around the bend for big companies, many question how much they will share with employees."[203] "(The) 'implicit social compact' that 'gave force to the simple proposition that American prosperity could include almost everyone' has been breaking down. Under the compact, Reich (departing labor secretary) said, it was believed that everyone should get access to education; that the safety net of Social Security, welfare and other programs was needed to guard against misfortune that might befall anyone; and that as companies did better, so should workers."[204] "The ranks of the working poor have been swelling. . . . (This) trend calls into question the unwritten bargain that the state (the body politic) has struck with business. The state accommodates and even encourages business development, which permits owners to profit; in exchange, business provides jobs to insure the general prosperity. The growth in poverty-level jobs, however, suggests that business may be reneging on the deal."[205] Thomas Hefty, chairman and CEO of health insurer United Health Services of Wisconsin adds, "You could say that capitalism has become more efficient and arguably more ruthless."[206]

Bottom line, what is important is to acknowledge the tendency of all of us to look out not just for our needs, but also for the wants of ourselves and our own at the expense of the very real and often desperate needs of others as a powerful factor in the capitalistic economic equation. Sadly it is as it always has been, a dog eat dog, every man for himself, survival of the fittest world. Therefore do the best you can to leverage any opportunity or luck you may have by saving, investing carefully, getting more education and whatever in-service training you can. Position yourself to market your skills. Life isn't fair. Nobody is going to do you any favors. You're going to have to do it yourself.

For almost two centuries (1776-1976) we were able to avoid facing the painful truth about what motivates us as individuals, societal structures and corporate entities. We were a new nation with a vast supply of land on our frontiers as we expanded westward. We had abundant resources, an expanding economy, countless opportunities to establish new businesses and a job market where demand exceeded supply. As long as there was more than enough to go around and the American Dream there for the taking for all who were willing to work for it, everybody was happy. The new economic realities have changed the paradigm; "inflation adjusted mean earnings for men" peaked in 1973. From then on more and more of us experienced the ruthless indifference of an economic system in which you are little more than a small, replaceable part, and where you had to look out for yourself, because nobody else will.

If you're more aware of what makes people tick and how the world works, you won't be blindsided. There is a reality out there that is not nearly as rosy as some would have us to believe; this leads to a discussion of the issue that has been given a big boost in awareness by the Occupy Wall Street (OWS) movement—income disparity in the US.

The Wealth Gap

It is not like the issue of the wealth gap just snuck up on us. There have been many articles about this trend in the print media for years. But warnings about these changes were disregarded. At what point do you cross the line when people realize that capitalism isn't working for them. It happens when enough people believe they aren't getting a fair shake, when they are worrying about the basics of a retirement where they will be able to be cared for with dignity, when they are truly worried about the future of their children and grandchildren, and when the political public relations consultants can no longer come up with rationalizations that citizens and voters believe. What has happened now is that we have crossed a line where the capitalist system clearly isn't "working" for an overwhelming majority of our households. There is a growing sense that the rich are getting richer, the poor are getting poorer and the middle class is disappearing.

"By the middle of Reagan's second term, official data began to show that America's broadly defined "rich"-the top half of 1 percent of the U.S. population—had never been richer."[207] "We are talking about a major transformation. Not only did the concentration of wealth intensify, but the sums involved took a mega-leap."[208] It is the immensity of the wealth gap that finally got our attention, triggered a national movement (OWS) and started a national debate.

We have been aware of the wealth gap for some time. "By 1989 the Congressional budget office projections showed the percentage of family income in the hands of the top 1 percent of Americans rising from 9 percent in 1980 to 12 percent in 1988."[209] "Reich presented statistics indicating that between 1979 and 1995, the poorest fifth of American families saw their incomes drop 9%, while the wealthiest fifth enjoyed a 26% increase."[210]

"The top 1 percent's take increased to 23.5 percent by 2007. CEOs who in the 1970s took home 40 times the compensation of average workers now rake in 350 times.[211] "In 2008 the top 1% took in more than 20%. . . . Other recent research, moreover, indicates that executive compensation at the nation's largest firms has roughly quadrupled in real terms since the 1970's, even as pay for 90% of Americans has stalled. . . . Repeated surveys by the National Opinion Research Center since 1987 have found that 60% or more of Americans agree or strongly agree with the statement that 'differences in income in America are too large."[212] Real median household income adjusted for inflation is almost exactly the same in 2010, $49,445 as it was in 1989, $49,075. Also, "Adjusted for inflation, median household income has fallen nearly 10% since December 2007."[213]

The Congressional Budget Office reports that income disparity is dramatic.

> (Between) 1979 and 2007 after-tax income going to each of the four bottom quintiles—the bottom 80 percent—has dropped. The only quintile that has increased its share is the top 20 percent. And the top 1 percent—the economic elites targeted by the Occupy Wall Street movement, which claims to represent the other 99 percent—has more than doubled its share.
>
> The top 1 percent saw its income skyrocket by 275 percent. Those between the 80th and 99th percentile also did pretty well,

seeing their incomes rise by 65 percent. Income for the bottom 20 percent, meanwhile, grew by just 18 percent.[214]

Here is another way to get a perspective on the extreme wealth gap between the haves and the have-nots. "While the income share of the nations top 1% is hovering around 20%—near what it was in the Gilded Age and up from about 8% in the 1970s—the rest of us haven't gotten a raise in nearly four decades."[215]

The most recent figures confirm that the trend of a widening wealth gap continues.

> The richest Americans got richer during the first two years of the economic recovery, while average net worth declined for the other 93% of U.S. households. . . .
>
> The upper 7% of households owned 63% of the nation's total household wealth in 2011, up from 56% in 2009.
>
> . . . The average net worth of households in the upper 7% of the wealth distribution rose by an estimated 28%, while the households in the lower 93% dropped by 4%.[216]

Middle-Class Paychecks Shrinking while Corporate Profits Set Records

The wealth gap increased in an economy where there was also a growing gap between corporate profits and employee compensation.

> Paul Krugman, the resident economics scold of The New York Times, made a good point in his "Conscience of a Liberal" blog the other day. He . . . explain(ed) why the average person may not want to root for General Electric, as GE boss Jeffery Immelt counseled on "60 Minutes" last weekend. "I think this notion that it's the population of the U.S. against big companies is just all wrong," Immelt said. In theory, Immelt is right. In practice, not so much. That's because GE and other corporations have done far better than the average person over the past 10 years—and have sent millions of jobs overseas at a time that income inequality in the country grew.[217]

Using the same scale, employee compensation had gone up 34 points, while corporate profits had increased by 176.2 points. "Also cited as factors contributing to the rapid growth of income at the top were the structure of executive compensation; high salaries for some 'superstars' in sports and the arts; the increasing size of the financial services industry; and the growing role of capital gains, which go disproportionately to higher income households."[218]

In addition, globalization and the rise of China have generated huge profits, which are earned and kept abroad. Back home workers with less education and skills are getting squeezed.

> America was once the great middle-class society. Now we are divided between rich and poor, with the greatest degree of inequality among high-income democracies. The top 1% of households takes home almost a quarter of all household income – a share not seen since 1929. The poor and working classes are squeezed. Identifying with the 99% OWS has stimulated a national conversation about the wealth gap. The rich are absenting themselves from the country's troubles. Their businesses sell goods and outsource jobs to China; their homes are behind gated walls; much of the corporate income is in offshore tax havens.[219]

A word you hear more frequently today is "aspirational." It means that we are ok with a considerable degree of income inequity, as long as we feel there is an opportunity to climb the ladder of success and realize our aspirations. However, there is a point at which we begin to question how realistic it is for us to get ahead even if we're hard-working, honest and make the most of our opportunities. Foroohar said, "Americans are . . . likely to tolerate high levels of income inequality. . . only when they feel the system isn't rigged against them."[220] Tom Saler, author and freelance financial journalist gives a little more insight into this issue. "There is a pervasive sense that most Americans are working harder for less and that employer loyalty is a thing of the past. Those perceptions have been decades in the making but were mostly hidden for a quarter-century by easy credit and the paper wealth generated by a powerful bull market in stocks and two massive asset bubbles."[221] Author, journalist and editor Jon Meacham addresses the same issue. "The perennial conviction that those who work hard and play by the rules will be rewarded with a more comfortable present and a stronger future for their children faces assault from just about every direction. The great enemy of democratic capitalism, economic inequality, is real and growing."[222]

How Did We Get Blindsided?

Some people saw it coming and tried to sound the alarm. Many others were content to keep quiet about what they saw and keep making money. On the back of the book jacket of *The Politics of Rich and Poor* Mario Cuomo says, "Phillips says convincingly what Democrats have not been bold enough to say and Republicans won't admit: we have redistributed our wealth from the poor and working middle class to the rich. We have compromised our fiscal integrity and risked our world position. Phillips says that people will compel what politicians have failed to do." Now people are really upset and angry about it.

How come it took so long for the issue to surface? Why did our capitalistic system get so far out of balance before there was a public outcry. Here are some of the factors that led to the middle class perception that they were still doing well, and to accept the *status quo*. First, "National majorities, and sometimes large ones, agreed when pollsters asked if Reagan favored the rich. . . . However, the President's personal job ratings remained high, propped up by over-all U.S. prosperity, personal affection and public support for his 'America is back' muscle-flexing. . . ."[223] Second, voters weren't even phased by "Budget Director David Stockman's thoughtless admission that supply-side economics was actually the latest version of old GOP trickle-down theory and practice."[224] "David Stockman introduced the arithmetic of taxation and spending. He warned President Reagan early on that Voodoo economics did not compute. But the president went blithely on his way, allowing the national debt to triple on his watch."[225] Third, Democratic strategist Robert Beckel thinks "'Ronald Reagan convinced . . . voters that their interests were with the wealthy. They bought into trickle-down theory.' But since then, Beckel said, they have become convinced that 'where they are losing out is not to the poor but to wealthy people. They believe the dollars they have lost have gone up, not down.'"[226] Fourth, there is "a . . . public demand for stability, for 'normalcy'. . . . Traditional values are, of course, conservative, even though conservative economic policy . . . would have radical effects."[227]

The final point is summed up very well by Jeff Sachs.

> The new globalization has accelerated the hollowing out of U.S. industries. . . . Although American consumers have been the beneficiaries of a flood of low-cost and high-quality Chinese products, America's industrial workers have paid for it in wage cuts and higher unemployment. . . . This deterioration in Main Street earning prospects was covered up for more than

20 years by debt. First, there was mortgage debt. Washington encouraged housing construction at every turn through Fannie Mae and Freddie Mac, Wall Street deregulation and the Fed's low-interest-rate policies. The housing sector seemed like an employment winner, creating construction jobs that at least partly offset the lost manufacturing jobs. A winner, that is, until the bubble collapsed in 2007. (Second), (eager) to keep voters feeling prosperous, Washington also fed the fever of consumer credit. If people could no longer earn their way to affluence, they could try to borrow their way instead. Only in 2008 did households come to understand the precariousness of their balance sheets.[228]

The surge of financial inequality and recklessness has been a bipartisan affair, aided and abetted by every administration and Congress since 1981. And leaders in both parties have yet to accept the magnitude of the shifts in the world economy and the scope of the solutions needed.[229]

It seems to me that neither party could have missed the seismic shifts in the world economy. As noted earlier, Phillips described the changes as "a major transformation. Not only did the concentration of wealth quietly intensify, but the sums involved took a mega-leap."[230] My sense is that they chose to ignore these developments, as it is in their best interest not to rock the boat and alienate the electorate by responsibly addressing a politically hot potato. I believe they know exactly what they are doing; this will be the focus of the next chapter. But without significant intervention, today's middle class is well on the way to becoming tomorrow's poor.

The middle class just didn't get it. They just didn't understand. They weren't hurting bad enough for the issue to get their attention. They weren't bleeding badly enough to really get angry. They hadn't yet realized how radical the shift in wealth had become, and how it would impact their pursuit of the American Dream.

A piece in "YAHOO! News" on March 9, 2011, caught my eye. It had a picture of a middle-aged guy standing by the front door of a McDonald's next to a poster in the window that said "Now Hiring." Here is the story that accompanied the picture. "When it comes to jobs, it's not just quantity that matters—it's also quality. It is great news that the economy is finally producing jobs again—even if it will take another few years of this kind of growth to get us back where we were before the Great Recession. But that also means it's time to ask what kind of jobs are being created. And on that front things are a lot less encouraging. Several recent studies suggest that the new jobs pay less and offer fewer work hours than the ones they have replaced. Let's look at the numbers. Lower wage industries—things like retail and food preparation—accounted for 23 percent of the jobs lost during the recession, but 49 percent of the jobs gained over the last year."[231]

It was d*eja vue.* Nineteen years earlier (1992) a cartoon on the editorial page of the Milwaukee Journal Sentinel caught my eye. It depicted a college grad standing next to a fast food establishment with a sign: "The GOLDEN ARCHES." The grad said, "The state made college unaffordable. But they told me not to worry, my prospects for employment looked **GOLDEN**." The cartoonist was Mike Thompson, State Journal Register, Springfield, Ill, our hometown for the ten years between 1975 and 1985. The editorial gave a striking historical perspective and an eerie parallel to what is happening as we speak. It was titled: "Falling behind: Glitter of '80s hid widening rich-poor gap."[232] Twenty years ago many recognized the widening gap between the rich and poor, and that the new jobs being created to replace those lost in the shift to a global economy do not pay as much and offer fewer benefits.

However, the powers that be were still peddling their magic potion, namely, that if you worked hard, you would succeed, even though they knew that world had ceased to exist. And the people, as noted, had not been able to see through the scam and weren't hurting bad enough because they had insulated themselves from the worst pain by taking out mortgages that were too big for their budgets and running up debt on their credit cards. They hadn't reached the point where they demanded change, and were ready to express their displeasure at the ballot box. We are at that tipping point right now.

Today people are extremely concerned about the widening wealth gap. A good way to sum it all up is in the words of Elizabeth Warren.

> The economic crisis has wiped more than $5 trillion from pensions and savings, has left family balance sheets upside down and threatens to put 10 million homeowners out on the street. .... (The) boom of the 2,000s resulted in an almost imperceptible 1.6% increase (in median family income) for the typical family. While Wall Street executives and others who owned lots of stock celebrated how good the recovery was for them, middle-class families were left empty-handed.

... Through it all, families never asked for a handout from anyone, especially Washington. They were left to go on their own, working harder, squeezing nickels and taking care of themselves. ... The contrast with the big banks couldn't be sharper. While the middle class has been caught in an economic vice, the financial industry that was supposed to serve them has prospered at their expense. Consumer banking—selling debt to middle class families—has been a gold mine. Boring banking has given away to creative banking, and the industry has generated tens of billions of dollars annually in fees made possible by deceptive and dangerous terms buried in the fine print of the opaque, incomprehensible and largely unregulated contracts.

And when various forms of this creative banking triggered an economic crisis, the banks went to Washington for a handout. All the while top executives kept their jobs and retained their bonuses. Even though the tax dollars that supported the bailout came largely from middle class families—from people already working hard to make ends meet—the beneficiaries of those tax dollars have been lobbying Congress to preserve the rules that let those huge banks feast off the middle class.[233]

There are those who hold that capitalism works best when the invisible hand is left alone as much as possible to do its work. Are they sincerely advocating this view so the invisible hand can work its magic and everybody will benefit fairly? Or are they taking this position because they know that convincing the lower and middle classes to agree and live within the conceptual framework of their belief system will serve as a smokescreen that will benefit them? What they really want is to be free to make business decisions that will result in outcomes favorable to them with little or no concern about how they will affect the lower and middle classes. We do have this tendency to look out not just for the needs of ourselves and our own, but also for our wants at the expense of the unmet needs of others. This same dynamic is foundational in shaping the recent major shifts in income distribution.

A New Baseline for the American Dream

The term *American Dream* was coined during the Great Depression. Historian James Truslow Adams published *The Epic of America* in 1931, in an atmosphere of even greater despair than today's. He wanted to call his book *The American Dream*, but his publishers objected. No one will pay $3.50 for a book about a dream, they said. Adams used the phrase so often that it entered the lexicon. The American Dream, he said, was of "a better, richer and happier life for all our citizens of every rank, which is the greatest contribution we have made to the thought and welfare of the world. That dream or hope was present from the start. Ever since we became an independent nation, each generation has seen an uprising of ordinary Americans to save the dream from the forces which appear to be overwhelming it." Today, those forces really do look overwhelming. But challenges like them have been beaten back before –and can be again. [234]

The idea of the American Dream describes a sense of "general prosperity and well-being for the average person."[235] It defines the baseline of well-being as having a job that pays a living wage, one that makes it possible to "raise your children, provide good housing, cover the costs of health care and retirement, and even insure an annual vacation."[236] Furthermore, it is framed within a context where there is an opportunity to move up the economic ladder.

The cherished American notion of upward mobility is no longer a slam-dunk. "America's story, our national mythology, is built on the idea of being an opportunity society. ... Modern surveys confirm what Toqueville sensed back then: Americans care much more about being able to move up the economic ladder than where we stand on it. We may be poor today, but as long as there's a chance we can be rich tomorrow, things are O.K."[237] We want our children to be able to live better than we did.

Today, many are disillusioned and angry.

JOE SCARBOROUGH. The belief that my kids can do better than me, and achieve whatever they want to achieve, this is part of the American Dream. ... The rich are getting richer, the poor are getting poorer, and the middle class is getting hollowed out. And the American Dream is on the run. ... My kids can't do as well as me, and I may not be doing well.

MIKE BARNICLE (broadcast journalist). This is such a complex issue. There is a huge social, cultural divide that's growing each day in this country that undercuts the hope and belief so many of us have about what America means. It means social mobility. It means the idea that you're going to get a job, and then you're going to get another job. And your kids are going to be able to get a job. (It means that) you're going to be able to buy a small house and then a larger house. Now we're getting to a point where a large group of ordinary Americans are the ones whose kids go to sub-par schools, the ones who get laid off first without much hope of getting another job, the ones whose sons and daughters fight our wars, the ones who bear the burden, while the 1% get richer, and richer and richer.[238]

These changes didn't just start happening yesterday. It was already happening during the farm crisis of the late '60s and early '70s. Now it has reached a point where inequality is rising and social mobility up the ladder as the essence of the American Dream has been decimated by technological advancement and emerging global markets. It's a different world. It's a different dream. Most lower and middle class Americans are having difficulty holding on to the dream. Here is a brief summary of the situation that I found helpful. "Does America still work like that ("there's a chance we can be rich tomorrow")? The suspicion that the answer is no inspires not only the OWS protests that have spread across the nation but also a movement as seemingly divergent as the Tea Party. While OWS may focus its anger on rapacious bankers, and the Tea Party on spendthrift politicians . . . there's a cabal of entitled elites on Wall Street and in Washington who have somehow loaded the dice and made it impossible for average people to get ahead. The American Dream, like the rest of our economy, has become bifurcated."[239]

Thomas Friedman's *The World is Flat* helps us to understand what happened. "In his opinion, this flattening is a product of a convergence of (the) personal computer with fiber-optic micro cable (and) with the rise of work flow software. . . . (He) recounts many examples of companies based in India and China that, by providing labor from typists and call center operators to accountants and computer programmers, have become integral parts of complex global supply chains for companies such as Dell, AOL and Microsoft."[240] "For Friedman . . . telecommunications have finally obliterated all impediments to international competition. . . . . . . The service sector (telemarketing, accounting, computer programming, engineering, and scientific research, etc.) will be further outsourced to the English-spoken abroad; manufacturing, meanwhile, will continue to be off-shored to China."[241] The obvious problem for the American worker is that the wage scale of workers in the countries where the work is outsourced is much lower than ours'. We have lost jobs and begun to question the continuing validity of the American Dream.

While businesses have a way to navigate this new world of technological change and globalization, the ordinary American worker does not. Capital and technology are mobile; labor isn't. American workers are located in America. And this is a country with one of the highest wages in the world, because it is one of the richest countries in the world. That makes it difficult for the average middle-class worker to benefit from technology and global growth in the same way that companies do.

. . . Technology and globalization are working together at warp speed, creating a new and powerful reality. Many more goods and services can now be produced anywhere on the globe. China and India have added literally hundreds of millions of new workers to the global labor pool, producing the same goods and services as Western workers at a fraction of the price. Far from being basket-case economies and banana republics, many developing countries are now stable and well managed, and companies can do business in them with ease. At some point, all these differences add up to mean that global competition is having quite an impact on life in the U.S.[242]

MIT economist "(David) Autor is cautious and tentative, but it would seem that technology followed by global competition, has played the largest role in making less valuable the routine tasks that once epitomized middle-class work."[243] **The result is that there has been a downward adjustment with a new and lower baseline for the American Dream.**

A TIME/Money poll indicates that the Dream is in flux. "We're making tough choices in a new age of austerity, yet we still believe in the American Dream. . . . We are less sure our children will achieve the American Dream."[244] Clearly Americans are trying to figure out what expectations are realistic for themselves and for their children. They are trying to come to terms with an American Dream that used to include the hope of a better life for our children, but now seems different, and we haven't adjusted to the change that is swirling all around us all over the world. It is indeed a new world. The protestant work ethic is no longer operative. The once widely held belief that hard work, initiative, honesty and integrity *alone* will get you a good job and your share of the American Dream has had its day. It's a whole new ball game, and since the old rules don't always apply people aren't sure what to do. The same confusion and uncertainty are evident on a Y(ahoo)! Finance Survey.[245]

41% say the American Dream is Lost

63% say the Economy is Getting Worse

53% still say America is a Land of Opportunity

45% still say their Children will do Better than they

It is clear that the capitalist system no longer works in the same way for a large majority of Americans. Income disparity and unemployment have changed the dynamics. OWS would say that the system is rigged. Technological developments, globalization and 30 years of changes in the tax code have had a tremendous impact on what we have come to know as the good life. We have seen a reset in our standard of living. It is harder to get ahead financially. For many lower income families it takes two wage-earners to maintain the standard of living with which we grew up, and it is going to get harder still for our children.

We also see a lot of stories like this one. "Beyond the 15 million Americans who have no jobs at all, millions more are caught in part-time or limited jobs that don't pay them enough to maintain their standard of living—much less contribute to the strong consumer spending needed to power the nation out of the economic doldrums. Economists have a technical term for these people: underemployed."[246]

Here is another article, based on an interview with Sherie Schwinninger of the New America Foundation. Her recent report, "The American Middle Class Under Stress," provides a "sobering" picture of what the middle class is up against. "Two recessions, a couple of market crashes, and stubbornly high unemployment are all wreaking havoc on America's middle class. . . . (Here are) some stunning facts that highlight the struggles the average American is having getting a decent-paying job and keeping up with the rising cost of living.

-There are 8.5 million people receiving unemployment insurance and over 40 million receiving food stamps.

-At the current pace of job creation, the economy won't return to full employment until 2018.

-Middle-income jobs are disappearing from the economy. The share of middle-income jobs has fallen from 52% in 1980 to 42% in 2010.

-Middle-income jobs have been replaced by low-income jobs, which now make up 41% of total employment.

-17 million Americans with college degrees are doing jobs that require less than the skill level associated with a bachelor's degree.

-Over the past year, nominal wages grew only 1.7% while all consumer prices, including food and energy, increased by 2.7%

-Wages and salaries have fallen from 60% of personal income in 1980 to 51% in 2010. Government transfers have risen from 11.7% of personal income in 1980 to 18.4% in 2010, a post-war high.

"The bottom line is simple, says Schwinninger: The middle class is shrinking which threatens the social composition and stability of the world's biggest economy. 'I worry that we're becoming a barbell society—a lot of money, wealth and power at the top, increasing hollowness at the center, which I think provides the stability and the heart and soul of the society . . . and then too many people in fear of falling down.'"[247]

It certainly appears that the fear described by Schwinninger is real. "(In) the U.S., The mood is sour. . . . Americans are glum, dispirited and angry. The middle class, in particular, feels under assault. In a *Newsweek* poll in September (2010) 63% of Americans said they didn't think they would be able to maintain their current standard of living. Perhaps most troubling, Americans are strikingly fatalistic about their prospects. . . . They fear we are in the midst of not a cyclical downturn but a structural shift, one that poses huge new challenges to the average American job, pressures the average American wage and endangers the average American Dream."[248]

My take is that gap between our standard of living as compared to that of the rest of the world is gradually going to decrease. . . . The advances in and availability of educational technology will gradually level the playing field in the global community. We will continue downward adjustments in the baseline for the American Dream until we arrive at the new realities of a global economy, and a "Global Dream" for all of our brothers and sisters in the human family, fellow citizens in the global community of nations.

Happiness, Contentment and Satisfaction

Adams original vision of the American Dream was of "a better, richer and happier life for all our citizens." What defines this life is different for each of us. If we just listen to people, they will tell us their story and how they define the meaning of life. If you've been listening to what I've been saying you know that as a Christian I understand the meaning of life as living modestly, giving generously and serving faithfully. Biblical teaching is clear: we are not entitled to have it all. If blessed abundantly, we are called on to be our brother's keeper. However, it is extremely difficult to sacrifice and deny yourself, when others around you are not making similar choices. Materialism and a consumer mentality permeate our culture.

We too live in the real world where you have to put food on the table, pay the mortgage, buy a car and save for college and retirement. But where do you draw the line after that when it comes to choices about big screen TVs, designer clothes for the kids, computers, music systems, music lessons and sports camps and how much to spend on vacations? It isn't easy, as we are tempted to want as much as our neighbor. Our culture would tell us that it is not just ok to strive to have what others have, it's downright American. It also stimulates the economy and creates more jobs.

Every once in a while you hear a lonely voice suggesting that even achieving the American Dream doesn't necessarily bring happiness. There is something more. Life has to have a deeper meaning. Money doesn't buy happiness. A study by Angud Deaton and Daniel Kahnman found that "there's a specific dollar number... after which more money has no measurable effect on day to day contentment. As people earn more money, their day-to-day happiness rises. That is, until you hit the magic number: $75,000 a year. After that it's just more stuff with no gain in happiness. ... Giving people more income beyond 75K is not going to do much for their daily mood ... but it is going to make them feel they have a better life."[249]

We simply are not passionate about and committed to helping provide for the unmet needs of others, and therefore never discover the path to true contentment and satisfaction. Some have never had it spelled out for them as I am doing. If they haven't been challenged to a life of surrender and sacrifice, that's one thing. Once someone lays it out there for them, and they still choose not to live a self-giving, selfless life of service, it is quite another. Tragically, as I see it, the nature of man will always hinder the experience of the joy and fulfillment found in relationship and service. But these are the things that lift the human heart.

Most of the time we give our eternal quest for meaning and satisfaction a half-hearted effort. It is the nature of man to look out not just for the needs of his own, but for their wants at the expense of the unmet needs of others who are often desperate. Barbara Tuchman's worldview is one that for me describes human nature—what makes us tick. "Tuchman's view of history is gravely classical. She is a tragedian who mounts the past against the fixed backdrop of human nature. Reason and goodwill exist but are like the stars in the heavens: flashes of enlightenment separated by vast expanses of darkness. 'Halfway between truth and endless error,' she concludes, 'the mold of the species is permanent.'"[250] To be obsessed by the quest to reach the American Dream is to miss out on all that is invigorating, liberating and celebratory; there is so much more to the meaning of life.

Excuse me! Did you say, "Give the Rest Away?"

Our country and our culture have entered an era of accelerating change: the shift to a green economy, a possible change in home ownership patterns, a gradual downward readjustment in our standard of living, and a more limited vision of the American Dream. What stays the same is human nature and how it will function in a changed paradigm of capitalism.

The American Dream has in no way become a nightmare. Nevertheless, how well you cope with the change will depend on your perception of economic reality, and your perception of the nature of man. Naively believing that those with resources will act in the interest of others goes against history and everything I have observed. Wars are fought among nations over resources and economic advantage, while labor unions bargain with management seeking what they perceive as their fair share of the pot. When our post WWII economy began to cook on all burners, unions overplayed their hand, seeking wage and benefit packages that contributed to a thriving middle class. Eventually, our high wages and benefits priced us right out of the world market. Jobs went to geographical areas of the country where wages were lower, and were then moved overseas to countries with a much more modest standard of living. Those who haven't realized that this is the way it is, that this is the way the world works, that it is dog eat dog, every man for himself, survival of the fittest world, may have a rude awakening when reality makes it impossible to avoid rethinking and reconsidering why their fundamental assumptions are no longer valid.

It is a whole different world from when Adams first used the term "American Dream"— a time when there was a unique configuration of circumstances. We had less people in our country. We had an abundance of land and natural resources, and energy was cheap. In the future it is going to be much more difficult for a large portion of the population to accumulate significant wealth. The Boomers lived at a unique moment in the history of our country and in the history of the world. There was a whole lot of luck involved in their realization of the American Dream. They were in the right place at the right time. The Boomers weren't any more hard working than the generations of Americans before or since. They simply lived at a time when there was more opportunity, when industrialization and an explosion in technology facilitated a steady increase in jobs, wages and the standard of living. We had gotten a great start educationally and technologically, and had not yet experienced any major negative effects from globalization, because many other nations hadn't started to catch up. Several generations of our people just happened to live at the right time. This alignment of the economic stars will likely not occur again. Then, "Beginning with Reagan, we've become two Americas, with a thin veneer of the wealthiest becoming even richer and (the) middle class shrinking."[251] "The widening gap between rich and poor suggests the Dream is becoming more and more elusive for more people than at any other time in our history."[252]

We are finding our way in a whole new economic world. I don't think that opportunity is out there in the same way that it was, and it will never be that way again. There aren't as many manufacturing jobs or jobs for laborers. All the economic pieces that made the American Dream possible for so many are no longer there, and realization of the dream will forever remain much more of a challenge.

Capitalism may be the best economic system out there. However, due to the nature of man, unbridled capitalism is dangerous. Its many damaging outcomes would suggest the need for some control and regulation. It is essential that we are having that discussion now. At least we are trying to learn something about the causes of the economic meltdown and near disaster that almost brought us to our knees. My purpose is not to lobby for specific changes in the fundamentals of our free market, free enterprise, capitalistic system. However, I most certainly am suggesting that we are not the generous, charitable, giving, compassionate people we think we are. And all of us, including those with money, power and influence will use it to take care of not just the needs, but also the wants of ourselves and our own, often at the expense of the unmet needs of others. We have to accept the truth about ourselves before any significant change is possible. This is a sermon nobody wants to hear.

So go ahead and be successful! Go ahead and make all the money you can! Take care of your needs and the needs of your own. Then give the rest away! In response you hear a deafening chorus: "Excuse me! Run that past me again!" If our purpose in life is simply to make money and accumulate stuff, investments and property for us and our descendants, we will never find peace and contentment. I am not against the idea of making a lot of money. If that is your gift, God bless you and more power to you. Nevertheless, I so very much hope that those whose gift is making money and being successful will use their wealth for the well being of others. My point is that we need to be reminded that there are others out there with great needs, and that God would nudge us as we make decisions about how we want to respond to those needs. We all understand when someone says: "We've earned it! We've put in some long hours. We've worked hard for what we have. We deserve a nice house and a nice car and traveling to some of the places we've always dreamed about." I would also hope that we all understand that not everyone has the same intellect, education, health, opportunity or luck. Some work hard just to pay rent or a small mortgage, and need some help to secure health insurance. Some are born destitute, in poor health and with little opportunity. There is a whole continuum of need, and all kinds of reasons why people are found all along the continuum.

Clearly the system is not working. The wealth gap is obscene. The erosion of the American Dream is threatening the foundations of our perceived economic reality. Many do not understand this and are really confused. They have played by the rules. They haven't done anything illegal. Nevertheless, so many who work hard have been snookered. They are victims of those who have gamed the system to their advantage. The majority have been sold a bill of goods. The majority have been used by those who had the smarts to intentionally deceive and mislead the weak and vulnerable, the trusting and naïve, hard workers and patriotic Americans. Many will say that hard work, initiative and persistence will lead to success. While this may have been true at one time in our country, it isn't true in the same way any longer. Today more than ever it is part education, part opportunity, part initiative, part skill, part connections, part luck and part policy. We are easy marks, ripe for the picking. We are taken advantage of by those who know how to manipulate the capitalist system in order to further their own interests. These are difficult and painful words to hear. We want to hold our hands over our ears. In a sense this is a sermon nobody wants to hear. Nevertheless, we need to be in the front pew.

Unfortunately, our fellow citizens are not all good people. They are not all nice people. We are naïve to assume that the basic goodness of people will result in capitalism working for the wealth and prosperity of all. There are plenty of movers and shakers who have caused gross inequities, lived unprincipled lives in pursuit of their own goals, hopes and dreams and adopted a scorched earth policy in pursuit of their own interests, seeking their own advantage without regard for the needs and interests of others. While a few have some sense of conscience, others have a winner-take-all mentality. Many have to rationalize the basic fairness of what they are doing so they can pursue an agenda (business plan) that will benefit them. Denial, repression and distortion make it possible for them to proceed with a clear conscience. They honestly don't see or believe they are doing anything wrong. There is enough of this in all of us to make it possible for us to understand the inequities in capitalism that get in the way of the fulfillment of the American Dream. Believing that capitalism is this great system that will lift everybody up discounts how human nature throws a monkey wrench into the system. The laissez-faire, capitalistic system is subject to decision makers who operate on the basis of self interest.

There are those who hold that capitalism works best when the invisible hand is left alone as much as possible to do its work. Are they sincerely advocating this view so the invisible hand can work its magic and everybody will benefit fairly? Or are they taking this position because they know that convincing the lower and middle classes to agree with and accept the conceptual framework of their belief system will serve as a smokescreen that hides their true intentions? What they may really want is to be free to influence economic policies in ways that will result in outcomes favorable to them, without having to be concerned about how those policies impact the lower and middle classes.

Trying to analyze intentions is extremely difficult, if not impossible. My sense is that there is a mixed bag of motivation. Some people are simply in favor of economic policy that creates a favorable business climate where they can succeed, and aren't aware of the larger issues. While they may have their views, they simply may not have taken into consideration the theoretical issues found at the next level of awareness. Others are aware of both levels of the conversation, and given my view of human nature, I would be shocked if they didn't know exactly what they were doing.

In the world view of Ayn Rand and Milton Friedman, everybody in the world is motivated purely by "self interest." There are "smart" people pursuing their own self-interest (also known as "the rich") and the "lazy" people pursuing their own self-interest by using an instrument of force (government regulations, and minimum-wage and collective bargaining laws, etc.) to extract wealth from the "smart" people for themselves. These latter people are labeled by Randians and Friedmanies as "parasites" and "moochers."[253]

How we address these issues is precisely what the next chapter is all about. One thing is sure, capitalism is a system where everyone involved is greedy, self-centered and self-serving, where everyone is trying to game the system in their favor, where everyone is seeking an advantage, where everyone is seeking an outcome from which they will benefit. Capitalism is not divinely inspired. It is a creation of the human mind and a very helpful one. However, believing that it is infallible, that it is self-regulating, that it has internal controls and will always work for the benefit of all is going to result in many people getting hurt, and hurt badly. It needs to be tweaked. It needs regulation, because all those who are involved in establishing the mechanisms that guide the operation of the system are guided by self-interest. These are the presuppositions on the basis of which the system functions. Human nature is always involved in the process of decision making about the mechanisms, and therefore the system will never function perfectly. There will be inequities. At this time in our history the differences are considerable.

"The mythology of the American Dream has made it difficult to start a serious discussion about how to create more opportunity in our society, since many of us still believe that our mobility is the result of our elbow grease and nothing more. But there is a growing truth seen in the numbers and in the protests that are spreading across our nation that this isn't so. (The other view says) we can no longer blame the individual. We have to acknowledge that climbing the ladder often means getting some support and a boost."[254] Everyone involved has their own interpretation of events, and their own ideas about how to resolve the issue. And what exactly does "some support" mean? Human nature has thrown a monkey wrench into the capitalistic system and conversations about the system for a long time, and will continue to do so in the future.

What is remarkable is that our political leaders have known about these issues for at least 25-30 years. During that time we have not had the political will to take on the tough challenges involved in addressing them early-on, making needed adjustments and nipping the problem in the bud; this will be discussed at length in Chapter 13. Truthfully, openly and honestly surfacing the growing gap between the rich and poor and the downward adjustment of the baseline of the American Dream create an environment where it requires the courage to make decisions that would increase the probability that you wouldn't be re-elected.

We probably need changes in the tax code, regulatory structure and how elections are funded before we can expect any meaningful change in the economic environment. The impact of the political environment on any attempt to address these issues is what the next chapter is about.

Chapter 11
The Morality of Government

". . . (Thomas) Hobbes pictured the life of man without government as 'solitary, poor, nasty, brutish, and short.' Without some authority to enforce law, there is no society, no order, only 'a war of every man against every man.' Men in general are inclined to 'a perpetual and restless desire of power after power.' So they set up a sovereign power (Leviathan) by agreement or contract (it makes no difference whether the sovereign is a king or a Parliament), by which all men agree to obey the sovereign. . ."
Thomas Hobbes

"Remind the people to be subject to rulers and authorities, to be obedient, to be ready to do whatever is good . . . to be peaceable and considerate, and to show true humility toward all men" (Titus 3:1).

Golf and Life: Using Triangulation to Calculate the Slippery "Slope" into Cheating

Playing golf for a preacher presents a unique challenge. If you don't know your playing partners, do you tell them you are clergy, and if so, when? Since we get to know each other on the course anyway, I tell them early on. Otherwise, you're setting them up to be embarrassed, which is not right and not a good witness to our faith. If they feel comfortable around you, it often opens the door for conversation or questions. If they don't care, they may tone it down, but will swear anyway—maybe out of fear reflecting uncertainty in their own spiritual journey and maybe in response to being hurt by a Christian in the past– perhaps even someone in the clergy.

A part of the code of etiquette in the game of golf is that you don't mess with another player's head on the course, unless you know them well and everyone enjoys the banter—especially so if its your son, brother or a good friend. If you're not sure how good of a friend they are, try messing with their head and you may find out in a hurry. This book is precisely about messing with people's heads and hearts and souls while they are traveling on down the road of life.

Playing golf with folks you don't know also provides opportunity to hear some great stories. While spending a few winter days in Mississippi, a good ole' southern boy shared this one after learning I was preacher and after listening to a little of what I have been writing about. Turned out he was a judge. He said, "Let me tell what it was like down south during prohibition. The bootleggers were making big money and didn't want prohibition repealed. They realized it was a good investment to generously support Baptist churches, where the preachers continued to rail against drinking and admonish their members not to vote for repeal. Prohibition continued, bootleggers kept making money, Baptist churches continued to receive an abundance of offerings and the pastors kept preaching fervently. Everybody was happy." I don't know if the story is true, or whether he was just blowing smoke, but it does serve as an apt metaphor for what this chapter is about. It was an interesting triangulation where everybody got what they wanted, except, perhaps, those Baptists who would have probably given their eye teeth for a cold beer.

In a round-about way it sounds like the today's triangulation involving politicians, campaign contributors and voters. Members of Congress vote for legislation favored by donors, while unsuspecting voters continue to elect politicians who have framed their public persona into a platform and voting record that appeals to the concerns of their constituency. The voters aren't aware of their true agenda. It's not illegal. It's just the way you do business in politics today. Today there is a growing perception that everyone in politics is on the take, that in government "Money Rules" and that politicians care more about the next election than with solving problems or the next generation.

The genius of our Constitution and the excellence of the governmental framework it establishes are sabotaged and corrupted by dishonest politicians. The problem isn't our form of government; it is that our elected leaders are corrupted by campaign contributions. Our system of government is not immoral. The source of the immorality that contaminates the system and disrupts how it functions is corrupt elected leaders. Human nature undermines the brilliant efforts of those who wrote the Constitution.

It is only by rationalizing and justifying their positions and votes that politicians can live with themselves. They convince themselves that they are not "cheating." They convince themselves that they have not sold their souls to the devil, that they have not been bought, that they do not vote in a way they know is not in the best interest of the country and that they have not framed and spun issues in ways that deceive voters into thinking they are getting what they want.

But voters are getting wiser.

> More than one-third of the country supports the Wall Street protests (37%), and even more—58%—say they are furious about America's politics. ... In January (just 9 months earlier) ... 49% said they felt that way. What's more, nearly nine in ten say they are frustrated with politics and nearly the same (number) say they are disappointed. ... Fewer are hopeful about politics than when the year began; 47% down from 60%. Only 17% of respondents say they feel proud or inspired. The poll was conducted October 13-17 (2011) by GK Roper Public Affairs and Corporate Communications.[255]

Priority One: The Next Election

Put us behind their desks and—operating on the basis of self interest, looking out not just for the needs of ourselves and our own, but also for our wants—we too would make the ethical compromises necessary to accept lobbyist contributions and vote for the interests they represent. The sad reality is that we are cut from the same cloth. We have the same depraved human nature. We know it from local politics, workplace politics and church politics.

Joe Scarborough summarizes the issue nicely. Then former US Congressman Harold Ford Jr. continues the discussion by talking about where we are now.

SCARBOROUGH. The 99% are being squeezed: the massive debt (in) Social Security, Medicare and Medicaid ... (and) at the same time we are facing a decline (in wages for men)—a decline that began in 1973. So (we have) these two things at the same time, the baby boomers are slouching toward retirement, (and) you have this decline in the middle class—the manufacturing base. It's so maddening when people say, 'It's Obama's or Bush's fault.' No! This is a crisis thirty years in the making. Could presidents over the past twenty years have done more to pay for this? Yes! They certainly could have. But the fact is right now there are two forces rocking this country and they are going to continue to squeeze and rock this country until we don't recognize America if Washington doesn't fix it. (author's note – Our presidents and Congress have seen this coming for at least the past 20 years, but didn't make much of an effort to address it. It served their own interests not to. They wouldn't have been re-elected if they had really been leaders and taken the unpopular positions needed to address these problems. At the same time a large majority of Americans were still doing well enough economically to continue to be able to believe in the earlier version of the American Dream. It was hard for the electorate to see the need for belt tightening and higher taxes. So why should politicians rock the boat by educating the public about what was going to happen and support unpopular corrective measures? Bottom line, they might very well lose the next election, as there is always another politician waiting in the wings to campaign on a platform that would conform to the way the voters see the world.)

CONGRESSMAN FORD. (The resentment expressed by) unions and "Occupy America" is simple. If you are going to ask for Medicare and Social security cuts, which we have to have, (saying) you're going to have to sacrifice in the middle class, then those who make a whole lot more than we around this table are going to have to pay more taxes.

SCARBOROUGH. So both sides are going to have to give, aren't they? We need shared sacrifice. . . . There is something we can do. I'm not talking about soaking the rich. I'm not talking about class warfare. But the entire tax system over the past 30 years has been geared toward helping rich people get rich much more quickly, creating exotic financial instruments on Wall Street, where the best and the brightest go to create them, instruments that do nothing to build Main Street. Wall Street gets rich while Main Street is withering. Guess what? We can adjust tax policy to encourage investment on Main Street, investment in manufacturing, investment in Middle America to rebuild the working class.

CONGRESSMAN FORD. There's no doubt (about) the growth excesses at the top of the economy; the top 1 percent had income grow by 275 percent in the last 30 years, others in the middle, the majority, have only seen 10-15 percent increases. Mike's (Barnacle) point is the most important in all this. The challenge we face and the overwhelming message coming from OWS for me is people don't believe they can attain a certain level or a certain (upward) mobility any more. When you lose that, you lose America.[256]

Yet, too many of our elected leaders in Washington often seem fixated on the next election.

"Land that I Love"

In 1998 Karen and I took a vacation to Williamsburg, Washington D.C, Philadelphia and Gettysburg. We wrote to try get passes for a White House tour. While none were available, Senator Kohl's office invited us to his weekly continental breakfast and conversation for any constituents who were in town. He and his staff took time to listen to each of us. We had an unexpected surprise when leaving, as we were directed unescorted to elevators that took us down to the underground tram that goes to the Capital. Sen. Lugar from Indiana was the only other person on the platform waiting for the tram. I recognized and greeted him, mentioning that I received my undergraduate degree from Concordia Senior College in Fort Wayne. When we arrived at the Capital, he graciously directed us to the main floor and rotunda. I recall that almost immediately we found ourselves going past Majority Whip Tom Delay's office. Less than two weeks later, an intruder was able to get past Capital security guards and make it as far as Tom Delay's office. The irony was poignant. While security has understandably been tightened since then, freely roaming in the Senate Office Building and the halls of the Capital unescorted was an extraordinary experience.

I love this great country and daily give thanks for the freedom we enjoy, the freedom that until just a few years ago allowed my wife and I to roam freely in the Capitol building. What a blessing to be able to go to sleep at night with a peace that comes from knowing that we, our loved ones and all of our fellow Americans are safe, protected by the brave men and women of our armed forces who stand guard over our freedom.

We live in a great nation! I wouldn't want to live anywhere else. I wouldn't trade our Constitution and our government for anything. The fact that we can have spirited conversations about issues and have our differences of opinion, knowing we have a mechanism for resolving those differences without resorting to violence is nothing short of priceless, and is worth fighting and dying for.

When I was just five, my Dad returned from the Navy at the end of WWII. He came to the door in uniform, and rang the bell. I answered, but didn't recognize him. He asked for Mom. I went and told her there was a man in a uniform at the door who was asking for her. When she came to the door and saw him, there were shouts of joy, tears, smiles, hugs and kisses—a scene I will never forget. What tears at my heart are the families whose loved ones did not return. My unending devotion goes out to them. A dear price has been paid for this treasured freedom we enjoy. When Mom died I asked for the flag from Dad's funeral. It's here in my study. Even as I write there is a flood of emotion, the same flood of emotion as when we visited Arlington National Cemetery, the battlefields at Williamsburg and Gettysburg, or when we drive past a military cemetery or watch a Memorial Day, Independence Day or Veterans Day parade.

A dear price has been paid for the priceless freedoms that are ours, a price paid in blood, and in the loss of life and limb. We can never repay their sacrifices and the sacrifice of their families, who also need always to be remembered and appreciated. We must provide all of the benefits and care needed by our veterans and the families of those who never returned. I will always remember with gratitude the sacrifices of those in our armed services.

A good friend moves in circles where people have different political views. One of them asked him, "Isn't there anything you would fight for?" His response: "I would be ready in a heartbeat to fight and die for this great country so that you will forever remain free to express views that I think are totally off the wall."

Our system of government and the freedom it brings are blessings to be cherished, to fight and to die for. The flag that flies on the front porch of our home symbolizes the freedoms we enjoy, the hope those freedoms give and the dear price paid for our freedom. The biggest question for me is, and always has been, how we choose to use this freedom. Where do our own interests infringe on the rights of others and the common good? For caring and compassionate folk, the plight of others is always of great concern.

The Purpose of Government

My hope is that we will always remain a beacon of freedom for all people. Still, we have to recognize that we are not perfect, and continually have the opportunity to be involved in discussions in the political arena about how we can do even better. While we have a great system of government, there is always room for improvement.

The essence of my thesis as it relates to this chapter is that we need to be protected from each other, as well as from any would-be foreign aggressor. The nature of man with his self-centered, self-serving, self-seeking nature is the reason we need a mechanism for resolving competing needs in a civilized way. Government provides the structure and defines the mechanisms used to maintain a balance, so that while meeting our needs, we do not infringe on the rights of others. Governing is the process of negotiation and compromise to the end that the needs of all can be met in a just, fair and equitable manner. In our country these issues are resolved within the framework of the treasure that is our Constitution, especially in the environment of a polarized electorate. It makes it possible to address hotly debated issues like what, if anything, to do about the disparity between "the 1% and the 99%."

How you view human nature determines how you structure society in terms of laws and law enforcement. The need for government presupposes that people act in their own interest without regard for the rights, needs and well being of others. The very fact that civilized societies develop a government structure organized around a constitution and laws presumes there is most certainly a need to protect its members from those who operate on the basis of self-interest, who don't respect the rights and property of others. We need government to protect us from each other. This is what it means to be a civilized society.

Certainly we have to look out for the needs of our families. However, all who celebrate and cherish the freedoms that are ours have to make choices between self-interest and the common good. Where our own interests intersect with and overlap the common good, we have choices to make. This is where our Constitution provides the mechanisms to resolve competing interests and preserve order.

As I've been saying, we look out for ourselves and our own. This is who we are. This is our nature. This is the way it has always been. The understanding of human nature described in this work impacts the ideal of a fair, decent and honest government. Just as this chapter was being written and being from Chicago, I noted that former Illinois Governor Rob Blagojeviich was sentenced to 14 years in prison for his crimes, the second Illinois governor to be sentenced in just a short time. His crimes were serious felonies. Nevertheless, from my point of view there is no doubt that the desire for money, power and prestige impact fair, decent and honest government at all levels. This is just how the system works today. It is a given. Why would we expect it to be any different? How else would we get to a place where we're discussing policy issues within the framework of "the 1% and the 99%?"

The electorate needs to understand what kind of legislation and regulation stifle business growth, negatively impacting job creation, and what policies and regulations foster competitiveness and profitability. The electorate needs to be informed about the percent of the profits allocated for the owner or stockholders, for reinvestment in the business and for wages and benefits that are reasonable and fair. Historically workers have more often than not come out on the short end of the stick. So workers have organized into unions to gain leverage in negotiating for what they felt was a fair and equitable distribution of profits. Chances are that the colonists would not have started a revolution if the English had been reasonable and fair.

We are currently engaged in an energetic and passionate debate about the formulation of government policy, and whether emerging policy will result in all of us having to make concessions, all of us having to experience a downward adjustment in lifestyle, all of us having to get used to a new normal that has a lower baseline for the American Dream. Folks in the upper class also need to recognize that they too will experience a reset of the baseline for their standard of living and the rate of growth of their portfolio.

As noted, the sermon people want to hear even less is that these readjustments will continue to occur until we come to a point where there is some semblance of global balance. These developments mean that we in the USA will continue to be involved in a long-term political conversation to find reasonable, balanced compromises through the processes of civilized government. If our intent is to foster a level of American economic superiority in a global economy that makes it possible for us to maintain our current standard of living, my sense is that even our best efforts to retrain workers and stoke creativity, research and innovation are temporary fixes that will delay the inevitable. As much as we would like to believe otherwise, there is no difference in intelligence or in the willingness of peoples everywhere to study hard and work hard. Better education and continued innovation will only take us so far.

We seem to be well along the way down that path to a more level global playing field. Huge numbers of manufacturing and white collar jobs have been outsourced across oceans and are now being filled in countries where the standard of living and wage scale are significantly lower than ours. What is critical to note is that a downward adjustment to a new normal for us is an upward adjustment to a new normal for others in the global economy. We are now dealing with a global labor pool. It appears to me that our economy is going through structural changes that for all practical purposes could ultimately lead to the elimination of the middle class. One of the purposes of our representative government is to provide the structure to manage the legislative process that will guide decision making amid potentially seismic changes in global economic policy.

My wife is from Wausau, Wisconsin, which was in Congressman Dave Obey's District. Since we have been married for 47 years, I've had a chance to follow his 41 year tenure of congressional service. The following interview was an eye-opener to say the least. Here are his remarks about economic fairness.

> We're right back where we were in 1929, a split-level society with the very wealthy gathering obscene amounts of cash and everybody else is struggling to make their car payments. The right wing will cry about, "Oh, the damn Democrats, they're redistributionists." Like hell. We've had income redistribution for the last 30 years and it's all gone up the income scale. . . . That's been our biggest collective failure over the past generation, to change that. It isn't just a matter of equity. It's a matter of economic survival.[257]

Dave Obey's interview was in Monday's paper. The next day the paper ran a story about the inauguration of our new governor, Scott Walker. It was reported (p 12A) he would introduce a number of bills, including one that would reduce business regulation. Given the lack of regulation that contributed significantly to the near economic collapse and the undo economic hardship experienced by the middle class, it would seem prudent to initiate a discussion about regulation to insure a level playing field. Less regulation can result in more profit and the accumulation of more wealth by business owners and stockholders. If the structural changes are unfair and come at the expense of lower wages and reduced benefits given the context of a global labor pool, we move closer to a two class society. How we pass legislation that finds a balance can be a contentious endeavor or cooperative effort.

We simply have to understand that policy discussions about proposed legislation or mechanisms that modify the functioning of a free market economy are not based solely on rational arguments. The unidentified elephant in the room is the self-serving, self-centered, self-seeking, selfish tendencies of everyone involved. We are all seeking outcomes that reflect our own interests. Factoring the powerful influence of human nature into the system results in legislation that tilts the playing field in ways that give the advantage to one of the participants. Acknowledging this reality as a presupposition of the principles of governing is essential if you want to make sense out of the issues and the positions of both parties. Those who haven't realized that this is the way it is, that this is the way the world works, that it is dog eat dog, every man for himself, survival of the fittest world, have to rethink their fundamental assumptions. Those who resist acknowledging the reality of this conceptual framework probably do so because it would result in having to make some changes in their worldview, one that no longer provides the same level of stability and security as they make decisions about their future.

Given the nature of man with his self-interest and greed, we can be certain that there will always be attempts to manipulate the system—to achieve advantage. There are times when the Federal government is the only entity big enough to protect the average citizen. We don't have the money or the muscle or the clout to do it ourselves. We as individuals cannot request a court order for a wiretap or issue a subpoena. There are issues where the need for federal government intervention needs to be carefully considered in order to find just the right balance between free enterprise, the size of government and the welfare of those who are vulnerable and in need. There are times when the issues are about wages and jobs. There are times when they are about the banking system.

Clearly, with my understanding that we all operate on the basis of self-interest, there are times when those with money and power have to be regulated. The question that remains is how much regulation is needed. We are currently involved in intense discussions about regulation, as well as the size of government, job growth, taxes, budget deficits and entitlement programs. I'm not in any way, shape or form suggesting that I know "the answer" to how our differences on these issues should be resolved; but I do have an opinion and a vote—as we all do.

But I am most definitely expressing my opinion about how our political system works. Given our human nature, we can assume that the powerful influence of self-interest is reflected in the views, positions, arguments and egos of everybody in the conversation. Thanks to the wisdom and common sense of those who wrote our Constitution we have the structure needed to have a spirited, yet civilized discussion. Again, this is reason why it is such a blessing to be an American. I try to stay informed so as to be able to participate in the conversation and vote intelligently. Within the framework of our constitutionally guaranteed freedoms, we can all participate in the decision making process.

One final note is necessary. We simply can't naively believe that freedom is never abused. It is abused all the time. Freedom is not this perfect, infallible entity. People manipulate the freedoms we have in order to further their self-serving, self-seeking, self-centered agendas. While freedom is a high and noble principle, one worth fighting and dying for, how it is implemented in the real world is less than perfect. The abuse of freedom is what the remainder of this chapter is about.

Leadership and the Next Election

Here is a piece about a good leader from our local paper.

> The first requirement of a leader is a vision, a dream. To lead, a person has to be going somewhere. Perceive and point us toward that glorious horizon.
>
> ... Lead by example. Be an expression of what we could be, what we should be.
>
> ... Today's pretenders to leadership are obsessed with money. A true leader would know that our lives are far richer and more meaningful than that. A true leader would understand that our professions, businesses and industries are how we live—not why we live. Our emphasis has shifted from the quantity of our possessions to the quality of our lives.
>
> A good leader would define us by the passions, hopes and fears that drive us and know that progress is not measured by how many bricks get stacked or how many miles get paved. (A true leader appreciate(s) our lives at home, at work and at play; respects our spiritual lives; understands our compassion and our avarice, our tenderness and our rage; knows us as true humans.)
>
> ... Today's pseudo-leaders invoke (a) notion of power that is more tyranny than leadership
>
> ... (Rather,)(b)uild bridges instead of walls. Bring us together to work on common ground. Do not divide and conquer us as enemies. Understand the diversity and the possibility of life, and help us to look beyond the follies that separate us.

> . . . Be willing both to admit mistakes and to forgive the offenses of others.
>
> It's considered naïve, but be principled. A leader's ethics need not mirror mine, but must have a philosophical framework by which we may know him or her. And be genuine, both in living by those principles and in expressing them. Cultivate grace.[258]

This is an insightful, sensitive, engaging vision. It almost sounds like a sermon. It is hopeful, uplifting and inspirational. It touches the soul. This is the kind of sermon people like. This is a paradigm for change that builds on all that is positive and hopeful; this is the way many would chose to frame the message in trying to motivate positive growth and change. He sees us as principled, on the way to becoming more than we are and living rich, meaningful lives that are not defined by money or possessions. It is a beautiful statement of principle, within the context of a worldview that sees people as more than civilized. Oh, how I wish that this was the way it would work. Given who we are by nature, what I understand about the history of the world and what I see going on around me, I do not hold out much hope for a positive shift in leadership values.

Again, our elected leaders are involved in the current national conversation about jobs, the budget deficit, the size of government, taxes, entitlements and regulation, and they are well aware that how they vote on these issues will affect campaign contributions and the next election. The unidentified elephant in the room is the self-serving, self-centered, selfish tendency of everyone involved in the debate to seek outcomes that further their own interests. To those who haven't realized that you have to factor in the powerful influence of human nature, it's time to re-evaluate some of the foundational assumptions of your worldview.

How our leaders frame their positions and vote will be consistent with the interests of those whose support they need in the next election. At times I wonder if they even bother considering any more whether they are compromising their values and integrity. They verbalize assurances about their ethics, morals and values, but with the approval rating for Congress being at an all time low, it doesn't appear that we trust them. We need to consider all of this in making our own assessment about how government works.

My cynicism has become apparent. My hope is that at the very least they make a conscious decision to play the game in the hope of positioning themselves where they can make principled decisions at critical moments. My sense is that at some point they might recognize that a willingness to compromise will serve the greater good.

A *Morning Joe* conversation on November 7, 2011 included comments that inform our discussion.

MIKE BARNICLE. The *Washington Post* this morning is reporting new government data that shows profits for American financial firms are reaching record highs not seen since before the financial crisis of 2008. In fact, Wall Street firms have earned more in the first 2½ years of the Obama presidency ($85.53 billion) than all eight years of the Bush presidency ($77.11 billion).

SCARBOROUGH. Their campaign contributions paid off very well for them.

MARK HALPERIN (MSNBC Political Commentator). There's something out of whack with our country if at a time of such hardship for so many families, our financial institutions—who got government help—can be doing well. And the slogan, "We need a bail out for the middle class," will be a winning slogan for the presidential candidate, whichever one uses it.

SCARBOROUGH. The thing is neither party can really do it.

WILLIE GEIST (co-host of MSNBC's *Morning Joe*). I just don't know how the President can go out on the stump and with a straight face talk about the fat cats on Wall Street. He gets more money from them than all the Republican candidates combined.

SCARBOROUGH. The biggest problem is not the massive profits . . . raking in cash. If it were just happening this year, or if it had just happened over the last three or four years, (that would be one thing). The problem is—and this is what I try to tell my conservative and Republican brethren—this is not about class warfare. . . . But (this is) . . . a thirty year trend (of falling average income for men), where you can see the trend lines of the middle class, a trend going back to 1973, as Jeffery Sachs says in his book (*The Price of Civilization*), (where) the rich are getting richer and the poor are getting poorer under Republican and Democratic presidents."[259]

Author Thom Hartman agrees with Geist.

Whether it was coincidental or consequential, a week after that Supreme Court (Citizens United) decision (asserting that even foreign corporations are persons with the constitutional protections of things like free speech), President Obama was backpedaling on his main criticisms of bankers and other companies who could easily outspend him and any other politician or political party (in the next campaign). . . . The President and Congress need to do something drastic, like amending the Constitution to say that corporations are not "persons."[260]

Our elected leaders do not seem to have the courage to do the right thing. They are not able to take positions divorced from political consideration. They seem to be willing to sell their souls by compromising honesty, integrity and the best interests of our citizens, rather than voting for legislation that gives everybody a fair shake. The upcoming election is the lens through which Washington sees all issues. The 2011 debate about the debt ceiling made this crystal clear. Washington is worried about the next election. Our elected leaders need the contributions of businesses and corporations. Businesses are worried about the next year's financials, and want our elected leaders help in furthering their interests by voting for measures that contribute to a positive business climate. Those with wealth and power use their influence to pass legislation favorable to their interests.

We live in a time when our politics has neutered the terms statesmanship and leadership. Our political system has become so polarized that except in the few situations addressing the pain and suffering resulting from natural disasters or threats to national security, we are unable to address even the most pressing needs. The next election is just around the corner and taking an unpopular position would be used against us in our own party's primary or by the opposing party in the general election. The members of Congress don't seem to have the courage to act in the interest of our citizens. Recent Congresses have been timid, ineffective and nearly irrelevant.

These are bright people. They know the issues. They don't need any more studies or commission reports, except to hide behind. Not one of them is, as my father used to say, "the third jerk from the end." But they act like it. We have known for years and years that the globalization of the economy, lower wages and the loss of jobs was inevitable. We have known for years that at some point changes in the global economy would wash ashore like a tsunami with blue collar and white collar jobs flooding our labor markets— jobs located in countries with a much lower standard of living and wage scale, but with a labor pool that was just as educated and qualified. Congress knew how cheap labor in underdeveloped countries would impact on our economy. They knew how globalization would impact our workforce and economy, but they also knew that it would be political suicide to address the issue and enact legislation that would have anticipated these changes and minimized their impact. Now you have large scale unemployment in places where manufacturing provided the blue collar jobs that sustained families and kept communities vibrant. We knew that these changes would have a powerful negative impact on our economy and standard of living. We knew these changes would precipitate vigorous debate about tariffs, protectionism and free trade agreements.

Political leaders in the legislative and executive branches of federal and state government have known all this for a long time, and that advocating and voting for the changes that needed to happen would jeopardize their re-election. They know there are opportunistic challengers waiting in the wings ready to push the old hot button arguments based on domestic and world economies that no longer exist. They don't want anyone misinterpreting or spinning what they say to make it sound like they don't believe in the greatness of America or the continuing viability of the American Dream. They don't want to be labeled as one of the "malaise" leaders who believe that America "is in a slow decline." Our leaders knew this was coming. They have access to the best studies and projections. Yet, they did nothing.

The point is that political leaders, motivated by a desire to maintain their sphere of influence and power, duck taking the positions and making the votes that leaders and statesman would. It is a hard sell when goods can be produced cheaper overseas, while wages decrease and jobs are lost at home. So they have to decide if they want to take the easy way out and get re-elected, or make the tough decisions that insure the long term well-being of the people they represent. If unions remain inflexible in wage negotiations, when gradual changes in wages and fringe benefits are discussed, and business resists consideration of lower profit margins, American jobs are lost overseas, and everybody loses. Or is business content to let the purchasing power of the U.S. consumer decline because emerging foreign markets will more than compensate?

Our political leaders aren't going to jump into the middle of this discussion and risk rocking the boat as long as there is more benefit to them in maintaining the status quo. To speak up would mean that they would lose votes. Being for free trade would alienate your union constituency. Favoring regulation would alienate business. Voting for a more progressive tax would alienate the wealthy. Supporting an increase in the capital gains tax would alienate investors. Being open to changes in entitlement programs would alienate seniors and the lower and middle classes. So they didn't vote for legislation that would address the coming reality and prepare for a time when wages would be lower, and the American Dream would not include the same level of affluence that it does today.

Courting votes for the next election means not taking any risks, when addressing issues like those on the table at labor-management negotiations, free trade discussions and immigration debates. As long as the economy is moving along, even though it needs a tune up, who cares about the rest of us? As long as incumbents have not had to take a stand one way or another on the tough issues facing us and as long as they have raised enough money to finance the next election, they are content, and will continue to vote in a way that assures campaign contributions keep rolling in. They and their constituencies have to discern whether they are acting on the basis of self-interest disguised by sophisticated spin doctors, or whether they are looking out for the well being of all of our citizens. Fundamental changes in the rules governing campaign financing are a pipe dream. It ain't gonna' happen.

I once asked someone in a position to provide an informed assessment, "How many in Congress have not been bought and maintain their integrity?" His answer was an eye opener: "You can count them on both hands." One Congress and one Administration after another is unable to deal with it. Perhaps their fragile egos require that they hold on for dear life to the position, power and influence they have. Who cares if at some point in the future our inability to act responsibly renders us economically vulnerable in a global economy? Our politicians know what to do about our nation's problems. They are afraid to do it. They are afraid to lead, if it means taking political risks and jeopardizing their careers, prestige, power and influence. They choose to not rock the boat and jeopardize the good thing they've got going.

Politics is the art of building consensus through compromise. Both sides need to make compromises that are hard to swallow. When elected leaders are paralyzed by the fear that any vote will be used against them in the next primary or general election, contrary to an over-riding concern for their own parents, children, grandchildren and future generations, the irony is that they do themselves a terrible disservice. Political leaders who fit this description fail to measure up to any standard of leadership.

Instead of voting for the policies that benefit most citizens, politicians succumb to the beast in all of us—self-interest—which translates into doing whatever will get them elected. It gets dicey when you have two opposing points of view. The rich don't want to pay for the poor. The poor feel the rich can help a little bit more. Positions harden. The electorate becomes polarized. We relate to each other with less and less civility.

Our elected leaders were aware that all of the current hot-button issues were coming, and did nothing. In their self-interest they kept looking only toward the next election, rather than advocating changes that would have left us better positioned to deal with the impact of the changing global economy. We may have had less discretionary income for the latest in communication technology, boats, snowmobiles and vacations, but we would have had a more stable foundation from which to compete in a world economy, and less apprehension about the well-being of future generations. It seems like the tough decisions can only be made in times of crisis when we are forced to make them. And, of course, we have to blame the other side for causing the problem, so we can try to justify why we voted for a compromise.

It would be inaccurate to characterize this process as one of repression and denial. Rather it is the result of avoidance and selective inattention motivated by self-interest: maintaining their office, power, prestige and influence. Raising these issues, participating in the process of educating the electorate and having a conversation about them is the quickest way to get defeated in the next election. So we plod along, complain about a situation as it gradually erodes, and wait for the next crisis when more of this change is crammed down our throats out of the necessity to survive. At the last possible moment they piece together a damage control plan that seeks to make the best of a bad situation.

The factors that come to bear on these issues are complex. The checks and balances in the global economy are complicated. But the truth is that we understand them and could have done something about them. We simply lack the political will to make the hard decisions. As with many issues that require leadership, statesmanship, conversations and compromises, politicians duck making the hard decisions that might jeopardize their re-election.

At the present time we have the world's largest economy and advantages when it comes to technology, innovation and education. But do we really think it will always be that way? Perpetuating that illusion is cruel hoax. While we have the advantage now, the playing field will level itself out. As long as we are still in front, however, we paint the future for our people and our nation positively and optimistically, because that is what wins elections. Then one day when the playing field starts to level out and other nations exercise leverage in their own interest, reality forces itself upon us. However, we could be better positioned for the future if our elected leaders made decisions that did not sacrifice wisdom and honesty for short term gain. We need something better from our leaders than a look into the future through rose-colored glasses that conveys an unrealistic sense of confidence and optimism.

To say that our political leaders have made a conscious decision to "game" the system, is to say they do the same thing preachers do when we set the bar way too low when it comes to teaching about discipleship, charity and loving service. They are guilty of moral conspiracy, fraud and deceit. We are, after all, kindred spirits, who operate from the same play book: greed and self-interest.

When considering the best interest of the people, our political leaders unfortunately do not openly discuss the elephant in the room. In the long run, it would be better if they did—so that we would be made aware of all the possible outcomes. I just don't see that happening. Our political leaders have also known about the coming shortfall in the Social Security Trust Fund and the growing federal deficit for a long time, and have chosen to do nothing about it. If they give us an honest assessment of an issue, and we say with our votes that we want to put off the "big" decisions until a crisis occurs, then we are responsible for the fallout. We can continue to elect leaders who put band aids on the wound until it gets so infected that our economic health becomes life-threatening.

It was a remake of an old script. "He (Obama) proposed a freeze in discretionary spending and federal salaries, a push to simplify the tax code and billions in cuts to the defense budget, and he made new calls for a bi-partisan effort to repair Social Security. Each of these had been proposed before by another third year President coming off a mid-term defeat in a period of high unemployment. 'Let us in these next two years – men and women of both parties, every political shade—concentrate on the long-range bipartisan responsibilities of government,' Reagan said in his 1983 State of the Union, 'not the short-range and short-term temptations of partisan politics.'"[261] Washington Politicians think short term, rather than in terms of what's best for our people in the long term. They think in terms of the next election, rather than in terms of what's best for all of our people, and for future generations. Politicians tend to think of their job, career, advancement, clout, celebrity and image.

Restructuring, rightsizing, downsizing, outsourcing, off-shoring—I'm not saying that these would have been easy issues to resolve, that there were any easy answers, that they would not have encountered intense public displeasure and opposition, that they would have been popular politically or that they would get re-elected. But at least everyone would have known and had the opportunity to plan accordingly.

We could have furthered our education. We could have begun training for new jobs in the fields of technology and information. We could have spent less and saved more, purchased more modest housing and avoided getting in over our heads with a mortgage we couldn't afford. Certainly it would not have been popular politically, as it could have been interpreted that we no longer believed that America was a great nation.

But if Americans understood that our early super-success as a nation was based upon a unique confluence of vast available real estate, an abundance of natural resources, and an influx of hard working, industrious immigrants that resulted in a booming economy in which there was enough wealth to spread around so that everyone could feel that they were sharing the wealth and had the opportunity to move up the economic ladder, over time they might have understood. Obviously we'll never know. What we can say is that there were vested interests that sought to control the conversation for short term gain. It has always been that way and it always will be that way. It's human nature.

As long as the average Joe gets a share of the pie and there is opportunity for upward mobility, it is reasonable to assume that when he votes, he will go along with the program. When the dividing up of the pie becomes overwhelmingly unfair, he will vote for change. When the system again bends enough, he will accept some improvement in a new status quo that politicians in Congress and state government have framed in a way he believes he's doing pretty well given the reality of a new playing field.

A once thriving local manufacturer, Briggs and Stratton, had a meeting about layoffs for several hundred more workers. I heard from one lady that her son had never seen as much hatred and rage as was evident at that meeting. The employees were angry at everybody who was in part responsible: Briggs and Stratton, the union, state government, the federal government and specific politicians. The group they didn't include was themselves. There has been a new economic reality out there for years, but none of the parties was willing to talk about the elephant in the room and suggest concessions and compromises of a magnitude that would have avoided the layoffs. It is a hard way to learn a lesson about human nature, including your own.

Preferential Tax Treatment: The Holy Grail of Politics

Insiders are able to cut through the distractions to the essence of the issue.

> When John McCain was still a raging reformer, he pointed to the tax code as the foundation of the corruption of American politics. Special interests pay politicians vast amounts of cash for their campaign, and in return get favorable exemptions or credits in the tax code. In other countries this sort of bribery takes place under bridges and with cash in brown envelopes. In America, it is institutionalized and legal, but it is the same—cash for politicians in return for favorable treatment from the government. The U.S. tax system is not merely corrupt; it is corrupt in a deceptive manner that has degraded the entire system of the American government. Congress is able to funnel vast sums of money to its favorite funders through the tax code—without anyone realizing it. The simplest way to get the corruption out of Washington is to remove the prize that members of Congress give away: preferential tax treatment.[262]

A piece from *USA Today* helps add both clarity and emphasis.

> President Bush, who has made tax-cutting the centerpiece of his domestic agenda, has held high-profile ceremonies to sign every tax-cut bill sent by Congress. Until last Friday. With no fanfare, he signed his fifth tax cut aboard Air Force One in route to a campaign stop. It's a $136 billion behemoth of breaks and payoffs over 10 years to corporations that lobbied hardest and executives who contributed the most to Congress.
>
> Little wonder Bush didn't want to advertise legislation that corporations can't justify and the nation can't afford in these times of record budget deficits.
>
> ... Corporations have worked hard since WWII to convince lawmakers that they shouldn't pay taxes. From a high of 35.4% of tax receipts collected by the U.S. Treasury, corporations now pay a mere 7.4% share despite the enormous growth in profits. The new measure will advance that trend.

It stands as an example of the symbiotic relationship between special interests that want tax breaks to improve their bottom lines and lawmakers who want donations to win re-election. Left out is the individual taxpayer, who is saddled with an ever growing burden to fund the government.

Corporate leaders say the legislation—named the American Jobs Creation Act—will make U.S. manufacturers more competitive so they can hire new workers.

In spite of the law's Orwellian title, independent studies suggest that the breaks will expand companies' profits more than their payrolls. That's nothing to trumpet, as Bush's stealth bill-signing only underscores.[263]

You can see from McCain's comments and Bush's signing of the corporate tax cuts, that everything Congress does is colored by self-interest—the color green needed for the next election campaign. All you have to do is give favorable consideration to legislation that will help improve their bottom line when they come to the floor for a vote.

The "Savings and Loan" Crisis

The S & L crisis (see Chapter 3) is a prime example of corruption in government. "While a few of the brigands got most of the publicity and the blame, they could not have flourished without an amazing run of mistakes by people who should have known better: Congressmen and cabinet officers, regulators, lobbyists and journalists who failed to see the clues. Some meant well. Others were driven by ideology, greed or self-interest. The net result of the cover-up was to cripple the nation's financial immune system."[264]

In 1982 the Garn-St. Germain bill allowed S & Ls to expand beyond home loans, and invest in high-risk, high-return ventures. Many of the principals agreed later that this was a huge mistake, as "it didn't force states to adhere to . . . federal regulations, (even) if depositors were going to get federal insurance on their accounts. . . . The stage was now set for anarchy and fraud. Thrifts could lend money at any rate and invest in a wide range of speculative ventures, all with taxpayer-backed insurance. . . . Scores of investors like Charles Keating moved in swiftly, turning the thrift industry into a huge casino where only the taxpayers could lose."[265]

Officials at the U.S. League of Savings Institutions, which supported the rules changes, now rue them. "We didn't see the buccaneers coming. We thought we were dealing with the traditional people we had always dealt with," admits Noel Fahey. Donald Regan (Secretary of the Treasury under Ronald Reagan), too, says he has learned that there is an "avaricious, greedy, criminal element in all industries. If he had known then what he knows now, would he have favored so much deregulation? 'The answer is no.'"[266] It is really hard to believe that he was that naïve and "got religion" so late. It was at that time the Senate Ethics Committee started investigating charges (involving) the "so-called Keating Five. . . ."[267]

This is just one window that gives us a peek into the inner workings of our government. On August 9, 1989 President George H.W Bush signed a bill granting the first $50 billion to begin the S & L bailout, saying: "This legislation comes to grips with the problems facing our savings and loan industry. It will stabilize [the system]."[268] Unfortunately, we the taxpayers were left holding the bag once again. We were the ones on the hook for the first $50 billion installment on a $500 billion bailout—yes, that is billion.

Jack Abramoff and the Lobbyists

Thom Hartman observes that giving "campaign contributions to politicians in the hopes of getting favors that would help my business . . . (and hiring) a lobbyist to try to amend laws that would serve my financial interest . . . (is) how big-time corporate America operates. To them making large campaign contributions and spending millions of dollars each year on lobbyists is just another investment that pays off handsomely."[269] Hartman titles one chapter "Making Members of Congress Wear NASCAR Patches," referring to the NASCAR practice of putting the logos of corporate sponsors on their cars and driver's suits. Then everyone would know who supports them. The only way these teams can afford to compete is through corporate sponsorships. Unfortunately, this also seems to be the way it works today if candidates want to have enough money to fund the next election campaign.

A Congressional Budget Office report said, "(Government) policy has also become less redistributive since the late 1970's, doing less to reduce the concentration of income. 'The equalizing effect of federal taxes was smaller' in 2007 than in 1979, as 'the composition of federal revenues shifted away from progressive income taxes to less-progressive payroll taxes. . . .'"[270] Policies suggested to address this issue are framed by some as wealth redistribution, socialism and attempts to start class warfare. Others would respond that class warfare is fought top down, and that those at the top of the income scale have been winning the battles for a long time, and that it is time for a counter offensive.

> Tom Delay . . . took all sorts of goodies from lobbyists when he was a Republican leader in the House of Representatives. . . . His major patron was Jack Abramoff, lobbyist, businessman, head of conservative organizations—and criminal, sentenced to prison for felonies related to defrauding Indian tribes and plying politicians with gifts in exchange for political favors. . . . In 2005, DeLay was charged with violations of campaign finance laws and money laundering, while two of his former aides were convicted in the Abramoff scandal.[271]

> (For) years now, reform efforts have focused on transparency and limits on campaign contributions and on pushing a system of publicly financing elections to take money out of politics. But all of that has been negated by the Supreme Court, and its latest ruling pretty much puts the nail in the coffin of public financing of campaigns. In 2010 the *Citizens United v. Federal Election Commission* case, the Supreme Court rules that corporations—even foreign corporations—and wealthy individuals can spend *unlimited* amounts of money to influence elections; they just have to spend it independently of the candidate's or party's official campaign.[272]

"So now if a candidate wants a few million dollars spent for his campaign, all he has to do is get the commitment (informally, of course) from a corporation that it'll do it. Assuming the corporation keeps its word, this pretty much blows up every strategy anybody has come up with so far to clean up the election's mess in the United States and will probably lead, over the next few years, to an entirely corporate-controlled and beholden Congress."[273]

On November 13, 2011, Jack Abramoff, the poster boy for lobbyists, was interviewed on CNN's *Piers Morgan Tonight*. He provides the ultimate insider's window into how lobbying influences legislation. The total spent lobbying Congress was $3.31 billion in 2010.

MORGAN. Sentenced to four years in prison for fraud, corruption and conspiracy, the once all powerful lobbyist now helps the Justice Department clean up influence peddling in the nation's Capital. He is now out of prison, has a new book called *Capital Punishment: This Is What Washington Is Like- I Got Caught*. One of the reasons many people believe America is in the shambles it's in financially and politically is because of people like you. Abramoff said he wanted to teach people what goes on there. (He acknowledged that power went to his head, and that he) crossed the line and was severely punished. However, it was still going on and he thought it was important for people to know what does go on, at least in terms of his experience. "Having an ability to have power got to me as it gets to others, and I stopped thinking about where the boundaries were."

ABRAMOFF. I entered a system that has structural issues, where some of the lines are vague, and some of the rules made purposely vague. While there was some tweaking in 2007, the truth is all the reform efforts to date are really feckless. ... The system still contains vast, vast amounts of loopholes

MORGAN (noting that Tom Delay is the constantly picked on archtypical legislator who is evil, then asked). How many other people are breaking the law?

ABRAMOFF. A healthy percentage—20%.

MORGAN. (Piers asked for Abramoff's reaction to the following comment.) George W. Bush denied knowing him, let alone meeting him. "I frankly don't even remember having my picture taken with the guy. I don't know him."

ABRAMOFF. He's the leader of the free world. I was in the middle of one of the biggest political scandals since Watergate. What's he supposed to do, come out and say, "He's my best friend, and I was hand and glove with him."

MORGAN. It's completely implausible that he would not have been aware of you. You were the Republican parties' top lobbyist."

ABRAMOFF. (I can't) speak for him, but he's a politician, and at the end of the day politicians are politicians. Republican and Democrat, there's a certain characteristic politicians have, and often they're with you when they need you, and often when you need them, they're not there. (As for) the level of corruption in American politics, I want people to know what this system is. The system is toxic for the United States. It has to be changed. So what I've done as somebody who was at a certain level of that system (is say) what no one else is saying: the system is wrong and here's how to change the system. These are the reforms that need to be made. Whether America wants to make them or not is another matter. Here is how to (do it: educate) people (and show) people what's going on. Whether it's criminal or not, whether it should be criminal, maybe is the question. There are things that are not technically against the law, because the law is made by Congress, and Congress has (an) interest in keeping many of the rules the same.[274]

On October 31, 2011 there was a segment on *Morning Joe* where Lawrence Lessig, Harvard Law Professor—Center for Ethics, discussed his book, *Republic Lost: How Money Corrupts Congress and a Plan to Stop it*. The book describes what Lessig believes to be the systemic corrupting influence of special-interest money.

LESSIG. Two-thirds to three-fourths of the public believes money buys results in Congress . . . enough to drive most people to think the institution is bankrupt, which is why confidence ratings hover around 10 or 11%. . . . The public isn't so stupid.

SCARBOROUGH. Tell me a way to get to the kind of big time structural reform you refer to in the book.

LESSIG. I think the big time structural reform is needed, because the inside the beltway plan cannot work. We cannot get this Congress to change the way it funds the system.[275]

He added that since the system is so corrupt and so entrenched that it cannot change itself. We have to do an end run around the system, a system where .05 percent has all of the money, power and control. They have hijacked the system, and can shape legislation to serve their interests. Because that's the way people are, that's the way the world of Washington works. The best system in the world is only as good as the decency, honesty and integrity of those who are in power.

The Atwater "Attitude"—Dirty Politics and Dirty Tricks

Candidates let the dogs out, and it's anything goes, as long as you win. Lee Atwater was one of the best that ever played the game. Atwater was a dog that could hunt. He died in 1991 of an inoperable brain tumor at age 40. He was an extraordinary political strategist who played hardball in the sport of negative campaigning. He was at the pinnacle of his political career when diagnosed. He was known as a dirty politician. "A reputation as a fierce and ugly campaigner has dogged me," Atwater once conceded. "While I didn't invent negative politics, I am one of its most ardent practitioners."[276] The article continues:

> Early in the 1988 campaign against Michael Dukakis, Atwater bluntly told a Republican audience, "If I can make Willie Horton a household name, we'll win this election."
>
> He succeeded on both counts. Horton was a convicted murderer who raped a woman while on a weekend furlough from a Massachusetts prison. The Bush campaign used the incident to portray Dukakis as a liberal who was soft on crime.[277]

The next day the Journal ran an editorial about Atwater.

> His political savvy was legendary. And feared. To him politics was "only a slightly politer form of ground battle." Scorched earth warfare might better describe it.
>
> In 1980, while running a congressional race in South Carolina, Atwater referred to the Democratic candidate, a man who had once received electro-shock therapy, as "someone who was hooked up to jumper cables."
>
> Such strategies worked—but at an awful cost. By exploiting racial fears, Atwater widened the rift between the GOP and the minority community and contributed to black-white tensions. . . .[278]

"*How to Spread a Smear: The Bickering on Capital Hill Takes a Vicious Turn*" is an article written when Lee Atwater was at the pinnacle of his career, before he had been diagnosed with cancer. It is an article that needs to be read in its entirety to get a sense of how our electoral process and governmental operation gets its business done. "Democrats like Beryl Anthony of Arkansas contend that this is another episode in the 'bad employee – good superior political mud wrestling that Atwater perfected during the campaign. Staffers, encouraged by their bosses, go on the attack, then—like a core of civilian Ollie North's—take the blame and are publicly rebuked. The superiors apologize."[279]

A pullout on the same page was headed, *"Sorry" Is Not Enough."*

From his early campaigns in South Carolina through the 1988 presidential election, Lee Atwater has displayed a talent for smearing opponents and then either apologizing or suffering memory lapses about his role.

"We should all remember the picture of bravery and regained perspective Lee brought us over these past months," (Democratic Party Chairman Ron) Brown said. . . . During the past year Atwater said he had "found Jesus Christ" and for the first time in his life didn't hate anyone. He mended fences with Brown and other political rivals, and apologized for some of his more brutal remarks during the 1988 campaign against . . . Dukakis.[280]

In his last months, his body ravaged by illness, he saw how wrong he was. "There is nothing more important in life than human beings, nothing sweeter than the human touch" he wrote. Would Atwater have been less of a man if he had let his humanity shine through when it mattered? Who really wants to be remembered more for savagery than for kindness?[281]

In an article titled "*Lee Atwater Sees Need for Spiritual and Moral Rebirth,*" Lee Atwater said, "'I acquired more wealth, power and prestige than most. But you can acquire all you want and still feel empty. . . . It took a deadly illness to put me eye to eye with that truth, but it is a truth that the country, caught up in its ruthless ambitions and moral decay, can learn on my dime. I don't know who will lead us through the '90s, but they must be made to speak to this spiritual vacuum at the heart of the American society, this tumor of the soul."[282] Nobody is going to learn on his dime. Tragically, others will also only "get religion" on their deathbed, or when they are convicted. Otherwise, it's business—no, politics—as usual. Why should we expect people to be any different after his conversion? We're all cut from the same cloth. We are all on a journey where it seems quite evident that we would do just what Atwater did, as long as it is consistent with our agenda, as long as we can rationalize and justify the behavior and as long as we can get away with it.

How do you tell the Lee Atwater story? Your heart goes out to his family for their loss. You're glad that he saw the "light." You're thankful he found peace before he died. You acknowledge that he tried to make amends. Nevertheless, before his conversion he was a vicious, cruel, mean attack dog of the worst order. He had mastered the art of mudslinging. He was a ruthless political operative who took no prisoners and left shattered lives in his wake. How do you tell the Lee Atwater story without appearing to engage in the character assassination that he did?

Forgiveness is certainly a part of my vocabulary. But just how do you make it right once you have messed with a person's character, their professional reputation, their professional future and how that future affects their family? Both he and Abramoff "got religion." Unfortunately, it was only after a whole lot of damage had been done. While you certainly get a second chance from God, and seventy-times seven more, you don't get a second chance to make things right once you've messed (with) the life of another person, and forever changed its course. If only a few of the cold, calculating, heartless "souls" like Atwater, Colson and Abramoff would experience a change of heart while still at the top of their game, it would mean a whole lot more.

Obviously, at the time he was doing his thing, he didn't care who got hurt. Are deathbed conversions sincere? You can look at what people did during the time they had left. It will give a clue as to whether they were just jerking us around again or not. Was Atwater's conversion sincere? Did he take the wealth he had accumulated in a career, which in his own words was described as "More than most", and give at least 90 to 95% of it to charity? Maybe that is unfair. Maybe nobody explained to him what it meant to be a disciple. Maybe he had enough on his mind and heart and didn't have time to become aware of and consider that option.

I found it interesting and intriguing to note the change of heart evidenced by the GOP's ruthless strategist. "Near death, he mellowed: (My illness helped me to see what was missing in society is) 'what was missing in me: a little heart, a lot of brotherhood.'"[283] And just what we have learned on his dime. Not much, I suspect. Politics hasn't changed. More germane to my thesis, there is a lot of Lee Atwater in all of us. We are willing to compromise our morals and our principles when it serves our purposes. He was just brighter, had a more acid tongue and was in a position where the damage he did influenced the course of history. Yet, through it all our Constitution is holding together and guiding us as we are trying to work things out as flawed individuals seeking our own interests. By nature that is just the way we are.

In terms of ethics, morals and values, politics has become a wasteland. Partisan wrangling has turned into uncompromising gridlock. The whole political environment has become poisoned. Both parties now live under a cloud of suspicion that the whole system has lost its moral compass.

Intentional Deception

We're still doing the same things Atwater did, only in a more deceptively civilized way. If you have money, you establish and fund think tanks that turn out studies that legitimize your views. Or, you purchase a newspaper to foster support for your political views, even though your circulation is small and you operate at a loss. We ask ourselves, "Why?" Some have suggested that the folks who own the paper buy books that support their political views, and then give them away to those who subscribe to their websites and publication. Why? "The answer is pretty straightforward: they do it because it buys them respectability and gets their con job out there. And one of their most important goals is lower taxes—for millionaires and billionaires like themselves."[284]

Al Gore addresses the same issue in a book titled *"The Assault on Reason."*

> Why do reason, logic and truth seem to play a sharply diminished role in the way America now makes important decisions? The persistent and sustained reliance on falsehoods as the basis of policy, even in the face of massive and well-understood evidence to the contrary, seems to many Americans to have reached levels that were previously unimaginable. . . . Faith in the power of reason – the belief that free citizens can govern themselves wisely and fairly by resorting to logical debate on the basis of the best evidence available, instead of raw power – remains the central premise of the American democracy. This premise is now under assault.[285]

> The potential for manipulating mass opinions and feelings initially discovered by commercial advertisers is now being even more aggressively exploited by a new generation of media Machiavellis. The combination of ever more sophisticated public opinion sampling techniques and the increasing use of powerful computers to parse and subdivide the American people according to their "psychographic" categories that identify their susceptibility to individually tailored appeals has further magnified the power of propagandistic electronic messaging that has created a harsh new reality for the functioning of our democracy.

As a result our democracy is in danger of being hollowed out. In order to reclaim our birthright, we Americans ought to resolve to repair the systemic decay of the public forum. We must create new ways to engage in a genuine and not manipulative conversation about our future. We must stop tolerating the rejection and distortion of science. We must insist on an end to the cynical use of pseudo-studies known to be false for the purpose of intentionally clouding the public's ability to discern the truth. Americans in both parties should insist on the re-establishment of respect for the rule of reason.[286]

While I would like to believe his hope and vision will become a reality, these are not reasonable expectations. People will use whatever advantage they can get. The best we can hope for is that with the right of free speech, we can refute their positions. The use of manipulation, pseudo-studies and the distortion of reason are simply reflective of our nature, and will not change. Again, I want to be wrong. Sadly, I just don't think I am.

This also speaks to the flip side of the question. How is it that many come to support a position that can be shot full of holes. All of the possible explanations involve some vested interest formulating an explanation that makes their case, even though the explanation involves reasoning that doesn't meet the test of logic. The process is intentionally deceptive and misleading. They have a vested interest in doing so. Let's start with the experts. We have many individuals who directly or indirectly receive benefit from advocating a position they know is wrong. There really isn't any hard research evidence: this allows them to make a case based on their interpretation of the information, research and evidence that is available. Public relations firms and spin-meisters are paid handsomely for coming up with a case that supports the position of the client who hired them. Trade organizations and even some high sounding foundations, associations, and councils have constituencies seeking an argument that validates their worldview and beliefs.

The reason people advocate a position they know is developed using flawed logic and false information is not difficult to understand. Their only concern is to make a buck. So they will sell a bill of goods they know to be false or a flat out lie, as they have no conscience, ethics, morals or values. That is just the way some people are.

Average folk often follow their leaders and swallow what they are saying hook, line and sinker. They believe what somebody has said on TV or the radio, or what they read in the paper or direct mail. Sadly, political leaders—perhaps most—are manipulative, deceptive and will say or do whatever it takes to get elected, more-so today than ever. They have no conscience and they could care less that their misinformation makes it even more difficult find a compromise settlement. If our elected officials were seeking the greater good, you would hope that they would simply provide an honest explanation to their constituency, and let the chips fall where they may. In so doing, they would have retained their integrity and the integrity of the political system.

Many folks have to rationalize the basic fairness of what they are doing so they can pursue an agenda that will benefit them. Denial, repression and distortion make it possible to proceed with a clear conscience, unable to see that they are doing anything wrong. Politicians influenced by political and public relations advisors telling them what they have to do to be elected are not being honest with themselves or their constituencies. Again, they aren't any different than the rest of us who rationalize that we are "good people: caring, charitable and compassionate." By any measure, we are a far cry from anything like that.

Insider Trading not Illegal for Congress

Steve Croft did a *60 Minutes* segment, a look at how America's lawmakers can legally buy stock using non-public information. It was based on the book *"Throw Them All Out"* by Peter Schweizer.

CROFT. Good things can happen if you are a ... member of Congress. Take Nancy Pelosi—while Speaker of the House she and her husband were offered an insider's opportunity to invest in a credit card company just as tough legislation of the industry was making it through the House. Would you (addressing Speaker Pelosi) consider that to be a conflict of interest? (My opinion is that her response was a political non-answer.) Do you (addressing the viewers) think it is all right for a Speaker to accept a very preferential, favorable stock deal? Well, we didn't. Few (in Congress) do it for the salary. (But there) is opportunity to become a Washington insider with access to connections and information that no one else has in an environment where rules that govern the rest of the country don't always apply to them. It contributes to a public perception of graft and corruption. This is a venture opportunity. This is an opportunity to leverage your position in public service and to use that position to enrich yourself, your friends and your family. Schweizer is a fellow at the Hoover Institute, a conservative think tank at Stanford

University. A few years ago he began working on a book about soft corruption in Washington with a team of eight student researchers who received financial disclosure records. Schweizer said he wanted to know why some Congressmen managed to accumulate significant wealth beyond their salaries, and proved particularly adept at buying and selling stocks.

SCHWEIZER. There are all sorts and forms of honest graft that Congressmen engage in that allow them to become very wealthy. So it's not illegal, but I think it's highly unethical, highly offensive and wrong.

CROFT. What do you mean, honest graft?

SCHWEIZER For example, insider trading on the stock market. If you are a member of Congress, those laws are deemed not to apply.

CROFT. So Congressmen get a pass on insider trading.

SCHWEIZER They do. The fact is you sit on a health care committee and you know that Medicare, for example, is considering not reimbursing for a certain drug. That is market moving information, and if you can trade stock off that information and do so legally, that's a great profit making opportunity. And that's the sort of behavior that goes on.

CROFT. Why does Congress get a pass on this?

SCHWEIZER It's really (just) the way the rules have been defined, and the people who make the rules are the political class in Washington. And they've conveniently written them in such a way that they don't apply to themselves. . . . But there is a long history of dealing in Washington, and it doesn't always involve stock trades. (When you know about earmarks in advance, that's insider information that can be used to make a profit on land and real estate deals.) Corporate executives, members of the executive branch and all Federal judges are held to strict conflict of interest rules, but not the people who write the laws. If you sit on the Defense Committee, you are free to trade defense stocks as much as you want, and that regularly goes on in all these committees. Brian Baird (is) a former Congressman from Washington State who served six years in the House.

BAIRD. There should only be one thing on your mind when you're drafting legislation: is this good for the United States of America. That's it. If you're starting to say to yourself, how is this going to affect my investment, you've got a mixed agenda, a mixed purpose for being there.

CROFT. ...The situation has gotten worse. In a few years a whole new totally unregulated $100,000,000 industry has grown up in Washington called "political intelligence." It employs former Congressman and former staffers to scour the halls of the Capital gathering valuable non-public information, then selling it to hedge funds and traders on Wall Street who can trade on it.

BAIRD. Now if you're a political intel guy and you get that information long before it's public . . . you can make real time trades before anyone else. . . . It's taken what would be a criminal enterprise anywhere else in the country and turned it into a powerful business model. This is the currency of Washington D.C. It's this kind of informational currency that translates into real currency. You can't trace it, and if you can't trace it, it's not illegal. You feel like an idiot not to take advantage of it.[287]

This is our Congress at work. This is how the members conduct themselves in the revered legislative body established by our Constitution. They make laws that don't apply to themselves in the same way they apply to the rest of us. Congress can trade on insider information, when it's illegal for the rest of us. These are the elected leaders to whom we look to run our country, and to do so in a way that seeks to find a way to meet the needs of every citizen, not just themselves, the wealthy and the connected. What they are doing is not illegal. Is what they are doing ethical? Do we want it to continue? How can we be confident that they are looking out for us, passing legislation that benefits all of us and insures the well-being of future generations? How can we trust them at all? The scourge of human nature infects everyone, even them. We are greedy and operate on the basis of self-interest. In the darkness of our souls we are self-centered, self-seeking, self-serving. Then we remember that we are no different than they are—no better, no worse. We dare not judge. We become delusional when we do not acknowledge and own the reality of what all humanity is like. Why would we expect any of our elected leaders to be different?

The *60 Minutes* feature highlighting the essence of Schweizer's *"Throw Them All Out"* was quite astounding. Less than five months later a big step was finally taken to correct the situation. President Obama signed the Stop Trading on Congressional Knowledge (STOCK) Act. People across the political spectrum were outraged, contacted their representatives in Congress, and Congress, realizing they were caught with their hands in the cookie jar, acted with unusual haste. The STOCK Act was a big first step, but they still didn't rectify all of the related issues. For example, it didn't address the issue of land deals. Why should we be surprised?

Caring for the Most Vulnerable

The question of how much funding is needed to insure the well-being of the weak and vulnerable involves a discussion that has to take place in the public arena. "It's one thing to say that government is inefficient in use of tax dollars, and has some pretty poor results. It's another to simply say, 'Therefore the only solution is to eliminate the government effort.'"[288] John Sununu observes, "We will always and should always respond to those in genuine need. But as a society, we should also be willing to ask, How much government dependence is too much? How much can we afford?"[289] These are the kinds of issues that have to be resolved at the ballot box and in the legislative process.

President H. W. Bush was very enthusiastic about fostering the concept of a thousand points of light. While many agree that this is a great idea that holds much promise and should be pursued, they do not think it comes anywhere near producing the results necessary to meet all of the needs that would no longer be met by government programs that are scaled down or completely eliminated.

> . . . It is a glittering phrase for an old idea – the notion that private charities and volunteers can take up the slack when the government reduces domestic spending.
>
> . . . Private giving certainly should be encouraged.
>
> However, he should not mislead himself or anyone else. The record indicates that private charity and volunteerism can go only so far in meeting human needs, and that dent is unlikely to become a great deal larger than it has been. . . . In the end it has to be admitted that the main responsibility for welfare, education and social services inevitably must rest with government.[290]

"A thousand points of light do not hold a candle to well-managed and adequately funded programs."[291]

My personal view is that there are some things we have to do together, or they simply won't get done. While I don't want to foster dependency, there are some basic areas of need where we don't want our fellow citizens to be left to fend for themselves and suffer harmful deprivation and indignity. My reason is that it is a dog eat dog world, a place where it's all about the survival of the fittest, the struggle involved in competing for limited resources, and where, bottom line, it is every man for himself. While we have to resolve these issues, even the process is flawed because of the way human nature influences the formation of policy and the making of laws, where think tanks can distort the true picture of poverty, need and how best to care for the poor and the vulnerable. They validate the view that there are too many welfare queens, that these people are lazy and don't want to work and that we are fostering a culture of dependency that sabotages the motivation to find a job and go to work.

The art of diplomacy is to find a way to avoid the extremes (regarding size of government and amount of taxation) and find a balance that will address the issues of homelessness, poverty, unemployment, medical care for the children of the poor, catastrophic health insurance and guaranteed care for the aging, the mentally ill and the disabled.

A review of Alan Brinkley's book, "*The End Of Reform: New Deal Liberalism in Recession and War,*" helps to frame the question in what he calls the "Age of Newt." "The book suggests that the question for liberals today is no different from the one they faced before and during World War II: What is the role of the state in remedying economic inequalities without eroding individual liberties? Or, as the question might be phrased for Gingrich: When does decreasing the role of the state unfairly increase the hardship on those whom the nation needs to help?"[292]

The conversation continued in the lead-up to the 2012 election.

> Some presidential campaigns—1960, 1980, 1992, 2008—are exhilarating, suffused with hope and excitement. This is not likely to be one of those. It is likely to be an election where no one wins and someone loses. It will be a reversal of politics past: a pragmatic democrat will be facing a Republican with all sorts of big ideas, promising an unregulated, laissez-faire American paradise.
>
> Obama will have to come up with a stronger argument than "It could have been worse," but in tough times the continuing presence of a government safety net is far more reassuring than the message that you're on your own. And in the end, all the Republican talk of repealing and defunding may prove too radical for an American public that is conservative in the traditional sense, and wary of sudden lurches to the left or right.[293]

Within the context of discussions about small government and big government we simply have to find a way to address the needs of the most vulnerable. In the State of the Union address on January 23, 1996 President Clinton said: "We can't go back to a time when Americans were left to fend for themselves."

The Corrupting Influence of Special-Interest Money

The landscape used as the backdrop for this chapter has been the issue of the ethics, morals and values of the leaders in our government, their advisors and the campaign contributors who seek support for legislation they favor. It is against that backdrop that we have to address the issue of the widening gap between the income and wealth of the upper class and lower class, and the decline of the middle-class. Again, my intent is not to suggest that I have the answer. I have my opinion. We all do. Rather my aim is to offer reflections and commentary that will stimulate consideration and soul searching about how our human nature influences the legislative process. Given human nature as I understand it, I am deeply concerned about the systemic corrupting influence of special-interest money on the decision making processes of American politics. The potential for mischief is gigantic.

For the most part I am at a place expressed clearly by Bill Babbitt. "We've evolved a cycle of dishonesty in our national discourse. Politicians don't tell the necessary but unpleasant truths because they are afraid that the voters will kill the messenger. So people learn not to expect the truth from politicians."[294] The system has been corrupted by the influence of campaign contributions. That the well-to-do prosper, while so many struggle to make ends meet, is outrageous. We need to have a good political conversation about all of the related issues.

Our Constitution and governmental structure are outstanding. When it comes to the people in government, there is no question that they are motivated by self-interest. But that is just human nature. To naively assume a more positive reality will lead to disillusionment and danger. "... Americans need to begin to realize that in a capitalist society, government—imperfect, clumsy, bureaucracy-driven government—is the only instrument we have for inserting a degree of fairness into a system that inherently does not value it."[295]

Chapter 12
What in the World Do You Do with Mother Teresa?

"The greatest evil is the lack of love and charity, the terrible indifference towards one's neighbor who lives at the roadside assaulted by exploitation, corruption, poverty and disease. . . ." Malcolm Muggeridge

"Dear Friends, let us love one another, for love comes from God. Everyone who loves is born of God and knows God. Whoever does not love, does not know God, because God is love. This is how God showed his love among us: He sent his one and only Son into the world that we might live through him. This is love: not that we loved God, but that he loved us and sent his Son as an atoning sacrifice for our sins. Dear friends, since God so loved us, we also ought to love one another" (I John 4:7-11).

Questioning Our Compassion

There is a huge gulf between the good people we think we are and what we're really like. Painting this picture of humanity with broad strokes doesn't sit well and isn't taken kindly by folks who have always considered themselves to be good people— decent folk who have acceptable morals, ethics and values. "What kind of people do you think we are? What about all of the good we do? What about all of our efforts as volunteers? What about our generosity in giving to church and charity! Look at the philanthropists who give huge sums of money. You've got a lot of nerve! Who do you think you are anyway?" This is exactly the type of reaction you expect toward someone who says that the perception of ourselves as having loving, charitable, servant hearts is nothing more than a delusion.

"And what can you possibly say about Mother Teresa? Doesn't she totally invalidate your thesis? You are losing it!" How can I bring the record of Mother Teresa's life under the umbrella of my thesis? How do I reconcile Mother Teresa with what I believe about the darkness of human nature?

Several times a year we have dinner with two other couples. Eunice had just lost her mother Gladys, who was 103. We listened as she recounted the inspiration her parents had been to her and to all who know their story. Right after Martin Kretzmann graduated from Concordia Seminary, St. Louis in 1930, he asked Gladys to marry him. He was ordained in late August and they were married two days later. Within weeks they headed for India where they served as missionaries for 33 years. That must have been quite a conversation: "Will you marry me and move to India?" At that time people traveled across the ocean by boat. They had few furloughs. Eunice was born in India and didn't move back to the States until it was time to go to college. Her parents decided to not return for her wedding. Rather, at the hour of the wedding they gathered with friends in India for support and for a little celebration.

So what do you say about Mother Teresa, the many other faithful, kind, compassionate, dedicated Sisters of Charity and other dedicated missionaries like the Kretzmanns? While they are the exception rather than the rule, worthy of being acknowledged and affirmed with thanks and admiration, integrity demands that their lives also be evaluated within the framework of my view of human nature.

When you pause to look at the facts, they don't seem to fit. They and many others like them live lives characterized by commitment, dedication, caring and service. Some people do contribute sacrificially to church and charity, and spend many hours serving as volunteers. Does my premise remain valid, namely, that these people have this tendency to look out not just for needs of themselves and their own, but also for their wants at the expense of the unmet needs of others?

Volunteers are Very Special People

Last evening I picked up our granddaughter from cheerleading practice at Grace Lutheran School; the two volunteer coaches were members of the congregation who attend college locally at our Concordia University—Wisconsin. Also waiting was a mom who had been the volunteer coach of the Grace upper grade girls' basketball team the previous year. These folks and the thousands and thousands of other volunteers who coach youth sports programs, serve as tutors, are Big Brothers and Big Sisters, lead 4H, Girl Scouts and Boy Scouts, and serve as role models for our young people are a national treasure. Volunteers are very special gifts to those they serve and an inspiration to all of us.

In this morning's paper there was a heartwarming story about how our community stepped up to help a homeless family in response to an article that ran a few days ago. The outpouring of concern was overwhelming, and led to increased support for agencies that serve the homeless, including gifts of $5,000 to each of five area shelters by an anonymous donor. As the article said, "It's Christmastime, and people feel a certain passion and compassion when you know that people are in need. . . ."[296] While many are moved to be more generous during the holiday season, we all know that examples of concern and compassion can be found all around us every day.

Wisconsin and Milwaukee are ranked in the top 10 for volunteerism, with a 34.9% rate for the state and 32% for the city. Their efforts were valued at $3.4 billion.

> More than one-third of the residents in the Badger State reported they served as volunteers for a nonprofit or community organization. Their donated time represented a total of 1.5 million adults and more than 159.1 million hours of service. In Milwaukee, 73.9% of the volunteers returned year after year, and the city led the nation in the retention category. "That dedication provides nonprofit groups with well-trained, effective volunteers to tutor, build homes and work in food pantries," said Bonnie Andrews, manager of the Volunteer Center of Milwaukee.
>
> . . . Paul Schmitz, the CEO of the volunteer group Public Allies, said the volunteers deployed in Milwaukee through AmeriCorps have helped bolster the ranks of those providing services in the city. Public Allies receives funding to coordinate the AmeriCorps efforts. "When you look at some of the challenges we're facing, and the budget cuts, it's a good sign that residents are stepping up and getting involved," Schmitz said.[297]

However, as you would expect me to say by now, while I am genuinely grateful that we are using some of our available time, what we are seeing is just a modest expression of care and concern for our neighbor's need.

We could be doing so much more. The potential is so much greater. While many live very full lives—working, raising their families and caring for aging parents—and don't have a lot of free time, they still set aside some time to serve as volunteers. But, the vast majority could do so much more. They aren't involved to the degree that their volunteering is an inconvenience that sometimes gets in the way of their routine and lifestyle. That's just our nature.

Those who volunteer are touched and moved to serve for many reasons. Some talk about their need to make a difference or how a profound personal experience opened their eyes and led them to reorder their priorities. Others want to give something back to their community. The religious of all faiths are encouraged to express themselves in all forms of charity. Some have found that material things have not brought the satisfaction they expected, and are searching for a deeper meaning in life. Still others are inspired by the deeds and kindnesses of others. Many who try volunteering find it to be satisfying and meaningful and decide to continue, and often move on to making charitable donations to the organizations where they volunteer.

You hear a familiar chorus from those who volunteer: I get so much more back than I give. "Diana and Rich Pine of Wauwatosa coordinate volunteers who staff a shelter for women without a home. . . . (Diana) doesn't feel so special for doing the work. She feels special for getting the opportunity. 'It's hard to put it into words what it gives you but I can tell you, if you go down there once, you'll want to come back,' she said. 'It's making an immediate and absolute difference to the women at the shelter.'"[298]

The cultural consensus of what is appropriate in terms of the percent of time we set aside for volunteering is so low. If less than half don't volunteer at all, we have to qualify any statements about the moral character of our nation. Personal sacrifice and inconvenience are not part of standard operating procedure. The way we talk about ourselves and our nation in terms of ethics, morals and values, you would assume that volunteering and generous charitable giving are part of our DNA. As individuals and as a nation, we have an inflated sense of the true levels of our concern and compassion for the needs of others.

Perhaps this is the best place to briefly address the proper place for a government-provided safety net for those of our fellow citizens in need. First, it is important to note the difference between those who experience misfortune and tragedy and those who are felt to be in some way responsible for their own plight due to laziness or an entitlement mentality. There is most certainly a consensus regarding the government's responsibility to step in during times of national disaster: floods, earthquakes, tornados, fire and the like. The discussion of regular government assistance (welfare) is where the issue becomes contentious. Some would say that government health, food and income-assistance programs are giveaways, a waste and "money down a rat-hole." My own personal views are consistent with an editorial that caught my eye several years ago.

> Sure, there is always going to be some waste in the welfare system... Conscientious, humane efforts to make welfare more cost-effective can only be applauded. And the government, by all means should look for better ways to move idle people into jobs so they will not become permanent welfare clients. Dependency tends to destroy people. . . . (However) even if the best imaginable welfare reform system were put into effect, a large number of people would still need assistance and other help. And the cost to taxpayers would still be large.
>
> Some . . . would have been able to make their way in simpler times, when less skill was needed in the workplace. But they are sadly redundant in the era of computers and automation. A decent society will not ignore such people; neither will a society motivated by enlightened self-interest. . . . Private giving is necessary but not sufficient. In a nation as large and diverse as the United States, private charities cannot possibly be the chief source of income support.[299]

Consistent with the previous chapter's discussion of government, I am not suggesting that my views are right or reflect an appropriate moral standard for government. We arrive at a national consensus of what defines our social safety net at the ballot box through those we elect to legislate and make policy for us. However, once government policy is established, each of us has to decide how to respond in terms of volunteering time and making charitable contributions to help address any needs that are still unmet—which is where we go next.

Shining Examples of the Millions of Volunteer Servants

Stories of people hearing about a need and being willing to step up to the plate touch us all. We appreciate the moving stories in the "Making a Difference" segment on the NBC Nightly News, or the "Positively Milwaukee" stories on our local NBC affiliate. Recently in the local paper, there was a story about a need for families to serve as temporary guardians.

Twenty-four families from Elmbrook Church in Brookfield are poised to open their homes to children in crisis. The families have been certified through a Chicago-based nonprofit to take in children temporarily while their parents or guardians work through personal problems. . . . "Families are under enormous stress—from medical issues, alcoholism, job losses—and the price is paid often by the children," said their lead pastor Rev. Scott Arbeiter. Tracy Weldie, director of Safe Families for Children Milwaukee added, "We're asking people to practice Biblical hospitality. Hospitality isn't having people over for coffee and doughnuts. It's about welcoming the stranger into your home."[300]

Then there is the story of Lori and Dan O'Brien. Supported by a community of fellow churchgoers who helped them build an eight-bedroom and five-bathroom home dubbed "Heaven House" to raise their three biological children and 10 adopted children. Most have special needs requiring love and structure.[301]

I am awed, humbled and inspired by all the good stuff happening right here in Milwaukee. Faith-based organizations like the Capuchin Franciscans, United Methodist Children's Services, Jewish Family Services, Mercy Housing Lakefront and the United Christian Church have partnered with federal, state, county and city governments to provide affordable housing for the homeless and mentally ill. Since 2007 nearly 300 apartments have become available, with 200 more due to come on line by 2012. One of the things that the faith-based organizations are also able to do is increase support services needed by the residents.

This has all happened in response to a Milwaukee Journal Sentinel series "highlighting the lack of safe, clean and affordable housing for the mentally ill in Milwaukee County. It prompted the creation of a city-county task force and housing trust whose funds would be used to help finance both profit and nonprofit projects aimed at serving that population."[302] People in the faith community responded, and hopefully will continue to do so as an additional 1,260 units will be needed in the next ten years.

The Milwaukee Journal Sentinel has raised the level of awareness about children who die before their first birthday through a feature titled "Empty Cradles: Confronting our infant mortality crisis."[303] The article included a list of 89 community agencies and programs, together with "a legion of volunteers" involved in wide range of support, assistance and encouragement, like . . . coaching expectant moms, running lactation counseling meetings, contributing to the city's Kids for Cribs program, giving new moms down the street a ride to the grocery store or helping a pregnant friend quit smoking.

Thousands of volunteers dedicate themselves to lives of humble, loving service. Some help the Salvation Army serve Christmas dinner or the daily meal at the rescue mission, mentor children and youth or work at their local shelter for battered women or the homeless. Then there is the story of John Bowen.

> I've been a teacher, coach and counselor at Milwaukee South Division High School for the past 27 years, usually working up to 80 hours a week. I believe that all of our children need at least one positive, significant adult in their lives (who expresses hope and success in their future).
>
> My mission has been twofold: To be that positive, significant person for as many students as possible and to find ways to bring other adults into our building who can provide positive role models for our students.[304]

Ace Backus, Booker T. Ash and Joel Ellwanger were cut from the same mold. An article in the paper was headed, *"Farewell to a Fighter for Fairness and Justice."* It described Ace Backus as one who, while born into privilege, chose to lead a simple life. "Money was not his goal; he had a habit of giving it away. A better world was his aim. (He) made his living as assistant program director at Neighborhood Houses, a west side community center. . . ."[305]

His obituary was headed "Backus devoted his life to helping the underclass," and read in part: "August 'Ace' Backus, a community activist whose life was a crusade for social justice . . . (was) 'a member of virtually every current community organization on the west side.' (He) made his living . . . at Neighborhood house, but his personal mission to help the underclass went far beyond that."[306]

Booker T. Ashe gave food, clothing and hope to poor families in Milwaukee as Director of the House of Peace for more than 25 years. "We show them what Christ is about by our action."[307] A cousin to tennis star Arthur Ashe, he was raised in the well-to-do suburb of Evanston, Illinois,

> . . . far from the poverty he later found surrounding him at the House of Peace. . . . In 1967, when the Capuchin fathers and brothers were looking for an outreach center apart from the large church structures, Ashe helped set up the House of Peace to distribute emergency food and clothing to the poor. . . . He often began his day at 4:30 a.m. and sometimes ended it long after the sun had set. He wore his monk's habit to church in the morning, but usually donned street clothes for the rest of the day, hanging his friar's

habit by the hood on an office door. . . . Ashe held his emergency center together with volunteers, some funds from the Capuchins and Milwaukee archdiocese, and contributions of cash, food and clothing from the community. . . . He refused to treat people like beggars, giving them self-respect along with food and clothing.[308]

"Social justice" defined the ministry of Rev. Joe Ellwanger, who served faithfully

. . . from his early years as a young white minister of a predominantly black congregation in the South through 30 years at Cross Lutheran. . . . Ellwanger will retire at the end of the year. . . . He will leave behind a record that has endeared him to his parishioners, sometimes made him an outcast among his Lutheran colleagues and led to the creation of MICAH— Milwaukee Intercity Congregations Allied for Hope . . . made up now of 43 churches (with an) in-your-face brand of non-violent confrontation on issues from open housing to school reform.

(He) graduated from Concordia Seminary, in . . . St. Louis in 1957. His master's thesis, 'Racism and the Christian World'— an unpopular topic at the time for a young white Lutheran minister—gave a glimpse of where his ministry was headed. . . .

. . . (He was) assigned to St. Paul Lutheran Church in Birmingham, Ala., a small Lutheran congregation that grew from 30 to 275 members by the time he left in 1967.

It was there he met Christopher McNair, a member of the (Lutheran Church – Missouri) Synod, whose daughter was one of four girls killed in the bombing of Birmingham's Sixteenth Street Baptist Church on Sept. 15, 1963.

Ellwanger was . . . among a group of ministers, led by Martin Luther King Jr., who took part in the girl's funerals.

"He wasn't like a lot of those ministers who came down from the North just to participate in Birmingham or the march on Selma," McNair said.

"He was a participant in the movement."[309]

Ellwanger moved to Milwaukee in 1957. He succeeded Rev. Reynold J. Lillie, who left Cross to serve Ashburn Lutheran, my home congregation in Chicago. Pastor Lillie was the person who was the biggest influence in my becoming a pastor.

Milwaukee would be a sadder and more emotionally barren place without them, and the efforts of thousands of others just like them. I am indeed inspired and humbled by the selfless dedication of many of my neighbors in the greater Milwaukee area. These folks are awesome! While Milwaukee is really just a big, little town, and in many ways a well kept secret, it's no secret that there are folks in your community and all over our country who share the same compassion and a willingness to commit much of their life and energy to those in need. What follows are the inspirational stories of some of those volunteers.

One of the most awesome national charitable service organizations is Habitat for Humanity and its mission of providing affordable housing. The absolutely magnificent efforts of thousands and thousands of volunteers and donors has led to a success story that now numbers 400,000 homes built or repaired worldwide—over 2 million when you add homes that were rehabilitated. It has taken an army of volunteers to help meet the need for housing for people living in or near poverty and would never be able to afford a home. Founded in 1976, it took 13 years to build the first 10,000 houses. The program took off after President Jimmy Carter joined Habitat in 1984. Carter was also instrumental in the eradication of the Guinea Worm in southern Sudan. As an ex-president, he could have made millions on the speaking circuit and corporate boards; instead he chose to devote his energy and influence to helping the disenfranchised.

Doctors without Borders (DWB) is there when conditions are the worst. Their field teams are positioned to respond quickly, as they "deliver emergency aid to people affected by armed conflict, epidemics, natural and man-made disasters in more than 60 countries. On any day, more than 25,000 (DWB) doctors, nurses, logisticians, water-and-sanitation experts, administrators, and other medical and non-medical professionals can be found providing assistance to people caught in crises around the world."[310]

Bobby MacGuffie, 69, a plastic surgeon from New City, N.Y. was on her way to help Rwandan refugees keep their children alive. The country's minority Tutsi clan overturned the Hutu government in a bloodbath after the Hutu president was killed. The war that followed left more than 500,000 dead and touched off a chaotic exodus as many Hutu fled to Zaire fearing revenge killings by the Tutsi. "'My kids were bleeding to death and I watched them die,' she says, remembering her two sons who died of AIDS. "When I hear thousands of mothers are going to go through the same thing, I know I've got to find a way to get over there."[311]

"So like hundreds of others, MacGuffie has updated her immunizations, canceled all appointments, packed a Swiss army knife and basic supplies.... For MacGuffie, it's a familiar trip. She has led aid missions to Africa since 1987 for an organization of doctors she heads: Society for Hospital and Resources Exchange, which collects donations and treats people in developing countries."[312]

The vivid images of suffering and death in the media have been so shocking that the response to this humanitarian crisis has been "unprecedented.... Agencies say that a fourth of the calls are people willing to get on a plane.... Among the volunteers: Lani Wishnie, 26, is a nurse getting a master's degree at Yale University. 'I have my summers off and logistics fall into place,' she says. 'I feel like I can do it, so I should.' ...Thomas Hadduck, 46, a family doctor in Aurora Colo., has experience in Africa. 'I've seen people die of cholera and I know how terrifying and devastating it is.... What I can do is a drop in the bucket compared to what needs to be done, but I'm going to just try to do what I can.'"[313]

These talented doctors could have had fancy offices and easy lifestyles. Instead they chose a different career path.

"I'm no role model" says Dr. Jennifer Furin. "I swear. I read romance novels. I watch bad television." But most of the year finds her working 70 hours a week or more inside dirt-floored shacks and dusty little clinics in the slums of Lima, Peru. Her face, surrounded by reddish curls, is usually animated but now it wears a look of pure concentration as she listens through her stethoscope to the lung sounds of yet another impoverished Peruvian afflicted with drug-resistant tuberculosis.

At 35, having completed both Harvard Medical School and one of the world's most coveted residencies at the Harvard-affiliated Brigham and Women's Hospital in Boston, Jen has the sort of credentials that guarantee a comfortable life. But she has chosen a different path. She belongs to a cadre of dedicated physicians who serve at Brigham's new Division of Social Medicine and Health Inequalities,[314] and with an affiliated public charity called Partners in Health. The heartwarming stories of their service in tragic and heartbreaking circumstances among desperately impoverished people are truly inspirational. Their names deserve mention as exceptional, exemplary volunteer servants: Howard Hiatt, Paul Farmer, Jim Yong Kim, Michael Rich, Keith Joseph, Heidi Behforouz. Their story will touch you deeply, and light candles of hope in a dark and cruel world.[315]

When Gen. Colin Powell left his post as Chairman of the Joint Chiefs of Staff in 1993, his vision of the future included his grandkids and many other young people as well. He "joined the Board of Governors of Boys and Girls Clubs of America, started working on behalf of the United Negro College Fund and other youth-oriented causes. Last year he found a way to consolidate his efforts as chairman of America's Promise—The Alliance for Youth. . . . Adds Connecticut Gov. John Rowland, 'He could spend his time making tons of money, but he has dedicated his star power, his resources and his energies to help kids.'"[316]

"From the top leadership of our country to the average citizen, our people do care. Following President George W. Bush's call for volunteers in his 2002 State of the Union speech, 18,000 people have asked how to join the Peace Corps. Enrollment in AmeriCorps is up 50%, and it is up 500% in the Senior Corps."[317]

As exemplified by "CNN Heroes" and the reciepients of the National Caring Awards, care, concern and compassion are certainly evident in communities all across America. Please know that I most certainly recognize and affirm their service with admiration. I am grateful for the very real needs they meet and the hearts they touch. Maybe I took too long to say it, but while questioning the totality of our commitment, and asserting that all of us are self-centered, self-serving, self-seeking individuals who look out for ourselves and our own at the expense of the unmet needs of others, it is especially important to make it clear that I do indeed see and give thanks for all who serve as volunteers. I do see it! I see it everywhere!

Mother Teresa—Giving beyond All Reasonable Expectation

And then there is Mother Teresa. "Mother Teresa, like Albert Schweitzer, . . . epitomize(s) the sort of person who casts off the world and goes to work amid the needy."[318] The motivation for all she did was love for her Savior Jesus. "The dying, the crippled, the mentally ill, the unwanted, the unloved – they are Jesus in disguise"[319] "She would often repeat the question, 'How can you claim to love a God you can't see if you fail to love the brother or sister standing right in front of you?'"[320] She served, labored and loved in the slums of Calcutta nearly 70 years.

> Mother Teresa describes the painful reality she encountered on (the) first day (she went into the slums). ". . .What dirt and misery—what poverty and suffering.—I spoke very, very little, I just did some washing of sores and dressings, gave medicine to some.—The old man lying on the street—not wanted—all alone just sick and dying.—I gave him carbarsone and water to drink and the old man was so strangely grateful. . . . Then we went to Taltala Bazaar, and there was a very poor woman dying I think of starvation more than TB. What poverty. What actual suffering. I gave something which will help her to sleep—but the woman is longing to have some care. I wonder how long she will last—she was just 96 degrees at the time. . . . I did everything I could but if I had been able to give her a hot cup of milk or something like that, her cold body would have got some life.—I must try and be somewhere close to the people. . . ."[321]

The Missionary Sisters of Charity devoted themselves "to the care of the poor and needy, who, crushed by want and destitution, live in conditions unworthy of human dignity."[322] "While going about the city to meet the needs of the poor, Mother Teresa often encountered people dying in the streets. Because these people were considered 'hopeless cases,' the hospitals would not accept them; they were destined to face the end of their life alone, unwanted and abandoned by all. Mother Teresa sought a home where they would be received with love and treated with dignity at least in the last moments of their lives."[323]

"The Rev. Charles Curran, ethics professor at Southern Methodist University, said Mother Teresa inspired praise because she represented the best of Christian tradition. 'She so totally lived out the twofold commitment of Jesus' love of God and love of neighbor' he said. 'Here you had this witness to it, which was so authentic. It was a witness that had integrity about it. Her words, deeds and lifestyle were all one."[324] Mother Teresa is the essence of what the Christian life is all about. Her ministry to the poor, sick and dying is the essence of charity. She gets it! She understands! She lives it!

"Her compelling compassion stood as a rebuke to those who would suggest that organized religion is frustrating and cramped. . . . Today, the Missionaries of Charity number somewhere around 4,500 sisters, and they have established hospices, orphanages and soup kitchens in the sorts of cities one might expect"[325] By 1988 they served at over 350 locations in 77 countries.

She expressed a part of the essence of what I see and what leads to my understanding of both humanity and Christian service. "There are plenty of nuns (pastors, ministers, priests, and Christian laity) to look after the rich and the well to do people—but for My very poor, there are absolutely none. For them I long—them I love."[326] "The work in Calcutta is so great—that there will never be enough nuns to do all that—still there are at least some to do it while for the slum poor—nobody."[327] Reflecting on the poor who she describes as the "Unwanted, Unloved, and Unclaimed," she says "Amen" to the powerful words of Malcolm Muggeridge: "The greatest evil is the lack of love and charity, the terrible indifference towards one's neighbor who lives at the roadside assaulted by exploitation, corruption, poverty and disease. . . ."[328] "At a time when humankind is being increasingly driven by selfish motive, she gave selflessly to those whom society has forsaken and forgotten."[329]

How well she summed it up when she accepted the Nobel Peace Prize in 1979. "I choose the poverty of our poor people. But I am grateful to receive it in the name of the hungry, the naked, the homeless, of the crippled, of the blind, of the lepers, of all those who feel unwanted, unloved, uncared for throughout society, people that have become a burden to the society."[330] We tend to look on the poor, the abandoned and the forsaken as a problem to be solved, rather than people to be cared for and served. "She often stated, 'God still loves the world through you and through me today.'"[331]

"Now," you ask, "how can you possibly reconcile the life of Mother Teresa and the lives of the other examples of extraordinary volunteers with my thesis, namely, that human nature is inherently self-centered, self-serving and self-seeking?" The apparent contradiction needs to be resolved. Before attempting to do so, I'm going to add charitable giving and philanthropy to the mix and then apply the resolution both to volunteers and to those who give generously.

Contributions to Church and Charity

There are a variety of motivations for donating time and treasure to religious institutions and charities. Some give out of a deep and abiding concern for suffering and the unmet needs of others in the human family.

Some give in response to values instilled by parents. Many give in a way that maximizes tax benefits through the charitable deduction and estate tax provisions. My sense is that for a huge majority the experience of charitable giving is more like getting a root canal, rather than a joyful experience reflecting thankfulness for having been blessed and as a celebration of being able to help less fortunate brothers and sisters in the human family.

In an article about philanthropy, Nancy Gibbs writes: "As though the motives even matter. America's first billionaire, Standard Oil titan John D. Rockefeller, was described as 'a monster; merciless in his greed; pitiless in his cold inhuman passions'—and that was by his brother. But the robber barons were complex, competitive men who emerged from the Industrial Revolution with way more money than the church offering plate could hold. So they industrialized charity, tackling immense problems—hunger, disease, the root causes of poverty—in ways that saved enough lives to salvage their legacy."[332]

I would agree with Gibbs comment, "with way more money than the church offering plate could hold," if she is referring to worshipping communities that reflect "naval gazing" and "maintenance," communities where they are only concerned about themselves and their own needs, and give little if anything to help reach the un-churched, the suffering, the needy and the abandoned. However, in worshipping communities where the emphasis is on outreach and social concern, there is no end to what good can be done with large contributions. In religious communities that look outward there is never "way more money than the church offering plate (can) hold." Rather, the congregation becomes a conduit where by consensus contributions are re-directed to a never ending list of prioritized needs.

Back in 2000 Bill and Melinda Gates were worth $65 billion, $22 billion of which was given or pledged. Their foundation "sees its role as filling the breach where the private sector is not addressing a crisis. The industrialized world's ailments, from indigestion to breast cancer, are already the focus of drug-company research. Cure a first-world disease, and reap millions in profits. But cure a third world disease such as malaria—the No. 1 killer in tropical climes—and there is hardly a penny to be earned. Those patients don't have health insurance. That's why the Gates Foundation has made finding a malaria vaccine a priority, along with eradicating scourges such as hookworm, hepatitis B, leishmaniasis (a parasitic disease transmitted by sand flies that affects 15 million people each year), HIV, guinea-worm disease and tuberculosis. The foundation is spending nearly $400,000 million a year on its global-health initiative, mainly by developing new vaccines and cures and making existing cures more accessible to the people who need them."[333]

We've all heard how Mark Zuckerberg, the founder of Facebook, gave $100 million to help improve schools in Newark, N.J. Less well known is Pierre Omidyar, founder of eBay, who says "he has given away $100 million and plans to give away all but 1% of his wealth—more than $4.2 billion—within 20 years."[334] Then there's Charles Feeney, who was listed on the Forbes list of the 400 richest Americans, but who probably should have been taken off years ago. Secretly and anonymously and without seeking any tax deductions, he has given away and placed in charitable foundations over $4 billion, keeping only $5 million on hand for himself.[335]

Many other wealthy philanthropists are well known: Warren Buffet of Berkshire-Hathaway, George Soros, Microsoft co-founder Paul Allen, Oracle Corp CEO Larry Ellison, New York Mayor Michael Bloomberg, Joan Kroc, widow of the former McDonald's chairman, and cable TV mogul Ted Turner. George Soros, the financier-philanthropist, has already donated $1 billion to charities around the world—as much as Turner is pledging over a decade."[336]

In 2010 40 American billionaires pledged to give at least 50% of their fortunes to charity. They are the first to join Bill and Melinda Gates and billionaire investor Warren Buffet in an effort known as the "The Giving Pledge," which they co-founded. Recently, Warren Buffet donated $1.6 billion to the Gates Foundation, and has pledged to donate 99% of his $47 billion dollar wealth to charity. Most will go in installments to Bill and Melinda Gates Foundation.

They were joined by a group that included Ted Turner; Larry Ellison; Paul Allen; Pierre Omidyar; Silicon Valley venture capital titan John Doerr; oilman T. Boone Pickens; filmmaker George Lucas; Tom Steyer, head of hedge fund firm Farallon Capital; IAC/Interactive Corp. CEO Barry Diller; David Rockefeller and Michael Bloomberg. "'I've always thought that the best thing to do is to make the world better for your kids and grandkids rather than just give them some money,' said Bloomberg.'"[337]

"For every Bill Gates there are literally millions of Morris Popes. The 81-year old retired train engineer has given at least $500 to the Atlanta Food Bank every year since 1982. One year he gave $1,200. And this on his retirement income of about $1,700 a month. He is almost too shy to mention the $3,000 he annually tithes to his First Corinth Missionary

Baptist Church. 'I look at how God has blessed me during my working years and raising my family, and I can't tell you how many times I've come to these homeless shelters and heard people say, "My children haven't had a bite to eat today," says Pope."[338]

An accurate measure of charity and generosity "is measured not by the number of dollars given, but the number of dollars given relative to the giver's wealth."[339] Rich, middle class or poor, the joy of giving brings peace and satisfaction. However, we all struggle with our human nature when we near the threshold of emotional pain we experience when we don't want to give any more. It's tough for the rich, and by the world's standard's that includes most of us in the United States.

So Exactly What in the World Do You Do with Mother Teresa?

"How can you possibly reconcile the life of Mother Teresa and the lives of the other examples of extraordinary volunteers with your thesis, that human nature is inherently self-centered, self-serving and self-seeking?" "How can you hold that we have the tendency to look out not just for the needs, but also for the wants of ourselves and our own at the expense of the unmet needs of others, when confronted with life of Mother Teresa? What in the world are you thinking?" I wondered too. Then I read her book and she provided the insights needed for resolution to the apparent contradiction.

You might be surprised to learn that arguably the most well known volunteer servant of our time experienced a powerful internal conflict. On the one hand, she bravely ventured into the world of absolute poverty, surrendering her whole being into His service. Her heart's desire was to give herself in absolute poverty to Christ and dedicate herself to the service of His suffering poor. "God wants me to give myself completely to Him in absolute poverty, to identify myself with the Indian girls in their life of self-sacrifice and immolation by tending the poor in the slums, the sick, the dying, the beggars in their dirty holes and the little street children."[340] Here's how she defined absolute poverty: "By absolute poverty I mean real and complete poverty—not starving—but wanting— just only what the real poor have."[341] It was her intent that self-denial become a way of life. Mother Teresa is certainly to be numbered among those who have most faithfully modeled a life that is self-sacrificing, self-giving and selfless.

On the other hand, she was also well aware of her humanity and began her journey afraid of how it might become a roadblock to fulfilling her commitment. "I am so afraid Jesus—I am so terribly afraid—let me not be deceived—I am so afraid.—I am afraid of the suffering that will come—through leading that Indian life—clothing like them, eating like them, sleeping like them—living with them and never having anything my way. How much comfort has taken possession of my heart."[342] The way she sees herself and the words she uses to describe herself are striking. "I am sinful and unworthy of his love...."[343] She refers to "my many sins."[344] "My own Jesus—what You ask it is beyond me—I can hardly understand half of the things you want—I am unworthy—I am sinful—I am weak.—Go Jesus and find a more worthy soul, a more generous one."[345]

It doesn't compute! How could she feel this way, when she humbly submitted to a life of absolute poverty, and surrendered her whole being in loving service? We simply don't understand why she felt this way. The powerful tension Mother Teresa experienced only makes sense in the context of her faith in Jesus Christ. She established as the norm for her life the self-sacrificing, self-giving, selfless life of Christ who permitted himself to be sacrificed on a cross in our place, as our substitute, so that we might be assured of the gifts of forgiveness of sin and eternal life. She so loved Him for what He had done for her that she was eager to offer her life back to Him in loving service.

If she could have read my thesis, I believe she would understand. She would get it. She wouldn't take it personally. She wouldn't get angry. She wouldn't take offense. She would include herself under the umbrella of my thesis together with all of us in the human family. The seeming contradiction in her own experience is the clue. While others would deem her life exemplary, based on the norm of the self-giving, selfless, self sacrificing life of Christ, she did not share that perception of herself. It wasn't necessary for me to reconcile her life with my thesis. An exemplary Christian life together with the testimony that she was painfully aware of her own sinfulness is the key to resolution.

When you preach one of those sermons that nobody likes, it is the mature, faithful, obedient Christians who understand. They don't take offense or get defensive. They get it! They understand. They appreciate it whenever they are made aware of how their self-serving, self-centered, self-seeking nature influences their behavior. They want to hear it, because they always want to be as faithful to Christ and as much like Christ as they can. They want to hear it, because they want to become accountable. Upon being reassured that they are forgiven they are overcome with emotion, thankful for the relief that brings peace. They are eager to live lives that show how thankful they are and how much they love their Savior. They get it as Mother Teresa got it.

Resolving the Internal Conflict
about How to Live

It is in trying to understand Mother Teresa that we learn so much about ourselves and the inner conflict we experience in the process of deciding how much we will contribute and how much time we spend as volunteers. We try to avoid the tension and push it out of our awareness as much as possible. Yet, each of us has to face it squarely and resolve it for ourselves. Each of us has to come to terms with the meaning of life. Each of us has to resolve the internal conflict about how to live.

So where does that leave us? What's next? Each of us has to ask what level of charitable giving and volunteer service is sufficient. Answering the question requires that we become aware of the norm by which we measure. Are we flowing along with the current of culturally accepted norms? Or, do we want to consider another norm for service and sacrifice? This issue needs to be surfaced and brought into our awareness, so that we can make a conscious choice about the standard by which we will measure ourselves.

We are blessed in our country with the freedom to choose. We have every right to choose the course of hard work in pursuit of getting more stuff and our share of the American Dream. Or we can work hard so that we can provide for the basic needs of our families, and as many of the unmet needs of others as we can. We could consider a commitment to the practice of charitable giving and volunteer service that seeks to do everything possible to meet the basic unmet needs of others. But how much is enough? Enough is enough. When have we served enough and given enough? No one can answer that question for us. Only we know when we have done enough. Mother Teresa chose a standard and measured herself carefully by that standard.

The sermons that I've preached and that I've heard others preach far better, sermons about being transformed into people who are more caring, compassionate servants are indeed a beautiful vision. However, the vision is flawed because we fall into the trap of measuring ourselves by culturally accepted norms. There is another norm. Mother Teresa's norm was the sacrificial, self-giving, selfless life of Jesus, which we can use to determine whether we are truly caring, compassionate servants and by which we can evaluate our charitable giving and volunteer service. She concluded that she didn't measure up to the standard by which she measured herself—God's standard as taught in His Word. We have to go through that same process. We have to be clear about the standard by which we evaluate ourselves, and then determine whether we "measure up," whether we think we are loving, decent and morally upright, or not.

What can be said about all the folks we hear about on "Making a Difference" or "Positively Milwaukee? All of their efforts are most certainly meaningful, valued, beneficial, helpful and appreciated, especially by those helped and served. As Brian Williams often says, "There is no shortage of Americans (45 percent) willing to help." They make a huge difference. They are most certainly positive. But there is a bigger picture and a larger question. Forgive me for asking even with reference to the 45 percent, how much are they giving within the framework of their situation and resources? How much are they helping and giving when measured against their potential? Is there a danger that we have whitewashed the meaning of life, and in the end have to ask whether we have wasted our lives?

Prince Michael of Greece met Mother Teresa after experiencing a profound personal tragedy, the loss of a six year old girl he had come to know and who he had helped. His words bring needed encouragement to me. "I saw that in her work, in her very being, Mother Teresa brings hope where there would not be any hope left. Now I understood that each one of us can follow her example. We must hope—and act."[346] I want so much to feel hopeful about the way we in the human family will treat each other. I want so much for the world to be different. I'm running out of hope that my thesis will be shown to be invalid. I need to hear the words again: "I saw in her work, in her very being, Mother Teresa bring hope where there would not be any hope left." I need to hear those words again, and again, and again.

The "Wow" people are those who have been transformed by the Gospel, who offer themselves as a living sacrifice, who give their all in service as dedicated disciples. In addition to our friends, the Kelms, we know another couple with two children who serve in a remote and undeveloped region of the world and a middle aged couple who serve in the foreign mission field. The same can be said about those who serve with the Lutheran Bible Translators, translating the Bible into new languages and dialects, in some cases having to write the language for cultures that have not had one before. Many of these men are married and have children who go with them. I think of the many faithful nuns and priests, some of our older pastors who served faithfully while living in parsonages, not worrying about how they would make ends meet in retirement, trusting that the Lord would provide.

These are some of the most selfless people I know, people representative of many others just like them. I believe that they would say the same thing about themselves that Mother Teresa said about herself, and I would say the same things about them that I said about Mother Teresa. They would get it! They would understand! They would be the first ones to agree with my thesis. They wouldn't take offense. Folks who are humbly submissive daily rejoice in and are thankful for all that Christ has done for them, and seek the Holy Spirit's help in serving Him even more faithfully. They are not offended and do not get angry. They understand.

It is those who are resisting the call and invitation to walk more faithfully as his servants, who are most likely to get upset and angry by my thesis. When you preach the sermons nobody likes, those who are growing in Christian maturity welcome the message, understand and do not get offended. It is those who are struggling to let go of the attractions of a materialistic and pleasure-oriented culture who take offense. Those caught in this tension are the ones who are furious and irate when anyone dares suggest that we are not as compassionate and generous as we could be, because they have been misled by accepted cultural and religious norms into believing that they are caring, kind, loving and generous. There is no question that for the vast majority my thesis hits a raw nerve. Again, this discussion can be helpful in putting our own stuff into perspective. My intent is not to judge, blame or criticize anyone, but simply to surface the issue and how it triggers powerful internal tensions and struggles for people of good will who have always considered themselves compassionate, caring and generous.

We have been richly blessed, and have the potential to do great things in the realm of volunteer service and charitable giving. And, as noted, we are blessed to live in a country where our government provides the structure for an ordered, civilized society where folks are free to make these choices for themselves. Even those concerned about fostering a culture of dependency can give to causes that meet desperate needs or that foster independence, individual initiative and personal responsibility.

Many do give to church and charity. As made clear, however, my sense is that we give enough to salve our consciences, and nowhere near our potential. Our level of charity is only a hint, a glimpse of what it might be. Our cumulative record of charitable giving and volunteer service does not provide pervasive evidence of man's humanity to man. It appears to me that we have made a choice to accept the lower cultural standard of compassion, generosity and charity. We have allowed ourselves to become comfortable with a bar that has been set way too low. We have watered down concepts like caring, kindness, compassion, service and generosity to the point where they have lost much of their meaning and much of what draws us to them and stirs the deepest of emotion and passion.

When you say that you can see love, compassion, mercy, commitment, dedication, caring and service in the hearts and lives of donors and volunteers, it sounds awesome. However, being precise requires that we carefully define the meaning packed into the word "awesome." Again, I'll use scale of 1-100 to try to define be more specific. One designates a person who does not make charitable contributions and does not volunteer, and 100 a person who gives all in excess of what they absolutely need and volunteers every available hour beyond their commitments to family and friends.

There are many decent people, who care for those in their household and are helpful neighbors and good citizens, and move beyond that to the first level of being charitable givers and volunteers. It would seem that this group would fall at about level 16 on the continuum. Level 31 would be those who had moved to the place where they give 5-10 percent of their income to church and charity and volunteer an average of 2 hours per week. Level 43 might be those who contribute 10 percent of their income to church and charity and volunteer 4-5 hours per week. Then let's say there is a mom who works two jobs, is raising a 16 year old son and an 11 year old daughter, and who still gives many hours of her time as a volunteer and is generous in her charitable giving. She exemplifies what it looks like for people with full, busy lives to make a significant, sacrificial commitment to a life of service, rather than being selfish, and content with a life of selective inattention to suffering, hunger, poverty and need   Let's say she is at level 62. We'll put Mother Teresa at level 96 rather than 99, only because she herself has acknowledged her sins, her shortcomings and her unworthiness.

If we just want to be civilized and even decent, that's one thing. Being kind, caring and compassionate in a way that reflects a concern that goes to the very depth of our being and defines who we are is a whole different ballgame. Those who have a deep and abiding concern for the needs of all of humanity, and a willingness to make a sacrificial commitment to do everything possible to alleviate human need and suffering are few.

Requests to support a charitable cause lift up the need and seek to touch hearts and motivate a response within the framework of charitable giving and volunteering defined by our culture. My hope is that the call for a compassionate response would be far more encompassing. Our sense of compassion is limited by what has become an acceptable norm. If we measure ourselves by that standard, we look pretty good. It works for us. It allows for a perception of the meaning of life that hardly inconveniences us, cramps our style or urges us to consider a sacrificial, selfless response.

Even when circumstances of suffering and desperate need "bring out the best in us," I grieve when reflecting on how we still don't come anywhere near realizing our full potential to serve and to give. Mother Teresa got it! If anyone could experience joy and celebration about her life of sacrificial service, if anyone could feel a sense of peace and fulfillment that she had done enough, it would be Mother Teresa. Yet it was she of all people who recognized how far she was from reaching the standard of love and service defined by the Biblical norm for holiness and measured by how well she was following in the steps of the "suffering servant," her Savior, Jesus. She knew she was forgiven and that eternal life in heaven was a certainty. Her response to the simply astounding love, mercy and forgiveness of God was the offering of a sacrificial life of loving service as her way of expressing the gratitude and gladness that filled her heart.

"The Good Life"

In our earlier years life is all about friends and family, work and relaxation, playing baseball and bowling, hiking and skiing, hunting and fishing, biking and boating, shopping and going to the movies, partying and fun. Life is dancing and music. Life is energy and laughing. Life is all of this and so much more. Yet, you learn that if this is all that fills your leisure time, you are missing so much. There is an aching and an emptiness. There are fleeting moments when you wonder about the meaning of it all, and about the possibility of making a difference.

When you get older family becomes more important. Life is watching your children and grandchildren reach for their dreams. Life is getting together with friends over lunch or coffee and a light breakfast at the local restaurant. Life is about exercise and tennis. Life is about cards and golf. And to the degree that health permits, life is about doing all of things you enjoyed when you were younger. Yet, you learn that if this is all that fills your leisure time, that there is a void that results in a continued search for meaning and purpose. You learn, perhaps from your own isolation, loneliness and need, that life is oh so much more.

I would suggest that from our childhood days to our golden years we carve out a generous portion of time for service as a volunteer. There is more to life than pleasure and fun. Life is serving at the soup kitchen or women's shelter. Life is tutoring and mentoring disadvantaged kids. Life is being a "Big Brother" or "Big Sister." Life is visiting the lonely and lending a hand to the aging. Life is taking the blind to the symphony and pushing those confined to a wheelchair through the park. Life is about adopting the hard to place child or being foster parents to children whose dysfunctional families are trying to get it together. Life is about listening to the war stories of our veterans, and the "poor" stories of the aging. Life is finding beds, mattresses, a kitchen set or sofa for those who live in bare apartments and sleep and eat and sit on the floor. Life is doing all you can to see that all people can live in dignity and peace.

Life is treating yourself to a piece of apple pie and cup of coffee after you have spent an hour in the morning one day a week listening to someone who is so narrow minded and opinionated that everybody else tunes them out or avoids them completely. Life is treating yourself to a glass of wine after spending an hour a week with someone in the early stages of Alzheimer's or dementia, or with one of the ragamuffins in your congregation or community who nobody pays attention to or cares about. For me as a Christian, this is what Jesus did, and because He gave His all for me on the cross, I am eager, I am honored, I am privileged to do what He would do and to do it in His name. And, come to think of it, it would also be nice to have a miraculous, inexhaustible source of wine readily available after the time of caring, sharing and service had ended for the day. Smack me down!

Don't say you can't do it. There are volunteer service-centers where they will help you find the right match for your skills and interests, and train you if necessary. There is a place that needs you in your church or community. Having been known to frequent the "burger-biggies," you can't help but notice the retired folks who gather faithfully with their friends, especially in the morning. We all need the opportunity for social interaction and conversation. But I do wonder how these folks spend the rest of their day. If they have time on their hands, they could become a powerful force of volunteers, whether visiting the lonely and forgotten at nursing care facilities or veteran's homes, helping out at their place of worship or with meals on wheels or mentoring or tutoring disadvantaged youth. This group has so much untapped potential as volunteer servants.

None of us wants to do things we find difficult or that for personal reasons elicit too much painful emotion. Some members of our church have said they would find it hard to serve someone who is grieving the loss of a loved one, or whose cancer is in stage three or four and they might die. Nobody expects us to be all things to all people, but we can be his love to someone.

Oh yes, you can substitute cherry or French silk for the apple, and a couple of cold beers for the wine. For the women it could be an hour at the spa, for the men a smooth whiskey or good cigar. Life is all of this and so much more. Just close your eyes and dream, and catch a glimpse of what might be. Then at the close of the day you will find quiet and peace, leaving all that is undone in the hands of our heavenly Father until we arise renewed and refreshed, and joyfully greet the new day in anticipation of once again being His love and presence to those in need.

Caring, Kind and Compassionate vs. Humane, Decent and Civilized

On April 18, 2010 the Ted Abernathy Show on WMVS was about how President Carter through the Center for Law and Justice, which he founded, has been able to eradicate the scourge of the Guinea worm in southern Sudan. The program also referred to his mother's work with lepers, which he wrote about in one of his books.

The relevance for our discussion is again in no way minimizing the importance of this wonderful charitable work with which they are involved. While he is certainly leveraging his prestige and reputation as a humanitarian servant as he does with Habitat, the question for him, for his mother and for all of us is whether or not we are using our personal wealth to provide not just for our family's needs, but also for their wants at the expense of the unmet needs of others. Certainly there is no question in applauding all he has done. Rather, the question and challenge for all of us is to measure our charitable giving within the context of the totality of our personal financial situation and resources. This applies to the Buffets, to the Carters, to those who contributed toward desks for Africa and to all of us who contribute to religious and charitable institutions.

On December 22, 2011 Tom Brokaw was on "Piers Morgan Tonight." Here's what he said. "Like you I've won the lottery. I'm paid very well for what I do. I have enough money to keep myself comfortable. . . . My kids who are working . . . have that thrift gene passed down from their grandparents. At the same time if their needs really get critical, they've got dad around to help out." Obviously, not everyone has parents with the means do the same thing for their kids. My wife and I are blessed with the means to be able to help our kids or other relatives in a pinch.

Not everybody has parents who can. We are their brothers and sisters in the human family.

Managing our life as stewards means that we carefully monitor how all of our time is spent, and what percent of our financial resources we contribute to church and charity. Certainly there is no one answer that fits all situations. We have to evaluate the circumstances in our household and establish goals for the giving of both time and treasure. First, giving 5, 10, 25, 40, or 60 percent of our available resources does not determine whether we are generous or not generous. It is our potential for giving—how much we give beyond what we really need—that determines whether or not our response is generous. While the value to the recipients who benefit does not change and is so very important, if we are not as generous as we could be, others who might also benefit will go un-served. If you donate 60 percent of your potential, does that still mean you are indifferent? Indifference is a virus that spreads and contaminates the soul.

To say that most of us in our country live pretty well is a gross understatement. Truth is that compared to the standard of living of most of the world, a large majority of the 99% are wealthy and live like kings. We have plenty of food, warm clothes, a nice house, one or two cars, cell phones, a large flat screen TV, a computer, an iPod or iPad, enough for a few meals out and a couple of movies or a concert each month, a boat or snowmobile, usually enough money for at least a little vacation. This is the "Ritz." We take so much of this for granted.

We may be civilized. We may even be decent people. We may have a reasonable standard of ethics, morals and values. We may be touched by some of the tragedy and misfortune we see in our community and our country. Nevertheless, it is imperative that we search the very depths of our being in order determine whether or not we truly have compassionate, generous, servant hearts. Can the starving and suffering turn to us to help meet needs related to nutrition, clean drinking water, basic health care, shelter, sanitation and education? Mother Teresa wrestled with those questions every day. I do too, and I invite you to join me.

Chapter 13
Power, Leverage and Advantage

"Freedom is not simply the absence of tyranny or oppression. Nor is freedom a license to do whatever we like. Freedom has an inner logic which distinguishes it and ennobles it: freedom is ordered to the truth and is fulfilled in man's quest for truth and in man's living in the truth. Detached from the truth about the human person, freedom deteriorates into license in the lives of individuals, and in political life, it becomes the caprice of the most powerful and the arrogance of power." Pope John Paul II

"Hear this, you who trample the needy and do away with the poor in the land, saying, 'When will the New Moon be over that we may sell grain, and the Sabbath be ended that we may sell wheat?'—skimping the measure, boosting the price and cheating with dishonest scales, buying the poor with silver and the needy for a pair of sandals, selling even the sweepings with the wheat" (Amos 8:4-6).

A few notes of explanation for Amos 8:4-6 describe the essence of the use and abuse of power, leverage and advantage. As God's spokesman,

> Amos addresses …the greedy merchant class. Their offense is not wealth itself but the way they are gaining it at the expense of their needy fellow-countrymen. They treat the poor like dirt under their feet. … In order to get enough food for himself, his wife, and his children, a poor Israelite may be forced to sell himself and his family into slavery … for the price of a pair of sandals, just to have enough to eat. Even then, Amos says, the grain he brings home from the marketplace may not make good

bread, because the merchants sweep up what has fallen to the ground and mix the sweepings with the wheat.[347]

Theory of Change

We live in a world of competing interests. The powers that be support the *status quo*. If anyone wants to change the *status quo* in order to gain a greater share of wealth, they are going to have to leverage enough power to take it. It won't be given to them. Those who currently possess and control the wealth have the power and use whatever leverage they have to see to it that it stays that way. That is just the way the world works. Accept it. In today's vernacular, "Deal with it!"

Change in the *status quo* occurs when external pressure is brought to bear on the way things are currently being done. Change occurs when a person or group has sufficient power, money and influence to exert enough leverage to force the current system to change. Change occurs when enough people share a common concern, get organized, raise awareness, build coalitions, develop a strategy, formulate a plan and manage the implementation of that plan. When the current system is challenged, a tension develops between those who benefit from the way things are being done and those who feel the system is not fair and needs to be changed. Both parties are operating on the basis of self-interest. These competing interests need to be resolved. While the issues and specifics are different in each situation, the fundamental dynamics of the change process remain the same in terms of how power, money and influence are leveraged.

We all want society structured in a way that will serve our interests. When the current system functions in a way that has resulted in one group having power, money and influence, the "advantaged people" don't want to give up that advantage and the perks and privileges that go along with it. They don't want things to change. In our world of competing interests, it is our nature to seek to protect and retain whatever economic advantage, power, privilege and influence we have. We want to retain the *status quo* if it is favorable to our interests.

Those who are receiving the most benefits from the way things are will not willingly or voluntarily concede or give up any of the advantage they enjoy. It is just not in our nature to do that. Power, leverage, advantage and influence are not conceded, not compromised, not given away unless and until pressure is exerted on the system. If the way things are gives you an advantage, if the way things are is the best deal for you, why in the world would you ever want to change. Somebody has to lean on you really hard before you will change. When you're top dog, somebody is going to have to fight you to take away that bone. Why negotiate or compromise when you have a vested personal interest and you hold a winning hand. It is tough to try to change things, if the other party has most of the power, money and influence. Besides, they have come up with a conceptual framework that serves to rationalize and justify that the current way of doing things is both fair and best for everybody. They have to in order to maintain their perception of themselves as kind, decent, good people.

Powerful interests have the advantage over the little guy. The rich have the advantage over the poor. And the people with power and money aren't going to give it up. They've worked hard for it. They've earned it. They deserve it. And in many cases they have. The reluctance to want to change on the part of those who have the advantage is perfectly understandable in terms of our tendency to look out not just for the needs, but also for the wants of our own at the expense of the unmet needs of others. The fallacy is that their conceptualized rationalizations and justifications are flawed. There is the matter of whether the system has operated in the past in a manner that treated everybody fairly and gave everybody an opportunity; this is a highly charged, controversial issue.

We all have choices to make about how we are going to live our lives within the context of our worldview. I've described my worldview, which in turn determines how I desire to function within that world. The exception is personal relationships, where the foundation is trust, and where you have a mutual commitment to looking out for the other's best interest. While I would hope that trust could be the foundation of all of my relationships, the reality is that I can't make that assumption. When I am party to any economic transaction involving more than a few dollars, I need some sort of contract or legal document that defines the transaction. It would be naïve to proceed otherwise, as there would be a risk that someone could take advantage of me. I wish it were different. The reality is, it's not.

While my understanding of people and systems and how they work is not pretty, it is the reality that is out there. Whoever has the power and money and leverage will get their way. They will seek to maintain their advantage. We simply need to recognize that this is how the world works. Self-interest supported by power, money and advantage, leverage and influence will carry the day. This dynamic is evident in all spheres of life. The strategies of individuals, governments, political parties, elected leaders, the business community and unions are designed to further their own interests. The goal is to position yourself in a way that allows you to maintain the most advantageous situation possible for as long as possible. People and systems won't give up power, money, clout, leverage or influence until they have to. While they may not be happy about it, they adjust to the new reality if there is no choice. Here are some specific examples of how change occurs within systems.

Sources of the Power and Leverage Needed to Change Our Laws

In our country the vehicle designed to facilitate change is the secret ballot—where the views and wishes of the majority result in the election of candidates who will represent their views in the process of enacting legislation. While the system for electing the members of Congress remains the same, two developments have resulted in monumental changes in how the process works.

First, our daily way of life is so very different from what it was in the early years of our nation. As recently as in my lifetime I can remember when there was no television, no computers, no space flight, no satellite communication and no cell phones. Technological progress has resulted in fundamental changes in political campaigns. The use of modern technology, media consultants, pollsters and advisors makes it possible to have your interpretation of the issues broadcast directly to the public in a powerful, compelling manner. Cable news and talk radio use their talking points to defend and reinforce their perceptions and preferences, while discrediting the positions of the opposition. The sheer volume of political discourse has multiplied beyond anything imagined not that long ago.

Second, somebody has to pay for all this communication. Campaign contributions, super-PACS and lobbyists have also changed the landscape dramatically. Depending on the importance of the issue in furthering your personal interest, considerable sums are contributed to political campaigns and super-PACs and paid to lobbyists. While the dollar amounts can be huge, large political contributions and astronomical fees for lobbyists are simply considered a "good investment," one that usually brings handsome returns. It takes money to organize a campaign. It takes a lot of money to maximize the use of media advertising. Money is the source of the power that buys leverage, influence and advantage. "It was also the systemic and ever cleverer manipulation of laws and rules by those able to pay lobbyists, legislators, lawyers and accountants to do their bidding. As income and wealth have risen to the top, so has the power to manipulate the system in order to acquire even more money and more influence."[348] When money speaks, legislators listen—it's human nature.

A third factor contributing to the power and leverage needed to force change in the *status quo* is grassroots movements like "The Tea Party" and "Occupy Wall Street." Both want to change the *status quo* by seeking to influence both public opinion and the legislative process. Bottom line, the political process is driven by the self-interest of those who have social or economic issues that are of significant importance to them, as well as the self-interest of the lawmakers who need campaign contributions to get re-elected. Power, leverage and advantage are for sale. Anyone with the means can turn to public relations consultants and political advisors for help with the spin, the rationalization and the justification they hope will make it seem that their views and votes are the right ones.

Using the political system to gain power, leverage and advantage has become an art. Under constitutional guidelines and the dynamics of election campaigns, the political process often becomes an exercise in futility. It used to be that with a relatively even balance of power you could have a spirited discussion about all facets of an issue, resulting in legislation that reflected the good ideas of all who participated in the discussion. Today it is extremely difficult to resolve the differences between competing interests in the process of writing legislation. With the election of so many whose positions are rigid and inflexible, the two major political parties are so polarized that the process has become paralyzed. Do we have to wait until one party controls both houses of Congress and the Executive Branch? That would be tragic. We will not get the benefit of the wisdom of all of the participants.

We will not see the passage of legislation that addresses the tough issues, unless the problem poses an immediate threat to all of us. "It is now conventional wisdom that the U.S. faces an acute fiscal calamity. America's problems are severe: a deficit that is more than 10% of GDP (Gross Domestic Product) and total debt that is more than 70% of GDP, but all evidence suggests that the U.S. does not face an immediate crisis. In fact the real problem for America may well be that it does not face a short-term crisis. . . . The great danger is that the American economy will outperform expectations and relieve politicians from having to make hard choices about entitlements and taxes. But it will only postpone the day of reckoning and make the crash more painful."[349] "One of the most difficult things to do in a democracy is react to a problem that is real, but not immediately threatening."[350]

It makes sense. Those who are making money and feel the current configuration of economic policy is working for them, also have the money, power, clout and influence to keep the playing field tilted in their favor. They certainly don't want any change that will result in having to give up any of their advantage. It takes a crisis to get people's attention and develop the momentum for change.

House Budget Committee Chairman Representative Paul Ryan (R – Wis.) touched on a number of the important related issues. "Ryan said government actions ought to combat inequality by making it easier for everyone to be successful rather than through policies he said would punish the wealthy. 'Justice is done when we level the playing field from the starting line and rewards are proportionate to merit and effort. . . .' He scoffed at the 'false morality that confuses fairness with redistribution' and presumes 'most differences in wealth and rewards are matters of luck or exploitation and few really deserve what they have.'"[351] Rep. Ryan is someone who has integrity and is well respected. Yet, his statement includes several thoughts that call for comment.

Trying not to misinterpret or read more into his statement than is there, there are several clarifying questions that need to be asked. Is it really possible to level the playing field "from the starting line?" It seems to me that there is no way we can go back to the starting line, even if we wanted to. We are a nation where there are vast differences in economic well being. The playing field is already tilted. Less government and less regulation have been factors in getting to our current situation. Those with wealth, power and influence already have the advantage. Those who currently have more financial resources are the ones who can hire the lawyers, accountants and lobbyists to advocate for them, to advocate for a playing field that is favorable to their interests. By being able to do so they can maintain their position of advantage.

If we want to have a playing field where "rewards are proportional to merit and effort," we all need to have the same chance to succeed. My sense is that enormous differences in the quality of education affect who is successful and who is not. This is a huge issue. To even begin to imagine going back to a level playing field "from the starting line" we have to have programs that will move people to economic and educational levels where market forces can take over and offer the opportunity to lift them further. Even with all of our nation's resources, wealth and potential, the philosophy of a free market, small government and minimum regulation is not effective in improving the lot of all Americans. Power, money, influence and advantage have short-circuited the system. It's human nature.

Also, we have to ask whether he is overstating the case when he says, "the 'false morality' that presumes 'most differences in wealth and rewards are matters of luck or exploitation and few really deserve what they have.'" The overwhelming majority of those who are doing well have worked very hard to get where they are. Yet, if he is overstating the case, then his comments are both misleading and inflammatory.

One has to ask, however, whether or not there was indeed fraud and exploitation by mortgage lenders and investment bankers, who lobbied for less regulation of the financial industry? Then there's the practice of giving members of your family the inside track when jobs open up at the plant where you work. There's nothing illegal about this practice. However, if the circle of your family, relatives and friends does not include folk who own businesses or have good jobs in good businesses, then you simply don't have the same opportunities that others do.

If he has overstated the case, and I realize that is an "if," then is he contributing to the emotionally charged atmosphere surrounding the discussion of issues by Congress, which makes it more difficult to deal with the very critical, substantive issues that his economic plan attempts to address? It just seems to me that talking about going back to the starting line is a stretch. When you start with a playing field that is already tilted, "less government" favors those with means over the poor. There is a danger that we could even tilt more toward an economy and political system that works far better for the rich than for the poor.

Next, we need to touch on the issue of how much government is needed to protect the poor, the disadvantaged and most vulnerable among us. How much government is needed to protect average, hard-working folk? How do you balance the needs of those who are financially well off, with the needs of average people? As a nation and a people, are we interested in the common good or only in our individual well being? What policies help to level the playing field, and which foster dependency and an entitlement mentality? President Clinton put it this way in a State of the Union address: "'the era of big government is over' with the caveat 'but we cannot go back to the time when our citizens were left to fend for themselves.'"[352]

We all have our personal views and convictions. Resolution of any differences in our system comes from a consensus determined by election results; this is the way our system works. We elect people who will support legislation that we favor. However, given the meteoric rise of candidate media exposure, campaign contributions and contributions to super-PACs, those with money definitely have the inside track.

"Members of Congress are people too; they're likely to embrace change only when it's easy, popular and rewarding."[353] Assuming less is both naïve and dangerous. Balance can only come from a counterforce of the middle-class, the disadvantaged and the vulnerable expressing their views on Election Day.

The Need for Regulation

The excessive risks taken by Wall Street nearly led to the collapse of our economy, and riveted the country's attention and focus. Given my understanding of human nature there is no question that regulation is needed. The only question is how much. Where is the right balance between free enterprise and regulation? There was enough concern in Congress to pass the Dodd-Frank Wall Street Reform and Consumer Protection Act. The serious problems that were addressed by the bill and the watered-down, final version of the bill, attest again to the self-interest of the principals. Some of the specifics were discussed in an earlier chapter.

Dodd-Frank addressed a number of issues. Here are two examples. First, it responded to the conflict of interest involving credit ratings agencies.

> Before buying corporate bonds, or the more exotic debt instruments, like those that fueled the subprime lending bubble, an investor might turn to a ... review— those of credit ratings agencies such as Standard and Poor's or Moody's. Their ratings measure how likely the issuer of these products is to default, and therefore whether they are safe investments.
>
> There is, however, one huge (issue). ... The debt rating is paid for by the issuer of the debt, creating an obvious conflict of interest.
>
> If you ever wondered why the agencies slapped AAA ratings on bundles of toxic mortgages, helping to create an epic credit crisis, the answer is simple: because they were paid good money to do so. Banks wanted to sell these products to generate huge fees and bonuses, and the last thing they wanted was a ratings agency to warn investors away.
>
> To help police this highly conflicted world and prevent the next meltdown, ... Congress (agreed to) make the ratings game

more transparent so that investors can make some independent judgments about their quality. . . .

This is an example of what happens when you have too little regulation. "Until . . . issuers of debt are not able to shop around for a ratings agency that will do their bidding, investors will not know whether a credit rating is fact or fiction."[354]

Second, Dodd-Frank also addressed "the kind of predatory lending practices at the heart of the subprime mortgage crisis."[355] An article titled "Mortgage Companies Agree to $25 Billion Settlement" says, ". . . the nation's five largest mortgage lenders have agreed to overhaul their industry after deceptive foreclosure practices drove homeowners out of their homes. . . . (The) agreement could reshape long-standing mortgage guidelines and make it easier for those at risk of foreclosure to restructure their loans. And roughly 1 million homeowners could see the size of their mortgage reduced."[356] A $25 billion settlement is not pocket-change, indicating there was significant wrongdoing. Regulation is needed. The regulation will be enforced by the Consumer Financial Protection Agency, which "is envisioned as a bulwark against . . . the 'tricks and traps' that banks hide in credit-card agreements and mortgages."[357]

Dodd-Frank will also help to rein in Wall Street with tough regulation on derivatives—those complex financial instruments known as CDOs and CDSs. They "were the deadweights that dragged down many a balance sheet. The aim is to make sure that most derivatives are traded on transparent, regulated exchanges."[358]

Business, money, and power usually argue for smaller government and unfettered free enterprise by keeping regulation to an absolute minimum. Given the abuses that have occurred over the years, the nature of man and the need for a stable economic system, it is clearly evident that some regulation is needed. Nobody wants to tie the hands of business leaders behind their back, and nobody wants them to pull a fast one behind ours. Balance is needed and has to be continually monitored, evaluated and updated. The Glass-Steagall Act was passed in 1933 to increase regulation by prohibiting consumer banks from getting into the investment banking business. It was repealed in 1999 under President Clinton, who in hind-sight regrets the decision which many believe contributed to the financial crisis of 2008.

When there is too little regulation, it is the average household that will bear the burden and pay the bill, which is what happened after both the Savings and Loan crisis (a bailout) and the near economic collapse of 2008 (a stimulus package). The big boys with the power, money and influence, adopt practices that get us into trouble and leave us holding the bag for their greed and recklessness. "(The Captains of Finance) represent an eternal truth that this country seems destined to learn eternally—a free market should never be allowed to become a recklessly freewheeling one. There's a difference. . . . A market free to innovate in search of more profit, yes. But not one with so little oversight and regulation that its practitioners feel free to snooker folks. . . . Our wish: a regulatory framework that makes sense for a 21st century global economy."[359] Bottom line—we need to be protected against the greed and self-interest that are lurking around every corner.

Negotiation and Compromise

When two groups have conflicting interests, and both believe their positions to be reasonable, just and fair, then you need a method for resolution. Differences need to be negotiated and resolved or there will be chaos. We have this tendency to look out for ourselves and our own at the expense of the unmet needs of others. The truth is that the plight of others is often of no real consequence to us. Once we have leverage and advantage, we do not want to concede such power. When involved in negotiations, we reluctantly give up as little as possible. For example, those who have the wealth, who also believe they have earned it and deserve it and who believe others have the same opportunity if they would just work for it, favor a tax policy (income, capital gains, and estate) that is favorable to the retention of as much of their wealth as possible.

If those who have less agree that the current system is just and fair and that they have the same opportunity as everyone else, all is well. If those who have less feel that the current state of affairs has been the result of a playing field that was tilted against them, if they feel they need some consideration in rectifying past unfairness, or some help to jump-start their efforts, you have got a conflict, a difference of opinion, an issue that needs to be resolved. Those who feel they need the help believe their cause is just. Those who would be asked to provide the funds for immediate assistance and to help jump-start the catch-up process have their reasons for feeling that what they are being asked to do is unfair and unjust, and will only serve to reinforce an entitlement mentality.

I am just so thankful that we live in a country where we have a Constitution that provides the mechanisms for working out such differences. In broad strokes, one group believes that there are growing inequities in the American system and that government has the responsibility to address such inequalities. Others feel that system is working just fine and doesn't need any adjustments. The question is whether the two parties can find some common ground.

While I am not without an opinion on this issue, my vote is just one of many that will decide the outcome. There are, however, several observations I believe need to be considered when participating in the resolution of contentious issues. While human nature is characterized by self-interest, there is also this thing called enlightened self-interest, where the key is to figure out where your self-interest overlaps with the self-interest of others. It is in the overlap that you find the common ground that becomes the basis for a compromise. Even when there is legislative gridlock, you reach a point where the proponents of each position begin to be affected. When both are hurt badly enough by their refusal to compromise, they may reach a point where self-interest begins to overlap and some degree of compromise is possible. When legislative gridlock no longer serves the interests of either group, we have to find a way to achieve resolution.

On the list of TIME's top 100 leaders for 2010 was former Arizona Senator Jon Kyl, someone known for trying to move the legislative process forward. He has "encyclopedic knowledge of domestic and foreign policy issues. ... His command of policy, his knowledge of its nuances ... is why so many of his colleagues look to him for advice. Kyl, 68, is a principled conservative who knows what is attainable."[360]

"Jon Kyl is a great persuader. As minority whip, the No. 2 position in the Senate Republican leadership, he is responsible for rallying his Republican colleagues for key legislative votes. What is unique is his single-minded focus on convincing them that a particular vote is in the best interests of their state and nation. Jon demonstrates continually that the essence of Senate power is the power to persuade."[361]

Another Republican leader who also seems genuinely committed to finding answers is Mike Huckabee. He said, "'I'm a conservative, but I'm not mad at everybody over it.'" "I'm (Leonard Pitts) writing this to say just one thing: I like Mike."

> That would be Michael Dale Huckabee, former Baptist preacher, former Governor of Arkansas, former GOP presidential candidate, current Fox News personality, the guy quoted above

being flagrantly reasonable during an interview on "The Daily Show."

. . . We have points of concurrence. But on any number of issues . . . the distance between us yawns like canyons. Indeed, Huckabee has said things I find downright appalling.

But here's the thing. Just when you've got him figured as another guy glued to his talking points, he will surprise you by showing evidence of actual thought. Like the John McCain of yore, he will deviate from what his ideological kin are all tonelessly repeating and follow conscience to some other conclusion.

In his debates with Stewart on "The Daily Show," Huckabee comes across as a guy you can reason with. Not necessarily a guy you will agree with, but one who will willingly join you in an honest search for common ground. That is a rarity.

Sometimes you wonder if anyone is still on the *country's* side. You couldn't prove it by most of what passes for leadership these days. Which is why we never seem to reach national consensus, never seem to find compromise, never do anything but boil with a free-floating, self-perpetuating anger.

But Huckabee seems to have the novel idea that it is more important to find answers than to win arguments, more important to speak conscience than parrot talking points. That's why, even when I disagree with him, I like Mike.

And why I wish other politicians would take note.[362]

Sadly, we negotiate and treat others in a fair, equitable manner only when forced to. GM didn't make needed changes until they went into bankruptcy and were forced to. It took the reality of the pressures of a global economy to get the United Auto Workers to make concessions in salaries and benefits so GM could again become competitive. We bargain and negotiate in an effort to reach a settlement that is in everyone's best interest. People need to feel that at least some of their interests are considered in the final compromise. Everybody saw the crisis in the auto industry coming. Yet the union wanted the best salary and benefits package for its membership. Management wanted to be competitive while making enough of a profit to stay in business.

I come from a union family. "What matters is the balance of power that unions provide. It is human nature for those who have more to resist giving it away, and it is just as natural for those who have less to demand a larger share.[363] Unions were organized in response to management overplaying its hand (self-interest). Once the unions had established a base of power and leverage, they overplayed their hand. Then management pushed back.

There was a time in our growth as a nation that our economy was just exploding, and there were simply many more job opportunities with a smaller population in a rapidly growing economy. It was much easier to be in the right place at the right time. The right place and the right time was everywhere. Not any more. Today many who start down the path to economic progress and *the good life* already have an advantage over those with less education, opportunity or good fortune. Your perception may be different. You work very hard and deserve everything you have. You have gained some degree of advantage, which you're not about to give up. You will not vote for candidates who will compromise the advantage you have gained; that's human nature.

We are now in the situation where we have the 1% and the 99%. There has been a shift in wealth from the middle class to the upper class, and now that the upper class has it, they don't want to give it up. They are able to rationalize, justify and explain their position. They have a certain spin they put on their views. They have their "take" on the issue. They have come to a place where with a clear conscience they can say they are right, and that what they believe and how they live are just and fair. Those with money, power and influence are not inclined to share it. While living in this tension and trying to resolve it, it is so very important to keep in mind that we all operate on the basis of self-interest. When we have money, power, leverage, we are going to try to keep it and maintain the advantage we have. We all have this tendency to look out not just for the needs of ourselves and our own, but also for their wants at the expense of the unmet needs of others.

The bigger reality is that if we were honest and if the shoe was on the other foot, any of the 99% who somehow were able to join the 1% would adopt the views of the 1%. They too would be inclined to use their financial resources to take care of not just the needs of themselves and their own, but also their wants at the expense of the unmet needs of others. And remember, the big picture is that our tendency to be self-centered and self-serving influences all areas of life, our views about taxes, about volunteering and about giving to church and charity.

The Bully Pulpit

The "bully pulpit" is aptly named as the platform where popes and presidents preach, plead and persuade. George H.W. Bush began his presidency with an inaugural speech that in many ways sounded as if he were using the podium as a "bully pulpit." His first "sermon" reflected a re-commitment to his quest to make the United States a kinder and gentler nation. (He) called on Americans to forsake materialism and work for the benefit of fellow citizens.

> America is never wholly herself unless she is engaged in high moral purpose. . . . We as a people have such a purpose today. It is to make kinder the face of the nation and gentler the face of the world.
>
> I am speaking of a new engagement in the lives of others – a new activism, hands-on and involved, that gets the job done.
>
> . . . Bush spent the heart of his inaugural address exhorting his fellow Americans to return to the nobility of work and sacrifice on behalf of others.
>
> "My friends, . . . we are not the sum of our possessions. They are not the measure of our lives. In our hearts we know what matters."
>
> Bush said he hoped as president to help the nation celebrate the quieter, deeper successes that were not made of gold and silk, but of better hearts and finer souls.
>
> "My friends, we have work to do. . . . There are the homeless, lost and roaming; there are children who have nothing, no love and no normalcy; there are those who cannot free themselves of enslavement to whatever addiction. . . ."
>
> Like his predecessor, however, Bush said that public money alone could not solve the nation's problems. He said there was deficit to bring down, and the nation had more will than wallet.[364]

He also lifted up his familiar "thousand points of light" theme, encouraging volunteerism. It was a great "sermon." George Bush brought to the presidency a dedication to traditional American values determined to make the U.S. "a kinder and gentler nation." My question is whether or not his "sermon" and other messages spoken from the "bully pulpit" of high office "get the job done." It is my sense that he and others who try the same approach, while sincere, are sadly misguided and naïve in terms of expecting meaningful change, which will only occur when pressure is brought to bear and there is no choice.

The same question needs to be asked about the "sermons" of the popes delivered over the years. While acknowledging upfront that advocating for the inclusion of Christian principles and values in public policy involves nuanced and complex judgments, I applaud and enthusiastically support their efforts to speak out about the issues of war and peace, suffering and poverty, economic injustice and social injustice. However, my sense is that they are not very effective and that the impact is minimal. Here are a few examples of papal use of the "bully pulpit."

In a July 6, 2000 papal encyclical "Caritas in Veritate," or "Charity in Truth," Pope Benedict said, "Financiers must rediscover the ethical foundation of their activity"[365] In that same encyclical Benedict "criticized the world's economic systems . . . and called for a new global structure based on social responsibility, concern for the dignity of the worker and a respect for ethics. . . . 'Without a doubt, one of the greatest risks for business is that they are almost exclusively answerable to their investors, (and) thereby limited in their social value.'"[366]

On October 24, 2011 the Vatican released a document it referred to as a "note":

> The Vatican called . . . for the overhaul of the world's financial systems and again proposed a supranational authority to oversee the global economy, calling it necessary to bring more democratic and ethical principles to a market-place run amok.
>
> The document grows out of the Roman Catholic Church's concerns about economic instability and the widening inequality of income and wealth around the world, issues that transcend the power of national governments to address on their own.
>
> . . . The document (is) . . . a reminder that the Catholic Church, without getting involved in policy-making, still seeks to shape its principles. "To function correctly the economy needs ethics: and not just any kind, but one that is people-centered (paraphrasing a 2009 encyclical). . . ."

In the United States, the report was embraced by politically liberal Catholics who are concerned about the widening gap between rich and poor.

Politically conservative Catholics, meanwhile, hastened to assure their camp that the document does not carry the full force of church teaching, since it was produced by a Vatican office, not by the Pope himself.

And some dismissed the report as nothing new or simply misinformed.[367]

There have also been other discussions and teachings from the "bully pulpit" of the Catholic Church which have addressed the U.S. economy and capitalism.

"The deprivation and powerlessness of the poor wounds the whole community. The extent of their suffering is a measure of how far we are from becoming a true community of persons."

. . . The new draft still makes poverty its paramount concern. . . . The time has come for "the creation of an order that guarantees the minimum conditions of human dignity in the economic sphere for every person."

(It) is aimed at stimulating America's 50 million Catholics to rethink their social and economic attitudes in light of Catholic moral teaching urging compassion for the weak and condemning selfishness.

. . . In a nation as wealthy as the United States, the fact that 33 million Americans are poor and another 20 million to 30 million could be classified as needy "is a social and moral scandal that must not be ignored. . . ."

Justice demands that society establish "a floor of material well-being on which all can stand. . . ." Such justice does not mean arithmetical equality of income, but demands a narrowing of great disparities in income that lead to social conflict…

(It also noted) an absence of political will to eliminate disparities.[368]

US bishops expressed their views in an article subtitled "Church leaders chastise Democrats, GOP for ignoring children, poor." Children and poor families "are the missing dimension of the debate on the budget, welfare and taxes. They have the greatest needs, but the weakest voice and littlest influence. Today we can become their voice."[369]

Here is some insight into the papacy's concern about capitalism. "In 1990 in Durango, Mexico—when NAFTA was but a gleam in the eye of corporate America—(Pope John Paul II) said of capitalism: 'We cannot be silent about the defects of an economic system which has money and consumption as its main power source, which subordinates the person to capital in a way which, without taking personal dignity into account, considers him or her to be only a gear in production's mammoth machine.'"[370]

When you are trying to raise awareness and effect change from the "Bully Pulpit" of the papacy or the presidency, you must be clear about your target audience. When you are speaking to Christians, praying and hoping that they will try to influence the political process, you have the power of the Holy Spirit at work as their motivation. When you're speaking to Democrats, Republicans, libertarians and independents, you simply have the power of moral persuasion. These are two vastly different motivators for change. It just doesn't seem to me that the "Bully Pulpit" is all that effective in addressing the issue of economic justice. I wish it were.

Pope John Paul II's 1991 statement (Centesimus Annus)

> . . . urged the world toward an enlightened capitalism that cared less about profits and consumer goods and more about its responsibilities to the poor.
>
> The Pope said capitalism was far preferable to either socialism or the welfare state.
>
> . . . He said the West must share its know-how and wealth with developing countries, allowing them a stake in the dazzling opulence just beyond their reach. In a clear signal to American society, he said cultures must move away from a lust for "having" and be far more concerned with moral concerns of "being."
>
> "The pope more clearly than ever recognized the limits of the marketplace in a way most right-wing Catholics are not willing

to acknowledge," (economist and social-justice advocate Sister Amata) Miller said. "If capitalism is limited in its ability to meet human needs, that strengthens the argument of those on the liberal side who argue that the state must have a stronger role."

In the 114-page document, the pope stressed that there were many basic needs, such as human dignity, education and a decent wage that the free market could not supply to all.[371]

In 2008 in his *Urbi et Orbi* message (to the city and to the world), he said, "If people look only to their own interests, our world will certainly fall apart."[372]

It just doesn't seem to me that the "Bully Pulpit" is all that effective in addressing the issue of economic justice. This is by no means to say that Church leaders shouldn't continue to speak up, pray and encourage Christians and all of our brothers and sisters in the human family to work toward making progress in addressing these important issues. Sadly, their efforts just don't cut it. Not much happens. While sermons from the "bully pulpit" are certainly important and needed, it is simplistic, naïve and unrealistic to think that the impact will be more than minimal. I would caution against undue optimism about their effectiveness in facilitating change. Remember that my premise for this chapter is that it is unrealistic to expect any change without the infusion of external leverage. In the real world money, clout, power, influence and leverage are the factors that facilitate change; these are the factors that get the job done.

My purpose in this chapter is not to take sides on specific issues. Rather, it is to point out the realities that define how we live our lives. We are all self-serving and self-centered and we make decisions based on self-interest. Those of us who have the leverage, power, advantage and influence will use it to our advantage, and to further our own self-interest. Whether we have more or less, we will leverage whatever power and influence we have to further our interests. If the shoe were on the other foot and power, wealth, advantage, influence were given to those who currently do not have it, my sense is that they would do exactly what those who currently have the power, money, leverage and influence are doing. In our country, we are free to make that choice.

This is our nature. This is what we're like. This is who we are. Then we find a way to rationalize and justify our views and our actions. The point is to become aware that this is the way we are and that this is how things work. Granted, this is how I see things. This is my world view.

This is my organizing principle. This is a part of my belief system. You may have a different worldview and different beliefs, and a different take on people and life. However, within the framework of what I believe, this is how I experience the world and people. We all have a worldview. It is reflected in the decisions we make.

My intent is to bring all of this into our conscious awareness. My hope is to surface all of this so that we can make conscious decisions about these issues, rather than remaining caught in the swiftly flowing current of our present worldview and beliefs. What we do with this awareness is up to each of us. Nevertheless, it is true for all of us that we have this tendency to look out not just for needs, but also for the wants of ourselves and our own at the expense of the unmet needs of others. Those of us who have leverage, power and influence will use them to further our own interests. We need to be more clearly aware of these tendencies, own them and then make conscious decisions about how we are going to live our lives in the future.

Chapter 14
Is There a Message for Me in All This?

*"Two roads diverged in a yellow wood,
And sorry I could not travel both
And be one traveler, long I stood
And looked down one as far as I could
To where it bent in the undergrowth;*

*Then took the other, as just as fair,
And having perhaps the better claim,
Because it was grassy and wanted wear;
Though as for that the passing there
Had worn them really about the same,*

*And both that morning equally lay
In leaves no step had trodden black.
Oh, I kept the first for another day!
Yet knowing how way leads on to way,
I doubted if I should ever come back.*

*I shall be telling this with a sigh
Somewhere ages and ages hence:
Two roads diverged in a wood, and I –
I took the one less traveled by,
And that has made all the difference."* Robert Frost

Matthew 25:35-40: "For I was hungry and you gave me something to eat, I was thirsty and you gave me something to drink, I was a stranger and you invited me in, I needed clothes and you clothed me, I was sick and you looked after me, I was in prison and you came to visit me." Then the righteous will answer him, 'Lord, when did we see you hungry and feed you, or thirsty and give you something to drink? When did we see you a stranger and invite you in, or needing clothes and clothe you? When did we see you sick or in prison and go to visit you?' The King will reply, "I tell you the truth, whatever you did for one of the least of these brothers of mine, you did for me" (Matthew 25:35-40).

So What's the Bottom Line?

While many hold that we Americans are "basically, good people," truth is that when it comes to the suffering and pain of others, we are just as indifferent as everyone else. Any description of us as good people or decent human beings is rhetoric that is so misleading. We are not any more caring and kind than others. Our hearts do not burn with compassion for the weak and vulnerable. The outward appearance of decency is little more than camouflage for our inner "survival of the fittest" instinct and "every man for himself" mentality.

So, what's the bottom line? What are you asking us to do? What moved me to take the time to write all this down, knowing that the time could have been used serving rather than writing? Remember, it was my hope that at least our boys, their wives and our grandchildren would know who this Grandpa is and what he believes in the very depths of his being. What makes him tick? What is he passionate about? Who does he live for? Does he have any fire in his belly? Is he the real deal or a phony? Perhaps these reflections may be helpful to them as they consider the meaning of life, and create their own future—their own sense of mission and purpose.

Our sons and their wives and a few relatives and friends have a pretty good idea of who I believe I am and what I believe is important. Yet, even for them there was a need to fill in some of the pieces that they had no way of knowing, so they could connect more of the dots. This book is a gift from a Dad and Grandpa who dearly loves his Lord Jesus to his children and grandchildren and to anyone else who might be interested. My fervent prayer is that they too will find that the meaning and purpose of life is found in loving service.

It was my hope that raising these issues would also serve as a springboard for reflection, prayer and conversation, a guide of sorts for some serious soul searching about how meaning and purpose are reflected in how we live each day. We all have to figure out how we are going to live out our lives in the tension between good and evil, right and wrong, black and white, indifference and compassion, selfishness and selflessness, accumulating and sharing.

Man is not kind, Americans are indifferent and we Christians are the worst of the lot. All of us have this tendency to look out not just for the needs, but also for the wants of ourselves and our own, at the expense of the unmet needs of others. That is the bottom line of my thesis. Accepting it can be a bitter pill to swallow. To hear it suggested that we may be delusional if we think otherwise is like getting punched in the gut. Asking us to volunteer that much is just not practical. Making all the money we can, providing for the needs of ourselves and our own and giving the rest away is lunacy.

Here are four translations of I Corinthians 13:5 which taken together provide a helpful summary of the meaning of love as it relates to my thesis. "(Love) is not self-seeking". "Love does not pursue selfish advantage" (The New Testament in Modern English). "Love is never selfish" (The New English Bible). The People's Bible Commentary puts in this way: "Love always seeks the welfare of others."[373]

Either you get it or you don't. Those who get it, those who understand, those who hear the call to live as self-sacrificing, self-living, selfless servants of others aren't offended and don't get upset. Those who get upset, ticked off, angry, irate or defensive are the ones who don't agree with the premise; they are still resisting and are not ready to submit and accept this calling.

Again, it is not my intent to criticize or judge, but rather to raise awareness so that we can be honest in facing the truth about ourselves. It is only when the truth about our nature is acknowledged as a presupposition that we can have good conversation and make good decisions. Are we going to make a conscious decision to continue go with the flow in the river of cultural tradition or consider making some changes? Living life without considering the reality that, basically, we are not good people, results in our living in an alternate reality. It was my intent to bring all this out in the open so that it becomes a part of our awareness. I hope we no longer repress, deny or distort the truth about ourselves, but rather see ourselves for whom and what we are. What we do with that awareness is another matter. My sense is that unless and until we see and accept ourselves for whom and what we are, we will not be fully alive.

Those who celebrate, enjoy and exercise freedom in a democratic country have to make choices between self-interest and the common good. If the poor were to become middle class or even wealthy, my hunch is that they would exercise only a bit more concern for the needs of those they left behind than the rest of us do. For the most part, they too would look out for themselves and their own at the expense of the unmet needs of others. You would think that having been poor once would make a big difference. My sense is that it doesn't.

The better parts of ourselves, our better angels, are those reflected in our being decent people, good neighbors and law abiding citizens who work hard for a living, take care of our own and share a little with others. The picture of us as concerned, kind and caring seems to me to be nothing more than blowing smoke. I have to call it like I see it and tell it like it is, and then take time to listen to what others have to say. I'm still on the journey and looking forward to the conversations this work may precipitate. What we are in the process of becoming is yet to be known.

Are we motivated by greed and self-interest? Part of the answer comes from taking a look at our thoughts about having it all or at least our fair share. Our perspective on the American Dream and the consumer mentality has to be a part of the big picture when asking ourselves how much we really care about the unmet needs of others. How we relate to "stuff," as well as our giving to church and charity will give us a clue as to our priorities. You can find another clue by asking whether you are willing to commit to a significant number of hours of volunteer service each week. Accurately perceiving reality and acknowledging the truth about ourselves is essential if we want to commit ourselves to serving others.

When you preach the sermons nobody likes to hear, the folks who are growing welcome the message and don't get offended. They "understand!" They "get it!" They know what you are trying to do. They understand what you're getting at. They welcome the reminders because they are constantly fighting the battle to stay focused and to resist the pull of our consumer culture. Those who are Christians know they have to ask for the help of Holy Spirit every day in order to have any chance of resisting the temptation to live the lifestyle to which our culture says we are entitled.

It is those who are struggling to let go of the attraction of a materialistic and pleasure-oriented culture who don't like these sermons. They are the ones who really get perturbed when anyone dares to suggest that they are not any where near as compassionate and charitable as they could be—because all along they have seen themselves as caring, kind, loving and generous. There is no question that my thesis hits a raw nerve. Hopefully what is shared here can be helpful in putting our own stuff in perspective. My intent is not to judge, blame or criticize anyone, but simply to surface an issue that will hopefully trigger powerful internal tensions and struggles for those who have always thought of themselves as "basically, good people," as people of good will who have always considered themselves to be compassionate, caring, charitable and generous. Sadly, even for most church-goers these are almost non-issues because most sermons are so generic and watered-down. Because my read is that preachers set the bar so low that there is enough wiggle room to allow their members to remain comfortable with their lifestyle, most don't even have to deal with the impact of a powerfully challenging sermon.

Most people think they are making an acceptable effort to live by the "Golden Rule: Do unto others as you would have them do unto you." Frankly, I'm surprised we even want to admit we know the "Golden Rule," because unless I am badly mistaken, we sure don't live by it. We either do not understand it *or* we do not really want to understand it. Yet, we have somehow convinced ourselves that we do. We believe that we have at least done a halfway decent job of living according to it.

Why don't we ask the parents of the children who put their children to bed hungry how well we're doing? Why don't we ask parents whose children have no medical care how well we're doing? Why don't we ask the parents of children who have no chance to get an education how well we're doing? Why don't we ask the parents who are watching their children starve to death how well we're doing? Why don't we ask the parents who are watching their children die from disease caused by unsanitary living conditions that could be eliminated, how well we're doing? Why don't we ask the parents watching their children die from diseases for which we have the cure, how well we're doing? When push comes to shove, the only thing that counts is, "What's in it for me?" Will it help me be able to claim my fair share of the American Dream? All the while, we somehow maintain the belief that we are kind, caring, generous folk who live by the "Golden Rule."

We will Always be Motivated by Greed and Self-Interest

Is all of this cause for despair? Is anything ever going to change? Will we always be characterized by greed, self-centeredness and self-interest?

On January 23, 1996 in the State of the Union speech President Clinton spoke of a basic sense of decency and community. In his response to the President, Senator Bob Dole said he believed in the charity and goodness of the American people. Sadly I have to respectfully disagree with both. My sense of it all is that the negative traits noted in this book have been and will continue to be the defining characteristics of human nature. At times there will appear to be some forward movement. We will make some progress in fits and spurts. However, the nature of man is so primitive that we are a pushover for the influence of the culture. Most of the progress that is made is undermined, sabotaged and eroded by the relentless forces of self-interest swirling around us. The threshold at which our basic instincts are triggered is quite low. It happens when I feel I'm being unfairly asked to sacrifice my standard of living for your well being. The issues converge when considering tax policy and entitlement programs.

As communities we pull together and help each other in times of natural disasters like floods, tornados, hurricanes and earthquakes. As friends and neighbors we pull together and help each other in times of personal loss and tragedy, like when miners are trapped underground or a little girl has fallen into a well. While being there for each other at times like these is such a blessing, it is helpful to keep in mind that these usually involve short term commitments. The existential danger is that they reinforce and contribute to the illusion that our nature is that of being kind, caring, compassionate people. We have a need to believe that we are decent folk—good people, good neighbors.

Honesty should compel us to understand that these are only fleeting glimpses into all we can be. Once in a while we see a little peak into what it could be like if we lived lives of sacrifice and compassion. They are not, however, pervasive evidence of man's humanity to man. In the grand scheme of things they involve minimal sacrifice and little inconvenience. Rarely do they demonstrate the type of long term concern for the needs of others that involves inconvenience or a disruption of plans and dreams. Rarely do they lead to long term commitments of time or require significant economic sacrifice. Then just this morning I heard that we have 9,000 Peace Corps workers on assignment, and many more volunteers waiting in the wings.

We all admit that we are not perfect and continually need to be looking for ways we can do better. Some of these discussions need to take place in the political arena. We have the best form of government going, one that has put in place a social safety net. Yet, we need to have ongoing discussions about how much of a safety net is needed.

Unfortunately, our self-centered, self-serving nature *does* influence the process of making decisions about the laws that govern us, and about how much our capitalistic economy should be regulated. We have a good economic system, but due to the nature of man, those with power, money and influence find a way to rationalize and justify keeping what they have and positioning themselves to accumulate more. Then they use what they have accumulated to take care of their own, often at the expense of the unmet needs of others. The egregious, damaging outcomes we have witnessed would suggest the need for some control and regulation. It is essential that we are having that discussion now while the causes of the near economic meltdown of 2008 are still fresh in our mind.

When passing legislation and establishing regulations that govern politics and the economy, we have to realistically consider the nature of man. If left uncontrolled, the results in countless households can be devastating. There are vultures out there that prey on the weak and the vulnerable. As a consequence of the recent economic crisis, too many have lost their jobs and homes, and had their savings depleted, while the vultures had a feast.

One could take the position that we can use both money and power as a means to a loving goal. A political career may be motivated by wanting to help work toward the betterment of the human race. The wealthy may use their considerable resources to create jobs and meet human need. However, my sense is that with rare exceptions the bottom line is that we are always seeking our own interests.

If any of us were in the banker's shoes, I'm not sure things would have been any different. I would like to believe that we would have acted with a higher standard of ethics and values. But I can't. We aren't any more concerned about who gets hurt by the fallout from our decisions than they were. It's the nature of the beast. I would like to believe that if any of us held elective office, we would maintain the highest standards of ethics, morals and values, but I can't. I would like to believe that if a quality education were available to all, and the poor realized significant improvement in their standard of living, that they would remember what it was like for them and would be extraordinarily compassionate toward those who are still poor and need a hand extended to them—but I can't.

If we could live a self-giving, self-sacrificing, selfless life of loving service, it would be cause for jubilation. I would hope that all of us in the human family would adopt this lifestyle. But from what I've observed of the world, it just doesn't happen. Thankfully our "basic" goodness has moved beyond the primitive. We are civilized, but not a whole lot more. The sense of "decency" cited by President Clinton in his inaugural address is, at most, minimal. For Christians, however, following in the footsteps of Christ-like loving service is not an option. This is who we say are and what we are supposed to be about. We are not free to take it or leave it, and still think we are "walking with the Lord." The God who has done it all for us in Christ, calls us to respond to his love by living a life of total surrender.

One certainly can not say that God has brought about the current reset of the American Dream in order to bring us to our senses about what is really important. But losing half the value of your 401(k) or retirement savings in the last economic downturn, losing your job, having to accept a new job at 65 percent of your previous salary and being unable to find anywhere to invest the funds you have left at more than a low rate because you can't afford to risk losing any more makes you angry and leaves you confused and bewildered. It also provides an opportunity to redefine the meaning of the American Dream in a way that is far more meaningful and satisfying. What one can say is that the current environment does afford the opportunity to do some soul searching as to what you think life is all about. What is really important? Maybe we've forgotten and this is a chance to sort it all out.

What do I hope will happen? What do I expect to happen? Sadly for me the gap between hope and expectation is huge. Everyone has issues, burdens, problems and challenges. As previously noted, we all need time to come to terms with them, and to heal enough to start the process of dealing with them. However, my sense is that in the larger scheme of things, the perception of being overwhelmed is often far more self-imposed and overstated than real, and serves to provide justification for the "choice" not to respond more positively when it comes to volunteering and giving sacrificially to church and charity. For a Christian who thinks he is living a good enough life to get to heaven but has never heard the full teaching about discipleship before, he may realize that he has a lot to pray about and even more to repent of when the Holy Spirit begins to work in him. For most the response will be minimal at best. Most don't see the world realistically. Truth is that in America almost all of us are wealthy, richly blessed people who have the means and opportunity to live self-giving, selfless lives of sacrifice and loving service. I wish I were more hopeful. In our consumer-driven economy where it is so easy to get distracted, it just doesn't seem like there will ever be much of a change. The situation won't ever be much different.

As to our being "good people," we have to remember that "good" is a relative term. By what standard are you measuring "good"? Do *we* choose the standard? Do we use the generally agreed upon societal norm for good? It seems to me that we have a greatly inflated sense of our own goodness. While we may be civilized, decent, hard working and law abiding, that is a long way from being compassionate, kind and caring. We may be charitable enough to be able to salve our own consciences and rationalize that we meet societal norms for being charitable and to be able to see ourselves as good people.

We may even be numbered among those who would help someone in need by giving them the proverbial shirt off our back. But what about the millions of others who need a shirt? What about the millions of others who are starving to death? What about the millions of others dying because they have no medical care? What about the millions of parents who are watching their children die? It is one thing to give someone the shirt off your back and quite another to be sacrificially compassionate.

It becomes compassion when it consumes your life. It becomes compassion when it consumes the part of your day that comes after you've worked hard to support your family. It becomes compassion when it consumes the part of your day that comes after you have fulfilled your commitments as a spouse, parent, child, relative and friend. It becomes compassion when it consumes that part of the day that comes after you have exercised and taken time to be renewed, re-energized, and recreated by doing whatever it is that you enjoy, or that allows your brain to switch gears.

You need time for rebuilding cars and showing cars, knitting or sewing, hunting or fishing, hiking or climbing, biking or camping, ceramics or wood carving, TV or the movies. The key issue relative to use of time is balance. Is leisure activity what you live for? Spending a total of 35 to 40 hours a week watching TV, reading, sewing, knitting working in the garden or playing cards or golf, but only 2 to 5 hours a week as a volunteer servant doesn't cut it in terms of coming anywhere near being a caring and compassionate person. Perhaps you've never thought about it this way. If so, this may provide an opportunity to do some soul-searching about what it's like to live a life full of meaning and purpose. Perhaps you feel like saying it's none of your business, so quit sticking your nose in where it doesn't belong. And if you're trying to make me feel guilty, it won't work. We are again at the core of the delusion that "basically, we're good people."

The same dynamic applies to retirement, only in spades.

The older generation has contributed so much to America, so I wouldn't begrudge retirees anything. But I shake my head at the way so many 60-and-70 somethings have chosen to live out their remaining years. . . . People who could be offering so much to their kids and the country have opted instead for a mad pursuit of golf courses, early-bird dinner specials, flea markets and elder hostels.

"We've earned it," was the retort from one retiree I know after he and his wife returned from a four-month hiatus at a condo along a Southern coast. They worked hard their entire lives and were ready to take it easy. But how satisfying can it be when the biggest decision of the day is whether to order a large frozen yogurt or a small one?

The transformation of intelligent, productive adults into aimless "elder-lescents" is most pronounced in sunny retirement meccas. . . . It is nice to see older people out and about on a February day rather than huddled indoors watching TV, as they would be up north (like in Wisconsin).

Yet there is something disquieting about the place. Most everyone there was busy—busy hunting bargains at Poultry King, busy standing in line to get the $1.99 breakfast special at the deli, or busy strolling around the mall for exercise.[374]

With their skills and wisdom seniors have tremendous potential as volunteer servants. And those who live in colder climates can find opportunities in the churches they attend and communities where they live when they head to a warmer climate for the winter. Those who want to be active, volunteer servants have no difficulty finding meaningful opportunities to do so.

It is tough to be honest with ourselves and see ourselves for who and what we are—folks looking out not just for the needs of our own, but also for our wants at the expense of the unmet needs of others. Our tendency is to repress, distort and deny what we're really like, rather than acknowledge that in our core we are self-centered, self-seeking and self serving. This is who we are. We simply don't want to acknowledge the truth. We rationalize and justify in order to insulate and protect ourselves from the truth—truth that is often too painful to bear.

You're a Possibility

I would suggest that America's uniqueness offers us yet again a vast frontier and awesome opportunity, but of a different kind. We are positioned to lead the way to a world where all people have the opportunity to realize their dream, as we already have. Ours is truly a wonderful country. There is no better form of government than that which is set forth in our Constitution, and there is no other place where I would want to live. Still, our best and brightest days could be out there before us. We could be a beacon of freedom, hope and opportunity for all of the world's peoples yet again. As a people, we have to decide what we want that future to look like.

At the same time my gut is screaming at me to be honest. While I would like to say we will do better, I can't and we won't. It is and always has been the survival of the fittest. We will continue to give lip service to national benevolence, while dealing with the reality of a dog-eat-dog world. That's the way we do things as individuals and as a nation. I just can't block out the memory of the yellow and black signs that marked our school building as a bomb shelter.

It seems to me that this is how the world works. It always has, and it always will. Everybody does their little dance to try to work out the best deal for themselves. We all operate out of a self interest that is self-centered, self-serving, self-seeking. "What a depressing message. You won't catch me going to his church. The sermons stink. You go home feeling worse than when you came."

But just maybe there is enough sanity and common sense to recognize that to leave the world a better place for our children, we as a global community have to find a way to continue to muddle along as we work through our competing interests. We have made it so far, but at a cost of incalculable human suffering and hardship. I don't expect that much to change among the community of nations. I want so very much to believe it can be different, but I just can't. As for our better angels, they simply aren't all that good.

Rich and poor alike all operate on the basis of greed and self-interest. Those who favor less regulation and those who favor more both operate on the basis of self-interest. Everybody operates on the basis of self-interest. What both frightens and saddens me is how someone operating on the basis of self-interest, one who has more power, influence, competitive advantage and money will impact the lives of those who have less, are financially vulnerable and can be taken advantage of. Ethically and morally, we are all in the same boat. To be sure, these ethical concerns do not only apply to capitalism. They are operative in all political and economic systems. Any system operates in a way that is reflective of those who have the power to control that system and who will manipulate that system to their advantage.

Just talk to Mother Teresa and the Sisters of Mercy and they will tell you what life is about, namely, that when your basic needs are met, meaning in life is found in helping see to it that others also have food, shelter and medical care. And if you would ask, my hunch is that they would make no claim of goodness, let alone sainthood.

What would it be like to get near the end of your life and only then realize that you had wasted it? Tolstoy asks, "What if in reality all my life, my conscious life, has not been the right thing?"[375] We either have to find a way to escape reality, or boldly and courageously ask ourselves the hard questions.

"Mother Teresa had great sympathy for those who felt rejected and unwanted: the forgotten parents left in an old people's home, the lonely youth whose family did not care. . . ."[376] You know, there are many people all around us who need to be cared for. "Having taken Christ's words 'Love one another as I have loved you,' and made them a reality in her life, she invites us to travel along the same path...reached by simple means. Starting by loving the unloved, the unwanted, the lonely closest to us in our homes, communities and neighborhoods, we can follow her example of loving until it hurts, of doing always a little more than we feel ready to do."[377]

Would I hope to see positive changes? Yes!! Do I believe the situation can improve? In some isolated instances, yes. A modest improvement in our culture and around the world is possible. Do I expect to see major changes in human behavior? No! I want so very much for people to change. I just don't see it happening. I wish I could be a whole lot more hopeful.

As I shared before, if the shoe were on the other foot and power, wealth, advantage, influence and leverage were in the hands of those who currently do not have it, my sense is that they would live the same way as those who currently have it. This is precisely why ours is such a great country: we are free to choose. All of the blood that has been shed and all of the lives that have been lost remind us just how precious our freedom is. I am willing to fight to safeguard that freedom, and the right of every American to express and advocate for their views and convictions. Once people are lifted up economically, they may in their freedom choose to be just as self-centered and self-serving as everybody else. That is their choice.

"Big Time" Reasons to Make "Big Time" Changes

It would be my hope that Christians would be different. The motivation generated by the promises of forgiveness and eternal life in Christ has the potential to be life changing. The never-failing love of a God who always forgives can be transformational. When we are exposed for what we are—self-centered, self-serving and greedy—and yet are assured he continues to love and forgive and gently invites us to grow, it would seem that we would be overwhelmed with love and gratitude, and moved to live self-giving, self-sacrificing, self-less lives of love and service.

When our lifestyle as Christians comes no where near what could be considered transformational, questions and doubts arise about the credibility, validity and reliability of our beliefs—and understandably so. It gets worse when others get a sense of the arrogance and conceit that comes from the disconnect between our self-righteous assertions of morality and the lack of any noticeable difference between the level of our compassion and the norm. We shoot ourselves in the foot. They look at how we live and they don't want anything to do with Christianity. As noted earlier, all too often we are the sermons that others don't like.

If preachers are bringing it to our attention, we Christians daily deal with Jesus' call to submission, surrender and compassionate service, and the tremendous tension it generates in our lives. The pull to adopt the lifestyle accepted as the cultural norm is just as powerful for us as it is for anyone else. We miss the mark all the time. Nevertheless, we plead for forgiveness, and in being forgiven find the power to persevere. Dietrich Bonhoeffer writes about the call from God to walk with the Lord and our struggles in doing so. "Only the man who follows the command of Jesus single-mindedly, and unresistingly lets his yoke rest upon him, finds his burden easy, and under its gentle pressure receives the power to persevere in the right way. The command of Jesus is hard, unutterably hard, for those who try to resist it. But for those who would willingly submit, the yoke is easy and the burden is light. . . . The commandment of Jesus is not a sort of spiritual shock treatment. Jesus asks nothing of us without giving us the strength to perform it."[378] We are called to a life that reflects obedience to the will of Christ. However, we try to find a way to combine our affection for worldly goods with loyalty to Christ.

The teachings of the Bible set the bar as high as it will go when establishing a guide for living. Some would say that if you set the standard too high, people will get discouraged. It is a daily battle for us. It is only with the help, inspiration and motivation of the Holy Spirit that we try as hard as we can to imitate the self-giving, self-sacrificing, selfless love of Christ as a response to what he has already done for us. Christ was sacrificed for us on the cross so that we have the extraordinary gifts of forgiveness and eternal life. With His help we then keep trying as hard as we can to live up to the very high standard God sets for us. But, remember, we don't try to live a good life in an attempt to earn forgiveness and eternal life. It is because we have already been given the gift of heaven that we try to live the best life we can.

Too many of us are in denial. We tinker and dabble in religion. We Christians don't embrace it with its challenging and life changing implications: a call to discipleship, a mandate for love and caring and service. We resist humble submission to a Lord who gave his all for us, brought us into a close personal relationship with him and calls us to walk with him and follow in his steps. Guided and moved by the Holy Spirit, a vision for the future has become crystal clear. As for me personally, I'm ecstatic about the future. I can't wait to walk down that road more faithfully in a life of humble service in the Name of Jesus.

What Those Who Matter Most to Us Think of Us

At the beginning of this chapter I shared that these reflections are intended to help all those who mean the most to me to know who I am, what is most important to me, what lights my fire and what turns me on. Only then can they hold me accountable. Once they know what makes me tick, they will know whether I'm blowing smoke, whether this preacher practices what he preaches. We all need to look at ourselves in the mirror. And I wonder what those who matter most to me really think of me.

My joy is simply to have been able to write and reemphasize what the Bible says, what many other faithful Christians have taught me and how they lived their lives down through the centuries. The anticipation of the future for me is to find great joy in walking the walk every day, and in some small way leading others to know that they are indeed important to God and loved by him.

My wife and family have always been my first priority in ministry, but there is no question that they were shortchanged. Now I'm trying to make up for too much time spent in ministry. I've come to understand that the hours I spent away from home reflected my own insecurities and inadequacies, not just a desire to serve the Lord. The healing is taking time, but I'm coming to peace about it. Currently I am serving as a volunteer in our congregation, assisting our pastors by making shut-in calls and hospital calls and coordinating our Stephen Ministry. We presently have 22 members receiving one hour of Christ-care a week as an extension of the senior pastor's office.

When this book is finished I plan to add significantly to my volunteer hours—continuing to serve at St. John's and finding a few more places to serve— possibly among the ragamuffins, at a veteran's home or in the city of Milwaukee. There are children to be tutored and youth to be mentored. There are all of the lonely, forgotten and those who are hard to get along with who need a friend. Some of the mentally ill seek companionship. Whenever and wherever possible, I want to be there for the lost, the last, the least and the lonely.

From a Grandpa Who Shares His Heart

My hope and prayer was to shine a little light into what I have come to believe is the vast darkness of human nature, and to suggest that we haven't hardly begun to uncover the treasures that are hidden. It's like we are at the place in the movie "National Treasure: Book of Secrets" where Harrison Ford used a torch to light the dark cavern full of treasure. Light can still reveal the treasure that is our lives. The need to discover this treasure is as great as ever. Yet, the treasure almost always remains hidden and undiscovered in the darkness. We haven't made much progress on the journey to be more caring toward all in the human family. The forces of darkness in our nature are formidable to say the least.

I want so very much for it to be different for me. I want so very much for it to be different for all of us. I pray for a life that leads to joy and gladness, peace and contentment. It is my intent to try to bring more light into the darkness of the sphere of life in which I live. Even having been on a journey through life in the Christian community, I missed too much of it. I missed it "big time." Oh, there were fits and starts, but the thrust that comes with putting the pedal to the metal in one of those old "muscle cars" just wasn't there. I got it, but only in part. I understood, but only in part. The Holy Spirit has helped me gain a whole new awareness of and thankfulness for just how much I have been forgiven through the suffering, dying and rising again of Jesus Christ. I am overwhelmed with joy and gratitude that God continued to love and forgive me even while my commitment was limited, tentative and lukewarm. I want so very much to have the Spirit's help to enlighten me and empower me so I can walk in his steps more faithfully to the end that more light shines in the darkness.

Karl Menninger wrote the book, *"Whatever Happened To Sin?"* The point being made is that now we find other ways to repress, deny and rationalize behavior that used to be called sin, and now describe that behavior in ways that relieve us from any culpability. The point that I want to make is that you have to call something for what it is. And what it is in terms of caring, loving, volunteer service and charitable giving isn't much when compared to what it could be.

Some of you might think that this book sounds like one of those hell, fire and brimstone sermons. Brothers and sisters, if you think that's what this is, then I want to invite you to come to services. You don't have any idea what hell, fire and brimstone sounds like. If you really want to hear some, here's a taste. "All of you think that, 'Basically, we're good people.' What a crock! What arrogance! What self-deception! What have you been smoking? You are all greedy, selfish, egotistical vultures who could care less about the burdened and suffering. You don't seem to care whether they live or die. While you see yourselves as pious and devout, you are really self-righteous hypocrites, not the least bit concerned about seeking out and caring for the lonely, the abandoned, the weak and the vulnerable. You are cold and unfeeling, spending your time and energy talking about the declining morals and values in our country and how our country is going down the tubes, rather than reaching out to and taking time for the rejected, the unwanted and the forgotten."

"And as for those of you in finance and banking, you are predators who don't care how many lives you destroy, as long as you get your year end bonus. You make Ebenezer Scrooge look like a choir boy. Your concern about your image, your need for power and influence, your need to enhance your reputation as a success is nothing more than a desperate attempt to fill the emptiness in your soul. Rather than reaching out to those in great need out, you use some poor suckers mortgage as a chip to play at the 'Big Bank Casino.'" One could certainly add politicians, and the raising of campaign contributions needed for the next election. But that's enough hell, fire and damnation—probably too much. I hope and pray that I didn't come off that way anywhere else in this book.

Mom was a housewife and mother who did not work outside the home—Dad wouldn't hear of it. She was born in 1913. During the Great Depression she was fortunate enough to get a job to help support a family of nine: she had four brothers and two sisters. Several of them also worked and helped support the family. Her job was in the gut shanty of the packing house at Wilson and Co. in the Chicago Stock Yards. She never wanted much, and ended up having more that she ever dreamed. She would have been content with much less.

Mom had a saying, "If the shoe fits, wear it." When I express my belief that we have this tendency to look out not just for the needs of ourselves and our own, but also for their wants at the expense of the unmet needs of others, am I talking about you? Well, it's kind of like what my mother used to say: "If the shoe fits, wear it."

Dad went to heaven in 1971. Mom lived 29 more years. Her wants remained modest. Since she had what she needed and didn't want much beyond the few things she could buy for herself, getting her birthday and Christmas gifts was always a challenge. If you could come up with an idea for a present she would enjoy, you were as excited as she was. She did enjoy going out, to a stage show, a play, or for dinner, especially for the family style chicken at White Fence Farm. One evening Karen and I took her to the theatre to see Jessica Tandy play the lead in "Driving Miss Daisy."

Afterwards we stopped just down the block at the Ritz Carlton for cheesecake and coffee. While waiting for our deserts she asked me, "Was there supposed to be a message there for me?" Even though we were beginning to pay attention to her driving, the question caught me off-guard, as that wasn't my intention at all. At first I felt bad, concerned that she had not been able to fully enjoy the simply delightful performance because it triggered second thoughts about her own driving. After gathering myself and a quick prayer, I remembered something I once heard from a friend, and shared it with her. "Mom, if there's a message there for you, then I guess there is. And if there's not a message there for you, then I guess there isn't." It was then I saw the look she gave me on those occasions when I said something that wasn't easy to say nor easy to hear, but that needed to be said. That was the end of it. The cheesecake was served and we enjoyed more coffee.

You have to decide whether there is a message for you in all of this. You have to ask whether you are looking out not just for the needs of your own, but also for their wants at the expense of the unmet needs of others. You have to decide whether your behavior further reinforces the view of the nature of man that tells us it's "every man for himself." You have to decide for yourself whether your organizing principle is the "survival of the fittest." You have to decide for yourself whether the cultural pursuit of the American Dream is for you. We are not compelled to pursue it. We make a conscious choice to pursue it. Christians are called to be different. We are called to a self-giving, self-sacrificing, selfless life of loving service in response to all that God has done for us in Christ.

My wife is very much like my Mom in that she is asks for so little. Substitute working in the kitchen and feeding patients in the polio ward at Wausau Hospital for the gut shanty. She does on occasion "plant seeds," and did mention that she would really enjoy going to the Pops series at the Milwaukee Symphony Orchestra. We sat in the third balcony for a while, and then decided to switch our tickets to the main floor. We were given "prime rib" seats in the center of the eleventh row. She is thrilled. We started attending before my retirement. At that time Doc Severinsen was our Principal Pops Conductor. There were Friday evenings when I was so totally exhausted and on more than one occasion fell asleep even as pure and vibrant tones streamed from his trumpet not seventy five feet away. This should be of some consolation to our pastors if they see that I have joined the "fellowship of the snoozers;" perhaps they will cut me some slack.

Life isn't fair. Being fortunate enough to be born in this country is a definite plus, a wonderful blessing and a significant advantage over being born in other countries, especially those where the masses are poor and uneducated. Here education, initiative and hard work open all kinds of doors. However, historically, even here the most poorly educated in the poorest states, cities and neighborhoods are still trying to play catch-up. Even within our country some are lucky enough to be born into families positioned to be more helpful on the journey to economic independence.

Yet, even some among those who have become successful have questions and have done some soul-searching. ". . . Richard Meyer, a thoughtful orthodontist from Little Rock, Ark., raised one possibility over dinner with his fellow dentists: 'Do we really need all this stuff we've accumulated? I can be a happy camper in a house half the size of the one I've got. I don't have to drive here in a BMW. Maybe we don't need to concentrate on consumer goods to be happy.'"[379]

Being about a constant process of soul-searching is an essential part of the journey through life for all of us.

"Gerry Felsecker, 65, has spent much of his life serving the poor in Milwaukee. A third-generation volunteer with the St.

Vincent de Paul Society, he is retiring as executive director after 40 years with the Catholic non-profit organization. Felsecker reflected on his tenure with the society. . . ."

Q. You talk about the importance of self-reflection by St. Vincent de Paul volunteers and their work in the context of a personal journey. Tell us about your own self-reflection and journey.

A. It's had its ups and downs. I was a child of the '60s. I marched with Martin Luther King. It was a period of great optimism. Then eventually everybody settled. I might have a great job. But you find it often questionable whether you're accomplishing much. You question constantly: is this just a job or is it really part of a journey that's going someplace? Maybe that's age and maturity or an understanding that one person is not going to significantly change the world. But I'm convinced the path I took is a good one and that it led to my own growth.

Q. There is a spiritual component to this work. How does that come into play in what volunteers do?

A. Spirituality doesn't mean kneeling down and saying the Our Father. It's really about understanding the message that God has for us and striving to understand the spiritual journey of other people. . . . I was in charge of a national committee that established a training program that . . . offers us excellent tools to help us reflect on . . . the attitudes we should embody toward the poor."[380]

While Felsecker didn't think "that one person is going to significantly change the world," he continued on down the path. Timothy Riordan expands on Felsecker's point. "I don't think we'll ever get to the point where everyone is wise, humane and just. But, he said, I don't think there will ever be an end to the good fight for equality and social issues."[381] What about our spiritual journey? Will we live a life of leisure, travel and the pursuit of hobbies and interests, or will we join the Gerry Felseckers of the world, bringing light into the darkness by living a life of humble, loving service to those in need?

A part of the challenge and dilemma in presenting my thesis while engaging the reader is what has become known as the Carter problem. Carter's "insistence on realism comes across as pessimism. This is our national character flaw, and it is what did in Carter: Ask us for sacrifice, and we'll show you the door."[382] Politicians can't say what I'm saying even if they believed it. Most preachers wimp out. Since I'm not actively serving, I can call it like I see it, because I don't have to worry about members who may want to get rid of me. I want to believe that's not true. I want to be more hopeful. I want to be positive. I want so very much to believe it is different than I see it and that I'm wrong. But I just can't. There may, indeed, be thousands of points of light out there; it is just that the darkness is so vast as to make all those points of light insignificant. Yet, we press on to achieve dominion over darkness by a life of humble, loving service.

From my early years I have looked up to The Rev. Billy Graham as a man of integrity. He is the most respected leader among protestant Christians. I wondered what he thought about all of this. "Graham said that one of his greatest concerns today was rampant greed. 'We have to overcome it,' he said. 'Greed causes a great deal of harm. . . . Over the years materialism became dominant—almost a God—in North America and Europe. Our hearts aren't satisfied by materialism,' he added. 'They can't be. That's why you see someone who has made millions driven on to make more millions. People confuse amassing money with security. But it is not so. What a pity to confuse real security with making money.'"[383]

While Dr. Graham expressed hopefulness about the future, he had no illusions about being able to solve all of our problems. While I see the world as being darker than he did, and while I'm less hopeful about the future, it doesn't mean that I don't still find amazing joy in life. I want to share with my grandchildren and all future generations that the joy and celebration that can be experienced each day is something they can look forward to with great expectation. Living the life of discipleship as a humble, loving servant will bring joy beyond measure. Others may live lives defined by greed. Others may look out not just for the needs of their own, but also for their wants at the expense of the unmet needs others. I want future generations of my descendants to know that the way most people relate to others in need in our country and all over the world may not change, but you can. You can be different. Just because others think it is a perfectly acceptable way to live, doesn't mean you have to. Just because that's the way most people are, doesn't mean you have to be that way too. A life of service to "the least of these" is the road less traveled.

> "Two roads diverged in a wood, and I—
> I took the one less traveled by,
> And that has made all the difference."

Is There a Message for Me in All This?

Frost's poem, "The Road Not Taken," reminds us all that there are different paths we can follow.

What about those who reject my thesis and choose another path? It is certainly not my place to be judgmental, blaming or be critical. It is not my place to get mad at them or be upset with them. I just hurt so much for those living in pain and misery, and who can't find relief from their suffering. The starving could be fed, but the distribution system has broken down. I am just so sad that so many could be helped, but aren't. This is what eats at my soul! What about the preachers who set the bar far below the Biblical standard of discipleship? It is certainly not my place to be judgmental, blaming or be critical. It is not my place to get mad at them or be upset with them. Maybe I need to cut them some slack. What hurts are the missed opportunities to share and be a reflection of God's love. People in need could be served, but aren't. Suffering could be alleviated, but isn't. The heartbroken could find peace, but don't. The forgotten could be visited and the abandoned could be found. Because of our inaction, there are millions out there who are falling by the wayside. This is what tears me up inside! "The worst sin towards our fellow creatures is not to hate them, but to be indifferent to them; that is the essence of inhumanity." If only we were more committed servants—more like the Good Samaritan—there would be so much less pain and suffering and misery in the world.

I look forward to living the rest of my life as Jesus' disciple. I've been trying to follow that path for years and have not been disappointed. We don't know what lies ahead. We can't see beyond where the road ahead bends into the undergrowth. We can't change the world. But we can be a reflection of God's love as we reach out and touch "the least of these" every day. Traveling that road will make all the difference in the world to those we serve, and to us, as we find joy, blessing and peace beyond measure.

These words are from a grandpa who is sharing his heart. He dearly loves his grandchildren, and wants more than anything for them and future generations to find the fullness of joy, celebration, meaning and purpose that is ours when we commit ourselves to a life of loving service to the Lord Jesus. At least I let them know who I am, what I am about, what makes me tick and what lights my fire. We hold our children close, love them and teach them when they are young, and prepare for a time when we will let them go and send them off on their own. I pray that all of this will have been a blessing for my children and their children's children for generations to come, as well as for all who have come along on this journey.

Endnotes

Chapter 1

1 Glenn Beck, "Glenn Beck: Restoring Love," Trinity Broadcasting Network, August 4, 2012

Chapter 2

2 "10 Questions" for the Dalai Lama," *Time*, June 14, 2010.
3 Winston Churchill, "Blood, Toil, Sweat and Tears," The History Place – Great Speeches Collection, May 13, 1940.
4 Jackson J. Spielvogel, *Western Civilization*, 6th ed. (Thomson-Wadsworth, Belmont, CA, 2003), 791.
5 Ibid.
6 Todd Gitlin, *The Sixties: Years of Hope, Days of Rage* (Bantam Books, New York, 1987), 98.
7 Ibid., 299.
8 Ibid., 300.
9 Ibid.
10 Associated Press, "U.N. War Crimes Office Tally of Kosovo's Dead Tops 2,100," *Milwaukee Journal Sentinel*, November 11, 1999, 4A.
11 Associated Press, "Bosnian Serb Leaders Accused in Genocide in U.N. Indictment, *Milwaukee Journal Sentinel*, November 17, 1995, 1A,4A.
12 Ibid.
13 George Will, "Ordinary Germans Guilty? That's Too Simplistic," *Milwaukee Journal Sentinel*, April 16, 1996.
14 Thomas Friedman, "The Struggle to Prosecute Rwandan Genocide," *Milwaukee Journal Sentinel*, February 7, 1996, 10A.
15 Editorial, "End Darfur Atrocities Now," *Milwaukee Journal Sentinel*, May 5, 2005, 12A.

16 Associated Press, "Powell Says Violence in Sudan is Genocide," *Milwaukee Journal Sentinel*, September 10, 2004, 2A.
17 Jeff Luger, "What Makes Us Moral," *Time*, December 3, 2007, 56-57.
18 Isabella Miram, letter to the editor, *Time*, June 2005.
19 William Golding, *Lord of the Flies* (New York: Capricorn Books, 1959), 192.
20 C.S. Lewis, *Mere Christianity* (New York: The Macmillan Company, New York, 1970), 38-39.
21 Ibid., 44.

Chapter 3

22 Roy Blount Jr., "America's Original Superstar," *Time*, July 14, 2008, 50.
23 Ron Chernow, "Blessed Barons,"*Time*, December 7, 1988, 74.
24 Ibid.
25 Ibid., 74-75.
26 Ibid., 75.
27 Cover, *Time*, December 5, 1988.
28 Kathy Rebello, Susan Antilla and Daniel Kadiec, *USA Today*, January 26, 1989, 1B.
29 Beth Belton, *USA Today*, December 28, 1989, 1B.
30 Editorial, *Milwaukee Journal Sentinel*, February 18, 1990, 5J.
31 Stefan Kanfer, *Time*, February 26, 1990, 53.
32 David A. Kaplan with Dody Tsiantar, "Wall Street: A Greed Apart," *Newsweek*, October 14, 1991, 48.
33 Ibid., 48.
34 Thomas McCarroll, "Fallen Master of the Universe," *Time*, May 7, 1990, 87.
35 John Greenwald, reported by Richard Hornik, William McWhirter and Frederick Ungeheuer, "Where's the Limit?," *Time*, December 5, 1988, 66.
36 John Greenwald, reported by Mary Chronin and Thomas McCarroll/New York and William McWhirter/Chicago, "Predator's Fall," *Time*, February 26, 1990, 47.
37 Ibid., 50.
38 Steven V. Roberts with Gary Cohen, "Villains of the S&L Crisis," *U.S. News and World Report*, October 1, 1990, 53.
39 Journal wire services, "Indictment of Keating Spotlights S&L Crisis," *Milwaukee Journal*, September 19, 1990, A10.
40 Steven V. Roberts with Gary Cohen, "Villains of the S&L Crisis," 53-59.
41 Ibid., 56.
42 Gregg Fields, "Tales of Greed, Lawlessness, (and) Loss Turn Business Pages into Tabloids," Knight Rider Newspapers, *Milwaukee Journal Sentinel*, January 1, 2003, D1.
43 Michael Duffy, "What Did They Know and … When Did They Know It?," *Time*, January 28, 2002, 16-20.
44 Marcy Gordon, "Inquiry Faults Enron Tax Schemes – Company Deceived IRS, Committee Says," *Milwaukee Journal Sentinel*, February 14, 2003, 6D.

45 Paul Gores, "Andersen's Descent into Greed Leaves Integrity Behind," *Milwaukee Journal Sentinel*, April 21, 2003, 4D.
46 Associated Press, "Enron CEO Stepping Down," *Milwaukee Journal Sentinel*, January 24, 2002, 1.
47 Greg Farrell, "Andersen Indicted in Enron Shredding," *USA Today*, March 15-17, 2002, 1A.
48 Gregg Fields, "Tales of Greed, Lawlessness, (and) Loss," D2.
49 Wikipedia, Enron Scandal, Kristin Hays, "Lay, Skilling Convicted in Enron Collapse," *The Washington Post*, May 26, 2006.
50 Wikipedia, Enron Scandal, Carrie Johnson, "Skilling Gets 24 Years for Fraud at Enron," *The Washington Post*, October 24, 2006.
51 Andrew Ross Sorkin, "Ex-Tyco Leaders Guilty of Fraud, Larceny," *Milwaukee Journal Sentinel* from *New York Times*, June 18, 2005, 12A.
52 Jennifer Bayot, "Tearful Ebbers Gets 25 Years," *Milwaukee Journal Sentinel* from *New York Times*, July 14, 2005, 1D.
53 Erin McClam, "Adelphia Founder Gets 15-Year Term," *Milwaukee Journal Sentinel*, June 21, 2005, 3D.
54 John Waggoner, "Greed is Good?," *USA Today*, December 31, 2003, 1B.
55 Ibid., 2B.
56 Ibid.
57 Jyoti Thottam, "Are They All Crooked?," *Time*, November 17, 2003, 55-56.
58 Bill Barol, "The Eighties Are Over," *Newsweek*, January 4, 1988, 42.
59 Greenwald, "Where's the Limit?," 67.
60 Chernow, "Blessed Barons," 74.

Chapter 4

61 Michael Grunwald, "How They Failed Us," *Time*, October 13, 2008, 43.
62 John M. Barry, "Words Offer Little Comfort," *Milwaukee Journal Sentinel* from *Washington Post*, July 17, 2002, 3D.
63 (David Pitt, "After 4 Years of 401(k) Volatility, There's Recovery," *Milwaukee Journal Sentinel*, March 22, 2011, 2D.
64 "Years Best Books for Making Sense of the Crisis," Money Bookshelf, *USA Today*, December 21, 2009, 6B.
65 William Cohan, *House of Cards: A Tale of Hubris and Wretched Excess on Wall Street* (New York: Doubleday, 2009), 195-196.
66 Ibid., 293.
67 Nancy Gibbs, "25 People to Blame: The Good Intentions, Bad Managers and Greed behind the Meltdown," *Time*, February 23, 2009, 24.
68 Cohan, *House of Cards*, 294-295.
69 Gibbs, "25 People to Blame," 23.
70 Cohan, *House of Cards*, 294-295.
71 Ibid., 300.

72 Ibid., 301.
73 Ibid., 318-319.
74 Gibbs, "25 People to Blame," 24.
75 Review of Michael W. Hudson's, "*The Monster: How a Gang of Predatory Lenders and Wall Street Bankers Fleeced America – and Spawned a Global Crisis*," (Times Books, 2010), by Andrea Sachs, *Time*, November 22, 2010.
76 Niall Ferguson, "The End of Prosperity," *Time*, October 13, 2008, 38.
77 Gibbs, "25 People to Blame," 23.
78 Ibid., 22.
79 Bill Saporito, "How AIG Became Too Big to Fail," *Time*, March 30, 2009, 28.
80 Gary H. Rawlins, "Year's Best Books for Making Sense of the Crisis," *USA Today*, December 21, 2009, 6B.
81 Richard Eisenberg, "Financial Meltdown Produced a Few Huge Wnners," *USA Today*, April 12, 2010, 5B.
82 Ibid.
83 Ferguson, "The End of Prosperity," 38.
84 Cohan, *House of Cards*, 331.
85 Barbara Kiviat, "A Brief History of: Ratings Agencies," *Time*, March 30, 2009, 18.
86 Ibid.
87 Cohan, *House of Cards*, 332.
88 McClatchy News Service, "Probe Finds Moody's Punished Workers Who Warned of Meltdown," *Milwaukee Journal Sentinel*, October 18, 2009
89 Bill Saporito, *Time*, November 22, 2010.)
90 Adam Zagorin and Michael Weisskopf, "Inside the Breakdown at the SEC," Time, March 9, 2009, 34.
91 Gibbs, "25 People to Blame," 22.
92 Karen Tumulty and Massimo Calabresi, "Three Men And a Bailout," *Time*, October 6, 2008, 40.
93 Bill Bradley, *We Can All Do Better*, (New York: Vanguard Press, 2012), 57.
94 Martin Crutsinger and March Gordon, "Greenspan admits mistake," *Milwaukee Journal Sentinel*, October 24, 2008, 4D.
95 Gibbs, "25 People to Blame," 22.
96 Verbatim, *Time*, September 21, 2009, 21.
97 Floyd Norris, "House Toughens Fraud Penalties," *Milwaukee Journal Sentinel* from *New York Times*, July 17, 2002, 1A.
98 Ibid., 1A & 9A.
99 John Barry, "Words Offer Little Comfort: Greenspan Testimony Upbeat Despite Dropping Dow," *Milwaukee Journal Sentinel* from *Washington Post*, July 17, 2002, 3D.
100 Michael Grunwald, "Person of the Year," *Time*, December 28, 2009, 48.
101 Gary Mann, April 23, 2010, CNN.
102 Editorial, *Milwaukee Journal Sentinel*, January 25, 2009, 14A.
103 Editorial, Milwaukee Journal Sentinel, August 22, 2010, 3J.

104 Stephen Gandel with reporting by Alex Altman, "Case Against Goldman Sachs," *Time*, May 3, 2010, 37.
105 Allan Sloan, "What's Still Wrong with Wall Street," *Time*, November 9, 2009, 27.
106 Ibid.
107 "Up with Chris Hays," March 18, 2012
108 Christine Harper, "Goldman Sachs Takes a Hit," *Milwaukee Journal Sentinel* from *Bloomberg News*, March 16, 2012, 2D.
109 Gregory Mott, "Wells Fargo to Pay $6.5 Million: Unit Didn't Do Enough Research on Securities It Sold, SEC says," *Milwaukee Journal Sentinel* from *Bloomberg News*, August 15, 2012, 3D.
110 Massimo Calabresi and Bill Saporito, "The Street Fighter," *Time*, February 13, 2012, 26.
111 Ibid., 27.
112 Ibid., 25.
113 Ibid., 25.
114 "Insider Trading Follow-up: Gupta Sentenced," Moneyline, *USA Today*, October 25, 2012, 1B.
115 "Gupta Sentenced to Two Years, Fined $5 Million," Business in Brief, *Milwaukee Journal Register*, October 25, 2012, 3D.
116 Christina Rexrode, "Countrywide Accused of 'Brazen' Fraud," *Milwaukee Journal Sentinel*, October 25, 2012, 3D.
117 Calabresi and Saporito, "The Street Fighter," Time, February 26, 2012, 26.

Chapter 5

118 Del Jones, "48% of Workers Admit to Unethical or Illegal Acts," *USA Today*, April 4, 1997, 1A-2A.
119 George Bernard Shaw, *The Devil's Disciple*, Act 2, 1901
120 Dr. Laura, "'Truly Human' Means Thinking of Others as Equals," *Milwaukee Journal Sentinel*, February 10, 1999, F1.
121 Francis D'emilo, "Pop Calls Power, Money 'Idols,'" *Milwaukee Journal Sentinel*, September 14, 2008, 3A.
122 Frank A. Aukofer, "The American Dream Adds a Social, Global Dimension," *Milwaukee Journal Sentinel*, April 17, 1996, 5A.
123 Baltimore Sun, "The Poor Are More Generous," *Milwaukee Journal*, October 19, 1988, 10A.
124 Tom Teepen, "Better Not Bet on Charity," *Milwaukee Journal Sentinel*, December 24, 1995, 3J.
125 Giving USA Foundation, "Charitable Giving to Education, Health, and Arts: An Analysis of Data Collected in the Center on Philanthropy Panel Study," 2003.
126 National Philanthropic Trust: Charitable Giving Statistics.
127 Frank Greue, "America's poor are its most generous donors," McClatchy Newspapers as it appears in the *Seattle Times*, May 23, 2009.

128 Marianne Sylva, letter to the editor, Time, August 22, 1994, 9.
129 Philip Chard, "World's Children Beg for Your Attention." *Milwaukee Journal Sentinel*, December 21, 2004, 2F.
130 Nancy Gibbs, *Time*, January 9, 1989, 20-21.
131 Urban Institute: National Center for Charitable Statistics.
132 2012 Statistical Abstract of the United States.
133 National Philanthropic Trust, Charitable Giving Statistics, 2011.
134 Nancy Schulins, "Savior of Homeless Is a Reluctant Hero," *Milwaukee Journal*, February 26, 1989, 1J, 5J.
135 John Sherlock, "'Narcissism' Loses Out in the USA's Crises" *USA Today*, November 27, 1989, 1A-2A.
136 Doris Hajewski, "Life on $3 a Day,"Milwaukee Journal Sentinel, December 31, 2000, p 4L.
137 Bill Clinton, "The Case for Optimism," *Time*, October 1, 2012, 38.

Chapter 6

138 Spielvogel, *Western Civilization*, 294.
139 Ibid.
140 John H. Kieschnick, *The Best is Yet to Come: 7 Doors of Spiritual Growth* (Friendswood, TX: Baxter Press, 2006), 26.
141 Ibid., 15.
142 Dr. Bill Knippa "True Repentance," *Lutheran Witness*, November 9, 2010, 26.
143 Kieschnick, *The Best is Yet to Come*, 56.
144 Adapted from Greg Cummins, "In a Plain Brown Wrapper."
145 Roland Bainton, *Here I Stand: A Life of Martin Luther*, (New York: Abingdon Press, 1976), 171.
146 Ibid., 177-178.
147 Ibid., 178-179.
148 Kieschnick, *The Best is Yet to Come*, 51.

Chapter 7

149 James M. Boyce, "Eternity's Dreams and Visions," *Eternity*, December 1988, 11.
150 Kieschnick, *The Best is Yet to Come*, 157-159, used with permission.
151 "Overcoming Selfishness," Stewardship Advisors, Birmingham, MI.
152 Kieschnick, *The Best is Yet to Come*, 147, used with permission.
153 Dietrich Bonhoeffer, *The Cost of Discipleship*, rev.ed.(New York: The Macmillan Company, 1959), 117.
154 Lewis, *Mere Christianity*, 42.
155 Ibid., 49.

156 Knippa, "True Repentance," 26.
157 Lewis, *Mere Christianity*, 44-45.

Chapter 8

158 Kieschnick, "*The Best Is Yet to Come*," 181.
159 Ibid., 182.
160 Ibid., 184.
161 Ezra Bowen, "Looking to Its Roots," *Time*, May 25, 1987, 29.
162 Ibid., 29.
163 Kieschnick, "*The Best Is Yet to Come*," 185.
164 Ibid., 194.

Chapter 9

165 Bonhoeffer, "*The Cost of Discipleship*," 45.
166 Ibid., 45.
167 Julia Lieblich, "U.S. bishops Call on Catholics to Change their Everyday Lives," *Milwaukee Journal Sentinel*, November 18, 1998, 8A.
168 Glen Thomas, "The Gospel of Wealth," Whataway (blog), *New York Times*, September 7, 2010, http://blog.whataway.org/blog/encourage-a-new-generation/0/0/the-gospel-of-wealth.

Chapter 10

169 Jeffrey D. Sachs, "Why America Must Revive Its Middle Class," *Time*, October 10, 2011, 32.
170 Michael Scherer, "Taking It To The Streets," *Time*, October 24, 2011, 24.
171 Spielvogel, *Western Civilization*, 472.
172 Justin Fox, "The Myth of the Rational Market," *Time*, June 12, 2009, 46.
173 Jo Sandin, "Author Urges People of Faith to Challenge World Inequities, *Milwaukee Journal Sentinel*, February 22, 1997, 2B.
174 Robert L. Heilbroner, "*The Making of Economic Society*," Revised for the 80's (Englewood Cliffs, N.J.: Prentice-Hall, n.d.), 279.
175 Ibid., 281.
176 Ibid., 282.
177 John Barton, "Modern Society Ruining the Meaning of Life," *The State Journal-Register*, Springfield, IL, May 7, 1981, 16-17.
178 Ezra Brown, "Looking to Its Roots," *Time*, May 25, 1987, 26.
179 Ibid.
180 Ibid., 3.

181 Ibid., 29.
182 Rana Foroohar, "When the Dismal Science Was Brilliant," *Time*, September 12, 2011, 18.
183 Ibid.
184 M. Scott Peck, *The Road Less Traveled* (New York: Simon Schuster, 1993), 166.
185 Stephen Koepp, "In the Shadows of the Twin Towers," *Time*, November 2, 1987, 46.
186 Ibid.
187 Angie Drobnic, "Buffet's Right: Mega Rich Get Tax Breaks", Milwaukee Journal Sentinel, August 23, 2011, 2A.
188 Fareed Zakaria, "Complexity Equals Corruption", *Time*, October 31, 2011, 27.
189 Kevin Phillips, "Risky Business: A Blind Belief in Wealth," *Milwaukee Journal Sentinel*, August 8, 1999, J2.
190 Editorial, "Capitalism, Too, Has Its Shortcomings," *Milwaukee Journal Register*, January, 23, 1990.
191 Ibid.
192 Justin Fox, "The Bailouts Biggest Flaw," *Time*, September 28, 2009, 44.
193 Ibid.
194 Justin Fox, "What would Adam Smith Say?" *Time*, April 5, 2010, 18.
195 John F. Stacks, "Dawn of the Living Dems," *Time*, March 11, 1996
196 Joe Klein, "Hard Choices," *Time*, July 20, 2009, 27.
197 Editorial, "Wean Wall Street Off Its Gambling Addictions: To Protect the Economy, Don't Let Big Banks Run In-House Casinos," *USA Today*, March 1, 2010, 15A.
198 Henry Paulson, "Ten Questions," *Time*, February 22, 2010, 4.
199 Philip Chard, "Almighty Profit Tugs at Values of Middle Class," *Milwaukee Journal Sentinel*, May 25, 1999, 2E.
200 Editorial, "Middle Class Lost: America Pulling Apart (Part Three)," *Milwaukee Journal Sentinel*, February 6, 1996, 1A.
201 Richard Longworth, "Workers in Middle as Globalization, Old Ways Collide," *Chicago Tribune*, May 24, 1998, Sec. 5, 5.
202 Augustus Napier, "Called by Families: The Therapist's Personal Journey", *Family Therapy News*, October/November 1997, 17.
203 Editorial, "Middle Class Lost," 6A.
204 Associated Press, "Reich Urges a Narrowing of Gap between Rich, Poor," *Milwaukee Journal Sentinel*, January 10, 1997, 3A.
205 Editorial, "Betrayal of Americas Dream," *Milwaukee Journal Sentinel*, November 18, 1996, 6J.
206 Associated Press, "Narrowing of Gap between Rich, Poor," 3A.
207 Kevin Phillips, *The Politics of Rich and Poor* (New York: Random House, 1990), 8.
208 Ibid., xxiii.
209 Phillips, *The Politics of Rich and Poor*, 164.
210 Associated Press, "Narrowing of Gap between Rich, Poor," 3A.
211 Robert Reich, "Middle Class Frustration Balloons With Pay Gap," *Kansas City Star*, August 21, 2010, A17.

212 Peter Whoriskey, "Income Gap? Try Chasm," *Milwaukee Journal Register*, June 22, 2011, 8A.
213 Tim Mullaney, "Protests Spotlight a Stressed Middle Class," *USA Today*, October 20, 2011, 2B.
214 Roth, Zachary, "New numbers: Income for top 1 percent skyrocketed over last 30 years," The Lookout on Twitter@YahooLookout, October 26, 2011. http://news.yahoo.com/blogs/lookout/numbers-income-top-ne-percent-skyrocketed-over...
215 Rana Foroohar, "Struck in the Middle," *Time*, August 25, 2011, 26.
216 Associated Press, "Report Finds Rich Got Richer in Recent Years," *Milwaukee Journal Sentinel*, April 24 2003, 4A.
217 Editorial, "Corporate Titans Shouldn't Be Surprised," *Milwaukee Journal Sentinel*, October 15, 2011, 9A.
218 Robert Pear (*New York Times*), "Rich Getting Richer," *Milwaukee Journal Sentinel*, October 27, 2011, 5A.
219 Jeffery D. Sachs, "Why America Must Revive Its Middle Class," 30.
220 Rana Foroohar, "It's the Stupid Global Economy," *Time*, September 3, 2012, 14.
221 Tom Saler, "American Dream Fading into Globalized Sunset," *Milwaukee Journal Sentinel*, September 2, 2012, 3D.
222 Jon Meacham, "The History of the American Dream," *Time*, July 2, 2012, 28.
223 Phillips, *The Politics of Rich and Poor*, 28.
224 Ibid.
225 Editorial, "It's Bush Who Must Understand," *Milwaukee Journal*, October 22, 1988, 10A.
226 Phillips, *The Politics of Rich and* Poor, 29,30.
227 Ibid., 55.
228 Sachs, "Why America Must Revive Its Middle Class," 30,31.
229 Ibid., 31.
230 Ibid., xxiii.
231 http://news.yahoo.com/s/yblog_thelookout/20110309/ts_ybog_the lookout/jobs-returning-b.
232 Editorial, "Falling Behind: Glitter of '80s Hid Widening Rich-Poor Gap," Milwaukee Journal, June 7, 1992, J4.
233 The Milwaukee Journal Sentinel, December 20, 2009, pp J-J2.
234 Fareed Zakaria, "Restoring the American Dream," *Time*, November 1, 2010, 34.
235 Ibid., 31.
236 Thom Hartman, *Rebooting the American Dream* (San Francisco: Barrett-Koehler Publishers, Inc, 2010), 200.
237 Rana Foroohar, "What Ever Happened to Upward Mobility?" *Time*, November 14, 2011, 28.
238 *Morning Joe* MSNBC, October 27, 2011.
239 Foroohar, "What Ever Happened to Upward Mobility?" 28.
240 Wikipedia – http://en.wikipedia.org/wiki/The_World_Is_Flat, 11/13/2011
241 http://thomasfriedman.com/bookshelf/the-world-is-flat, review by *Publishers Weekly*, 11/13/2011

242 Zakaria, "Restoring The American Dream,"32.
243 Ibid, p.33
244 Sachs, "Why America Must Revive Its Middle Class, 29.
245 http://finance.yahoo.com/blogs/daily-ticker/; 11/15/11
246 Don Lee, "Workers Stuck with Less," *Milwaukee Journal Sentinel*, September 11, 2010, 6B.
247 Peter Gorenstein, "America's Middle Class Crisis: The Sobering Facts," *Daily Ticker*, May 4, 2010
248 Zakaria, "Restoring The American Dream," 31-32.
249 Robert Frank and Phil Izzo, "Magic Number for Happiness: $75,000 a Year," The Aggregator, *Milwaukee Journal Sentinel*, September 12, 2010, 5D.
250 R.Z. Sheppard, review of *"The First Salute,"* by Barbara W Tuchman, T*ime*, October 3, 1988, 89.
251 Walter Mondale, no title, Milwaukee Journal Sentinel, Feb 6, 2011, 8A.
252 Meacham, "The History of the American Dream," 35.
253 Hartman, "Rebooting the American Dream,"55.
254 Foroohar, "What Ever Happened To Upward Mobility," 34.

Chapter 11

255 Laurie Kellman, "37% Back Wall Street Protests," *Milwaukee Journal Sentinel*, October 22, 2011, 10A.
256 *Morning Joe*, MSNBC, October 27, 2011.
257 Craig Gilbert, "The Unvarnished Obey," *Milwaukee Journal Sentinel*, January 3, 2010, 5.
258 Russell King, "Looking for One 'Good' Leader," *Milwaukee Journal*, October 21, 1994, A13.
259 *Morning Joe*, MSNBC, November 7, 2011.
260 Hartman, *Rebooting the American Dream*, 30- 31.
261 *Time*, Feb 7, 2011, 27.
262 Fareed Zakaaria, "Complexity Equals Corruption," *Time*, October 31, 2011, 27.
263 Editorial, "Yet More Breaks for Fat Cats," *USA Today*, October 25, 2004, 22A.
264 Roberts with Cohen, "Villains of the S & L Crisis," 54.
265 Ibid., 55.
266 Ibid., 55.
267 Ibid., 58.
268 Ibid.
269 Hartman, *Rebooting the American Dream*, 99.
270 Robert Pear, "Rich Getting Richer," *Milwaukee Journal Sentinel*, October 27, 2011, 5A.
271 Hartman, *Rebooting the American Dream*, 99-100.
272 Ibid., 110.
273 Ibid., 110, 111

274 *Piers Morgan Tonight*, CNN, November 13, 2011.
275 *Morning Joe*, MSNBC, October 31, 2011.
276 Associated Press, "Lee Atwater, 40, GOP Strategist Dies of Tumor," *The Milwaukee Journal*, March 29, 1991.
277 Ibid.
278 Editorial, *Milwaukee Journal*, March 30, 1991.
279 Margaret Carlson with reporting by Dan Goodgame and Nancy Traver, "How to Spread a Smear," *Time*, June 19, 1989, 33.
280 Associated Press, "Republicans Mourn Atwater's Loss," AP, *Wausau Daily Record Herald*, WI, March 30, 1991.
281 Editorial, *Milwaukee Journal* March 30, 1991)
282 "Lee Atwater Sees Need for Spiritual and Moral Rebirth" *Christians and Society Today*" March 1991, 1.
283 *USA Today*, Dec. 31, 1991 5A.
284 Hartman, "*Rebooting the American Dream*, 39.
285 Excerpted in *Time*, May 28, 2007, 39.
286 Eric Pooley, "The Last Temptation of Al Gore," *Time*, May 28, 2007, 41-42.
287 Steve Croft, *60 Minutes*, November 13, 2011.
288 David Van Biema, "Can Charity Fill the Gap," *Time*, December 4, 1995, 53.
289 John Sununu, "One Nation, on the Dole," *Time*, August 8, 2011, 27.
290 Editorial, "Thousand Points of Light Won't Do," Milwaukee Journal, February 20, 1989, 6A.
291 Nancy Shullins, Associated Press, "Hunger in US Increases Grip," *Milwaukee Journal*, May 13, 1990, 1J.
292 Richard Stengel, "When Liberalism Ruled, *Time*, April 3, 1995, 94.
293 Joe Klein, "The GOP's New Rules," *Time*, June 27, 2011, p 35.
294 Lance Morrow, "Who's in Charge," *Time*, November 9, 1987, 20.
295 Robert Rena, "GOP Shows Just How Much I Care," *Milwaukee Journal Sentinel*, November 11, 1995, 10A.

Chapter 12

296 Annysa Johnson, "Homeless Family Will Get to Have a Merry Christmas," *Milwaukee Journal Sentinel*, December 16, 2011, 5B.
297 Tom Held, "State Excels in Helping Out," *Milwaukee Journal Sentinel*, August 15, 2011, 9A.
298 Kathy Flanigan, "How You Can Give, without Spending a Dime," by Milwaukee Journal Sentinel, November 17, 2002, 12S.
299 Editorial, "Churches, Charity Can't Do It All," *Milwaukee Journal*, December 23, 1994, A6.
300 Annysa Johnson, "Church Members Open Homes to Children in Need," *Milwaukee Journal Sentinel*, July 5, 2011, 3B.

301 Laurel Walker, "Room for One More," *Milwaukee Journal Sentinel*, December 17, 2011, 3B.
302 Annysa Johnson, "Faith Groups Guiding Progress on County's Special Needs Housing," *Milwaukee Journal Sentinel*, June 20, 2011, 9A, 11A.
303 Crocker Stephenson, "Helping Out," *Milwaukee Journal Sentinel*, May 22, 2011, 1A.
304 John Bowen, "6 people who make a difference," *Milwaukee Journal Sentinel*, January 9, 1994, G10.
305 Editorial, *Milwaukee Journal Sentinel*, March 12, 1997, 10A.
306 Eldon Knoche, "Backus Devoted His Life to Helping the Underclass, *Milwaukee Journal Sentinel*, March 8, 1997, 4B.
307 Eldon Knoche, "Ashe Guided with a Deft Touch," *Milwaukee Journal Sentinel*, December 26, 2000, 1B.
308 Ibid., 5B.
309 Leonard Sykes Jr., "True Believer: Pastor Works to Bring Social Justice to All," *Milwaukee Journal Sentinel*, November 25, 2001, 1B, 6B.
310 Doctors without Borders, *Time*, May 10, 2010, 31.
311 Erin Einhorn, "Volunteers Drop Everything to Help," *USA Today*, July 27, 1994, 8A.
312 Ibid.
313 Ibid.
314 Tom Herd, "Hospital Leader Follows Dream of Helping Kids around the World," *Milwaukee Journal Sentinel*, September 9, 2000, 5B.
315 Tracy Kidder, "Because We Can, We Do," *Parade*, April 3, 2005, p 4-6.
316 E.J. McGregor, "The Power of Caring: Colin Powell's Promise: A Better Life for Kids," *Time*, August 31, 1988, 2.
317 Robert Morgan, "Bush Renews Appeal for Americans to Devote Time to Volunteering," *Milwaukee Journal Sentinel*, March 13, 2002, 7A.
318 Paul Hendrickson, "Inspiration for the Ages," *Milwaukee Journal Sentinel*, September 6, 1997, 10A.
319 Edward W. Desmond, "A Pencil in the Hand of God," *Time*, December 4, 1989, 11.
320 Joseph, Shimek, "Reflected in the Saints among Us," *Milwaukee Journal Sentinel*, October 26, 2003, 4J.
321 Brian Kolodiejchuk, ed., "*Come Be My Light*" (New York: Image-Doubleday, 2007), 132.
322 Ibid., 39.
323 Ibid., 44.
324 Deborah Kovach Caldwell, "Mother Teresa's Death Leaves Void for the World," *Milwaukee Journal Sentinel*, September 8, 1997, 10A.
325 Joseph Shimek, "Reflected in the Saints among Us," 4J.
326 Kolodiejchuk, ed., "*Come Be My Light*," 98.
327 Ibid., 86.
328 Ibid., 233.

329 Barbara Crossette, "Thousands Gather to Say Goodbye to Patron of the Poor," *Milwaukee Journal Sentinel*, September 8, 1997, 10A.
330 "Inspiration for the ages," by Paul Hendrickson, Washington Post, Milwaukee Journal Sentinel, September 6, 1997, p 10A
331 Kolodiejchuk, ed., *Come Be My Light*," 286.
332 Nancy Gibbs, "Friends in Need," *Time*, October 11, 2010, 68.
333 Karl Taro Greenfield, "Giving Billions Isn't Easy," *Time*, July 24, 2000, 53.
334 Karl Taro Greenfield, "Do Techies Give Back," *Time*, July 24, 2000, 56.
335 Romesch Ratnesar, "Charles Feeney," *Time*, December 29, 1997, 100.
336 Victor Keegann, "Can Turner Move the World's Wealth?" *Milwaukee Journal Sentinel*, September 28, 1997, 6J.
337 Patrick Cole, "40 Billionaires Pledge to Share 50% of Wealth," *Milwaukee Journal Sentinel*, August 5, 2010, 4A.
338 Karl Taro Greenfield, "A New Way of Giving," *Time*, July 24, 2000, 51.
339 Maureen Dowd, *New York Times*, "As Charity Becomes the Rope of Social Climbing," *Milwaukee Journal Sentinel*, December 4, 1996, 8A.
340 Kolodiejchuk, ed., *Come Be My Light*," 105.
341 Ibid., 110, 111.
342 Ibid., 97
343 Ibid., 85.
344 ibid, 88.
345 Ibid., 96.
346 "All The Lives We Touch", by Prince Michael, Parade Magazine, August 11, 1996 4.

Chapter 13

347 Paul E. Eichmann, *The People's Bible, Hosea, Joel and Amos*, 2nd. ed. (Milwaukee: Northwestern, 2002), 251-253.
348 Robert Reich, "Middle Class Frustration Balloons with Pay Gap," *Kansas City Star*, August 21, 2010, A17.
349 Fareed Zakaria, "In the Short Term, Good News," *Time*, May 2, 2011, 35.
350 Joe Klein, "Democracy's Discontent," *Time*, August 10, 2009, 34.
351 Brian Faler, "Obama Fuels Class Resentment, Ryan Says," *Milwaukee Journal Sentinel*, October 27, 2011, 4A.
352 Editorial, "As a Campaign Opener, Speech Succeeded," *Milwaukee Journal Sentinel*, January 25, 1996
353 Michael Grunwald, "Change," *Time*, April 13, 2009, 32.
354 Editorial, "Plans to Fix Credit Rating Agencies Deserve a C-minus," *USA Today*, March 22, 2010, 10A.
355 Ibid., 8A.
356 Associated Press Reports, "Mortgage Companies Agree to $25 Billion Settlement," *Milwaukee Journal Sentinel*, January 24, 2012.D1.
357 Michael Scherer, "The New Sheriffs Of Wall Street," *Time*, May 24, 2010, 24.

358 Editorial, "Rules of the Road," *Milwaukee Journal Sentinel*, April 21, 2010, 12A.
359 Editorial, *Milwaukee Journal Sentinel*, January 25, 2009, 14A.
360 Mitch McConnell, "The Senate's Great Persuader," *Time*, April 29, 2010, 52.
361 Ibid.
362 Leonard Pitts, "Why I Like Mike Huckabee," *Milwaukee Journal Sentinel*, August 24, 2010, 9A.
363 John Gurda, "Labor Day Is about Rights Hard Fought and Won," *Milwaukee Journal Sentinel*, September 3, 2009, 2J.
364 Frank A. Aukofer, "Bush Becomes 41st President," *Milwaukee Journal*, January 20, 1989, 1A.
365 Verbatim, *Time*, July 20, 2009, 21.
366 Washington Post, New York Times, "Pope Issues Call for New Economic Order," *Milwaukee Journal Sentinel*, July 8, 2009, 3A.
367 Elisabetta Povoledo, "Reform World Finances, Vatican Says," *Milwaukee Journal Register*, October 25, 2011, 3A.
368 New York Times, Newsday, "Bishops Soften Middle Class View," *The Milwaukee Journal*, October 7, 1985, 1A, 7A.
369 Associated Press, "Budget Rift Fails Moral Test, Bishops Declare," *Milwaukee Journal Sentinel*, November 15, 1995, 10A.
370 Colman McCarthy, "Eco selling: Consumerism on the Side of Angels," *Milwaukee Sentinel*, December 7, 1993, A13.
371 Newsday, "Pope Backs Enlightened Capitalism with Emphasis on Helping the Poor," *The Milwaukee Journal*, May 5, 1991, A4.
372 "Pope Appeals," *Milwaukee Journal Sentinel*, December 26, 2008, 10A.

Chapter 14

373 Carlton A. Toppe, First Corinthians (Milwaukee: Northwestern, 1987), 124.
374 Steven Greenhut, "Aimless Retirement is No Retirement,", *Milwaukee Journal Sentinel*, May 18, 1997, 1J.
375 Leo Tolstoy, *The Death of Ivan Ilych and Other Stories* (New York: Barnes and Noble Classics, 2004), 140.
376 Kolodiejchuk, ed., *Come Be My Light*, 292.
377 Ibid., 338.
378 Dietrich Bonhoeffer, "*The Call to Discipleship*," (New York: The Macmillen Company, 1961), 31.
379 Joe Klein, "Middle of the Road," *Time*, October 24, 2011, 34.
380 Anysa Johnson, "40 Years of Service a Spiritual Journey," *Milwaukee Journal Sentinel*, June 5, 2010, 5B.

381 "The Age Of Greed," Gary Rummler, *The Milwaukee Journal*, September 17, 1989, 2G.
382 Richard Cohen, "Obama's Carter Problem," *Milwaukee Journal Sentinel*, October 13, 2010, 5A.
383 Colin Greer, "Change Will Come When Our Hearts Change," *Milwaukee Journal Sentinel*, October 20, 1996, Parade 5.

Made in the USA
Lexington, KY
28 August 2014